HOLY LEGIONARY YOUTH

HOLY LEGIONARY YOUTH

Fascist Activism in Interwar Romania

Roland Clark

CORNELL UNIVERSITY PRESS ITHACA AND LONDON

First published 2015 by Cornell University Press
Printed in the United States of America

Library of Congress Cataloging-in-Publication Data

Clark, Roland, author.
Holy legionary youth : fascist activism in interwar Romania / Roland Clark.
pages cm
Includes bibliographical references and index.
ISBN 978-0-8014-5368-7 (cloth : alk. paper)
1. Fascism—Romania—History—20th century. 2. Fascism and youth—Romania—History—20th century. 3. Nationalism—Romania—History—20th century. 4. Romania—Politics and government—1914–1944. I. Title.
DR264. C613 2015
949.8′02—dc23 2014045991

Cornell University Press strives to use environmentally responsible suppliers and materials to the fullest extent possible in the publishing of its books. Such materials include vegetable-based, low-VOC inks and acid-free papers that are recycled, totally chlorine-free, or partly composed of nonwood fibers. For further information, visit our website at www.cornellpress.cornell.edu.

Cloth printing 10 9 8 7 6 5 4 3 2 1

For Laura

Contents

Illustrations

Acknowledgments

My first word of appreciation goes to Irina Livezeanu, who has followed this project since the very beginning. Her own research inspired the early chapters of the book in important ways, and her editing and wise advice are responsible for preventing any number of errors and misinterpretations. Thanks also to my other mentors: to William Chase, for his humor and interest in comparative history; to Lara Putnam, for her dogged commitment to logic; to John Markoff, for his unfailing ability to find any and every historical question fascinating; and to Árpád von Klimó, for his priceless knowledge of the European historiography. I would also like to thank my other editors—Shannon Woodcock, John Watts, and R. Chris Davis—each of whom discussed the ideas with me at length and who went through the manuscript with a fine-tooth comb.

An interdisciplinary project such as this necessarily requires the input of a large number of people, each of whom is a specialist in his or her own field. I owe thanks to a multitude of scholars who looked over specific sections and shared their disciplines with me: to Maria Bucur, on women's involvement; Evan Winet, on performance studies; Nancy Condee, on cultural studies; Cristina Albu and Izabel Galliera, on art history; Jean-Paul Himka and Ionuț Biliuța, on religious rhetoric; Adam Shear, on literary cultures; Amy McDowell, on social movement scenes; Gregor Thum and Radu Harald Dinu, on violence; Justin Classen, on commerce; and Adriana Helbig, Joe Grim Freiberg, Andra Draghiciu, Margaret Bessinger, and Victor Stoichița, on music. Others helped me think through crucial aspects of the project, including Alejandra Boza, Kenyon Zimmer, Madalina Vereş, and Joel Brady.

This research was funded by a variety of organizations, including the Council for Library and Information Resources; the Association for Women in Slavic Studies; the Society for Romanian Studies; and various departments and research centers at the University of Pittsburgh—the Department of History, the Center for Russian and East European Studies, the University Center for International Studies, the European Studies Center, and the Faculty of Arts and Sciences. Without the generous support of these organizations I could not have assembled the documentary base for this book. Research reassigned time from Eastern Connecticut State University was crucial for allowing me to revise the manuscript for publication, as was advice on publishing from Lavinia Stan. I would also like to thank *Arhiva Moldaviae* for allowing me to include material in chapter 3, which has already been published as "Conflict and Everyday Life at the Legionary Cultural Hearth in Iaşi (1924–1938)," *Arhiva Moldaviae*, 3 (2011): 139–61.

During the research stage I benefited greatly from archivists such as Dorin Dobrincu at the National Historical Archives of Romania, George Vişan at the National Council for the Study of the Securitate Archives, and Paul Shapiro and Radu Ioanid at the United States Holocaust Memorial Museum. Alongside them, an army of unnamed archivists and librarians deserve my thanks for the countless hours of assistance they gave me at every step of the project. Pompilica Burcică, Raul Cârstocea, R. Chris Davis, Valentin Săndulescu, Justin Classen, and Claudiu Oancea helped me find valuable sources and introduced me to important archival collections. Wolfram Nieß, Oliver Jens Schmitt, and Justin Classen provided me with hard-to-find documents from their own research. I also benefited greatly from discussions with Eleodorus Enachescu and Alexandru Belciu, who eagerly shared their knowledge and books on the Legion with me even though our politics are very different. I would also like to thank those who generously allowed me to read their unpublished manuscripts on questions relevant to my research—Cristina Adriana Bejan, R. Chris Davis, Joanne Roberts, Valentin Săndulescu, Shannon Woodcock, and Kenyon Zimmer. I am very grateful to Roger Haydon and Karen Laun of Cornell University Press, as well as to Romaine Perin for copyediting and to Judy Kip for indexing the manuscript. Finally, my infinite thanks to my wife, Laura, who has put up with a great deal to see this book through to the end, and to my parents, Geoff and Yvonne, who edited the entire manuscript, for their constant encouragement and support. The book is dedicated to Laura, without whom my life would be infinitely poorer.

Abbreviations

Organizations

ASC	Asociația Studenților Creștin (the Christian Students' Association)
CFR	Căile Ferate Române (the Romanian Railway Company)
CML	Corpul Muncitoresc Legionar (the Legionary Workers Corps)
CSB	Centrul Studențesc București (the Bucharest Student Center)
FNR	Fascia Naționale Române (the National Romanian Fascists)
LANC	Liga Apărării Național Creștine (the National Christian Defense League)
MNR	Mișcarea de Rezistență Națională (the National Resistance Movement)
PCR	Partidul Comunist Român (the Romanian Communist Party)
PNC	Partidul Național Creștin (the National Christian Party)
PNL	Partidul Național Liberal (the National Liberal Party)
PNȚ	Partidul Național Țărănesc (the National Peasant Party)
PSD	Partidul Social Democrat (the Social Democratic Party)
UNC	Uniunea Națională Creștină (the National Christian Union)
UNSCR	Uniunea Națională a Studenților Creștini din România (the National Union of Christian Students in Romania)

Archives

ACNSAS	National Council for the Study of the Securitate Archives, Bucharest, Romania
AN	Romanian National Archives—County Branches
ANIC	National Historical Archives of Romania, Bucharest, Romania
DGP	Direcția Generală a Poliției
MI-D	Ministerul de Interne—Diverse
USHMM	United States Holocaust Memorial Museum Archives, Washington DC, USA
USNA	United States National Archives, College Park, MD, USA

HOLY LEGIONARY YOUTH

Introduction

On Saturday, 15 January 1938, a group of forty schoolgirls gathered in Craiova, a regional city in southern Romania, for the funeral of their colleague Maria Cristescu (1922–1938). The girls were accompanied by seventy legionaries, mostly shopkeepers, tradespeople, and office workers, led by the tailor Dumitru Baiculescu. Sixteen-year-old Maria had become a legionary four months earlier.[1] The mourners who assembled in a military formation outside her parents' house were members of Legiunea Arhangelul Mihail (the Legion of the Archangel Michael), a fascist organization that had just won 15.58 percent of the votes in the national elections (26.92 percent in Craiova's county) and could boast a membership of at least 272,000 people, organized into 34,000 small groups known as *cuiburi* (nests), making it one of the biggest fascist movements in Europe.[2] Maria died from a sudden illness, but in her last months she had kept a diary in which she wrote about her love for her country and for the Legion's leader, her "Căpitan" (Captain)—Corneliu Zelea Codreanu (1899–1938). The diary

1. According to the 1924 Education Law, girls were obliged to attend four years of primary education and could then opt to study another three or four years before attending a more academically rigorous *gimnazium* that would prepare them for tertiary study. Ottmar Traşcă, "Aspecte ale educaţiei femeii în România în perioada 1926–1948. Studiu de caz: Liceul de fete 'Principesa Ileana' din Cluj-Napoca," in *Condiţia femeii în România în secolul XX: Studii de caz*, ed. Ghizela Cosma and Virgiliu Ţârău (Cluj-Napoca: Presa Universitara Clujeana, 2002), 103–4.

2. Armin Heinen, *Legiunea "Arhanghelul Mihail": Mişcare socială şi organizaţie politică*, trans. Cornelia Esianu and Delia Esianu (Bucharest: Humanitas, 2006), 357; "Alte rezultate de ieri," *Buna vestire*, 1/248 (22 Dec 1937): 3.

contained her prayers to die a "Christian death" and reflected on how heroically other legionaries had died.[3]

The theatricality, religiosity, and community spirit displayed at Maria Cristescu's funeral hint at how fascism transformed the lives of rank-and-file legionaries. The crowd stood to attention and gave a fascist-style salute when Maria's body was carried out of the house, following the coffin down to the nearby church. Maria's father, Ştefan Cristescu, was a manager in the county administration and her uncle, Father Grigore Cristescu (1895–1961), was a theologian at the University of Bucharest. Legionary connections brought in local celebrities such as the poet Eugen Constant (1890–1975) and extra priests who otherwise would not have bothered with the funeral of a schoolgirl. After leaving the church, the procession stopped in front of the offices of Partidul Totul pentru Ţară (the Everything for the Fatherland Party)—the Legion's official political party—where more people made speeches and held another religious service before continuing on to the cemetery.[4] The crowd sang "Imnul legionarilor căzuţi" (The hymn of the fallen legionaries) at the graveside before dispersing quietly.[5] Maria's affiliation with the Legion shaped her death just as it had dominated her diary, her friends, and her family connections.

Led by the charismatic Corneliu Zelea Codreanu, legionaries combined political assassination, street violence, and antisemitic hate speech with romantic nationalism, religious symbolism, and charity projects. They claimed that they followed a "religion," not a political party, and they described the Legion as a "spiritual" movement whose aim was to create a "new man" through suffering and sacrifice.[6] They "molded legionary character" by attending weekly meetings and occasional religious services, following strict disciplinary procedures, going on long marches, performing voluntary labor at summer work camps, paying weekly dues, and internalizing legionary doctrine through singing, speeches, and small-group discussions.

What does it mean to say that Maria Cristescu was a fascist? Was she horrified at the decadence of modernity and eager to stimulate a "cultural rebirth" by worshipping the nation, a position that Roger Griffin suggests lay at the heart

3. Fr. Ilie Imbrescu, "Maria Cristescu," *Buna vestire*, 2/270 (23 Jan 1938): 1.

4. Legionaries contested elections as Grupul Corneliu Zelea Codreanu (the Corneliu Zelea Codreanu Group, 1927–1931), Garda de Fier (the Iron Guard, 1933), and Partidul Totul pentru Ţară (the Everything for the Fatherland Party, 1934–1938). Totul pentru Ţara literally means "Everything for the Country," but I follow the translation of Ion Moţa, who rendered it in French as "Tout pour la patrie." Ion Moţa, *Corespondenţa cu Welt-Dienst (1934–1936)* (Munich: Colecţia Europa, 2000), 45.

5. This account of Cristescu's funeral is based on ACNSAS, Fond Informativ, dosar 258626, f. 103–105.

6. Corneliu Zelea Codreanu, *Pentru legionari* (Bucharest: Editura Mişcării Legionare, 1940), 286.

of fascist ideology?[7] Did she feel frustrated because she thought that Jews[8] were limiting her employment opportunities, or was she threatened by the thought of communist workers overthrowing capitalism?[9] Was she addicted to paramilitary violence?[10] Or seduced by the spectacle of uniforms, marches, rallies, salutes, and singing?[11] Historians have suggested all these as essential elements of interwar European fascism. As they look for an answer to the question "What was fascism?" observers have made fascism into a category of analysis to describe a wide variety of individuals, movements, and regimes, each arising in profoundly different circumstances. Scholars of comparative fascism lump Mussolini's transformation of Italy through corporatist labor relations, festivals, building projects, women's organizations, educational reforms, and mass media together with the terroristic violence, pogroms, church services, and emperor worship of the Black Hundreds in Russia.

Claud Sutton, a member of the British Union of Fascists, remarked in 1937 that *fascism* was "an inconvenient and awkward term to describe the world movement that has emerged in our time," but he acknowledged that its widespread popular usage made the word impossible to avoid. Aware of his movement's affinities with similar groups abroad, Sutton suggested that fascism was "an underlying similarity of outlook that can be detected in various modern national movements, and that may be seen to emerge with a kind of necessity from the

---

7. Roger Griffin, *Modernism and Fascism: The Sense of a Beginning under Mussolini and Hitler* (Basingstoke: Palgrave Macmillan, 2007).

8. In a long tradition occasioned by scholarly usage of emic terms when categorizing people in twentieth-century Europe, I use the words "Jew" and "Romanian" in the same way as they are used in my consistently racist sources. I do not wish to endorse these usages but know of no alternative that retains the embodying meaning that these terms had to contemporaries.

9. Historians who see antisemitism as a core element of fascism in east-central Europe include Radu Ioanid, *The Sword of the Archangel: Fascist Ideology in Romania* (New York: Columbia University Press, 1990). For a more balanced view, see William Brustein, *Roots of Hate: Anti-Semitism in Europe before the Holocaust* (Cambridge, UK: Cambridge University Press, 2003). Few historians consider anticommunism to have been foundational to fascism, but most consider that it played an important role. See John-Paul Himka, "The Importance of the Situational Element in East Central European Fascism," *East Central Europe* 37/2–3 (2010): 353–358.

10. Key works on the importance of paramilitary violence to fascism include Adrian Lyttelton, "Fascism and Violence in Post-war Italy: Political Strategy and Social Conflict," in *Social Protest, Violence, and Terror in Nineteenth and Twentieth Century Europe*, ed. Wolfgang Mommsen Gerhard Hirschfeld (New York: St. Martin's Press, 1982), 257–274; Richard Bessel, *Political Violence and the Rise of Nazism: The Storm Troopers in Eastern Germany, 1925–1934* (New Haven: Yale University Press, 1984); Sven Reichardt, *Faschistische Kampfbünde: Gewalt und Gemeinschaft im italienischen Squadrismus und in der deutschen SA* (Köln: Böhlau, 2002).

11. Key works on the importance of spectacle to fascism include Emilio Gentile, *The Sacralization of Politics in Fascist Italy*, trans. Keith Botsford (Cambridge, MA: Harvard University Press, 1996) and Simonetta Falasca-Zamponi, *Fascist Spectacle: The Aesthetics of Power in Mussolini's Italy* (Berkeley: University of California Press, 1997).

situation in which our European culture finds itself at present."[12] Unlike the followers of other "-isms" such as communism or liberalism fascists had no clearly articulated ideology or intellectual system. Instead, they built movements and regimes by using tactics, words, and symbols that came to be recognized all over Europe as fascist. In Romania, legionary ideologues more frequently used terms like *nationalist* to describe their movement, but—especially after 1933—they presented the Legion, Italian Fascism, and German Nazism as part of a global network of like-minded parties.[13]

With several important exceptions, many students of comparative fascism focus on the Italian and German regimes as ideal cases, describing movements that did not come to power as "failed" or "unsuccessful" fascisms, and sometimes as "minor" movements.[14] But prior to 1939, fascists in every European country except for Italy and Germany were members of social movements—not regimes.[15] I use the Legion of the Archangel Michael, also known as Garda de Fier (the Iron Guard), as a case study because it was one of the largest and most enduring fascist movements in interwar Europe.[16] At the time of Maria Cristescu's funeral, roughly 1.79 percent of ethnic Romanians were card-carrying members of the Legion—significant numbers given that, as Michael Mann notes, "these are higher percentages than the 1.3 percent attained by German Nazism and the 1.0 percent by the Italian PNF before their seizures of power."[17]

Fascism was not an entity or essence defined by certain characteristics, nor was it a set of ideas requiring intellectual assent. Rather, one *became* fascist,

12. Claud Sutton, "An Interpretation of 'Fascism,'" in *International Fascism: Theories, Causes, and the New Consensus*, ed. Roger Griffin (London: Arnold, 1998), 257–258.

13. Mihail Polihronade, "'Garda de Fier' şi statul democrat," *Axa*, 1/13 (31 May 1933): 1; Vasile Marin, "Extremismul de dreapta," *Axa*, 2/21 (29 Oct 1933): 1–2; ACNSAS, Fond Informativ, dosar 211932, vol. 1, f. 90–92.

14. For example, Roger Eatwell, *Fascism: A History* (New York: Allen Lane, 1996), 195–244; Robert Paxton, *The Anatomy of Fascism* (New York: Knopf, 2004); and R. J. B. Bosworth ed., *The Oxford History of Fascism* (Oxford: Oxford University Press, 2009). Exceptions include Philip Morgan, *Fascism in Europe, 1919–1940* (London: Routledge, 2003); and Michael Mann, *Fascists* (Cambridge, UK: Cambridge University Press, 2004).

15. Assuming that like most scholars, one does not classify Miklós Horthy's Regency in Hungary (1920–1944), Austria's Väterlandische Front (1934–1938), Antonio de Oliveira Salazar's Estado Novo regime in Portugal (1933–1974), or Francisco Franco's dictatorship in Spain (1936–1975) as fascist.

16. Corneliu Zelea Codreanu formed the Legion of the Archangel Michael as an ultranationalist social movement in 1927. He established the Iron Guard as a paramilitary subsidiary of the Legion in 1930. The Iron Guard was banned in 1933 and has not officially existed since, but it continues to be a popular way of referring to the Legion.

17. Mann, *Fascists*, 237. According to Ministerul Industriei şi Comerţului, *Anuarul Statistic al României, 1937–1938* (Bucharest: Institutul Central de Statistică, 1939), the population of Romania in 1937 was 19,535,398 people. Census data from 1930 estimated that 73 percent of the population was ethnically Romanian. Extrapolating the 1930 percentage into 1937, this gives a total of 15,237,610 ethnic Romanians in 1937.

integrating oneself into a network of like-minded individuals. I see fascism as a social category that had practical consequences for those who embraced it. The term *fascism* became popular in Romania from 1933 onward, when legionaries, Cuzists, and others used it to emphasize their similarity with far-right groups elsewhere in Europe. What fascism meant to Romanians emerged out of legionaries' interactions with each other, the state, other political parties, families and friends, and fascist groups abroad. Official repression, uniforms, and the frequency of legionary activities meant that becoming a legionary changed a person's everyday activities and relationships in profound ways.

A number of historians have asked what fascism meant to those who embraced it. A significant group of historians led by Roger Griffin have argued that at the heart of interwar fascism lay an "anti-modern revolt" catalyzed by World War I, which made people believe that a new world was necessary and that its apocalypse required the violent purification of Western civilization.[18] Alternatively, Michael Mann's study of Europe's six largest fascist social movements suggests that "fascists only embraced more fervently than anyone else the central political icon of our time, the nation-state, together with its ideologies and pathologies."[19] Nationalism—or in Mann's terminology, "nation-statism"—was certainly important for fascists, and Mann doggedly tries to understand why it appealed to some social groups more than others. Just because many nonfascists endorsed nationalism does not mean that fascists were part of the political mainstream. Their terror tactics, symbolism, and extremist views put them at odds with the political elites in their respective countries. As Juan Linz observes, fascists defined themselves more consistently by criticizing, rejecting, and seeking to overthrow their societies than by proposing a coherent ideology of their own.[20] Others have asked what might have motivated rational people to join fascism, and what role class, gender, and participation in other community groups played in stimulating fascist activism.[21] Finally, George Mosse has shown that leisure activities, mass gatherings, sexuality, gender norms, and political symbols

---

18. George Mosse, "Introduction: The Genesis of Fascism," *Journal of Contemporary History* 1/1 (1966): 1–14; Griffin, *Modernism and Fascism.*

19. Mann, *Fascists,* 1.

20. Juan J. Linz, "Some Notes toward a Comparative Study of Fascism in Sociological Historical Perspective," in *Fascism: A Reader's Guide,* ed. Walter Laqueur (Berkeley: University of California Press, 1976), 4–5, 15–23.

21. Rudy Koshar, "From Stammtisch to Party: Nazi Joiners and the Contradictions of Grass Roots Fascism in Weimar Germany," *Journal of Modern History* 59/1 (1987): 1–24; Detlef Mühlberger, *Hitler's Followers: Studies in the Sociology of the Nazi Movement* (New York: Routledge, 1991); Timothy Mason, *Nazism, Fascism, and the Working Class* (Cambridge, UK: Cambridge University Press, 1995); Karina Urbach ed., *European Aristocracies and the Radical Right, 1918–1939* (Oxford: Oxford University Press, 2007).

developed at the same time as European nationalisms and helped structure fascist ways of being in the world.[22] Following Mosse, other cultural historians have discussed the importance of uniforms, violence, parades and charity events, gender, art, theater, music, and sociality.[23]

I draw on the history of everyday life (*Alltagsgeschichte*) to show how historical actors "reproduced and transformed" social structures and ideologies through petty interactions and personal decisions.[24] Approaching fascism as an everyday practice leads one to ask how legionaries performed fascism and how being fascist marked legionaries socially. What emerges is a story of individuals working together to promote a unique and totalizing social identity in the hope that it would eventually become hegemonic. As did identifying with state-sponsored ideological projects in Nazi Germany or Stalinist Russia, identifying as a legionary changed activists' relationships within their families, churches, workplaces, and villages. Legionaries became intentional about their friendships, career choices, and religiosity. The emotional energy they invested in political activism and the extent to which they allowed legionary discipline to shape daily routines testifies to the attraction that illiberal subjectivities held for young people during this period.[25]

The potential efficacy of fascism was directly proportional to the number of people who identified as fascists and to the seriousness with which they embraced it. Viewing this equation from the perspective of rank-and-file legionaries raises other important questions about resource mobilization, the biographical impact of activism, movement frames, and political opportunity structures: How did legionaries recruit new members? How was legionary ideology produced and disseminated? How did one demonstrate commitment to the movement? What

---

22. George Mosse, *The Nationalization of the Masses: Political Symbolism and Mass Movements in Germany from the Napoleonic Wars through the Third Reich* (New York: H. Fertig, 1975); George Mosse, *Nationalism and Sexuality: Respectability and Abnormal Sexuality in Modern Europe* (New York: H. Fertig, 1985).

23. Julie Gottlieb, *Feminine Fascism: Women in Britain's Fascist Movement, 1923–1945* (London: I. B. Tauris, 2000); Michael Spurr, "'Living the Blackshirt Life': Culture, Community, and the British Union of Fascists, 1932–1940," *Contemporary European History* 12/3 (2003): 305–322; Paul Mazgaj, *Imagining Fascism: The Cultural Politics of the French Young Right, 1930–1945* (Newark: University of Delaware Press, 2007); Mark Antliff, *Avant-Garde Fascism: The Mobilization of Myth, Art, and Culture in France, 1909–1939* (Durham: Duke University Press, 2007).

24. Paul Steege et al., "The History of Everyday Life: A Second Chapter," *Journal of Modern History* 80/2 (2008): 361. See also Maria Bucur et al., "Six Historians in Search of *Alltagsgeschichte*," *Aspasia* 1/3 (2009): 189–212.

25. Cf. Jochen Hellbeck, *Revolution on My Mind: Writing a Diary under Stalin* (Cambridge, MA: Harvard University Press, 2006); and Sheila Fitzpatrick and Alf Lüdtke, "Energizing the Everyday: On the Breaking and Making of Social Bonds in Nazism and Stalinism," in *Beyond Totalitarianism: Stalinism and Nazism Compared*, ed. Michael Geyer and Sheila Fitzpatrick (Cambridge, UK: Cambridge University Press, 2009) 266–301.

risks and sacrifices did legionaries assume when they joined the movement? Answering such questions involves examining the role of organizational structure, the authority of leaders, the importance of social capital for promoting one's point of view, the degree of political freedom in interwar Romania, and the impact of police repression on fascist activism. The story of rank-and-file legionaries exposes the mechanics of a peculiar type of activism taking place throughout interwar Europe. Local incidents clarify how macrohistorical forces shaped individual experiences of fascism and how rank-and-file militants helped build the movement as a whole.

The story of the Legion begins in 1922, when a violent antisemitic student movement emerged in Romania's universities. The antisemitic students identified themselves with like-minded movements elsewhere in Europe and were supported by a loose but self-conscious network of ultranationalists scattered throughout the country. Ultranationalists simply called themselves *nationalists* or *antisemites*, but those labels risk confusing them with the majority of politicians, who articulated both nationalism and antisemitism as an ordinary part of Romanian politics. Ultranationalists made these ideas into guiding principles that they claimed directed all their other actions. In 1927 former student activists and ultranationalists formed the Legion of the Archangel Michael under the leadership of Corneliu Zelea Codreanu. The movement grew steadily during the 1930s, until government repression in 1938 left Codreanu and many of the Legion's other leaders dead and the rest in prison or in exile. The Legion became an underground organization for the next two years, after which it suddenly took power in a coup together with General Ion Antonescu (1882–1946), ruling for five months before the general destroyed the Legion in response to a failed legionary rebellion against the regime.

The Legion emerged in southeastern Europe rather than elsewhere on the continent and legionaries were comfortable looking abroad for their models. Adherents of most important Romanian intellectual and political movements of the eighteenth and nineteenth centuries, from the Enlightenment nationalists of the Transylvanian School (Şcoala Ardeleană) to the revolutionaries of 1848 and members of the antisemitic movements of the 1880s also took their lead from western European trends. Having been ruled by Habsburgs, Ottomans, and Russians for centuries, Romanians adopted a postcolonial mentality that insisted on ethnic Romanian dominance over the nation-state while legitimating local phenomena through western European connections.[26] Romanians—many of whom were rural peasants—had lacked equal access to courts, hospitals, and schools

26. Sorin Antohi, *Civitas Imaginalis: Istorie şi utopie în cultura română* (Bucharest: Editura Litera, 1994). Cf. Franz Fanon, *The Wretched of the Earth*, trans. Richard Philcox (New York: Grove Press,

while under imperial rule, leaving them at a distinct disadvantage in a Europe that privileged such institutions as markers of civilization. Legionaries mobilized peasants and other politically marginalized groups while appropriating language, aesthetics, and labels popularized by Italian Fascists and German Nazis in ways that situated the Legion symbolically within Europe's political avant-garde.[27] Fascism did not stamp its image onto empty space but emerged within and through existing institutions in a specific time and place. The individuals who constituted the Legion of the Archangel Michael did so within power relations shaped by postcolonialism, race, class, gender, and religion and this is the story of how they responded to conditions not of their own choosing to create a new and radical form of political activism in interwar Europe.

2004), 97–144; and Rebecca Bryant, *Imagining the Modern: The Cultures of Nationalism in Cyprus* (London: I. B. Tauris, 2004), 156–181.

27. Traian Sandu, "Le fascisme, révolution spatio-temporelle chez les Roumains," in *Vers un profil convergent des Fascismes? "Nouveau Consensus" et religion politique en Europe Centrale*, ed. Traian Sandu (Paris: Cahiers de la Nouvelle Europe, 2010), 217–230.

1

THE ROOTS OF ULTRANATIONALISM

One of the most popular songs among antisemitic student activists during the 1920s was "Deşteaptă-te, române" (Wake up, Romanian). Students sang it during street protests, when disrupting lectures and assaulting other students, or when throwing Jews off trains.[1] The words blamed foreign oppressors for the inert and apathetic state of ethnic Romanians and called on the latter to rise up as a people to overthrow the yoke of tyranny:

> Wake up, Romanian, from the sleep of the dead,
> Into which tyrannous barbarians immersed you
> Now or never, create your own fate,
> At which even your harshest enemies should bow.

The lyrics to "Wake Up, Romanian" were originally written by Andrei Mureşanu (1816–1863) during the 1848 revolution, when Romanians in Transylvania demanded autonomy for Romanians within the Habsburg Empire. Within weeks it was being sung in Bucharest and Iaşi against the Ottoman and Russian empires.[2] Today this song is the official Romanian national anthem, but to the antisemitic students of the 1920s it represented decades of nationalist struggle

1. AN—Iaşi, Fond Universitatea Alexandru Ioan Cuza, Iaşi, Rectorat, dosar 1022/1923, f. 467; dosar 1024/1923, f. 125–127; dosar 1057/1924, f. 22–23, 38–43; AN—Bucharest, Fond Universitatea din Bucureşti, Rectorat, dosar 4/1923, f. 65–66.

2. Viorel Cosma, *De la cântecul zaverei la imnurile unităţii naţionale* (Timişoara: Facla, 1978), 33–64.

to claim the land for ethnic Romanians. This was a holy struggle, the anthem claimed, blessed and patronized by the Orthodox Church:

> Priests, lead with your crucifixes! Because our army is Christian,
> The motto is Liberty and its goal is holy,
> Better to die in battle, in full glory,
> Than to once again be slaves upon our ancient ground!

The song divided the world into Romanians and foreigners, friends and foes, and portrayed the nationalist movement as a battle for "freedom or death!" It spoke of brotherhood and camaraderie, traitors, and a widowed mother evoking supernatural powers to curse her son's enemies. This anthem located the students within a tradition of patriotic warriors who were accepted as heroes by the state and by Romanian society at large. It provided legitimacy for their fight against Jews and "Judaized" politicians and affirmed the special calling of "elders, men, youths and boys, from mountains to the plains" to be defenders of the Romanian nation.

The belief that nations exist and are valid and meaningful collectivities deserving of allegiance is known as nationalism. Benedict Anderson describes nations as "imagined communities" similar to religions or kinship groups—collectivities extending through space and time that people identify themselves with.[3] The song "Wake Up, Romanian" commanded the students to "raise your broad forehead and look around you / Like fir trees, hundreds of thousands of heroes are standing tall." These heroes belonged to the feudal armies who defended the patrimonies of medieval princes, but nationalist propagandists claimed that they were simultaneously fighting for the modern Romanian nation. Mureşanu called on "Romanians from the four corners, now or never / Unite in thought, unite in feeling," as if a noblewoman from Timişoara would sit down together with a locksmith from Galaţi and a serf living on the outskirts of Siret. Anderson suggests that people feel solidarity with other members of their nation even though they will never meet them because technologies such as languages, maps, newspapers, and common time zones remind them that their basic everyday experiences are shared by other people who also identify with their nation. Nationalism is therefore closely connected to literacy and channels of communication. Rituals, myths, and symbols such as national histories, anthems, flags, and state weddings and funerals intensify that solidarity through moments of collective focus on the national community.

---

3. Benedict Anderson, *Imagined Communities: Reflections on the Origin and Spread of Nationalism* (New York: Verso, 1991).

Over the past two hundred years the idea of nations has been used to justify territorial claims, so cultural artifacts like history and language have taken on important political and geopolitical functions. The idea of nations is so important politically, in fact, that nationalists like Andrei Mureşanu began speaking about "the Romanian nation" at a time when nationalism was only a literary idea. Mihail Kogâlniceanu observed in 1891 that most peasants identified themselves according to the region or social class they came from instead of as Romanians, and in 1905 the ultranationalist activist A. C. Cuza (1857–1947) complained that "the popular masses are unaware even of their nationality."[4] For this reason, Rogers Brubaker has argued that nationalist discourses are not really based on nations at all but are actually political stances used by social actors for their own goals.[5] As those goals changed, so too did the purpose of speaking about nations: A discourse that in 1848 was used to justify a revolution became a war cry in 1916 and an excuse for antisemitic violence in 1922. When Mureşanu wrote that "the Danube is stolen / Through intrigue and coercion, sly machinations," he was referring to Hungarians, Russians, and Turks. But antisemitic propaganda of the late nineteenth century had connected words such as *intrigue*, *coercion*, and *slyness* with Jews and by the 1920s it was easy to apply Mureşanu's lyrics to a political platform seeking to limit Jewish influence in Romanian public life.

Jews and Foreigners

The historical context in which Romanian nationalism developed meant that nationalists frequently expressed anxieties about their identity, collective national purpose, and place in Europe through attacks on Jews and foreigners (*străini*). The territory of present-day Romania was ruled by the Habsburg, Russian, and Ottoman empires until these empires collapsed in the early twentieth century. Despite frequent rebellions, Wallachian princes (*domni* or *domnitori*) began paying tribute to the Ottomans in 1390 and the Moldavians did the same during the 1450s. In return they received self-governance, were spared the settlement of Muslim landowners in their territories, and princes generally had a strong say in the appointment of ecclesiastical officials.[6] The power of the native *domnitori* declined in the eighteenth century and they were replaced with Greek rulers

4. Alex Drace-Francis, *The Making of Modern Romanian Culture: Literacy and the Development of National Identity* (London: Tauris Academic Studies, 2006), 129–134.

5. Rogers Brubaker, *Nationalism Reframed: Nationhood and the National Question in the New Europe* (Cambridge, UK: Cambridge University Press, 1996), 60.

6. Charles King, *The Black Sea: A History* (Oxford: Oxford University Press, 2004), 121; Drace-Francis, *Making of Modern Romanian Culture*, 18–19.

known as Phanariots, who also owed their positions to the Ottoman sultan. Those regions of Moldavia that were not governed by the Ottomans—Bukovina and Bessarabia—fell under Habsburg and Russian control. Anti-Phanariot sentiment grew among the Romanians in these principalities and culminated in 1821 when Romanian forces supported the Ottomans against the attempt by Alexander Ipsilantis (1792–1828) to resurrect the Byzantine Empire, which was to include Wallachia and Moldavia.[7] Although technically still governed by the Ottomans, Wallachia and Moldavia both fell under Russian military occupation in 1826. Russian armies occupied the principalities eight times between 1711 and 1854, but this occupation involved thoroughgoing and unpopular agrarian reforms, the introduction of a cash economy, the subordination of the church to the state, and the consolidation of the legal rights of the Romanian boyars to their estates.[8] Even though they were officially under foreign rule, intellectuals in the Romanian principalities had the liberty to develop Romanian culture in relative freedom while being able to blame the region's economic and social problems on a litany of foreign invaders.

The principalities of Wallachia and Moldavia had their own national movements, and individuals claiming to be "working for the benefit of the Romanian nation" appear in the sources as early as the eighteenth century.[9] These national movements were facilitated by newspapers and a growing literary scene influenced by French intellectual culture and the rise of liberal nationalism throughout Europe and encouraged by the Romanian Orthodox Church. But the influence of nationalism was limited because it was rarely discussed outside elite circles—the leaders of the Romanian national movement in Transylvania during the later half of the nineteenth century were predominately bourgeois males or high-ranking clergymen.[10] Many Romanians in Transylvania were legally serfs up until the 1854 emancipation, and even then they remained in an economically subordinate position vis-à-vis their Saxon or Hungarian neighbors.[11] Similarly, most Romanians in Wallachia and Moldavia were impoverished and illiterate peasants who had little hope that they would benefit from the wave of nationalist uprisings that rocked the Balkan provinces of the Ottoman Empire during the first part of the nineteenth century. The abolition of serfdom in the principalities followed by the rise of a nascent capitalism left many former serfs without

---

7. Keith Hitchins, *The Romanians, 1774–1866* (Oxford: Clarendon Press, 1996), 141–152.

8. Mark Mazower, *The Balkans: A Short History* (New York: Modern Library, 2000), 90–91.

9. Drace-Francis, *Making of Modern Romanian Culture*, 10.

10. Keith Hitchins, *A Nation Affirmed: The Romanian National Movement in Transylvania, 1860–1914* (Bucharest: Encyclopaedic, 1999), 103–110.

11. Katherine Verdery, *Transylvanian Villagers: Three Centuries of Political, Economic, and Ethnic Change* (Berkeley: University of California Press, 1983), 219–222.

cultivatable land and in a position of dependency on the large landholders, creating a rural proletariat who remained in a state of "neo-serfdom."[12]

Imperial administrators and western European travelers categorized Romanians as backward and barbaric, and in turn Romanians classified Others according to how they, as a group, benefited from the imperial system.[13] As long as Romanians lived within multiethnic states, foreigners were neighbors as often as they were outsiders. The Romanian word *străin* referred equally well to Phanariot or Russian administrators, Turkish or Jewish traders, and Hungarian or German peasants, all of whom lived in the same towns and villages as Romanians. Nationalists used negative stereotypes about Roma—whom they called *ţigani* (gypsies)—as uncivilized people in need of wise rulers to justify their claim that Romanians were worthy of a nation-state, and they spoke about Jews and *străini* as a way of emphasizing that Romanians were not yet in full control of their own country.[14] With the gradual success of the national movement, Romanian nationalists slowly lost interest in Phanariots and Turks and came to see Jews as their most immediate enemies, closely followed by those Romanian elites who collaborated with Jews.

Jews had lived in the territory of present-day Romania since at least the late Middle Ages, but modern antisemitism in Romania dates to the wave of Jewish immigration from Polish Galicia during the eighteenth century. Phanariot princes gave the new immigrants a hostile welcome, and Greek and Bulgarian merchants stirred up antisemitic violence in Brăila, Galaţi, Giurgiu, and Iaşi to prevent the immigrants from taking their trade.[15] Over the next century, Romanian documents portrayed Jews as sly, deceitful, ugly, smelly, cowardly, and lazy. They spoke about Jews as Christ-killers who practiced ritual sacrifices with Christian babies to strengthen their pact with the devil. Romanians also accused Jews of corrupting morality by running taverns and of monopolizing commerce to the exclusion of Romanians, even though census data shows that only 2.5 percent of publicans and 21.1 percent of merchants were Jewish at the beginning of the twentieth century.[16]

---

12. Constantin Dobrogreanu-Gherea, *Neoiobăgia: Studiu economico-sociologic al problemei noastre agrare* (Bucharest: Editura "Viaţa Românească," 1910), 56–73; Virgil Madgearu, *Agrarianism, capitalism, imperialism: Contribuţii la studiul evoluţiei sociale româneşti* (Cluj-Napoca: Dacia, 1999), 22.

13. Sorin Mitu, *National Identity of Romanians in Transylvania* (Budapest: Central European University Press, 2001).

14. Shannon Woodcock, "'The *Ţigan* Is Not a Man': The *Ţigan* Other as Catalyst for Romanian Ethnonational Identity" (PhD diss., University of Sydney, 2005), 78–93.

15. Gabriel Asandului, *Istoria evreilor din România (1866–1938)* (Iaşi: Institutul European, 2003), 15–18.

16. Ibid., 32; Andrei Oişteanu, *Inventing the Jew: Antisemitic Stereotypes in Romanian and Other Central-East European Cultures*, trans. Mirela Adăscălţei (Lincoln: University of Nebraska Press, 2009), 176 and passim.

Antisemitism and State-Building

Once Romanians gained an independent nation-state in the mid-nineteenth century, earlier hatreds of Jews took on a postcolonial edge, as Romanian nationalists identified Jews with foreigners and attacked ethnic Romanians who collaborated with them. In 1859 great-power rivalries between Russia, Britain, and the Ottoman Empire provided an unexpected bounty when both Wallachia and Moldavia were granted independence at the end of the Crimean War. Few Romanians had discussed uniting the principalities between 1770 and 1830, but the "Romanian Question" was still a regular topic of conversation among the Great Powers, and among Romanian émigrés from the early 1850s.[17] Although the Convention of Paris in 1858 said nothing about joining Wallachia and Moldavia, the Romanians took the initiative and the following year the two principalities united under the personal rule of a leader of one of the Wallachian revolutionaries from 1848, Alexandru Ion Cuza (1820–1873). Alexandru Ion Cuza's regime increased Romanian society's contact with the West, borrowing heavily from foreign investors and importing consumer products in ever greater quantities.[18] New fears about foreigners emerged as Romania moved from the Ottoman periphery into a European periphery and discovered that once again its agricultural and industrial products were leaving the country for meager profits.[19] Romania's small bourgeois class included more Jews than ethnic Romanians, and as the economic importance of this class grew, concerns developed about who truly held the power in the country—the (Jewish) bankers or those (Romanians) who worked the land.

One of the most famous antisemites was the poet and journalist Mihai Eminescu (1850–1889). He wrote in 1879 that "the Jew does not deserve rights anywhere in Europe because he does not work. . . . He is the eternal consumer, never a producer."[20] Antisemites believed that Jewish power depended on the cooperation of Romanian politicians, and according to Eminescu, the ultimate cause of Romania's social and economic problems were the "red" (Liberal) governments who "lulled Romania to sleep with patriotic words while at the same time, whenever possible, doing the work of foreigners."[21] Andrei Oişteanu argues that

---

17. Drace-Francis, *Making of Modern Romanian Culture*, 23–25; Hitchins, *The Romanians*, 276–294.

18. Bogdan Murgescu, *România şi Europa: Acumularea decalajelor economice (1500–2010)* (Iaşi: Polirom, 2010), 113.

19. Ilie Bădescu, *Sincronism european şi cultură critică românească* (Bucharest: Editura Ştiinţifică şi Enciclopedică, 1984), 231–235.

20. Mihai Eminescu, quoted in Léon Volovici, *Nationalist Ideology and Anti-Semitism: The Case of Romanian Intellectuals in the 1930s* (Oxford: Pergamon Press, 1991), 12.

21. Mihai Eminescu, quoted in Bădescu, *Sincronism european*, 284.

from the mid-1860s onwards nationalist intellectuals appropriated antisemitic stereotypes from popular culture and then reintroduced them through polemical texts.[22] The stereotype of the swindling Jew, for example, expressed through sayings such as "Until he cheats, the Jew does not eat," is found in collections of popular fables gathered during the nineteenth century.[23] One of the many intellectuals who reformulated this stereotype was the famous historian Nicolae Iorga (1871–1940), who wrote in his newspaper, *Neamul românesc* (the Romanian people, 1906–1940), that "the Jews in Romania, especially those in Moldavia, live on trade, on exchange, *on double-dealing* to the prejudice of others, and they shun any hard work. *They are intelligent but cunning* and, pursuing solely their own interests, seek to corrupt the mores."[24] Iorga distributed free copies of *Neamul românesc* to teachers and priests in villages throughout Moldavia, giving a politicized and learned image to existing folk wisdom.[25] During the 1860s and 1870s, a number of intellectuals argued loudly against granting Jews more rights.[26] In 1879 the National Liberal politician Pantazi Ghica (1831–1882) described Jews as "a nation within a nation," warning that they constituted a fifth column that threatened to undermine Romania from within.[27] That same year the philosopher Vasile Conta (1845–1882) affirmed that "if we do not fight against the Jewish element we will perish as a nation."[28] Antisemitism was intimately connected with nationalist anxieties that the Romanian nation was weak and vulnerable. In the popular imagination, political corruption left ordinary Romanians at the mercy of the Jews.

Accusations of bribery, election rigging, and the corruption of justice at the highest levels were common and sometimes even demonstrated in court, making antisemitic slurs an effective means of discrediting political opponents.[29] Cuza was overthrown in 1866 and replaced by a member of the Hohenzollern dynasty, Prince Carol (1839–1914). Article 7 of the new constitution specified that "only foreigners of the Christian religion are eligible to become Romanians," effectively denying Jews political rights in the Romanian principality.[30] When a softened

22. Oişteanu, *Inventing the Jew*, 5.

23. Ibid., 143.

24. Nicolae Iorga, *Neamul românesc*, 5 June 1907, quoted in Oişteanu, *Inventing the Jew*, 144.

25. Oişteanu, *Inventing the Jew*, 144.

26. Victor Neumann, *Istoria evreilor din România: Studii documentare şi teoretice* (Timişoara: Amarcord, 1996), 173–191; Volovici, *Nationalist Ideology*, 12–15.

27. Carol Iancu, *Evreii din România: De la emancipare la marginalizare 1919–1938*, trans. Ţicu Goldstein (Bucharest: Hasefer, 2000), 150–151.

28. Ibid., 152.

29. Titu Maiorescu, *Istoria contemporană a României (1866–1900)* (Bucharest: Editura Universităţii Titu Maiorescu, 2002), 40–51, 62–66.

30. Neumann, *Istoria evreilor*, 169.

version of that article went before the legislature later that year, a crowd surrounded the building, drowning out the proceedings with angry shouting until the proposed amendment was dropped. Cheering, the protesters moved on to the center of the city where they destroyed a recently completed synagogue.[31] Cuza's dismissal and limitations on Jewish rights did little to solve the problem, however, and in 1871 Prince Carol published an open letter in which he laid the blame for the problems of a country that was "so well provisioned by nature and yet poor beyond belief" squarely at the feet of its indigenous political class.[32]

The workings of Romania's political system changed once Carol was proclaimed king in 1881. King Carol I personally appointed both the judiciary and the prime minister. Between 1881 and 1914 he negotiated with both the Conservatives and the National Liberals before deciding which group he would ask to form the next government. Carol's chosen government would organize the upcoming elections, which including appointing county prefects who supervised the elections. These county prefects and local officials then influenced the outcomes of elections, ensuring that the king's preferred party won.[33] As Keith Hitchins dryly notes, "No government designated by the king was ever disappointed at the polls."[34] Once a government was elected, only a dispute with the king could topple it. Political rivalries were of a very personal nature and on many occasions individuals crossed the floor of Parliament, agitated in the press against members of their own parties, or formed dissident alliances within the major parties.[35] Armed police were regularly used to intimidate political opponents, as were bands of armed thugs that police were unable or unwilling to control.[36]

Four events from the spring and summer of 1884 give a sense of the methods used by politicians of this era to maintain power: In April, a crowd protesting against "the disloyal and unpatriotic politics of the present government, the dilapidation of public funds, the arbitrariness and incompetence of the monarch in the administration of this unhappy nation, [and] the system of corruption

---

31. Paul E. Michelson, "Romanian Development, Nationalism, and Some Nationality Issues under Carol I, 1866–1914," in *Naţiunea română: Idealuri şi realităţi istorice*, ed. Alexandru Zub, Venera Achim, and Nagy Pienaru (Bucharest: Editura Academiei Romane, 2006), 336.

32. Prince Carol, *Augsburger Allgemeine Zeitung* (15/27 Jan 1871), quoted in ibid., 22.

33. Ultranationalist descriptions of how local elections were rigged in the favor of government candidates can be found in I. R., "Cum se fac alegerile la ţară," *Neamul românesc*, 2/57 (18 Nov 1907): 904–908; Ion Zelea Codreanu, "Discursul rostit în şedinţa Adunării Deputaţilor," 19 July 1920; reprinted in *Totalitarismul de dreapta în România: Origini, manifestări, evoluţie, 1919–1927*, ed. Ioan Scurtu (Bucharest: Institutul Naţional pentru Studiul Totalitarismului, 1996), 210–211.

34. Keith Hitchins, *Rumania, 1866–1947* (Oxford: Clarendon Press, 1994), 94.

35. Ibid., 96–127; Ion Bulei, *Sistemul politic al Romaniei moderne: Partidul Conservator* (Bucharest: Editura Politica, 1987), 201–203, 279–280, 304–317.

36. Florin N. Şinca, *Din istoria poliţiei române*, vol. 1 (Bucharest: Tipografia RCR Print, 2006), 85–89.

that threatens the new generations" was assaulted and beaten by the police with the prior knowledge of government ministers. In May, one hundred students marching to the Austro-Hungarian Legation singing "Wake Up, Romanian" were forcibly dispersed by the police prefect. In June, protesting students were attacked on the street by bands of thugs who had been organized and armed by the police. In July, the government used police and armed gangs in the provinces to prevent electoral propaganda by opposition parties.[37] This was ordinary politics for the period, and 1884 was not a particularly turbulent year.

Political violence often spilled over into violence against Jews. Romanians attacked Jews in Iaşi and Bucharest in 1891, 1898, and 1899.[38] In Chişinău, then still part of the Russian Empire, a large pogrom occurred in 1903. It was sparked by an antisemitic newspaper, *Bessarabeţ*, which was edited by Pavel Cruşevanu (1860–1909). A member of the Black Hundreds and an influential journalist, Cruşevanu claimed that a Russian boy from a nearby town had been murdered by Jews. Indignation over the murder led to widespread antisemitic violence even though the true murderer—one of the boy's relatives—was later found and convicted.[39] When hundreds of thousands of peasants from all over Romania rose up in 1907 to protest against absentee landlords and their *arendaşi* (estate managers), their revolt left at least eleven thousand dead and many Jewish families homeless.[40] Although the goals of the revolt were neither antisemitic nor nationalist, much of the rhetoric against *arendaşi* focused on their Jewish ethnicity. In Wallachia, where few *arendaşi* were Jewish, peasants generally left Jews in peace, but in Moldavia where the revolt began, peasants attacked Jewish homes and businesses together with manorial estates.[41]

Romania remained neutral when World War I broke out in August 1914, and its leaders negotiated with both sides before finally joining the Allies in August 1916. The drawn-out discussions over whether to support Germany or Britain and France polarized public opinion and a number of intellectuals who admired

---

37. Frédéric Damé, *J. C. Bratiano: L'ère nouvelle—la dictature* (Bucharest: Bureaux de l'Indépendance Roumaine, 1886), 241–304.

38. "10 Mai la Iaşi," *Universul*, 17/128 (13 May 1891): 4; Constantin Dobrogeanu-Gherea, *Carp und die Judenfrage* (Vienna: Buchdruckerei "Industrie," 1900), 9; Eugen Herovanu, *Oraşul amintirilor* (Bucharest: Minerva, 1975), 177.

39. Iurie Colesnic, *Basarabia necunoscută*, vol. 3 (Chişinău: Museum, 2000), 28–41; Monty Noam Penkower, "The Kishinev Pogrom of 1903: A Turning Point in Jewish History," *Modern Judaism*, 24/3 (2004): 187–225.

40. Philip Gabriel Eidelberg, *The Great Rumanian Peasant Revolt of 1907: Origins of a Modern Jacquerie* (Leiden: E. J. Brill, 1974); Carol Iancu, *Les Juifs en Roumanie (1866–1919): De l'exclusion à l'emancipation* (Provence: Éditions de l'Université de Provence, 1978), 230–233.

41. Ion Popescu-Puţuri ed., *Marea răscoală a ţăranilor din 1907* (Bucharest: Editura Academiei Republicii Socialiste România, 1987), 75.

Germany faced treason charges after the war.[42] One of Romania's primary war aims was to gain Transylvania, but according to the Conservative politician Constantin Argetoianu (1871–1955), "it was impossible to awaken the peasantry to the national cause."[43] Peasants, quite simply, cared less about the nationalist dream of bringing all Romanians into one nation-state and more about their own livelihoods. The Romanian army was not prepared for war and after some initial advances into Transylvania it was forced to retreat. The Central Powers occupied Bucharest in December 1916. Fighting continued in Moldavia, but here too the Romanians were forced to concede defeat in May 1918.[44] As native speakers of German, Jews fared well in occupied Romania, which further infuriated antisemites, who claimed (erroneously) that Jews had not supported the war effort sufficiently.[45] As the German army began to retreat, Romania reentered the war in November 1918, and King Ferdinand returned victorious to Bucharest three weeks later.

The end of the war caused a number of difficulties. Unlike in Western Europe, the state did little to help people rebuild. Moreover, Romania gained Transylvania, Bucovina, and Bessarabia, which meant that Hungarians, Germans, Romanians, and others who had fought in the Austro-Hungarian armies now experienced the Romanian state as an occupying force that did little to acknowledge or honor their dead.[46] Veterans were crucial supporters of fascist movements in Italy, Germany, Austria, and Hungary—all countries that had lost territory during the war.[47] Instead of facing a large group of disappointed veterans, Romanians had to contend with large minority populations who had previously dominated the occupied regions both economically and culturally. Antisemites complained bitterly about the peace treaties that denied Romania a serious role in regional politics and imposed an unwelcome Minorities Treaty on the country.[48] The treaty supposedly guaranteed rights for Jews and other minorities but it also underlined the fact that the Western powers did not trust Romanians to fairly govern the country.[49]

According to the 1930 census, Hungarians were by far interwar Romania's largest ethnic minority, followed by Germans, Jews, and Ruthenians and Ukrainians.

---

42. Gala Galaction, *Jurnal*, vol. 3 (Bucharest: Minerva, 1980), 43–57, 72–78, 84–90.

43. Quoted in Lucian Boia, *"Germanofilii": Elita intelectuală românească în anii primului război mondial* (Bucharest: Humanitas, 2010), 52.

44. Hitchins, *Rumania*, 262–279.

45. Boia, *"Germanofilii,"* 92; "Jidovii şi războiul mondial," *Apărarea Naţională*, 1/1 (1 Apr 1922): 13–14.

46. Maria Bucur, *Heroes and Victims: Remembering War in Twentieth-Century Romania* (Bloomington: Indiana University Press, 2009), 49–59.

47. Mann, *Fascists*, 68–69, 151–154, 213, 240.

48. A. C. Cuza, *Îndrumari de politică externă: Discursuri parlamentare rostite în anii 1920–1936* (Bucharest: Cugetarea—Georgescu Delafras, 1941), 11–19.

49. Carole Fink, *Defending the Rights of Others: The Great Powers, the Jews, and International Minority Protection, 1878–1938* (Cambridge, UK: Cambridge University Press, 2006), 133–265.

TABLE 1.1 Ethnic groups in Romania in 1930

ETHNIC GROUP	POPULATION	PERCENTAGE
Romanian	12,981,324	71.9
Hungarian	1,425,507	7.9
German	745,421	4.1
Jewish	728,115	4.0
Ruthenian and Ukrainian	582,115	3.2
Russian	409,150	2.3
Bulgarian	366,384	2.0
Roma	262,501	1.5
Other	556,511	3.1
Total	18,057,028	100.0

Source: Table based on Sabin Manuila, *Recensământul general al populației României din decemvrie 1930* (Bucharest: Institutul Central de Statistică, 1938), vol. 2, xxiv.

Jews were by no means the largest of these minority groups, but Jews and Roma—and to a lesser extent Ukrainians and Ruthenians—were the only minorities that did not have a strong state nearby to protect their rights. Romanian authorities restricted access to Ukrainian-language education and cultural societies in the early 1920s, and Ukrainian nationalist organizing had little success in Romania.[50] Ultranationalists and state officials alike ignored Roma during the interwar period because nationalists were concerned with establishing the authority of ethnic Romanians in the newly expanded state, and Roma's status as a powerless and disadvantaged group had been well-established in the nationalist imagination since the mid-nineteenth century.[51] Jews, on the other hand, had economic influence and occupied important positions within the country's educational and cultural institutions. As Romanians struggled to assert control over the new territories, the prewar rhetoric about Jews as the quintessential foreigners who dominated helpless Romanians once again came to the fore.

One of the ways that Romanian authorities tried to assert their dominance over the new provinces was by persecuting Jews. Although hostilities ceased in most of Europe in November 1918, Romanian soldiers continued fighting in Transylvania. The rhetoric of the war framed it as a crusade against communism after Béla Kun came to power in Hungary on 21 March 1919. That November police distributed antisemitic posters around the country on the orders of the short-lived government led by Arthur Văitoianu (1864–1956). These posters

50. Irina Livezeanu, *Cultural Politics in Greater Romania: Regionalism, Nation Building, and Ethnic Struggle, 1918–1930*, Ithaca: Cornell University Press, 1995), 49–88.

51. Woodcock, "The *Ţigan* Is Not a Man," 36–37.

identified members of Béla Kun's Communist Party as Jewish and denounced all Jews as Bolsheviks who had to be liquidated. Isolated attacks on Jews and on Jewish property followed, including some by Romanian soldiers acting under orders, with no legal repercussions.[52] In the Bessarabian town of Leova that year, which had also just come under Romanian control, Jewish travelers were arrested, beaten, and tortured before being transferred to Chişinău, where they were forced to bribe their way out of police custody.[53] In 1922 the Liberal minister of education, Constantin Angelescu (1870–1948), authorized the distribution of an antisemitic pamphlet titled *Înfruntarea Jidovilor* (Standing up to the Yids) to schools throughout the country.[54] The Romanianization of schools in Bucovina from 1918 onward involved creating special Jewish schools for students who had previously had access to the Austro-Hungarian Empire's best institutions. Jewish schools then faced budget cuts, staff replacements or demotions, and changes to the language of instruction.[55]

Electoral reform finally came in 1917, and universal male suffrage was implemented for the first time in 1919, radically changing the constitution of Parliament with 83 percent of those elected entering public office for the first time.[56] Despite these changes, 1920s politicians continued many of the corrupt practices perfected before the war. Partidul Naţional Liberal (the National Liberal Party, PNL) maintained close ties with bankers and industrialists, passing legislation and granting permits to benefit certain companies and excluding unwanted foreign competitors from the market.[57] Scandals filled the headlines when evidence of compromising links between supposedly patriotic politicians and Jewish financers or foreign arms dealers emerged that compromised the credibility of the political establishment as a whole.[58] When Ion I. C. Brătianu's PNL won the elections of January 1922, both the National Romanian Party and the Peasants Party openly accused the government of electoral violence and fraud.[59] Romania's constitution of 1923 granted citizenship to Jews, but the sixty-year-old

52. Iancu, *Evreii din România*, 143–144; "Memorandum on Roumanian Riots for Conference, 19 December 1926," USNA, Records of the Department of State relating to Internal Affairs of Romania, 1910–1944, f. 3.

53. Iancu, *Evreii din România*, 145.

54. Ibid., 150.

55. Livezeanu, *Cultural Politics*, 68–72.

56. Sorin Radu, *Electoratul din România în anii democraţiei parlamentare (1919–1937)* (Iaşi: Institutul European, 2004), 73.

57. Maurice Pearton, *Oil and the Romanian State* (Oxford: Clarendon Press, 1971), 109; Ludovic Báthory, *Societăţile carbonifere şi sistemul economic şi politic al României (1919–1929)* (Cluj-Napoca: Presa Universitară Clujeană, 1999), 54–55.

58. Nicholas M. Nagy-Talavera, *Nicolae Iorga: A Biography* (Iaşi: Center for Romanian Studies, 1998), 229–232; Mihail Chioveanu, "Afacerea Skoda," *Sfera politicii* 8/84 (2000): 16–20.

59. Scurtu ed., *Totalitarismul*, 247–249.

tradition linking Jews and political corruption meant that antisemitism flourished throughout the interwar period.

Organizing Ultranationalists

As long as Romanians were ruled by foreign empires, Romanian nationalist activism was largely peaceful and reformist. But the tradition of nationalist organizing developed during the nineteenth century established the basis for ultranationalist mobilization after World War I. In the Habsburg provinces of Transylvania and Bucovina, nationalists formed cultural associations, feminist groups, ethnic choirs, gymnastics groups, and reading societies that they then used to promote national sentiment and to mobilize the Romanian population around nationalist causes. These associations attracted the wealthiest and most civically active members of Romanian communities both inside and outside the country and directed their energies toward creating and sustaining the sense that a Romanian nation existed, was threatened, and was worth fighting for. But by the twentieth century it was not only the rich and the highly educated who were forming nationalist organizations. Ultranationalist leagues and political parties with significant numbers of members sprang up all over the country once the dust settled from the Hungarian-Romanian War of 1919, drawing on networks that clearly predated the parties themselves. Many used a vocabulary that was increasingly popular among members of the extreme Right throughout Europe, blending fraternity, militarism, and religious ideas into a new ultranationalist idiom.

The Frăție de Cruce (Blood Brotherhood) was founded in the Apuseni Mountains by Amos Francu (?–1933) in June 1919. Members wore white flowers on their cufflinks and a white cross on their left arms and practiced sport and marksmanship together.[60] The Blood Brotherhood still spoke about cultural propaganda, but the nonviolent tone of nineteenth-century nationalism was now gone. Antisemitism was a central feature of these organizations, and in April 1924 a high school teacher, two shopkeepers and a tenant farmer met together in the city of Ploiești to talk about establishing a Ligă Antisemită (Antisemitic League) after the Easter holidays. They planned to gather support by holding small gatherings in the suburbs as well as large public meetings. One of the four, the shopkeeper Moise Găvănescu, immediately began doing propaganda among his friends and acquaintances. He told them that the Jews controlled the press and the economy

60. Statut de organizare a Frăției de Cruce, 29 June 1919; reprinted in *Totalitarismul*, ed. Scurtu, 181–185; Heinen, *Legiunea "Arhanghelul Mihail,"* 98.

and that forming a common front to drive the Jews out of industry and commerce was the only way to reduce the cost of living. Gavanescu belonged to the local branch of Societatea Apărătorii Patriei (the Defenders of the Fatherland Society) and he used his connections there to promote the league among war veterans as well.[61] The police quickly lost interest in Gavanescu's proposed league so there is no record of how long it lasted or how many people joined.

I call people like Frâncu and Gavanescu *ultranationalists*. They simply called themselves *nationalists* or *antisemites*. According to ultranationalists, "practically and theoretically, antisemitism is the same as nationalism."[62] By the early 1930s some of ultranationalists had come to identify themselves as "fascists," though others continued to cherish core ultranationalist values while rejecting fascism because of the label's aesthetic, ethical, and geopolitical implications. Ultranationalists shared the nationalism and antisemitism that was common in Romania after the war, but rather than simply expressing such sentiments, they mobilized around them. Whereas Conservatives or National Liberals saw nationalism as the best means of promoting their own political programs, ultranationalists made attacking Jews and corrupt politicians their main raison d'être.

Ultranationalists embraced the central ideas of Romanian nationalism that had been developed during the nineteenth century, even while they rejected many mainstream intellectuals as Westernizers.[63] They saw Romanians as a downtrodden but noble people who had lived under foreign oppression for centuries.[64] Romanian nationalism was a moral imperative for them, and required sacrificing time, money and if necessary, respectability.[65] They blamed "politicianism" for their country's economic and social woes and charged that the democratic parties had sold Romania out to foreigners.[66] In the ultranationalist imagination, the quintessential foreigners were Jews, whom they considered the ethnic, religious, economic, and social enemies of their people.[67] They advocated expelling Jews from the country.[68] They believed that the solution to Romania's problems lay in cultivating autochthonous Romanian "traditions" and not in foreign imports,

61. ANIC, Fond DGP, dosar 16/1923, f. 8.

62. "Antisemitismul este naționalismul," *Străjerul*, 1/1 (4 Oct 1926): 1.

63. "Junimiștii și 'Adevărul,'" *Antisemitul* (Bucharest), 1/45 (12 Oct 1899): 1–2; Nicolae Iorga, *Istoria evreilor în țerile noastre* (Bucharest: Academia Română, 1913), 37.

64. Mina Savel, *Istoria Judaismului* (Iași: Tipografia M. P. Popovici, 1902), 158.

65. I. Manolescu-Mladian, "Invitare cordială frațească," *Strigătul*, 1/1 (19 Jan 1892): 4.

66. *Antisemitul* (Bucharest), 1/2 (17 Aug 1887): 1; "Jidovul P. P. Carp," *Ecoul Moldovei*, 2/65 (11 Feb 1893): 2; Gheorghe Roșianu, *Pățania lui Gheorghe Roșianu in Focșani* (Focșani: Atelierele Gh. A. Diaconescu, 1914), 4–5.

67. Comitetul antisemit din Bârlad, "Manifestul Program al partidului național-antisemit" (1899), in *Documents concerning the Fate of Romanian Jewry during the Holocaust*, ed. Jean Ancel (New York: Beate Klarsfeld Foundation, 1986), 3.

68. Un bun român, *Chestiunea Ovreiască* (Bucharest: n.p., 1913).

but that Romanians themselves needed to be reformed through discipline and sacrifice.[69] All these elements can be found in the discourses of Romanian nationalism and antisemitism that evolved over the course of the nineteenth century. Ultranationalists synthesized these notions into a single worldview and committed themselves to working toward its realization.

One of the leading ultranationalists of the late nineteenth century, Mina Savel, explained:

> For someone to be an antisemite today . . . means to be a devoted fighter against a materialist current that puts money above honor, virtue, and the highest sentiments worthy of human nature. At the same time, to be an antisemite is to be a martyr and defender of one's nation, of the rights and institutions that, together with the spirit of liberty, contribute to the progress of a nation. An antisemite fights not only against Yids, but also against those Judaized people who support them.[70]

Ultranationalists were spread out across the country but appeared most frequently in large urban centers like Bucharest, Iaşi, Galaţi, and Cluj. Carol Iancu writes about an "antisemitic movement" made up of "clergy, army officers, state functionaries, teachers and students," which manifested itself through "groupings, associations, and clubs whose members were recruited among the different professions with the declared goal of combating Jews economically and of organizing systematic boycotts against them."[71] Iancu uses the word *movement* because ultranationalists themselves spoke of an "antisemitic movement" at the beginning of the twentieth century, but this was not an organized group with a clear leadership or hierarchy. Ultranationalists maintained social ties with each other and regularly moved in and out of various antisemitic organizations, but before the mid-1920s no single organization united them all.[72]

When Nicolae Iorga and A. C. Cuza established Partidul Naţionalist Democrat (the Nationalist Democratic Party) in 1910 it was the first attempt by ultranationalists to form a traditional political party. It lasted only six years and had little success at the polls, but it brought ultranationalists together and promoted Iorga, Cuza, and activists such as Ion Zelea Codreanu (1878–?) and Corneliu Şumuleanu (1869–1937) to celebrity status among like-minded individuals. The party split during World War I, and the more antisemitic wing, led by Cuza and

69. Alexandru C. Cuza, *Naţionalitatea în arta: Expunere a doctrinci naţionaliste, principii, fapte, concluzii* (Bucharest: "Minerva," 1915), xiii.

70. Mina Savel, "Cine sunt antisemiţii," *Antisemitul* (Craiova), 1/5 (31 Mar 1898): 1.

71. Iancu, *Les Juifs en Roumanie*, 220.

72. "La mormântul lui Cruşevan," *Naţionalistul*, 1/3 (3 Sept 1922): 3.

Codreanu, rearticulated ultranationalist goals as "the purification of our social atmosphere, the ending of political parasitism, the abolition of club-house politics, of partisanship and toadyism."[73]

Another short-lived movement was Constantin Pancu's Garda Conştiinţei Naţionale (the Guard of the National Conscience). The guard mobilized workers and students in Iaşi against Bolshevism, provoking brawls with left-wing workers and bringing ultranationalist politics onto the streets. The guard called its agenda "national socialism," which it said involved preventing communist propaganda, economic speculation, and administrative corruption, but it also promoted workers' rights and women's suffrage through speeches and publications.[74] Pancu's guard continued the nineteenth-century practice of nationalist organizing through community events, but it introduced rallies and strikebreaking into the ultranationalist repertoire and shifted the emphasis away from antisemitism toward a more broadly defined program that included anti-Bolshevism and antipoliticianism.

In 1921 Elena Bacaloglu (1878–1947), a journalist living in Italy, gained Mussolini's begrudging support to form a Movimento nazionale fascista italo-romeno (Italian-Romanian National Fascist Movement), which merged with Fascia Naţionale Române (the National Romanian Fascists, FNR) in 1922.[75] FNR created branches all over the country, adapting the ideology and rhetoric of Italian Fascism to the Romanian context. Police reports from December 1924 estimate that FNR members throughout the country numbered in their tens of thousands.[76] FNR collapsed in 1924 as a result of leadership struggles and a scandal associating it with the National Liberal Party, but members carried the memories of its temporary success into other ultranationalist organizations.

In Cluj, a handful of ultranationalist intellectuals formed Acţiunea Românească (Romanian Action) on 7 June 1924. They hoped to continue the struggles of the pre-1918 national movement within the context of an expanded Romania. The group dedicated itself to "reducing the economic, cultural and political power of foreigners, especially Jews, to a just proportion" and to overcoming those Romanians who, "fallen prey to unjustifiable pessimism or excessive egotism, dishonor Romanians through their work and actions and prevent the economic and moral

73. Mihail Dragoş, "Frontul Nou," *Unirea*, 4/1 (29 Oct 1918): 3.

74. "Apel," *Conştiinţa*, 1/1 (30 Aug 1919): 4; F. Gugui, "Socialismul şi 'Garda Conştiinţei Naţionale,'" *Conştiinţa*, 1/2 (18 Sept 1919): 3; "Pentru muncitoare şi funcţionare," *Conştiinţa*, 1/13–14 (5 Jan 1920): 2. Codreanu later claimed that no one in the guard had heard of German National Socialism at this time. Codreanu, *Pentru legionari*, 24.

75. Heinen, *Legiunea "Arhanghelul Mihail,"* 102–104.

76. ANIC, Fond DGP, dosar 36/1923, f. 9–10, 16–21. Another report from 1924 gives much lower numbers, emphasizing that most FNR members had already joined the LANC by this time. Ibid., dosar 49/1924, f. 135–140.

renewal of our country."[77] Although Romanian Action's support base was limited, it included prominent elite figures and laid the basis for ultranationalist organizing in northern Transylvania.

The spoils of these various movements fell to Liga Apărării Național Creştine (the National Christian Defense League, LANC), which was led by a law professor from Iaşi named Alexandru Constantin Cuza. After the collapse of the Nationalist Democratic Party, Cuza formed Uniunea Națională Creştină (the National Christian Union, UNC) together with Nicolae Paulescu (1869–1931) in May 1922. As had the German National Socialists a year earlier, UNC took the swastika as its emblem. Cuza described the swastika as a cross-shaped symbol used by the ancient Pelasgians, who he said were the ancestors of modern Romanians.[78] According to its propaganda, the organization's main purpose was to solve the "Yid problem." Unlike other nations, Cuza wrote, the Jews have no territory, only "a doctrine of greed and hate" that constituted the core of their religious beliefs.[79] Religious antisemitism was typical of Paulescu's ideology, which rejected the Old Testament as the work of a vengeful God who had nothing in common with the Christian deity.[80] Most of Cuza's earlier writings concentrated on the economic threat that Jews posed to the Romanian state, but he had touched on religious themes briefly in the past.[81] Antisemitism took pride of place in UNC publications, overwhelming antipoliticianism and anticommunism as ultranationalist preoccupations.

UNC became LANC when UNC leaders met at one of the biggest churches in Iaşi on 4 March 1923 for a religious commemoration (*parastas*) for soldiers who died in the war. They arranged for the officiating priests to sanctify seventy flags bearing swastikas and swore an oath to the Church, Romania, and LANC.[82] The founding of regional branches followed a similar pattern. When a local branch of LANC was established six months later in Ungheni, a small rural district (*plasă*) to the east of Iaşi that was home to 650 people, all of them ethnic Romanians, the ceremony began with a church service and the sanctification of a LANC flag by the local priest.[83] According to the police report, two hundred people turned out for the event, which was held on a market day to ensure that the district was

77. Comitetul Central, "Cuvântul Acțiunei Româneşti către cetitor," *Acțiunea românească*, 1/1 (1 Nov 1924): 1–2.

78. A. C. Cuza, "Ce este svastica," *Apărarea națională*, 2/16 (15 Nov 1923): 1–6.

79. A. C. Cuza, "Uniunea Națională Creştină," *Apărarea națională*, 1/1 (1 Apr 1922): 4.

80. Nicolae Paulescu, *Spitalul, Coranul, Talmudul, Cahalul, Francmasoneria* (Filipeştii de Târg, Prahova: Antet XX Press, 2001), 34–35.

81. Cuza, *Naționalitatea în arta*, 287–300.

82. "Actul de cosntituire al LANC," and "SSI Nota privind constituirea LANC," reprinted in *Totalitarismul*, ed. Scurtu, 311–313.

83. On the ethnic composition of Ungheni, see Sabin Manuila, *Recensământul general al populației României din decemvrie 1930*, 10 vols. (Bucharest: Institutul Central de Statistică, 1938), vol. 2, 250.

as crowded as possible. Ion Zelea Codreanu traveled out from Iaşi for the occasion, and spoke about the importance of the church service, the Jewish peril, and LANC's program.[84] Not all LANC leaders knew a great deal about the party. In his memoirs the future legionary I. C. Crişan writes that when he was a student he gave a speech in a village, encouraging people to join LANC, even though he himself was not yet a member. They immediately made him the LANC representative for the region.[85] More important ultranationalist celebrities traveled to speak when LANC meetings were held in larger towns, and they were generally met at the station by cheering crowds, who followed them to the church for the sanctification of the flags.[86] Priests did not always agree to sanctify the flags, and when this happened they were roundly condemned by LANC speakers.[87]

A. C. Cuza established himself as a patron of the antisemitic student movement, using LANC periodicals, meetings, and channels of communication channels to link the ultranationalist community to the protests in the universities. LANC's obsessive antisemitism marginalized antipoliticianism and anticommunism, but its concerns broadened as ultranationalists from the smaller organizations began to swell LANC ranks. Through their cultural gatherings, balls, newspapers, banks, workers' unions, and political rallies, ultranationalist organizations connected like-minded people and spread their ideology throughout the country. This network of respectable members of society with its considerable financial and political resources was to prove crucial for sustaining the more radical student movement and its successor, the Legion of the Archangel Michael.

In the nineteenth century the idea that nations exist and are valid and meaningful collectivities deserving allegiance may have been new to most inhabitants of the region that became modern Romania, but nationalist propaganda soon caused people to interpret their economic and social problems through nationalist ideology. Barbara Jeanne Fields defines ideology as "the descriptive vocabulary of day-to-day existence, through which people make rough sense of the social reality that they live and create from day to day."[88] No longer simply propaganda or the belief of a small number of activists, by the beginning of the twentieth

84. ANIC, Fond DGP, dosar 16/1923, f. 13.

85. I. C. Crişan, "Amintiri despre Corneliu Zelea Codreanu," in *Corneliu Zelea Codreanu şi epoca sa*, ed. Gabriel Stănescu (Norcross, GA: Criterion, 2001), 56–61.

86. ANIC, Fond DGP, dosar 16/1923, f. 1. Descriptions of similar LANC meetings from this period can be found in USHMM, Fond MI-D, Reel #133, dosar 2/1922, f. 44, 76; ANIC, Fond DGP, dosar 16/1923, f. 156–157; and "Intrunirea LANC din T-Severin," *Ogorul nostru*, 1/11–1 (17 Sept 1923): 3.

87. USHMM, Fond MI-D, Reel #136, dosar 5/1926, f. 22; Fond SRI Files, Reel #105, dosar 1151, f. 12–14.

88. Barbara Jeanne Fields, "Slavery, Race, and Ideology in the United States of America," *New Left Review*, 181 (1990): 110.

century Romanian nationalism had become an ideology. Moreover, ethnicity is situational, in that national categories do not automatically generate close-knit national groups, nor does identifying oneself with a particular ethnic group in one context mean that one is willing to fight for a "national" cause in another.[89] Through their newspapers, rallies, and violence, ultranationalists articulated nationalism as an economically and politically urgent matter. People who may not have been particularly passionate about their nation did care about the dire situation of the Romanian peasantry; so ultranationalists framed what was effectively an economic problem as a contest between ethnic groups.

89. Rogers Brubaker et al., *Nationalist Politics and Everyday Ethnicity in a Transylvanian Town* (Princeton: Princeton University Press, 2006).

2

YOUTHFUL JUSTICE

While the "old" nationalism of the nineteenth century provided models and ideas for twentieth-century ultranationalists, and the "new" nationalism of LANC organized them into a united movement, the crucible in which legionary repertoires and relationships were forged was the antisemitic student movement that traced its origins back to the protests of 10 December 1922. That day between three thousand and four thousand students from all over the country met in the amphitheater of the Faculty of Medicine at the University of Bucharest, where they declared a general strike and complained about overcrowded living conditions in the dormitories and poor food in the canteens. At the top of their list of demands was a *numerus clausus*, meaning that they wanted the number of Romanian, Hungarian, and Jewish students enrolled at university to correspond to the size of their ethnic groups as a percentage of the general population.[1] This explicitly targeted Jews, who at the time of the 1930 census represented 14.2 percent of students but only 4.0 percent of Romania's population as a whole.[2] Of the 136 students who graduated from the Faculty of Medicine at Cluj in 1922, only 64 were Romanians.[3]

As soon as the protesting students left the amphitheater they were met by cordons of gendarmes and soldiers, and when they refused to back down the

1. Napoleon N. Crețu, "Acum 14 ani," *Sfarmă piatră*, 2/55 (10 Dec 1936): 4.

2. Manuila, *Recensământul general din decemvrie 1930*, vol. 2, xxxii; Livezeanu, *Cultural Politics*, 238.

3. Maria Someșan, "Mișcarea studențească din 1922," *Anuarul Institutului Român de Istorie Recentă*, 1 (2002): 192.

gendarmes fired on the crowd. Battles between students and soldiers continued all day, the dormitories and student canteens were evacuated, and the students went on strike indefinitely.[4] Similar protests took place on the same day in Iaşi and Cluj, where Jewish students were assaulted and prevented from attending classes.[5] Student violence had filled the newspapers for two weeks prior to the meeting on 10 December. On 21 November a crowd gathered outside the home of the chancellor of the University of Iaşi, calling him "Judaized" and demanding his resignation for dismissing a student leader in one of the dormitories and for starting administrative action against the dean of the Law Faculty, A. C. Cuza.[6] On 29 November protestors in Cluj ejected Jews from the campus and from their dormitories before devastating the offices of the Zionist newspaper *Uj-Kelet* (New East, 1919–1940), burning manuscripts and assaulting its editors and other journalists.[7] One Jewish student was killed and four badly wounded in the fighting.[8] The next day students in Cluj interrupted an opera performance with cries of "Down with the Jews!" and violence spread to nearby villages.[9] In Iaşi Jewish stores were closed on 6 December because of an antisemitic protest rally attended by four hundred students that ended with the office windows of two newspapers broken and with several students wounded.[10] Three days later students from Iaşi traveled to Braşov and Oradea Mare, where they attempted to stir up the inhabitants against the Jews.[11] Antisemitic violence spread throughout the country over the course of the following month. Students destroyed a Jewish coffee house in Bârlad, a Jewish child in Huşi was stabbed and left unconscious, windows of Jewish homes and synagogues were broken, crowds of students clashed with police in Cernăuţi, and Galaţi witnessed the looting of Jewish shops and street fighting between groups of Jews and antisemitic students after roughly two hundred students—mostly from Iaşi—congregated

4. "10 Decembrie 1922, Mărăşeştii studenţimii române," *Porunca vremii*, 5/599 (11 Dec 1936): 3; "Manifestaţia studenţeasca de Duminica," *Universul*, 11/284 (13 Dec 1922): 3; "Agitaţiile studenţeşti," *Dimineaţa*, 14/5788 (13 Dec 1922): 3; USHMM, Fond MI-D, Reel #133, dosar 4/1922, f. 1.

5. "Membrii Marelui Colegiu Universitar şi agitaţiile antisemite," *Lumea* (10 Dec 1922); reprinted in *Totalitarismul*, ed. Scurtu, 260–261; "În jurul manifestaţiunilor din Iaşi," *Dimineaţa*, 14/5788 (13 Dec 1922): 4.

6. Stelian Neagoe, *Triumful raţiunii împotriva violenţei: Viaţa universitară ieşană interbelică* (Iaşi: Junimea, 1977), 175–176.

7. "Manifestaţia studenţilor creştini din Cluj," *Universul*, 11/274 (1 Dec 1922): 7; "Incidente sângeroase la Cluj între studenţi," *Dimineaţa*, 14/5775 (30 Nov 1922): 7.

8. "Dezordinile studenţeşti din Cluj," *Dimineaţa*, 14/5776 (1 Dec 1922): 7.

9. "O punere la punct," *Universul*, 2/276 (3 Dec 1922): 7; "Dezordinele antisemite din Cluj," *Dimineaţa*, 14/5777 (2 Dec 1922): 7.

10. "Tulburările antisemite din ţară," *Dimineaţa*, 14/5783 (8 Dec 1922): 3.

11. "Agitaţiile studenţeşti din ţară," *Dimineaţa*, 14/5786 (11 Dec 1922): 3.

outside the Central Theater, where a Yiddish play was being performed, waiting for Jewish youths to come out.[12]

Romanian universities had been plagued by ultranationalist student violence since 1919. In Iaşi small groups of ultranationalist students scuffled with communists and stole their distinctive buttons or hats, disrupted lectures by shouting antisemitic slogans, tried to prevent Jewish students from attending courses, and hindered the university's opening ceremony.[13] They also quarreled with the press, assaulting journalists and newspaper salespeople, vandalizing newspaper stands, and burning newspapers that criticized them.[14] One of the leaders of the student gangs was Corneliu Zelea Codreanu—the son of the Nationalist Democrat politician Ion Zelea Codreanu, a protégée of A. C. Cuza, and an activist in Constantin Pancu's Guard of the National Conscience. He was expelled from the university in June 1921 for assault and vandalism, but he continued to play an active role in student politics and his expulsion did little to curb the radicalism of the ultranationalist students.[15] Similar problems occurred in Cluj, where the university had been newly "Romanianized" and professors as well as students complained about the number of "foreigners"—particularly Hungarians—who still worked there.[16] Members of Centrul Studenţesc "Petru Maior" (the "Petru Maior" Student Center) published an ultranationalist newspaper called *Dacia Nouă* (New Dacia), wrote libelous articles against their professors, held raucous parties, and vandalized medical laboratories that they said were used by a disproportionate number of Jews.[17]

The issue that sparked the new wave of protests in 1922 was a debate over the use of Jewish cadavers for dissection by medical students. Eastern European Jews believed that the soul would stay with the body longer if the dead person was not buried before sunset on the day that he or she died and that, even then, it remained attached to the body for up to twelve months. They therefore strongly resisted the use of Jewish bodies in medical classrooms, and rabbinic *responsa* from the eighteenth and nineteenth centuries permitted autopsies only when

---

12. "Anti-Semitic Riots Spread in Rumania," *New York Times* (20 Dec 1922): 2; "Attack Jews in Rumania," *New York Times* (27 Dec 1922): 4; USHMM, Fond MI-D, Reel #132, dosar 1/1922, vol. 1, f. 14–15; ACNSAS, Fond Penal, dosar 013207, vol. 2, f. 320; "Manifestaţii antisemite la Bârlad," *Dimineaţa*, 20/5809 (3 Jan 1923): 4; "Turburările antisemite la Huşi," *Dimineaţa*, 20/5815 (11 Jan 1923): 2.

13. Codreanu, *Pentru legionari*, 40–52; Neagoe, *Triumful raţiunii*, 78, 83, 90–99.

14. Neagoe, *Triumful raţiunii*, 99–100; *Totalitarismul*, ed. Scurtu, 200–202, 250–253.

15. Neagoe, *Triumful raţiunii*, 90–91.

16. Vasile Puşcaş, *Universitate, societate, modernizare: Organizarea şi activitatea ştiinţifică a Universităţii din Cluj (1919–1940)* (Cluj-Napoca: Eikon, 2003), 202.

17. "Tinerime universitară română," *Apărarea naţională*, 1/1 (1 Apr 1922): 20; Stelian Neagoe, *Viaţa universitară clujeană interbelică*, vol. 1 (Cluj-Napoca: Dacia, 1980), 163, 187, 204.

they could be used to help an existing patient. Vienna's antisemitic mayor Karl Lueger had created a scandal over this very issue in 1903 and it was far from being a new problem for Jewish-Christian relations in east-central Europe.[18] The students said that during November 1922 Jewish students had begun to steal Jewish bodies from the medical stores to protect them from dissection, even though they were willing to dissect Christian cadavers.[19] C. M. Râpeanu, one of the leaders of the antisemitic students at this time, later claimed that the Jews attacked Romanian students with swords when they gathered to protest the thefts.[20] Antisemitic student rioting broke out in Cluj the next day.

It is crucial to keep in mind the social and intellectual environment of Romanian universities to understand why students were so easily mobilized behind ultranationalist causes. A large proportion of students enrolled in Romanian universities during the 1920s were the first in their families to attend university. Professors complained that their students were hopelessly unprepared for university educations, stating that they were "ignorant of even the most fundamental and elementary notions" of biology or the classics.[21] Only 10 percent of students who enrolled in Romanian universities between 1929 and 1938 actually graduated with a diploma.[22] Confronted with an academic environment that they were not equipped to succeed in, poor living conditions, overcrowded classes, and little hope of having successful careers after graduating if they did not have the right connections, students needed an outlet for their frustrations. With free rail passes that let them travel to student congresses cheaply and just enough education to find the politics of ultranationalist professors such as A. C. Cuza convincing, the predominantly male student population found that outlet in antisemitic violence.

Hooliganism

The university authorities in Romania responded to the provocations of 10 December 1922 by closing the universities and expelling the leading troublemakers. They also gave in to several of the students' demands. On 4 January 1923 the minister of education decided that everyone who was not a Romanian citizen

18. Tatjana Buklijas, "Cultures of Death and Politics of Corpse Supply: Anatomy in Vienna, 1848–1914," *Bulletin of the History of Medicine*, 82 (2008): 598–605.

19. Delaromanu, "Cadavrele . . ." *Cuvântul studențesc*, 1/3 (15 Jan 1923): 3.

20. C. M. Râpeanu, "Începuturile mişcării studențesc," *Sfarmă piatră*, 2/55 (10 Dec 1936): 5.

21. AN—Cluj, Fond Universitatea din Cluj, Facultatea de Ştiință, dosar 204/1930, f. 18.

22. Antoine Roger, *Fascistes, communistes et paysans: Sociologie des mobilisatinos identitaires roumaines (1921–1989)* (Brussels: Editions de l'Université de Bruxelles, 2002), 117–118.

should be ex-matriculated. This measure did not affect Romanian Jews, nor did it come into effect immediately.[23] Later that year the Senate of the University of Iaşi decreed that Christian students would dissect Christian cadavers, and Jewish students, Jewish ones. If the Jewish students were unhappy about cutting up Jewish cadavers then they could go to the museum and study the exhibits there.[24] By this time the issue of cadavers had taken second place to demands for a *numerus clausus* and for more power to student bodies. Ultranationalist students continued intermittent protests until the establishment of a royal dictatorship in 1938.

In Bucharest, the student newspaper *Cuvântul studenţesc* (the Student word, 1923–1940) announced that a gang of 150 Jews armed with clubs, boxing gloves, and revolvers had attacked twenty-five to thirty Romanian students in class during January 1923.[25] The paper also reported that eight students—including one woman—were attacked and "tortured" by Jewish gangs when the students entered the mostly Jewish suburb of Văcăreşti to sell copies of *Cuvântul studenţesc.* When Romanian police intervened, the Jews apparently assaulted them too.[26] Neither of these accounts is recorded in nonfascist sources. In fact, several students were arrested that month for committing acts of violence in Văcăreşti, which casts doubt on the reliability of ultranationalist accounts of Jewish violence against Romanians.[27] This manner of framing the incident as a Jewish attack on Christians was common in the right-wing press at the time. In August 1925, a major newspaper with nationalist sympathies reported that "groups of Jews [in Băceşti] molested young Christians caught on the street alone or in pairs."[28] Jews reportedly assaulted taxation officials in Chişinău and Romanian students in Haţeg, and one Romanian teacher was attacked by his Jewish students.[29] In Piatra Neamţ, the right-wing press reported that Jews beat up schoolchildren who threw a rock through the window of their synagogue during a service.[30]

According to police and university records, it was usually the Romanian students who attacked Jews. Throughout the spring semester of 1923 ultranationalist students in Bucharest intermittently entered classrooms and laboratories and demanded that everyone leave the room. If people refused to move, the intruders shouted, sang songs, banged on doors, and made continuing the lesson

23. AN—Bucharest, Fond Universitatea din Bucureşti, Rectorat, dosar 4/1923, f. 264.

24. AN—Iaşi, Fond Universitatea A. I. Cuza, Rectorat, dosar 1022/1923, f. 372–375, Reel #121, dosar 1025/1923, f. 21–25.

25. "Jidovii ne-au declarat război," *Cuvântul studenţesc*, 1/5 (31 Jan 1923): 2.

26. N. N. Creţu, "Vănătoare de creştini," *Cuvântul studenţesc*, 1/6 (1 Feb 1923): 1.

27. Someşan, "Mişcarea studenţească," 199.

28. "Măsuri de ordine în toată Moldova," *Universul* (18 Aug 1925).

29. USHMM, MI-D, Reel #135, dosar 2/1926, f.111; "Incidente regretabile la Haţeg," *Universul* (23 June 1926); "Învăţătorul Bodrugă a încercat . . . asasinarea elevilor evrei?" *Universul* (24 July 1926).

30. "Incăerările dela P.-Neamţ," *Universul* (1 Oct 1926).

impossible. Sometimes they attacked Jewish students as the latter left the room.[31] Ultranationalists forced anyone whom they suspected of being Jewish to present his or her identity card; the cards had students' ethnicity written on them.[32] The police arrested student leaders and confiscated copies of their newspaper, but to no avail.[33] Parts of the city were blocked off and barriers were still in place in late February 1923; gendarmes were brought onto campus during April; and in December they were replaced by the Romanian army.[34] Even though they were supposed to be policing student unrest, many of the soldiers admired the students' ultranationalism, and two army officers were arrested in February 1923 for participating in a student demonstration.[35]

In May University Senates in Bucharest, Cluj, and Iaşi began expelling students who were known troublemakers and collecting identification cards when students entered the building as a way of blacklisting problem students.[36] Later that month Romanians in Bucharest assaulted Bulgarian students in the canteen of the Faculty of Medicine.[37] Trouble continued once studies started again in the fall, with Jewish students complaining that they were insulted, threatened, and attacked on a daily basis.[38] In 1925 the authorities decided to immediately expel students for acts of violence, but then they welcomed them back on the condition that the students recognize their mistakes and ask for forgiveness. The students responded that such measures were offensive and humiliating, but many availed themselves of the opportunity nonetheless.[39]

In Cluj, students continued to disturb classes and prevented Jewish students from attending lectures throughout January 1923.[40] The strike continued, and individual students gave declarations to the faculty saying that "the spirit of collegiality and national consciousness dictates that so long as the Jewish students are

---

31. AN—Bucharest, Fond Universitatea din Bucureşti, Rectorat, dosar 4/1923, f. 61, 65–66, 76.

32. Mihail Sebastian, *De două mii de ani: Roman* (Bucharest: Editura Nationala-Ciornei, 1934), 19, 31–32.

33. USHMM, Fond MI-D, Reel #132, dosar 1/1922, vol. 1, f. 45.

34. Aladin, "Tâlcul Scandalului," *Contimporanul*, 2/29 (3 Feb 1923): 1; "Jandarmul în universitate?" *Cuvântul studenţesc*, 1/10 (15 Apr 1923): 1; "Armata în universitate," *Cuvântul studenţesc*, 1/46 (18 Dec 1922): 1.

35. Dana Beldiman, *Armata şi mişcarea legionară* (Bucharest: Institutul Naţional pentru Studiul Totalitarismului, 2002), 53–54.

36. AN—Bucharest, Fond Universitatea din Bucureşti, Rectorat, dosar 4/1923, f. 91–92; AN—Cluj, Fond Universitatea Ferdinand I, Facultatea de Ştiinţa, dosar 76/1922, f. 53, 95.

37. AN—Bucharest, Fond Universitatea din Bucureşti, Rectorat, dosar 4/1923, f. 80–81.

38. Ibid., dosar 4/1923, f. 137, 140–141. Cf. Sebastian, *De două mii de ani*, 7, 17, 19, 53; Saşa Pană, *Născut în '02: Memorii, file de jurnal, evocări* (Bucharest: Minerva, 1973), 137–145.

39. "În preajmă deschiderei Universităţilor," *Lancea*, 1/7 (1 Nov 1925): 1; AN—Iaşi, Fond Universitatea A. I. Cuza, Rectorat, Reel #121, dosar 1084/1925, f. 34–36; AN—Cluj, Fond Universitatea Ferdinand I, Facultatea de Ştiinţa, dosar 76/1922, f. 110–113.

40. AN—Cluj, Fond Universitatea Ferdinand I, Facultatea de Ştiinţa, dosar 76/1922, f. 3, 6.

at work I cannot return to the laboratory."[41] In February they attacked the offices of minority newspapers again, and threatened police with revolvers when they tried to intervene.[42] On March 10 a handful of students were arrested for wandering through several suburbs shouting insulting remarks and assaulting Jews.[43] In April, Jewish medical students were attacked again outside their classrooms, and a meeting of 346 students voted to continue their boycott of classes.[44] In May the faculty began keeping class attendance lists, which were submitted to the dean at the end of each day. Sometimes no students showed up at all, and the majority of names of those students who did attend classes are recognizably Jewish.[45] The antisemitic students became increasingly brazen and later that month several shots were fired into the chancellor's home.[46] In 1924 a crowd of students broke down the door to the chancellor's office in order to assault the prefect of police, Ovidiu Gritta, who was hiding inside. While they did so, the students shouted to the chancellor to be careful and to stand back from the door so as not to get hurt.[47] As of February 1925, forty gendarmes permanently occupied the campus with strict orders to arrest anyone who caused trouble.[48]

The story in Iaşi was similar, albeit even more violent. Here the worst troublemakers were law students, who disrupted classes in the Faculty of Medicine.[49] The authorities suspended courses in March 1923, but trouble continued as soon as classes began again.[50] Student demonstrations and meetings often ended with the participants marching through the streets singing nationalistic songs.[51] When the police tried to stop students singing they were greeted with volleys of vinegar and rotten eggs.[52] On 5 December 1923 Jewish students in Iaşi reported that they could not go to classes because armed students guarded the entrances to the buildings.[53] Another forty-four Jewish students wrote to the chancellor that they were attacked in Corneliu Şumuleanu's class on 11–12 December 1923. Şumuleanu was a leading member of LANC, and he apparently turned a blind

---

41. Ibid., dosar 76/1922, f. 4.
42. Ibid., dosar 76/1922, f. 9.
43. Ibid., dosar 76/1922, f. 21.
44. Ibid., dosar 76/1922, f. 24, 26, 41–42.
45. Ibid., dosar 76/1922, f. 61–82, 88–89. Often the professor explicitly noted which of the students in attendance were Jewish.
46. Ibid., dosar 76/1922, f. 92, 216.
47. Ibid., dosar 96/1923, f. 5–8.
48. Ibid., dosar 109/1924, f. 42.
49. AN—Iaşi, Fond Universitatea A. I. Cuza, Rectorat, Reel #121, dosar 1024/1923, f. 2, 42–44.
50. Ibid., Reel #121, dosar 1024/1923, f. 45–46.
51. "Acţiunea studenţilor naţionalişti," *Lumea* (9 Dec 1922), reprinted in *Totalitarismul*, ed. Scurtu, 259–260.
52. "Provocătorul Manciu," *Naţionalistul*, 10/44 (4 Nov 1923): 3.
53. AN—Iaşi, Fond Universitatea A. I. Cuza, Rectorat, dosar 1022/1923, f. 511–512.

eye when his Romanian students began beating the others with clubs. The Jews ran outside to wait for the chancellor, but had to return to get their hats and coats because of the cold weather. The Romanians were waiting for them when they returned and now they attacked them with metal rods. This time it was medical students who were disrupting lectures in the Faculty of Law.[54] Attendance lists were introduced at Iaşi that month and the Romanian army occupied the campus.[55]

Romanian students learned from the German student movement while it was in its most radical phase at the beginning of the 1920s. They formed an "Association of Romanian Students in Berlin" in 1921 to promote cultural exchanges, and Corneliu Zelea Codreanu traveled to Germany in fall 1922 to observe the antisemitic movement there.[56] Students from Iaşi borrowed eight thousand lei from one of the LANC's financers to pay for Codreanu's journey, and he arrived in time to witness student violence on the streets of Berlin that November.[57] He later wrote that the reason for his trip was that "from the study we had done we realized that the Yid problem has an international character and that the reaction must also be on an international scale."[58] Codreanu did not get to know German students, but he avidly purchased every antisemitic book and pamphlet available.[59] On his return from Berlin, Codreanu promised that in March 1923 he would hold a "great student gathering" in Iaşi that would include delegates from Germany, Poland, and Czechoslovakia.[60] But the promised meeting never took place, and when Czechoslovak students did visit Romania in September 1923, their letter of thanks never mentioned the antisemitic struggle, though they did say that they felt very welcomed by the Romanian students and hoped for closer collaboration between student centers in the two countries.[61]

Codreanu was still in Berlin when student protests broke out in Romania during December 1922, but when he returned in February 1923 he brought with him new organizational ideas as well as broaches and tie clips with swastikas on them, which immediately became popular among the Romanian students.[62] He also commissioned female students to begin making flags bearing swastikas in their

---

54. Ibid., dosar 1022/1923, f. 474–477. Cf. Sebastian, *De două mii de ani*, 33.
55. Ibid., dosar 1022/1923, f. 538, 546.
56. AN—Iaşi, Fond Universitatea A. I. Cuza, Rectorat, dosar 966/1921, f. 41.
57. ACNSAS, Fond Penal, dosar 013207, vol. 1, f. 248–250, 320.
58. Codreanu, *Pentru legionari*, 68.
59. Interrogation of Corneliu Zelea Codreanu on 31 October 1923, reprinted in *Totalitarismul*, ed. Scurtu, 387.
60. ACNSAS, Fond Penal, dosar 013207, vol. 1, f. 321.
61. "Relaţiile dintre studenţii Cehoslovaci şi Români," *Cuvântul studenţesc*, 1/34 (25 Sept 1923): 2.
62. ACNSAS, Fond Penal, dosar 013207, vol. 1, f. 324.

dormitories.[63] Victims of student violence in Iaşi identified their attackers by the swastikas they wore, showing that in a short time these pieces of jewelry had become a distinctive characteristic of ultranationalist fashion.[64] Within a couple of years Jews traveling on trains at night learned to wear swastikas on their coats so as to avoid being attacked.[65] Codreanu continued to import fascist jewelry from Germany until late 1924, but by mid-1923 the Bucharest Student Center had already designed its own insignia, which it sold to raise money.[66]

Students from other university cities expressed sympathy with the ultranationalist cause. Those in Cernăuţi declared a strike on 28 December 1922 and promised that they would prevent Jewish students from sitting their exams.[67] Students in the law school at Oradea Mare wrote to the chancellor of the University of Iaşi declaring their solidarity with the antisemitic movement there.[68] Those at the Technical School (Politehnica) in Timişoara voiced their support for the movement in Bucharest and emphasized that they too struggled with overcrowded living conditions and underresourced facilities.[69] Individuals traveled between these cities to share news and to learn what was going on in other universities.[70] From 1923 onward students also began traveling to nonuniversity towns and villages where they distributed pamphlets and carried out ultranationalist propaganda during their holidays.[71] As had prewar nationalist organizations, the students also held national celebrations and fund-raisers where they spread their message and raised financial support.[72]

Student violence usually took place in groups, and most descriptions of these attacks mention forty to one hundred students assaulting only a handful of Jews. Victims could usually identify only the ringleaders and most attackers remained anonymous.[73] Sometimes the attackers were not even students, or did not eat

---

63. ANIC, Fond DGP, dosar 15/1923, f. 8–10.

64. AN—Iaşi, Fond Universitatea A. I. Cuza, Rectorat, dosar 1087/1925, f. 15, 18–19.

65. USHMM, Fond MI–D, Reel #135, dosar 1/1925, f. 162.

66. ACNSAS, Fond Penal, dosar 013207, vol. 1, f. 119–120; "Insigna studenţească," *Cuvântul studenţesc*, 1/22 (10 July 1923): 4.

67. AN—Iaşi, Fond Universitatea A. I. Cuza, Rectorat, dosar 1021/1923, f. 222–224.

68. Ibid., dosar 1087/1925, f. 41. There was no university in Oradea Mare, but the city did have a law school, which was affiliated with the University of Cluj.

69. Aurel Ciochină, "Studenţii Timişoarei," *Cuvântul studenţesc*, 1/4 (28 Jan 1923): 4.

70. AN—Iaşi, Fond Universitatea A. I. Cuza, Rectorat, dosar 1085/1925, f. 30–34; AN—Cluj, Fond Universitatea Ferdinand I, Facultatea de Ştiinţa, dosar 109/1924, f. 60.

71. AN—Iaşi, Fond Universitatea A. I. Cuza, Rectorat, Reel #132, dosar 1/1922, f. 75–76, 84, 142; "Studenţi în propagdandă," *Cuvântul studenţesc*, 1/19 (19 June 1923): 4; "Pentru studenţi," *Cuvântul studenţesc*, 1/22 (10 July 1923): 4.

72. "Informaţiuni," *Cuvântul studenţesc*, 1/20 (26 June 1923): 4; "Din activitatea studenţească," *Cuvântul studenţesc*, 1/32 (18 Sept 1923): 2.

73. AN—Iaşi, Fond Universitatea A. I. Cuza, Rectorat, Reel #129, dosar 1057/1924, f. 9.

at the canteens where the attacks took place.[74] The size of the groups suggests that perpetrators joined in if and when they wanted to and that this was not the work of hierarchical, tightly bound gangs or paramilitary squads. Nor was it the work of veterans accustomed to violence as a result of World War I, as was typical of paramilitary violence elsewhere in Europe at this time.[75] Nonetheless, the students did have clear leadership, the violence was usually premeditated, and targets were chosen to maximize publicity.

As the singing, shouting, and hooliganism of antisemitic demonstrations suggest, student crowds were also fun. During one protest in 1927, students carried a boiler full of food down the street with the sign "Taste it to convince yourselves how badly we are fed."[76] Two examples from the mid-1930s give a sense of the convivial, less-than-serious atmosphere associated with student crowds. After students were shot during demonstrations in Bucharest on 25 January 1933, the leaders there sent a telegram to Teodor Mociulschi (1903–?), who was the leader of Asociația Studenților Creștin (the Christian Students' Association, ASC) of Iași, asking him to arrange for a protest that weekend.[77] In response, on Sunday students in Iași attended a church service, after which Mociulschi gave a speech and the crowd began a peaceful protest march before making a sudden turn toward an old building undergoing renovations that was owned by a prominent Jewish family. The students began tearing down the walls, and when a professor named Eugen Pavlescu arrived they spoke back to him and refused to show their identity cards. The police in attendance refused to intervene, even when the students began throwing tiles at them. Eventually Pavlescu himself marched into the middle of the crowd and the students immediately changed their tone, cheering, "Long live the professor!" and swearing to him that they had not been the ones throwing tiles.[78] These students seem to have thought of their vandalism as little more than a joke, of police as harmless playthings, and of their professors as people who could be friends or foes depending on the whims of the students.

On another Sunday evening in 1935, groups of students wandered through Cișmigiu Park in the center of Bucharest, where they stopped passers-by and demanded to inspect their identification cards. If someone turned out to be Jewish, they promptly assaulted the person. Eventually the groups of students grew in

74. Ibid., dosar 1125/1926, f. 6.

75. Reichardt, *Faschistische Kampfbünd*, 96; Robert Gerwarth, "The Central European Counter-Revolution: Paramilitary Violence in Germany, Austria, and Hungary after the Great War," *Past and Present*, 200 (2008): 175–210.

76. "The Government and the Needs of the Students," USNA, Records of the Department of State relating to Internal Affairs of Romania, 1910–1944.

77. ACNSAS, Fond Penal, dosar 000324, vol. 8, f. 126.

78. AN—Iași, Fond Chestura de Poliție, dosar 52/1933, f. 83–89; Fond Universitatea A. I. Cuza, Rectorat, Reel #305, dosar 1596/1935, f. 32.

number and drifted onto the nearby boulevards, where they continued harassing passing Jews until they became concerned about police retaliation and returned to the park. By now numbering roughly one thousand students, the crowd began a cheer of "Down with the Jews!" and moved on to the medical students' dormitory two blocks away. The balconies of the dormitory were full of students and someone made a speech about how holy and just the student cause was. Becoming bored, students returned to the street, where they checked identification cards on passing buses and vandalized shop windows. Police and gendarmes intervened when the crowd reached the Jewish commercial district of Lipscani Street. They fired several shots and hit students with their rifle butts, so the troublemakers dispersed and went home.[79] Afterward, Centrul Studenţesc Bucureşti (the Bucharest Student Center, CSB) wrote to the minister of the interior that it had carried out its own investigations into the incident and "discovered that agents provocateurs of this movement are members of the National-Liberal Party Youth, and some of them are Siguranţa (secret police) agents. We even surprised police sergeants and commissars who mingled with the protesters and cried out, pointing at individuals: 'Hit him, he's a Yid!'"[80]

The students appear to have had no specific goals in mind, and the locations where they congregated were places where they would normally have spent their leisure time. The speeches were ad hoc and vague. The aggressors targeted any Jews, and not specific enemies of the student movement. Checking identification cards is something that police do, and the students were mimicking legitimate authority figures as they distributed their vigilante justice, but they seem to have treated it more as a game than as a serious attempt to rid the area of Jews. When they did encounter armed resistance, the students immediately yielded. When called to account, they made farcical claims about liberals and secret police having engineered the whole incident. Sven Reichardt notes in his comparison of Italian *squadristi* and German *Sturmtruppen* that violence became more entrenched in Italian Fascist culture than in German Nazism because there was less serious opposition to Fascist violence in Italy. The same pattern holds true in Romania, where student violence was anarchic, not a struggle for life and death.[81] Hooliganism and violence was a serious matter for Jews, university faculty, and officers of the law, but for the ultranationalist students it was an excuse to enjoy themselves, to be part of a group, and to insist that the Romanian students—not Jews or police—dominated the country's streets and public spaces.

79. ACNSAS, Fond Documentar, dosar 012694, vol. 1, f. 32–45.
80. "Măsurile represive împotrivă dezordinelor," *Adevărul* (12 Apr 1935).
81. Reichardt, *Faschistische Kampfbünd*, 75, 98.

Student Congresses

The universities whose students took part in the ultranationalist student movement were separated by hundreds of miles, but students met in congresses that were held at least once a year. Student congresses were usually accompanied by acts of vandalism and violence, and the authorities were always wary when students asked to meet, placing extra guards on the trains and at stations in case students began attacking Jews on their way to the congresses.[82] The first of these congresses was to be held in Cluj during July 1923, with university professors and prominent ultranationalists from a variety of organizations being invited to speak on antisemitic themes.[83] The government refused the students permission to hold the congress but they met anyway in Iaşi, forcing their way through a cordon of gendarmes into the university's assembly hall and then finishing the last two days of the congress at nearby Cetăţuia Monastery.[84] They spoke about reorganizing the student centers; supporting Romanian populations in Macedonia and the Serbian Banat; and continuing their battle against Jews, the government, and the university authorities.[85] The discussions at later congresses stuck to similar themes but were supplemented by church services and musical and artistic performances.[86]

The most notorious student congress of the decade took place in Oradea Mare, a city in Transylvania near the Romanian border with Hungary. When a student congress at Oradea Mare was first proposed, local officials protested because of the potential for student violence. Their objections were overruled by government ministers, who promised to provide the troops necessary to keep order.[87] An edition of *Cuvântul studenţesc* from 24 November 1927 carried two articles

---

82. USHMM, Fond MI-D, Reel #132, dosar 1/1922, f. 161–162, 171, 178, 190; Fond SRI Files, Reel #106, dosar 1151, f. 301–305; AN—Braşov, Fond Chestura de Poliţie, Serv. Exterioare, dosar 253/1927, f. 5.

83. The invited speakers were I. C. Cătuneanu, A. C. Cuza, Vasile Dumitru, Mihail Dragomirescu, Găvănescul, Gheorghiu, Iuliu Haţieganu, I. Mândrescu, S. Mehedinţi, Ec. C. Nazarie, Cezar Papacostea, Nicolae Paulescu, M. Ştefănescu, Octavian Goga, C. Vasiliu-Bolnavu, Alexandrina Gr. Cantacazino, Leonte Moldovanu, and Amos Francu. "Programul congresului," *Cuvântul studenţesc*, 1/27 (14 Aug 1923): 1; AN—Iaşi, Fond Universitatea A. I. Cuza, Rectorat, Reel #121, dosar 1024/1923, f. 194.

84. "Congresul studenţesc oprit," *Cuvântul studenţesc*, 1/26 (7 Aug 1923): 1; "Congresul delegaţilor întregei studenţimi române din ţara," *Cuvântul studenţesc*, 1/30 (4 Sept 1923): 1. Romanticized later accounts claim that after the initial clashes with gendarmes, the students held their congress in the woods. Lorenzo Baracchi Tua, *Garda de Fier*, trans. Cesar Balaban (Bucharest: Editura Mişcării Legionare, 1940), 40–41.

85. "Hotărârile studenţimii române în congresul de delegaţi," *Cuvântul studenţesc*, 1/30 (4 Sept 1923): 1–2.

86. "Programul congresului," *Cuvântul studenţesc*, 4/1 (26 Nov 1926): 2; USHMM, Fond MI-D, Reel #135, dosar 1/1924, f. 163.

87. Téreza Mózes, *Evreii din Oradea*, trans. Liviu Borcea (Bucharest: Hasefer, 1997), 140.

that were to prepare students for the congress. The first was written by Lorin Popescu, the president of Uniunea Națională a Studenților Creștini din România (the National Union of Christian Students in Romania, UNSCR), an organization created in 1925 to represent ultranationalist student groups throughout the country. Popescu called for students to come to the congress "with calm faces and open spirits."[88] The second listed thirty examples of Christian students who had been the subject of recent Jewish attacks.[89] Such mixed messages did not bode well for a peaceful few days. By 1 December, police circulars were warning of antisemitic brochures being circulated on trains in order to stir up the population.[90] Three days later, the young journalist Mircea Eliade (1907–1986) defended the "adorable idealism" of the student agitators in the pages of *Cuvântul studențesc*, interpreting the disturbances as the growing pains of an "authentic rebirth of religiosity."[91] Attacks on Jews began the same day.

Students had free train travel to the congress and some were accommodated in hotels, but the citizens of Oradea—including Jews—were asked to accommodate the rest of the students in their homes.[92] Students used their trip across the country to vandalize train stations and to visit sympathizers in towns along the way.[93] An estimated six thousand students entered Oradea Mare for the congress, which was held in a hall with a capacity for fifteen hundred. Plenty of students attended the discussions about a *numerus clausus* in day one, but fewer and fewer students stayed on to discuss minor details.[94] The rest, according to the American Legation in Bucharest, "were running through the streets shouting, carrying long sticks that they had stolen at a marketplace, their pockets loaded with stones which they had collected from the edge of a river in the town, and gendarmes pursuing them everywhere."[95] According to the American account, most shops were closed, and the streets were deserted except for the rioting students, who stole, destroyed four synagogues, and assaulted Jews on the streets and on the trains. The police later wrote that students "destroyed all window displays and businesses, breaking shutters and destroying shops, right up to the most ordinary

88. Lorin Popescu, "La Oradea," *Cuvântul studențesc*, 4/1 (24 Nov 1927): 1.

89. "La Răboj," *Cuvântul studențesc*, 4/1 (24 Nov 1927): 5.

90. "Circulara Ministerului de Interne," 1 Dec 1927, reprinted in *Ideologie și formațiuni de dreapta în România*, ed. Ioan Scurtu, vol. 2 (Bucharest: Institutul Național Pentru Studiul Totalitarismului, 2000), 87.

91. Mircea Eliade, "O generație," *Cuvântul studențesc*, 4/2 (4 Dec 1927): 1.

92. Mózes, *Evreii din Oradea*, 141.

93. Scurtu ed., *Ideologie*, vol. 2, 91–92, 95.

94. Ibid., vol. 2, 98–100.

95. "A Bird's-Eye View of the Students' Congress, the Riots, and the Effects," USNA, Records of the Department of State relating to Internal Affairs of Romania, MII98, Reel #7, American Legation Dispatch 510, Enclosure 3.

things."[96] One Jewish man recalled being beaten by students and then chasing them into the synagogue, begging them to stop destroying sacred objects. "These reckless [students] broke and destroyed everything that they came across, he reported. "They took cult objects with them and, dressed in prayer mantles, they began a wild dance in the courtyard."[97] Another Jewish man protected Torah scrolls with sword in hand.[98] After the congress some students went on to Cluj and other nearby towns, where they continued rioting for several more days. Roughly forty Jewish houses, a tube factory, and a synagogue were destroyed in Cluj. Only one Jew and the police subcommissar were assaulted.[99] Students traveling directly to Bucharest jumped off at various train stations on the way to destroy things or assault anyone they identified as Jewish while the train was stopped. Approximately four hundred students were arrested when they alighted from the trains in Bucharest.[100]

When challenged, the students responded by blaming the government for the disturbances. They protested against the expulsion of 380 students who had not been formally charged with crimes.[101] During the trial of two students, Gherghel and Disconescu, the UNSCR president, Lorin Popescu, testified that the chief of police in Oradea Mare had warned them that they would be provoked by communists and that ten thousand armed factory workers had been mobilized to attack the students. Moreover, argued Popescu, "the first student protest took place in perfect quietness, but then . . . the butchers Friedman and Gutman beat the students Gherghel and Disconescu. Due to the number of soldiers, students were prevented from responding to these provocations."[102] Later, in 1928, Popescu led the students in a general strike to protest the treatment that they had received at the hands of the police, and the chancellor of the University of Bucharest tried unsuccessfully to dissolve the UNSCR that May.[103]

For most students, what mattered most about such violence was that it changed their everyday lives so dramatically. Biographical accounts of activists who joined terroristic or highly marginalized social movements in the late twentieth century shows that more often than not, their decisions were shaped by situations when they or their friends were involved in violence as a result of movement

96. Scurtu ed., *Ideologie*, vol. 2, 98–100.
97. Marţial Magrini, quoted in Mózes, *Evreii din Oradea*, 142.
98. Ibid., 142.
99. Scurtu ed., *Ideologie*, vol. 2, 98–100.
100. Ibid., vol. 2, 118–119, 123–124.
101. USHMM, Fond MI-D, Reel #135, dosar 8/1925, f. 74–76.
102. "Procesul studenţilor la Cluj," *Cuvântul* (3 Mar 1928).
103. "Studentimea va declara greva generală," *Cuvântul* (13 Dec 1927); "Dizolvarea organizaţiilor studenţeşti," *Cuvântul* (13 May 1928).

politics.[104] Violence creates difference, establishing boundaries between victims and perpetrators and forcing bystanders to take sides, even passively. Unlike with earlier ultranationalist groups, in which organization had preceded violent action, in Romania's universities of the early 1920s violence was constitutive of ultranationalist politics.[105] Students formed transitory communities of violence in response to real or imagined threats, they used these communities to protest a broad range of social issues, not just antisemitism, and these transitory communities became permanent when their members organized into formal associations. Based on communities of violence, ultranationalist student groups institutionalized violence in turn. The universities were often either closed or occupied by gendarmes and soldiers, dormitories and canteens were evacuated and closed, and students were insulted or physically attacked almost on a daily basis. Such events must have made the ultranationalist student movement very difficult to ignore. Being thrown out of a dormitory or attending congresses such as the one in Oradea Mare are likely to have been defining moments in many students' university careers, causing them to either violently reject antisemitism or to join in and become ultranationalists themselves.

Youthful Heroism

Most disturbances in the universities had involved gangs of ultranationalist students, but in late 1923 Corneliu Zelea Codreanu and a small group of friends became national celebrities for planning a series of assassinations. Their subsequent trial united the dispersed ultranationalist community with student leaders and provided an opportunity for them to articulate ideas about justice, youth, and heroism that became central to legionary ideology. On 8 October 1923, police in Bucharest charged Codreanu and five other young men with plotting to "spark a civil war" by assassinating government ministers and Jewish bankers, at which signal they apparently hoped that Romanians would rise up and murder Jews throughout the country. Not all the would-be assassins knew who their victims were or what they looked like, the prosecutor general said, but they had instructions on how the plot was to be carried out and had met in Bucharest

---

104. Quintan Wiktorowicz, *Radical Islam Rising: Muslim Extremism in the West* (Lanham, MD: Rowman and Littlefield, 2005), 85–128; Donatella Della Porta, "Political Socialization in Left-Wing Underground Organizations: Biographies of Italian and German Militants," in *International Social Movement Research: Social Movements and Violence; Participation in Underground Organizations*, ed. Bert Klinderman Klandermans (Greenwich, CT: JAI Press, 1992), 259–290.

105. Cf. Lyttelton, "Fascism and Violence in Post-war Italy," 257–274; Bessel, *Political Violence and the Rise of Nazism*.

the night before to assign targets and procure revolvers.[106] A number of students were allegedly involved in the plot, though only six took the spotlight—Corneliu Zelea Codreanu, Ion Moța, Ilie Gârneața, Radu Mironovici, Teodosie Popescu, and Corneliu Georgescu.[107] These men were all leaders in the student movement but collectively they came to be known as the "Văcăreşteni" after the Văcăreşti prison, where they were held for six months awaiting trial. All six had different stories about why they had met in Bucharest, but a written declaration signed by Ion Moța (1902–1937) explains that at the August student congress in Iaşi he had become convinced that the majority of students were "tired, exhausted, ready to return to normal (that is, to abandon their holy movement) unconditionally." Moța decided that only a small, dedicated group ready to sacrifice everything could save the movement, and when hiking together with Codreanu and his girlfriend in September, Moța spoke to them about a plan "to shake the country once again, to wake it up to the danger that threatens it."[108] In a letter written from prison at the beginning of 1924, Codreanu admitted that he and his friends had plotted against "this march of our people toward death," and against "an attack on the Romanian soul" by the Jews.[109] Codreanu and Moța set about recruiting other conspirators, and the plot of the Văcăreşteni was born.

All the Văcăreşteni had activist pasts. Corneliu Zelea Codreanu had been expelled from the University of Iaşi two years earlier for numerous acts of vandalism and assault.[110] In June 1923 he led a gang of youths around Huşi, where his family lived, breaking windows, assaulting Jews, and burning a house down.[111] Ion Moța was a law student in Cluj and the president of the belligerent Petru Maior Student Center, which constituted the vanguard of the student movement in Cluj. He was expelled from university just two weeks before being arrested as part of the Văcăreşti plot.[112] Teodosie Popescu was a theology student at Cernăuți, where he had been instrumental in organizing FNR and was president of the Cernăuți Student Center.[113] Corneliu Georgescu (1902–1945) studied pharmacy first at Cluj and then at Iaşi, taking an active part in the student movement in

---

106. ACNSAS, Fond Penal, dosar 013207, vol. 2, f. 16–18.

107. Other people implicated in the plot included Leonida Bandac, Nicolae Dragoş, Aurelian Vernichescu, C. Dănulescu, Traian Breazu, and Ion Zelea Codreanu.

108. ACNSAS, Fond Penal, dosar 013207, vol. 2, f. 178–180, vol. 3, f. 206–207. Interrogations of the others are found in f. 185–199, 218–285; Codreanu, *Pentru legionari*, 162.

109. Corneliu Zelea Codreanu, *Scrisori studențesti din închisoare* (Bucharest: Ramida, 1998), 14–15.

110. Codreanu, *Pentru legionari*, 13–16, 40–45; Neagoe, *Triumful rațiunii*, 90–91.

111. "Dezordinele cuziste dela Huşi continua," *Aurora* 3/530 (30 July 1923): 4.

112. Neagoe, *Viața universitară clujeană interbelică*, vol. 1, 209–210, 213; ACNSAS, Fond Penal, dosar 013207, vol. 3, f. 19.

113. ANIC, Fond DGP, dosar 36/1923, f. 18–21; ACNSAS, Fond Penal, dosar 013207, vol. 1, f. 2.

both cities.[114] Ilie Gârneaţa (1898–1971) studied law at Iaşi, and was president of ASC in Iaşi at the time of his arrest.[115]

The last of the group, Radu Mironovici (1899–1979), studied electrical engineering at the University of Iaşi, where he quickly became involved in the student movement. His family disagreed with his political involvement and broke off relations with him when he refused to abandon Codreanu.[116] According to a declaration he made years later, some of Mironovici's closest friends at this time were Mille Lefter (1902–?), a law student who together with Codreanu and Pancu had been one of the ultranationalist strikebreakers in Iaşi during 1920;[117] Constantin Buşilă, an engineering student who led attacks on Jewish villages in Tutova County during July 1924;[118] Candiani, one of the most violent thugs on campus;[119] Constantin Antoneanu, who came from a vehemently ultranationalist family and was later arrested in connection with the plot;[120] Nellu Ionescu, a former president of the antisemitic Society of Law Students;[121] and C. Ifrim, the president of the Student Circle at Bacău.[122] The ties formed during this period were binding, and together with the Văcăreşteni, all these men remained committed followers of Codreanu until his death in 1938. Although Mironovici does not mention them, one might add to this list the three law students Ioan Sava, Iulian Sârbu, and Gheorghe Urziceanu, who were at the forefront of most of the gang violence at the University of Iaşi in 1923–1924; and Constantin Capra, a literature student who organized groups of high school students to carry out antisemitic violence in Ilie Gârneaţa's hometown of Darabani.[123] The Văcăreşteni were part of a larger group of committed students whose activism spearheaded the movement in Iaşi.

This trial was the first opportunity that ultranationalists had to support the student movement by rallying around a specific cause. Gifts of money, prison visits, or letters of support were well publicized. One letter published in *Cuvântul studenţesc* described a gift "sent by the Moţi from the Apuseni Mountains. They each scraped together two, three, or five lei out of the corner of a drawer or out

---

114. ACNSAS, Fond Penal, dosar 013207, vol. 1, f. 2.

115. Codreanu, *Pentru legionari*, 171.

116. ACNSAS, Fond Informativ, dosar 234687, vol. 1, f. 7–9; vol. 3, f. 48.

117. Ibid., dosar 259143, vol. 1, f. 222–228.

118. "Din Bârlad," *Aurora*, 612 (9 July 1924).

119. ACNSAS, Fond Penal, dosar 013207, vol. 1, f. 248–250; AN—Iaşi, Fond Universitatea A. I. Cuza, Rectorat, dosar 1125/1926, f. 7.

120. ACNSAS, Fond Penal, dosar 013207, vol. 2, f. 319; vol. 3, f. 3.

121. Neagoe, *Triumful raţiunii*, 101.

122. ANIC, Fond DGP, dosar 79/1927, f. 1.

123. AN—Fond Universitatea A. I. Cuza, Rectorat, Reel #129, dosar 1057/1924, f. 4; ACNSAS, Fond Informativ, dosar 211932, vol. 2, f. 35–43; Scurtu ed., *Totalitarismul*, 535–536.

of a handkerchief, and they walked the valleys, over the paths that [Avram] Iancu traveled, to send this money together with their best wishes a long way away, over the mountains to Văcăreşti, where they had heard that their children were locked up because they wanted to save them from need and injustice, from poverty and malice."[124] The Moţi were a people who live in the Apuseni Mountains in Transylvania. They were notoriously poor during the interwar period but were loved by Romanian ultranationalists because of their connection with the uprising led by Avram Iancu (1824–1872) in 1848.[125] Some ultranationalists—including Corneliu Georgescu's mother—were horrified at the idea of the Văcăreşti plot, but their voices never entered ultranationalist publications.[126] In general, the Văcăreşteni reveled in the encouragement they received. Codreanu wrote letters, published in a booklet in 1925, thanking their supporters from prison. The list of addressees in the collection of letters reveals what sort of admirers ultranationalists valued: students from Piatra-Neamţ and Cluj; a child, a high school class, and older men from Vaslui; Codreanu's mother; a major; a captain; two young women; two married women; a nationalist group from Bucovina known as Archers; and high school girls from Sibiu. Selecting letters to children and women was clearly intended to convince readers that the Văcăreşteni enjoyed widespread support from the most disempowered elements of society. This volume reinforced the idea that the Văcăreşteni were fulfilling their duty as young men to defend those who could not defend themselves. The old aristocracy no longer had the power to protect ordinary Romanians, Codreanu wrote, so they were duty bound to form a new "aristocracy of the sword" and to earn their titles in battle.[127] At this time Romanian liberals, conservatives, nationalists, and ultranationalists all believed that politics was a man's responsibility and that men should protect and guide women as one would children. Neither women nor children could vote, own property, or represent themselves in court, but this booklet suggested that had they been able to, women would have chosen the Văcăreşteni as their champions.[128]

Codreanu's letters emphasized the important contribution of children who loved their country and of girls who sewed national flags, but the student movement

124. "Obolul moţilor," *Cuvântul studenţesc*, 2/7 (4 Mar 1924): 2, reprinted in Codreanu, *Pentru legionari*, 176–177.

125. "Situaţia disperată a moţiilor: Răportul alarmant al Dl. Ion C. Pop adresat primului ministru," *Calendarul*, 461 (2 Sept 1933): 2; A. Vântu, "Tragedia Moţiilor," *Axa*, 1/14 (15 June 1933); N. Mladin, "Problema motiilor," *Sfarmă piatră*, 3/73 (22 Apr 1937).

126. ACNSAS, Fond Penal, dosar 013207, vol. 2, f. 331; vol. 3, f. 126; Ion I. Moţa, *Axa*, 1/4 (1933): 5. One exception, which criticized student hooliganism ten months before the plot was uncovered, is "Mişcarea studenţească şi armata neamului românesc," *Apărarea naţională*, 1/19 (1 Jan 1923): 22–26.

127. Codreanu, *Scrisori studenţesti*, 44.

128. Ibid., 52–55.

spoke even more often about the virtue, strength, and courage of young men during these years. One song from May 1923 proclaimed:

Brother students, great apostles
Good and strong Romanians,
Today our gentle nation
Awaits its salvation!

From a danger that threatens it
With a consuming flood
Of leprous Yids
Who spread out ever further

We are its apostles
Young and spotless,
Our nation calls out together with us
To pay the valleys their tribute.[129]

Militant students are referred to here as "brothers" and the nation is described as feminine and gentle because even though women were well represented within the student movement, ultranationalist writers typically thought of virtue, strength, and courage as male characteristics, whereas they characterized women as nurturing, caring, pious, and self-sacrificing.[130] Female acts of bravery or heroism during World War I went unnoticed even by non-nationalist Romanians, in part because society expected women to be mothers rather than fighters.[131] Youth was as important to ultranationalist masculinity as virtue was because, in the words of one student manifesto, young people "represent the energy of the nation."[132] Ultranationalist ideologues emphasized that only the new generation could make a new future because it could lead Romania in a new direction.[133]

In the ultranationalist imagination, the importance of the Văcăreşteni lay not only in the fact that physically and mentally they epitomized Romanian masculinity but also in the notion that this perfection was threatened. If they rotted in prison then the Jewish bankers and Judaized politicians who apparently controlled the country would have destroyed the very best of Romania's present and future. The Christian resonances of innocent men dying for others were not lost on contemporaries.

---

129. S. Şiciovan, "Înainte," *Apărarea naţională*, 2/4 (15 May 1923): 21.

130. Maria Bucur, "In Praise of Wellborn Mothers: On the Development of Eugenicist Gender Roles in Interwar Romania," *East European Politics and Societies* 9/1 (1995): 129.

131. Maria Bucur, "Between the Mother of the Wounded and the Virgin of Jiu: Romanian Women and the Gender of Heroism during the Great War," *Journal of Women's History* 12/2 (2000): 30–56.

132. "Tinerime universitară română," *Apărarea naţională*, 1/1 (1 Apr 1922): 20.

133. Benone Negreţu, "Tineretul LANC," *Apărarea naţională*, 6/17 (22 Apr 1928): 1; Codreanu, *Scrisori studenţesti*, 37.

Cuvântul studențesc spoke of the Văcăreşteni as a "sacrificial group" who had decided to lay down their lives to defend Romania from the Jews.[134] A newspaper of the Archers pushed the metaphor even further: "The students were determined to die to give us life. And they gave us, without dying, proof that Christ is with us."[135]

The ultranationalist press threw its full support behind the arrested students. Father Moța's newspaper, *Libertatea,* received poems that children had written in support of the students.[136] FNR newspapers praised the students for their acts of heroism.[137] *Apărărea națională*, the official LANC periodical, ridiculed the idea that such a plot even existed, and claimed that the liberal press had exaggerated the threat that six young men posed to the state.[138] *Naționalistul* asserted that the students were being unfairly imprisoned and were persecuted because of their patriotism.[139] *Frăția creştină* spoke of how the Văcăreşteni had saved "the honor of a great and holy struggle."[140] The student newspaper *Cuvântul studențesc* published thank you messages to people who supported the Văcăreşteni by donating money, food, and clothing during their time in prison.[141] It reasoned that because the prime minister was not on the list of victims, the alleged plot was obviously a warning, not an attempt at revolution. The newspaper portrayed the trial as a test of whether the justice system was "unbiased" enough to identify the true traitors. "For over a year," the anonymous journalist wrote, "20,000 young people have been raising the alarm about an enormous plot that two million murderous Yids have launched against our country."[142] As the day of the trial approached, *Cuvântul studențesc* emphasized that "to fight to ensure that the Romanian people have an ethnically Romanian ruling class by excluding the Yids is not an attack on the Romanian state! . . . Nor is defending a people threatened with destruction a crime punishable by law."[143] On the contrary,

> It will not be the students who will be judged, but current and past governments, all of whom have collaborated with the Yids who are ruling

134. "Pedepsirea trădătorului Vernichescu," *Cuvântul studențesc*, 2/11 (29 Mar 1924): 1.

135. "Jertfă pentru jertfă," *Arcaşul*, 1/1 (14 Apr 1924): 6.

136. ACNSAS, Fond Penal, dosar 013207, vol. 1, f. 68.

137. Alexandru Uimara, "Complotul," *Fascismul*, 1/10 (22 Oct 1923): 1; Th. Voinea, "Atentatul," *Fascismul*, 1/10 (22 Oct 1923): 1–2.

138. "Un complot monstru," *Apărarea națională*, 2/14 (15 Oct 1923): 18.

139. "Protest," *Naționalistul*, 10/4 (4 Nov 1923): 3; Tăzlăuanu Huşi, "Dl. Ion Zelea Codreanu în lanțuri! . . ." *Naționalistul*, 10/4 (4 Nov 1923): 3.

140. "O aniversare," *Frația creştină*, 2/4 (12 Oct 1924): 1.

141. "Mulțumiri," *Cuvântul studențesc*, 2/11 (1 Apr 1924): 2.

142. "Complotul," *Cuvântul studențesc*, 1/38 (30 Oct 1923): 1. Romania had only 748,115 Jews, according to the 1930 census. The estimate that there were twenty thousand people involved in the antisemitic student movement is also an exaggeration.

143. "Procesul studenților arestați la Văcăreşti," *Cuvântul studențesc*, 2/10 (25 Mar 1924): 1.

> Romanian lands today. . . . The judiciary will determine if the Yids are the mortal enemies of our people, if a Yid problem exists, and if its immediate solution is a problem of life and death for us. Through the verdict which it gives, the judiciary will decide if it is with us or with them: if it recognizes truth and reality, or negates them.[144]

On the day of the trial students in Cernăuți staged a demonstration supporting the Văcăreşteni, while others traveled to Bucharest, where thousands filled the streets around the courthouse dressed in national costumes.[145] A newspaper of the Archers described how on 29 March 1924, the accused entered the courtroom wearing national folk costumes that one would usually wear for a festival, and it commented that "both in the courtroom and on the streets, among numerous military cordons, [there were] crowds of male and female students and other Romanians dressed in traditional holiday garments [*haine de sărbătoare româneşti*]." These crowds joined together with "mothers, sisters, brothers, and parents" all over the country who were awaiting the verdict with baited breath. "This is what Romanians are like," the article concluded; "their spirits are so great that they wear holiday garments both for life and for death."[146] The trial ended up involving both life and death, because in the middle of the proceedings Ion Moța pulled out a gun and shot a student named Aurelian Vernichescu, who had originally been part of the plot but then betrayed the plotters to the authorities. Despite the students having confessed to planning murder, the jury found them innocent of attempting to cause a revolution and they were released to a cheering crowd.[147]

After the trial the Văcăreşteni returned home as heroes. When Ilie Gârneața arrived in Darabani, where his family lived, he was welcomed by a crowd of 100–150 high school students organized by Constantin Capra, who followed him down the street shouting, "Long live the Romanian students!" and "Romanian youth!"[148] Corneliu Georgescu and Teodosie Popescu returned to leading roles in the ultranationalist movement in Cluj and Cernăuți, respectively.[149] Codreanu was greeted warmly by the students in Iaşi but angry police officers attacked him when they saw him back on the streets of their city.[150] Ion Moța

144. "La 29 martie," *Cuvântul studențesc*, 2/10 (25 Mar 1924): 1.

145. Scurtu ed., *Totalitarismul*, 410–413.

146. "Jertfă pentru jertfă," *Arcaşul*, 1/1 (14 Apr 1924): 6.

147. Codreanu, *Pentru legionari*, 183. The defense lawyers argued that the plot could not have been treasonous or revolutionary because none of the intended victims were heads of state. ACNSAS, Fond Penal, dosar 013207, vol. 2, f. 140, 143–148, 151–155.

148. ACNSAS, Fond Informativ, dosar 211932, vol. 2, f. 36.

149. ACNSAS, Fond Penal, dosar 013207, vol. 1, f. 62–63, 153.

150. Codreanu, *Pentru legionari*, 184.

remained in prison awaiting trial for Vernichescu's murder until October 1924, as did Vlad Leonida, who was charged with smuggling Moța's gun into the prison. Both received enthusiastic support from students and ultranationalists in Cluj, where they had been students. Their supporters distributed numerous fliers and wrote to the judge and jury members defending their innocence and condemning Vernichescu for not even having the courage to hang himself, as Judas had after betraying Jesus.[151] In Orăştie, Moța's father received letters and money from Romania and the United States, expressing solidarity with Vernichescu's murder and telling him how proud he must be to have such a son.[152] *Acțiunea românească* reported that when Moța was acquitted, "in every place he passed through he was received with triumph as an apostle of a holy cause. In his birthplace, Orăştie, they called local peasants out from their modest villages to see his homespun ancestral costume, to feel his Romanian soul, and to understand from him that there are still some who put the needs of the people above their own."[153]

Vigilante Justice

Student violence did not abate in the universities, and conflict soon developed between the ultranationalist community and the police prefect in Iaşi, Constantin Manciu. Prefects were political appointments, and Manciu had been chosen specifically to suppress the student movement. When he was appointed in September 1923, Manciu immediately set about removing corrupt police officers, arresting students, and directing the military occupation of the campus. From then on, police officers in Iaşi began receiving regular death threats in the mail, and a police sergeant was beaten when he tried to prevent four students from breaking into Manciu's house in November 1923.[154] Manciu reported that from this time ultranationalists in Iaşi identified him as their worst enemy, and "failed politicians" such as Constantin Pancu, Ioan Butnaru, and Ioana Voicu and "elements forced to resign from the army," including Major Ambrozie and Major I. Dumitriu, launched a campaign against him.[155]

At 4:00 a.m. on 31 May 1924, Manciu led a group of police officers to Constanța Ghica's garden, where they found Codreanu speaking to a group of roughly sixty

151. ACNSAS, Fond Penal, dosar 013207, vol. 1, f. 101–106.

152. Ibid., dosar 013207, vol. 1, f. 68–73, 107.

153. "Un simbol: Ioan Moța," *Acțiunea românească*, 1/1 (1 Nov 1924): 4.

154. "Complotul studentesc," *Cuvântul*, 1/4 (9 Nov 1924): 4; ACNSAS, Fond Penal, dosar 013207, vol. 1, f. 2, 244–246; AN—Iaşi, Fond Universitatea A. I. Cuza, Rectorat, Reel #121, dosar 1022/1923, f. 518–523, dosar 1025/1923, f. 28–39.

155. ACNSAS, Fond Penal, dosar 013207, vol. 1, f. 244.

young people and holding a floor plan of Manciu's house in his hand. The police arrested a number of those in attendance. They interrogated them at the police station and then released them the following day.[156] In less than twenty-four hours the students collected sixty signatures asserting that the arrests were illegal and demanding that Manciu be punished.[157] Some of the arrested individuals were high school students, and Manciu claimed that those whose parents were not ultranationalists were grateful for his intervention. Others accused him of abusing their children and laid formal charges against him, complete with medical examinations taken immediately after the children were released. Codreanu later claimed that they had been beaten with canes and riding crops for hours on end.[158] On the first day of Manciu's trial for abuse, Codreanu followed Manciu out of the courtroom after an argument with the prosecuting attorney and shot Manciu repeatedly on the steps of the courthouse, killing him and wounding two of his companions in the process.[159]

Codreanu was immediately arrested, as were the other Văcăreşteni, and rumors circulated that the Liberal Club in Iaşi had sworn to kill him before he stood trial.[160] As it had a year earlier, the ultranationalist community rose in his defense, sending money, writing petitions, and filling its newspapers with supportive articles.[161] Thousands of people sent forms to the president of the jury requesting that their names be recorded as Codreanu's defenders.[162] Students protested first in Iaşi and then in Bucharest, where they distributed pamphlets defending Codreanu and staged demonstrations in his support.[163] ASC in Iaşi claimed responsibility for the assassination, but few people took much notice of it.[164] Some students faced legal charges for trying to justify the crime but were acquitted on the grounds that they had done so for patriotic motives.[165] Together with numerous other pamphlets and posters, LANC published a collection of

---

156. Ibid., dosar 013207, vol. 3, f. 383–384.

157. Ibid., dosar 013207, vol. 4, f. 4.

158. "A început judecarea procesului Corneliu Z. Codreanu," *Universul*, 43/115 (22 May 1925): 4; "Sălbăteciile fostului prefect de poliţie din Iaşi C. Manciu," *Ogorul nostru*, 3/34 (11 May 1925): 2.

159. ACNSAS, Fond Penal, dosar 013207, vol. 1, f. 4–8, 244–246; Codreanu, *Pentru legionari*, 201–221.

160. ACNSAS, Fond Penal, dosar 013207, vol. 1, f. 367.

161. Ibid., dosar 013207, vol. 1, f. 264–265, 293, 449–451, vol. 4, f. 179–181; Scurtu ed., *Totalitarismul*, 473–477, 479–484, 488–492.

162. Examples are collected in ACNSAS, Fond Penal, dosar 013207, vol. 4, f. 167–171, 175–178, 182–297, 302–321, vol. 5, f. 1–145, 200–220. Codreanu writes that 19,300 petitions of this nature were submitted. Codreanu, *Pentru legionari*, 230.

163. Neagoe, *Triumful raţiunii*, 275; "Descoperirea organizatiei teroriste din Capitala," *Cuvântul*, 1/1 (6 Nov 1924): 3; Scurtu ed., *Totalitarismul*, 514.

164. Neagoe, *Triumful raţiunii*, 291.

165. "Achitarea studentului Răpeanu," *Curentul studenţesc*, 1/5 (13 Apr 1925): 3.

twenty-five songs honoring Codreanu and promising to support him at his upcoming trial in Turnu-Severin. Many of the songs were hymns and anthems written by university students, while others reflected more popular, folkloric song forms. These used simple rhyming schemes and botanical references common in peasant music at the time: "Green bay leaves / Let's go, brother, to Severin, / To stand in defence of Cornel, / When he's judged by Mârzel!"[166]

A testimony to the effectiveness of ultranationalist propaganda is that two previously neutral cities were overtaken by antisemitic sentiment in the wake of concerted campaigns by students and other Codreanu supporters. The trial was originally scheduled to be held in Focşani, which Codreanu considered to be "the strongest Liberal citadel in the country." Focşani was a minor regional center, with only thirty thousand inhabitants. Its nine factories employed Romania's fast-growing industrial working class, and the town was useful to its hinterland as a center for wine distribution.[167] The students from Iaşi, Codreanu writes, were "very worried" when they heard that the trial had been moved here, and hundreds of students flooded the town carrying antisemitic literature.[168] Despite its reputation as a "Liberal citadel," Focşani also had a strong nationalist heritage. The Cultural League had an active presence in the city, and a number of national commemorations were held there in the early 1920s because Focşani and its surrounding villages were the site of some of the hardest fighting of World War I. LANC had been active in the city since 1924. It was led by a relative of Constanţa Ghica and already had three antisemitic newspapers that appeared sporadically.[169] By the time the trial was scheduled to start, support for Codreanu was so strong that riots broke out when it was suspended on the first day. He was quickly transported to Turnu-Severin, on the other side of the country. The rioters were only an estimated one hundred students and two hundred to three hundred hooligans, but the lack of police control meant that they were able to inflict considerable damage.[170] Even if many of the rioters were outsiders, it is notable that for a few days at least, the voices of 300–400 ultranationalists were more prominent than those of the 4,240 local Jews who had lived in Focşani all their lives and were active participants in the city's civic life.[171]

---

166. E. L. *Cântecele lui Corneliu Zelea Codreanu* (Turnu-Severin: Editura Ziarului Ogorul Nostru, 1925), 20.

167. Dumitru Gusti ed., *Enciclopedia româna*, vol. 2 (Bucharest: Asociaţiunea Ştiinţifică pentru Enciclopedia României, 1939), 623–624.

168. Codreanu, *Pentru legionari*, 225.

169. Cezar Cherciu, *Focşanii: O istorie în date şi mărturii (sec XVI–1950)* (Focşani: Andrew, 2010), 318–352, 360, 368–374, 381–382.

170. Dinu Dumbrava, *Fără ură! Pregătirea şi deslănţuirea evenimentelor din Focşani în zilele de 17 şi 18 martie 1925* (n.p.: n.p., n.d.); Livezeanu, *Cultural Politics*, 283.

171. Manuila, *Recensământul general din decemvrie 1930*, vol. 2, 350; Cherciu, *Focşanii*, 361, 381, 386.

Whereas it is difficult to know what most of Focşani's population thought about the rioters devastating their town, in Turnu-Severin many locals came out in support of Codreanu. Turnu-Severin was not an antisemitic stronghold any more than Focşani had been, but hundreds, and eventually thousands, of students descended on the city, as did two battalions of gendarmes and one battalion of soldiers.[172] This time the students did not riot, and when some tried to destroy Jewish stops they were stopped by the soldiers.[173] Drawing on eyewitness testimonies, Irina Livezeanu writes,

> Local antisemitic merchants put Codreanu's portrait in their windows. Daily meetings, involving ever larger groups of the local population, were organized by Codreanu supporters under different pretexts. . . . On the eve of the trial, the whole town was wearing national colors, people sported swastikas, and walls were covered with incendiary manifestoes. Postcards with Codreanu in national folk costume had been sent by the thousands to the provinces, and the route he was supposed to travel to the courtroom was covered with flowers.[174]

In contrast to the groundswell of ultranationalist support, communists who were planning a protest rally against Codreanu were arrested before they even finished their preparations.[175]

As it had the trial of the Văcăreşteni, the ultranationalist community framed Codreanu's trial as a problem of "justice." Ultranationalists were quick to distinguish between justice as a fair recompense for moral actions and justice as a product of the legal system. The "supreme law" was not a written code but "common sense and human logic."[176] They condemned judges as corrupt and did not think that true justice could be secured through legal means in a Romania controlled by Jews and Masons. *Ogorul nostru* (Our field, 1923–1926), an ultranationalist newspaper from Turnu-Severin, argued, "The justice system is profaned in an odious manner by those who by interfering and applying pressure from above influence judges to change their beliefs and to alter justice for political and personal motives."[177] Nellu Ionescu, a former president of the Law Students Society in Iaşi, wrote in an ultranationalist student newspaper that the students had tried bringing Manciu to court for abusing students twice before

172. "Procesul Corneliu Zelea Codreanu," *Cuvântul*, 2/161 (23 May 1925): 2.
173. C. "Procesul Corneliu Zelea Codreanu," *Adevărul*, 38/12713 (24 May 1925): 7.
174. Livezeanu, *Cultural Politics*, 284–285.
175. Cuţana, "În jurul procesului Codreanu," *Adevărul*, 38/12709 (20 May 1925): 6.
176. Paul Iliescu, "Asasinatul dela Iaşi," *Ogorul nostru*, 3/31 (19 Mar 1925): 2.
177. "Apelul naţiunei," *Ogorul nostru*, 3/31 (19 Mar 1925): 1.

but without success.[178] A. C. Cuza complained during the trial that "the Romanian legal system has to be badgered repeatedly before it will act, and justice can only be achieved by forcing the issue."[179] Codreanu had done just that by murdering Manciu. Rather than judging Codreanu, ultranationalists asserted that the purpose of the trial was to bring the justice system into line with the moral values of Romanian ultranationalism. Once again, it was the state that was on trial, not Codreanu. Valeriu Roman, one of Codreanu's lawyers, argued that "if the members of the jury believe that the time has come to correctly apply the law in the Romanian lands, then they have the duty to acquit Codreanu."[180]

The message of Codreanu's trial was conveyed as much through its theatricality as through the arguments and newspaper commentaries that accompanied it. The trial was held in the ballroom of the city's largest theater so as to accommodate the largest possible audience, but spectators still lined up an hour and a half early to get a seat.[181] Codreanu and the other defendants were dressed in folk costume—as were the multitudes who filled the streets—and this time one jury member also wore a folk costume, while the others wore swastikas on their jackets.[182] The jury's choice of lapel pins suggests that the ending of the trial was decided before it had begun.[183] The selection of defense lawyers reinforced the trial's message that the whole country supported Manciu's killer. Codreanu's lawyers included senior LANC figures as well as representatives from the bar associations of thirteen different cities. Valer Pop spoke on behalf of Acțiunea românească (Romanian Action) and Ioan Sava on behalf of the students from Iași, and each of the other student centers also sent a representative. One of the jurors who would have tried Codreanu in Focșani signed on as a lawyer for the defense, and not to be outdone, the mayor of Turnu-Severin enrolled himself as another of Codreanu's lawyers.[184] Rather than discussing Codreanu's deed, the testimonies for the defense focused on Manciu's persecution of the students, his violent character, the "noble" goals of the student movement, and Codreanu's

178. Nellu Ionescu, "În jurul morții lui Manciu," *Cuvântul Iașului*, 2/Ediție specială (27 Oct 1924): 1.

179. "Procesul lui Corneliu Codreanu," *Adevărul*, 38/12710 (21 May 1925): 6.

180. N. Clocârdia and Leontin Iliescu, "Procesul Corneliu Z. Codreanu: Ziua IV-a," *Universul*, 43/119 (27 May 1925): 6.

181. Leontin Iliescu, "Procesul Corneliu Z. Codreanu: Ziua II-a," *Universul*, 43/117 (24 May 1925): 3; Cuțana, "În jurul procesului Codreanu," *Adevărul*, 38/12709 (20 May 1925): 6.

182. Livezeanu, *Cultural Politics*, 285; N. Clocârdia and Leontin Iliescu, "Procesul Corneliu Z. Codreanu: Ziua IV-a," *Universul*, 43/119 (27 May 1925): 4.

183. Newspapers hostile to Codreanu also believed that the verdict was predetermined. N. D. Cocea, "Achitarea Corneliu Codreanu," *Facla*, 7/27 (29 May 1925): 1; Ad. "Achitarea lui Codreanu," *Adevărul*, 38/12716 (28 May 1925): 1.

184. Leontin Iliescu, "A început judecarea procesului Corneliu Z. Codreanu," *Universul*, 43/115 (22 May 1925): 4; N. Clocârdia and Leontin Iliescu, "Procesul Corneliu Z. Codreanu: Ziua IV-a," *Universul*, 43/119 (27 May 1925): 6.

allegedly distinguished record in high school. The prosecution witnesses, on the other hand, focused entirely on reconstructing the moment of the assassination, rarely even alluding to Codreanu's violent past.[185]

The trial resembled a LANC rally more than a murder investigation. Manciu's widow withdrew from the trial after the second day and left town in disgust, together with one of the wounded police officers. The prosecutor general, C. G. Costa-Foru, later wrote that both in town and in the courtroom Adelina Manciu was the object of "hostile glares, offensive remarks and threatening gestures."[186] When Costa-Foru began to speak on the third day, the proceedings took on elements of melodrama. Costa-Foru argued that "we should not spread the idea that assassination leads to glory and apotheosis. That would be dangerous for the country." He then asked rhetorically, "Who among the parents in this room would like to see their son in the defendants' box?" The room immediately filled with cheers of "All of us! All of us!" The president of the jury then continually interrupted him when he began to speak about antisemitism, telling Costa-Foru that no pogroms had ever taken place in Romania and that introducing the question of minorities into the discussion was irrelevant. When he mentioned that he had a Jewish son-in-law, Costa-Foru was heckled so badly by the crowd that A. C. Cuza had to intervene to quiet the audience.[187] Codreanu was acquitted on the fifth day to the sound of thunderous applause.[188] Students in Bucharest celebrated the acquittal with singing, shouting, and demonstrations, while those in Iaşi held a banquet.[189] As had the trial of the Văcăreşteni in 1923, Codreanu's trial polarized the country between those who agreed with Manciu's murder and those who did not. Among those who disapproved of Codreanu's action, N. D. Cocea (1880–1949), a socialist activist and prolific journalist, blamed the government for Manciu's murder, because its excessive use of force gave the students the moral high ground.[190] The editorial staff at the center-left newspaper *Adevărul* (The truth, 1888–1913, 1924–1938) suggested that perhaps the jury had acquitted Codreanu because it was really A. C. Cuza who was responsible for most of the ultranationalist violence.[191]

---

185. Leontin Iliescu, "A început judecarea procesului Corneliu Z. Codreanu," *Universul*, 43/115 (22 May 1925): 4; Leontin Iliescu, "Procesul Corneliu Z. Codreanu: Ziua II-a," *Universul*, 43/117 (24 May 1925): 3.

186. C. G. Costaforu, "Impresii dela procesul Codreanu," *Adevărul*, 38/12715 (26 May 1925): 1.

187. Leontin Iliescu, "Procesul Corneliu Z. Codreanu: Ziua III-a," *Universul*, 43/118 (25 May 1925): 3.

188. N. Clocârdia and Leontin Iliescu, "Procesul Corneliu Z. Codreanu: Ziua IV-a," *Universul*, 43/120 (28 May 1925): 2.

189. "Manifestaţia studenţilor din capitală," *Universul*, 43/120 (28 May 1925): 3; "După achiterea lui Corneliu Codreanu," *Cuvântul*, 2/166 (29 May 1925): 1.

190. N. D. Cocea, "Achitarea lui Corneliu Codreanu," *Facla*, 7/27 (29 May 1925): 1.

191. Ad. "Achitarea lui Codreanu," *Adevărul*, 38/12716 (28 May 1925): 1.

It did not take long before the whole episode was dramatized as a four-act play. That year another of the Văcăreşteni, Corneliu Georgescu, led a team of students from town to town performing a play he had written called *Vremuri de restrişte* (Hard times).[192] The first act presents Herşcu, a treacherous Jew, selling information to the Germans during World War I and then accusing a Romanian publican from his village of espionage in order to steal his wealth. In the second act, set several years after the war has ended, Herşcu is now a multimillionaire and controls the entire region, including the police prefect. When the prefect beats peasants and steals their vineyards, the student Ileana explains to her father, who has just lost his land, that "justice is decided by money these days, Father, and we have no money to buy some." When Ileana protests to the prefect, he tries to rape her. She is saved just in time by the student Ştefan Dascălul, the son of the publican who was ruined by Herşcu during the war. The third act opens with Dascălul chained up in a dungeon, where the prefect tries to bribe him to join their side. Dascălul resists and is saved by five students, singing "Imnul studenţesc" (The student hymn). Justice comes in the fourth act, when the prefect poisons himself and Herşcu is sent to Palestine.[193] The references to Codreanu's murder of Manciu are all too obvious. We do not know how local audiences reacted to the play, but ultranationalist students certainly appreciated it. Iustin Ilieşiu (1900–1976), one of the movement's leading poets and songwriters, described the play as "very necessary food for the soul" because of Georgescu's "Romanian sentiment that throbs with power from the beginning to the end."[194]

After his acquittal in Turnu-Severin on 26 May 1925, Codreanu returned to Iaşi. He had been in prison for twelve out of the twenty months since he had first achieved national prominence in October 1923. Crowds met him at every station, and Codreanu estimated the gathering at Bucharest to contain over fifty thousand people.[195] A police report from Buzău stated that when Codreanu passed through "he got out off the train, and was lifted up and carried on the arms of university and high school students from that town, making a grandiose parade and shouting 'Down with the Yids!' Codreanu shouted together with them, as did his fiancé, who remained in the train." Jews who were found on or near the train were beaten by the students.[196]

192. USHMM, Fond MI-D, Reel #132, dosar 1/1922, f. 141.

193. This summary is based on Iustin Ilieşiu, "Cuvinte în jurul unei cărţi," *Înfrăţirea românească*, 4/2 (15 Nov 1927): 6–7. The second act was changed when the third (extant) edition was published in 1940. Ileana's conversation with her father was edited out, as was the prefect's attempt to rape her. Corneliu Georgescu, *Vremuri de restrişte* (Bucharest: Muntenia, 1940).

194. Ilieşiu, "Cuvinte în jurul unei cărţi," 6–7.

195. Codreanu, *Pentru legionari*, 235.

196. Scurtu ed., *Totalitarismul*, 519–523.

Codreanu and his fiancé, Elena, traveled through the country in this manner and when they arrived in Focşani, he says, they were met by a delegation who told him, "If we were not given the pleasure of having the trial in our town, you have to have your wedding here. Come to Focşani on 14 June, and you will find everything arranged."[197] As they had promised, the ultranationalists in Focşani hosted and organized the wedding, actively participating in a spectacle that presented ultranationalists as a warm, sharing, and hospitable community celebrating together as a family.

Between eighty thousand and one hundred thousand people attended the wedding, which was filmed and broadcast in Bucharest.[198] In his memoirs the legionary Mircea Dumitriu mentions his attendance at the wedding as a twelve-year-old child as a formative moment in his life.[199] One high school girl committed suicide when her parents told her that she was not allowed to attend the wedding, and after the ceremony the wedding guests collected money to help pay for her funeral.[200] Police blocked off roads to ensure that wedding guests did not travel through Jewish districts, and Jewish shops and taverns were closed for the day. Local Jews telegrammed the authorities that "the city is in a state of terror. Peaceful Jewish citizens are beaten in their houses."[201]

The ultranationalist presence in Focşani only increased after Codreanu's wedding, with more antisemitic vandalism and a new LANC newspaper established in late July and August.[202] Codreanu and A. C. Cuza returned to Focşani two months later to act as godfathers to children born since the wedding. Once again, activists distributed invitations widely, inviting "all good Christians" to come and have their children baptized, and locals were asked to bring food to feed the guests.[203] When mothers arrived in Focşani to have their children baptized they found the area cordoned off by gendarmes because a state of emergency had been declared several days before.[204] The crowd of roughly five thousand people moved on to the village of Goleşti, which was also sealed off by gendarmes, and then to Slobozia. Sixty-five babies were eventually baptized, including some whose parents were Seventh-day Adventists. The LANC newspaper *Lancea* (The spear,

197. Codreanu, *Pentru legionari*, 235.

198. Petre Abeaboeru, "Nunta lui Zelea Codreanu: Un exemplu de marketing politic," *Historia* 10/100 (2010): 38.

199. Mircea Dumitriu, "Istorie comentată a mişcării legionare, 1927–1999," in *Corneliu Zelea Codreanu*, ed. Stănescu, 62–82.

200. ACNSAS, Fond Penal, dosar 011784, vol. 14, f. 134.

201. Cherciu, *Focşanii*, 388–389.

202. "Asupra pretinselor vandalisme antisemite dela Focşani," *Lancea*, 1/1 (6 Aug 1925): 1; Scurtu ed., *Totalitarismul*, 529–531.

203. ANIC, Fond DGP, dosar 16/1923, f. 134, 137.

204. "Cum se aplică starea de asediu la Focşani," *Adevărul*, 38/12785 (18 Aug 1925).

1925–1926) said that "Father Dumitrescu from Bucharest, a saint in our eyes, jostled his way through the bayonets dressed in his robes and with a cross in his hand. Many mothers gave their children to the soldiers, telling them to take them because they did not want to return home with pagan babies."[205] Asking mothers with small infants to clash with armed gendarmes pitted ultranationalists against the state, and by provoking the state into forbidding a baptism, LANC made it look like the Romanian state was anti-Christian. Baptisms proved to be such an effective local propaganda exercise that they continued the following month, with other important LANC figures baptizing small groups of children in more isolated areas.[206]

Violence and the Courts

LANC pursued a strategy of provoking official reactions and then portraying its members as victims for the next few years. The University Senate lost patience with A. C. Cuza after Manciu's murder and the disturbances of 10 December 1924, and in April 1925 Cuza faced the court, charged with being the "moral author" of the student unrest. The Senate refused to allow classes to take place in the Faculty of Law until its leadership officially condoned the punishments handed out to belligerent students. Six professors, including Cuza, resigned, but they were soon reinstated.[207] Students argued that Cuza was the victim of political machinations, and they held demonstrations in Bucharest during his trial.[208] Cuza appeared in court once again, after a Jew named Ghern Lerman approached him on the street and punched him in the face on 1 August 1925.[209] Later that year the student Gheorghe Urziceanu fired four bullets into a Jew who he claimed had planned an assassination attempt against Cuza.[210] Writing in Urziceanu's defense, Ion Delapoiană said, "The jury in Iaşi will not have to decide whether Urziceanu is guilty or not according to the law, which has been shown so many times to be too restrictive, but it will ask: 'Does the Romanian people have the right to defend

205. "Cum s'au efectuat botezurile oprite," *Lancea*, 1/3 (1 Sept 1925): 1.

206. USHMM, Fond MI-D, Reel #132, dosar 2/1922, f. 112; Reel #136, dosar 5/1926, f. 3, 98.

207. Neagoe, *Triumful raţiunii*, 304–308; Gabriel Asandului, *A. C. Cuza: Politică şi cultură* (Iaşi: Fides, 2007), 21. One of the six, Matei Cantacuzino, had actually handed in his resignation earlier in protest against A. C. Cuza's refusal to submit to university policies. The other four resigned together with Cuza.

208. "Cronica," *Apărarea naţională*, 4/1 (20 Apr 1925): 21.

209. ANIC, Fond DGP, dosar 16/1923, f. 131; Corneliu Şumuleanu, *Atetnatul jidănesc împotriva profesorului A. C. Cuza* (Bucharest: Tipografia "Cultura Poporului," 1925).

210. "Procesul Urziceanu," *Naţionalistul*, 13/5 (28 Jan 1926): 2; "Informaţiuni," *Chemarea*, 1/7 (10 Mar 1926): 3.

its life and honor or not?'"[211] Within days of Urziceanu's acquittal, the peasant Mihai V. Budeanu, from the village of Brehueşti, near Botoşani, was tried for murdering a Jewish landowner named Avram Abramovici with an ax. Cuza and other LANC lawyers came to Budeanu's defense and Budeanu too was acquitted on the grounds that it was not an individual crime but an act of social protest against the Jewish menace threatening the country.[212]

The most widely discussed ultranationalist trial of the later half of the decade was that of a student named Nicolae Totu (1905–1939). The conflict began with protests by Jewish students over the administration of the newly introduced baccalaureate examination for high school graduates. Results from the exam's first year in 1925 showed that examining committees disproportionately failed Jewish and other minority students during the oral sections of the exams. Traian Brăileanu (1882–1947), a sociology professor from Cernăuţi University and an outspoken LANC supporter, led the 1926 committee, sparking concerns that Jewish students would be discriminated against once again. Crowds of disgruntled students followed the examining committee around town, heckling them and at times threatening violence.[213] One of the committee members, Emil Diaconescu, distributed a pamphlet after the protests claiming that the Jewish students had thrown rocks at him and that a student named David Fallik told him, "You've come from the Old Kingdom to ask tricky questions so that students will fail. But we know more than all the students from the *Old Kingdom* put together, and even more than the teachers!"[214] Diaconescu circulated his pamphlet around town for free, stirring up ultranationalist sentiment against what he called an insult "to the prestige of the Romanian state's authority."[215] Nicolae Totu, a student in Iaşi, responded to this insult by shooting David Fallik.

The population of Jews numbered 42,500 in Cernăuţi—a city of 112,427 people—and an estimated 30,000 of them turned out for Fallik's funeral.[216] Jewish homes and businesses displayed black flags and closed for three hours in the middle of the day as a sign of mourning.[217] Ultranationalists reacted just as strongly, describing the murder as necessary vigilante justice and as a display of youthful heroism. In LANC newspapers Paul Iliescu labeled Totu's act a "supreme sacrifice," and N. Mucichescu-Tunari called it an expression "of the

211. Ion Delapoiană, "Dela procesul Gh. Urziceanu," *Înfrățirea românească*, 2/9 (1 Mar 1926): 8.

212. H. Vasiliu, "Achitarea lui M. V. Budeanu," *Chemarea*, 1/7 (10 Mar 1926): 1.

213. Livezeanu, *Cultural Politics*, 79–84.

214. Emil Diaconescu, *Agresiunea de la Cernăuţi din ziuă de 7 octombrie 1926 împotriva profesorilor din Comisiunea No. 1 a examenului de bacalaureat* (Iaşi: Tipografia "Albina," 1926), 4.

215. Ibid., 10; ACNSAS, Fond Penal, dosar 015671, vol. 3, f. 27.

216. Manuila, *Recensământul general din decemvrie 1930*, vol. 2, 120.

217. ACNSAS, Fond Penal, dosar 015671, vol. 3, f. 21–22.

entire Romanian revolt" against the Jews.[218] Students distributed pamphlets about how, despite official apathy in the face of the attacks on Diaconescu, "the young Totu took revenge and washed away [Romanian] shame."[219] Supporters in Iaşi collected twenty-two thousand lei to give to Totu, but it was stolen by Aurel Morărescu, the lawyer responsible for taking it to Cernăuţi.[220] Thousands traveled to Câmpulung for Totu's trial in February 1927, staying in the homes of ultranationalist supporters there. Both before and after the trial, they attacked Jews on trains and vandalized Jewish property near train stations, as well as breaking up a Jewish wedding in Paşcani and assaulting the partygoers.[221] The jury acquitted Totu eight to two, after only ten minutes of deliberations.[222]

Such widely publicized acquittals encouraged more and more acts of individual and group violence against Jews, including an attack by high school boys on a synagogue in Bălţi, which they burned down one night before it had even been finished.[223] Other boys threw rocks at Jews while on a school excursion.[224] In Piatra Neamţ, a group of students left a masked ball in the middle of the night armed with sledgehammers and axes and destroyed graves in a Jewish cemetery.[225] In Buzău, high school students marched down the street singing nationalist anthems and then vandalized a Jewish pharmacy.[226] Just as perpetrators were acquitted during the major trials, the justice system rarely punished such vandals and assailants to the full extent of the law. When a young clerk in Tulcea, Constantin Teodorescu, assaulted three Jews without provocation in August 1925, the local police officer gave him a warning and advised him to improve his behavior.[227] Officers of the law were not immune to antisemitic sentiments, and the next month a candidate enrolled at the Gendarmerie School in Oradea Mare traveled to the Black Sea, where he and a friend beat up Jews who were sunbathing on the beach.[228] One particularly interesting strategy for harassing Jews was the *pluguşor*, a song usually sung by children walking through a village on New Year's Day. A *pluguşor* tells a story appropriate to the season and declares

218. Paul P. Iliescu, "Procesul studentului Neculai Totu din Bucovina," *Chemarea*, 2/29 (14 Feb 1927): 2; N. Mucichescu-Tunari, "Achitarea elevului Niculae Totu," *Unirea*, 2/30 (28 Feb 1927): 2.

219. ACNSAS, Fond Penal, dosar 015671, vol. 3, f. 38; ANIC, Fond DGP, dosar 44/1927, f. 23.

220. ANIC, Fond DGP, dosar 44/1927, f. 4.

221. ACNSAS, Fond Penal, dosar 015671, vol. 3, f. 30, 54, 69–74; ANIC, Fond DGP, dosar 44/1927, f. 7.

222. Livezeanu, *Cultural Politics*, 86.

223. USHMM, Fond MI-D, Reel #135, dosar 1/1925, f. 180.

224. Ibid., Reel #136, dosar 5/1926, f. 77.

225. "Profanatorii de morminte din Piatra-Neamţ," *Luptă* (12 Jan 1928).

226. USHMM, Fond MI-D, Reel #136, dosar 5/1926, f. 122.

227. Ibid., Reel #135, dosar 1/1925, f. 12.

228. Ibid., Reel #135, dosar 1/1925, f. 156.

blessings for the listeners in return for gifts of apples and nuts. LANC *pluguşor* songs added antisemitic themes, recounting how Jews had stolen the country's wealth and calling on Romanians to rise up against them. In 1926 groups of LANC members circulated around Jewish neighborhoods singing antisemitic *pluguşor* songs and taking money from Jews in return for their singing.[229]

When Jews assaulted Romanians, ultranationalists came to the victim's defense, making sure that the perpetrator received the maximum penalty for his or her crime.[230] Given that police officers and judges were also often antisemites, Jews rarely escaped harsh penalties when they got into fights with Romanians. Reporting interethnic violence as Jewish attacks on Romanians was common in ultranationalist publications, such as in an article in *Svastica* (Swastika, 1926) that claimed that bands of hundreds of Jews armed with revolvers, rocks, and metal rods attacked a peaceful student congress in Chişinău in 1926.[231] In another incident a year earlier, gangs of Jews apparently roamed the streets of Piatra Neamţ looking for Romanian boys walking alone, and any they found were mercilessly beaten.[232] Reports about Jewish violence against Christians portrayed Romanians as victims who were only defending their rights if they retaliated. Neither of the incidents just mentioned were reported in any of the mainstream newspapers, suggesting that the reports might not have been entirely credible.

Capitalizing on the publicity provided by high-profile trials and acts of violence, LANC worked to turn public sympathy into electoral success and consolidated their ties with other nationalist groups, such as the Archers of Stephen the Great. Cuzists began infiltrating Archers groups when the Dacia student society at Cernăuţi took an interest in them in 1923. Ultranationalists took control of at least one existing group but mostly formed their own, which in turn traveled to nearby villages and established new groups there. By 1928 twelve of the fifty-five Archers groups in Bucovina were affiliated with LANC. The others were influenced by Valerian Dugan, who worked at the county office in Rădăuţi and had taken responsibility for reorganizing the Archers after World War I. Dugan insisted that the Archers remain apolitical, and his conflict with the Dacia society effectively split the five hundred thousand Archers in Bucovina.[233] LANC leaders actively cultivated their ties with the nationalist group, and Corneliu Zelea

229. USHMM, Fond MI-D, Reel #136, dosar 5/1926, f. 154–160.

230. Ibid., Reel #135, dosar 1/1925, f. 189, 207, 235; "Lupta contra Cuzismului în Basarabia," *Apărarea naţională*, 6/10 (4 Mar 1928): 1.

231. "Atentatele jidoveşti de la Chişinău," *Svastica* (1926): 2, in USHMM, Fond MI-D, Reel #136, dosar 5/1926, f. 147.

232. "Agresiunea dela Piatra Neamţ," *Unirea*, 1/1 (1–15 Oct 1925): 2.

233. ANIC, Fond DGP, dosar 25/1926, f. 24–25, 32, 39–42; Scurtu ed., *Totalitarismul*, 506–507; USHMM, Fond MI-D, Reel #135, dosar 2/1924, f. 87, 110.

Codreanu visited an Archers congress in 1924 after they had expressed their support for the Văcăreşteni.[234] His father attended a meeting of 120 Archers in September 1926, when he told them, "Captains of the Archers must hold meetings in their villages two or three times a week, teaching theory and giving instruction, so that the Archers will be as well trained as they were in the days of Stephen the Great. They will make every effort to extend their propaganda and to organize as many Archers as possible, for in time the Cuzists will come to power and will have need of these Archers, and the country will trust only them."[235] In addition to trusting the Archers, LANC merged with FNR and Romanian Action in 1925, strengthening its voting base and geographical reach.[236]

Propaganda meetings involved church services and speeches to audiences made up of several hundred peasants, priests, and teachers at a time in villages scattered throughout Moldova.[237] In cities, LANC members rallied with flags and singing and paraded in groups according to gender, age, and social category.[238] Sometimes such meetings were specifically aimed at women, workers, or other clearly defined groups.[239] When LANC gathered in the town of Piatra Neamţ in March 1926, the police blocked off major streets to allow the two-thousand-person strong procession to pass by, led by ten mounted students carrying maces with swastikas on their tips.[240] The democratic newspaper *Adevărul* noted that the riots that sometimes accompanied these events were not spontaneous affairs. Excuses such as sanctifying a flag were used to gather people, who were told that they had "orders" to meet at a specific place and time. Once a crowd assembled, LANC propagandists then incited the crowd to violence against nearby Jews.[241]

Ultranationalist violence escalated during the 1920s as Romanian authorities implicitly condoned LANC's notion of vigilante justice by acquitting Codreanu, Moţa, Totu, and others and consistently failing to protect minority rights. Violence mobilized ultranationalists in support of specific causes, keeping the message of the student protests of 10 December 1922 alive throughout the rest of the decade. High-profile trials, weddings, and baptisms helped build personal

234. ANIC, Fond DGP, dosar 49/1924, f. 81.

235. USHMM, Fond MI-D, Reel #135, dosar 2/1926, f. 81.

236. Ibid., Reel #135, dosar 1/1925, f. 103.

237. ACNSAS, Fond Penal, dosar 011784, vol. 14, f. 373; ANIC, Fond DGP, dosar 16/1923, f. 156–157; USHMM, Fond MI-D, Reel #135, dosar 1/1925, f. 42–43, 130, 135.

238. USHMM, Fond MI-D, Reel #135, dosar 2/1926, f. 121, 131; Reel #136, dosar 5/1926, f. 6–14.

239. Ibid., Reel #136, dosar 5/1926, f. 106, 113.

240. USHMM, Fond SRI Files, Reel #105, dosar 1151, f. 6–8.

241. "Cum se pregătesc dezordinilie: Constătuirile "Ligii creştine" la Tecuci," *Adevărul* (5 Sept 1925); "Incidente antisemitice la un bâlci," *Politică*, 113 (14 Oct 1926); USHMM, Fond MI-D, Reel #135, dosar 3/1926, f. 38; Reel #136, dosar 5/1926, f. 26–28.

connections between ultranationalists scattered throughout the country, consolidating LANC's role as the organizational face of ultranationalism. Simultaneously, these events reinforced the idea that there was something noble about fighting politicians, Yids, and police; that ethnic Romanians could rule their own country only through violent struggle; and that the cause needed youthful heroes to establish justice in the land.

3

MOBILIZING SUPPORT

In a front-page article reflecting on the meaning of Easter, Ion Popescu-Mozăceni, a leading figure in LANC and a deacon in the Romanian Orthodox Church, reminded the readers of *Apărarea națională* in 1927 that when the Son of God came to earth, "the 'Truth' was followed by 'the Lie' and by 'the children of lies.' The Lie (treason), even sat with him at mealtimes." Two paragraphs later, he mentioned that treason had entered "the divine sanctuary of our fight for purifying the nation."[1] The story of the Legion of the Archangel Michael begins with a split within the ultranationalist community, as Codreanu and his followers broke away from A. C. Cuza. Codreanu's legionaries spent their first years trying to justify breaking away from LANC, which involved bringing antipoliticianism and the cult of youth to the forefront of their ideology and emphasizing that they were the legitimate heirs of the student movement of 1922. Being a legionary initially meant supporting Codreanu against Cuza, but a distinctive legionary identity emerged once legionaries found symbols, rituals, and organizational structures that differentiated them from LANC.

The treason, or "Yid conspiracy," that LANC publications referred to frequently during the spring and summer of 1927 officially began when A. C. Cuza accused LANC deputy Paul Iliescu of opposing the student struggle, of trying to take control of the party in Bucharest, and of using LANC's bank for his own

1. I. G. Popescu-Mozăceni, "Înviere și trădare," *Apărarea națională*, 5/2 (24 Apr 1927): 1.

purposes.[2] Cuza suddenly and unilaterally expelled Iliescu without consulting the other leaders of the party. Led by Corneliu Şumuleanu and Ion Zelea Codreanu, five of the other nine deputies protested vehemently against the lack of due process in Iliescu's dismissal, and Cuza responded by expelling them as well. He claimed that they had formed an alliance with Jews and had tried to turn LANC into a political party.[3] Even if possible family quarrels had taken place between the Cuzas and the Codreanus in 1925, conflict between A. C. Cuza and the Codreanus came out in the open in early 1926. Most likely, a power struggle for control of LANC lay at the heart of the conflict, with A. C. Cuza trying to establish himself as the unquestioned leader of the movement, while the Codreanus and their supporters sought a more open decision-making process. Ion Zelea Codreanu clashed with Cuza in July over the selection of LANC candidates for the elections in December 1927. At the same time, Ion Moţa began preparations for forming a new, independent student movement while the younger Codreanu was still in France.[4] When student hooliganism escalated during Nicolae Totu's trial in February 1927, Paul Iliescu and Ion Zelea Codreanu loudly criticized the students' lack of self-control.[5] Dr. Ioan Istrate and Teodosie Popescu were arrested in Bucharest as part of a "fascist plot" in March 1927. They had allegedly been planning to break away from LANC and to direct its youth wing into the Codreanus' faction, which now included the former leaders of Romanian Action in Cluj, LANC leaders in Focşani, and a handful of prominent ultranationalists in Iaşi.[6] LANC was badly divided by the scandal, but most of the students swore their loyalty to Cuza. Student hooligans demonstrated their allegiance by interrupting a meeting held by the dissidents and forcing the hotel where it was held to be evacuated.[7]

A New Faith

Corneliu Zelea Codreanu had spent 1926 in France, and when he returned to Iaşi in May 1927 he immediately gathered sympathetic students and tried to

---

2. "Conspiraţia jidanilor în LANC," *Apărarea naţională*, 5/1 (17 Apr 1927): 2.

3. "Excluderea deputăţilor LANC," *Apărarea naţională*, 5/6 (30 May 1927): 1; "Uneltirile contra LANC," *Apărarea naţională*, 5/11 (6 Oct 1927): 1; ACNSAS, Fond Penal, dosar 011784, vol. 18, f. 46–51.

4. USHMM, Fond MI-D, Reel #135, dosar 2/1924, f. 86, 126–127, dosar 2/1926, f. 6–7, 22.

5. ANIC, Fond DGP, dosar 44/1927, f. 1.

6. "După arestări politice," *Luptă* (9 Mar 1927); Codreanu, *Pentru legionari*, 269.

7. USHMM, Fond SRI Files, Reel #106, dosar 1151, f. 312–313, 320–321; "Ridicole înscenare dela Bucureşti," *Apărarea naţională*, 5/4 (10 May 1927): 2.

form an independent group under his leadership.[8] Accusing the older generation of destroying LANC through self-interested bickering, Codreanu drew on the image of the purity of youth to propose "an idealistic, youthful, voluntary movement organized hierarchically."[9] He managed to convince only roughly twenty students to join the new movement, which he dubbed the Legion of the Archangel Michael.[10] The name came from an icon of the archangel that Codreanu's father had shown the younger Codreanu and his colleagues were they were in Văcăreşti prison in 1923. Corneliu Zelea Codreanu had commissioned several copies of the icon at the time. He deposited one at the St. Spiridon Church in Iaşi and gave another one to his mother, which he later borrowed to use in the legionary offices in Bucharest.[11] In his 1847 epic poem *Mihaida*, Ion Heliade Rădulescu (1802–1872) used the archangel Michael as a heavenly messenger who inspired the early modern prince Michael the Brave (1558–1601) in his battles against the Ottomans. Historians such as Nicolae Iorga claimed that Michael the Brave had "united" the three Romanian principalities, thereby laying the foundations for the modern nation-state, and his skull was kept at the Dealu Monastery in Dâmboviţa County where it was honored on 8 November, the feast day of the archangel Michael in Romanian Orthodoxy. Codreanu attended a military academy next to the monastery and it is likely that he had heard his teachers connect the cult of the archangel with Romanian nationalism, but he never explicitly made this connection in his writings.[12] The archangel Michael is an important figure in Eastern Orthodoxy, and given Codreanu's obsession with lucky days and omens, it is more likely that he chose the archangel on the basis of his religious experience in prison and as part of a widespread Orthodox practice of adopting patron saints as the protectors of individuals and groups.[13]

---

8. Codreanu later wrote that he first tried to reconcile the two factions, but this is not mentioned in police reports from the time. Codreanu, *Pentru legionari*, 271; ACNSAS, Fond Penal, dosar 011784, vol. 14, f. 97; ANIC, Fond DGP, dosar 79/1927, f. 5.

9. Corneliu Zelea Codreanu, "E ceasul vostru: Veniţi!" *Pământul strămoşesc*, 1/1 (1 Aug 1927): 5.

10. Codreanu, *Pentru legionari*, 271, 275.

11. ACNSAS, Fond Penal, dosar 011784, vol. 13, f. 124.

12. Constantin Iordachi, "God's Chosen Warriors: Romantic Palingenesis, Militarism and Fascism in Modern Romania," in *Comparative Fascist Studies: New Perspectives*, ed. Constantin Iordachi (London: Routledge, 2009), 329–333.

13. John Charles Arnold, *The Footprints of Michael the Archangel: The Formation and Diffusion of a Saintly Cult, c. 300–c. 800* (New York: Palgrave Macmillan, 2013). On Codreanu's superstitions, see Corneliu Zelea Codreanu, *Însemnari*, MS, 1934 and in other legionary writings, Vasile Marin, *Crez de generaţie* (Bucharest: Tipografia "Bucovina" I. E. Torouţiu, 1937), 25, 27; Ion Moţa, "Cei din urma articli," *Libertatea*, 34/15 (8 Apr 1937): 1; and Ion Dumitrescu-Borşa, *Cea mai mare jertfă legionară* (Sibiu: Editura "Totul pentru Ţară," 1937), 31, 49–50, 74–75, 96.

Cuza's most biting accusation was that the dissenters were engaging in "politics" when LANC was a movement, not a political party.[14] In an article from the first issue of the Legion's new newspaper, *Pământul strămoşesc* (the Ancestral land, 1927–1930, 1933), titled "To the Icon!" Ion Moţa responded. "We do not do politics, and we have never done it for a single day in our lives," he wrote. "We have a religion, we are slaves to a faith. We are consumed in its fire and are completely dominated by it. We serve it until our last breath." Admitting that "we lost our way for a while, carried along by worldly values," he said that if the ultranationalist movement was to succeed it must submit itself afresh "to a life as God wanted it: a life of truth, justice, and virtue." In Moţa's vision Christian virtue was not a goal in itself, but a means for the ultranationalist movement to overcome its enemies with divine assistance. "In this consists salvation," he wrote, "with freedom from the Yids and from all the deadly plagues that consume us: *in restoring fruitfulness* in the godly way [*în via dumnezeească*], which today is sick and barren, in our nation (at least here), fallen into satanic claws that lay waste to the soul and bring it loss."[15] Subsequent issues of *Pământul strămoşesc* continued Moţa's focus on virtue, insisting that the foundational elements of legionarism were "youthfulness of the soul, that is, purity in life, drive and selflessness in battle," as well as "deeds, not words."[16] The increased emphasis on virtue did not mean that the legionaries had renounced violence. Ion Banea (1905–1939) affirmed legionary violence in an early issue of *Pământul strămoşesc* by quoting Jesus' words: "I have not come to bring peace, but a sword."[17] When a Bucharest newspaper accused Nicolae Totu of being involved in antisemitic violence on a train near Dorna in August 1927, he replied that he had been in Iaşi at the time but that he regretted having missing the opportunity to assault Jews.[18] Ultranationalists who remained loyal to Cuza began arming themselves for fear of legionary attacks.[19]

Ion Moţa's father printed the first issues of *Pământul strămoşesc* at the *Libertatea* press in Orăştie, and legionaries sold them in Iaşi as well as sending free copies to former LANC supporters and to villages in Moldova.[20] Scattered support for the Legion soon emerged. According to the second issue, one man from Panciu sent a two-hundred-lei donation to the newspaper, and another immediately found them five new subscribers in his city of Adjud. Newspaper sellers in

14. A. C. Cuza, "Marea adunare naţională," *Apărarea naţională*, 5/1 (17 Apr 1927): 1.
15. Ion Moţa, "La icoană!" *Pământul strămoşesc*, 1/1 (1 Aug 1927): 9–10.
16. "Legiunea Arhanghelul Mihail," *Pământul strămoşesc*, 1/2 (15 Aug 1927): 3.
17. Ionel I. Banea, "La luptă!" *Pământul strămoşesc*, 1/4 (15 Sept 1927): 12.
18. "P. S. Avertisment," *Pământul strămoşesc*, 1/2 (15 Aug 1927): 8.
19. Scurtu ed., *Totalitarismul*, vol. 1, 618.
20. ANIC, Fond DGP, dosar 79/1927, f. 6.

the villages of Sâmnicolaul Mare and Prundul Bărăului asked that their orders be doubled. Another supporter, in the village of Văculeşti, near Dorohoi, found fifteen unsold copies that had been incorrectly addressed so he sold them himself, sending the money to the legionaries in Iaşi.[21] The newspaper's editors published similar stories in each subsequent issue, thanking supporters for donations or for signing up large numbers of subscribers; they printed letters from individuals—young and old, male and female—who praised the new initiative. Some influential LANC figures allied themselves with the Legion immediately, among them Gheorghe Clime, an engineer who was the former LANC vice president for Iaşi County; Ioan Blănaru, a former president of the Christian Students' Association in Iaşi; I. C. Cătuneanu, a leader of Romanian Action in Cluj; Mille Lefter, the president of LANC in Galaţi; Valer Danileanu, the LANC president in Câmpulung County; and Ioan N. Grossu, Victor M. Tilinca, and I. Mihailă, presidents of LANC in their respective villages.[22] Such prominent defections hint at the extent of disillusionment within LANC and were important for boosting the prestige of the Legion amongst ultranationalists. The Legion boasted three hundred members at the end of its first month, and by December 1927 individuals from fifty towns and villages around the country were subscribing to its newspaper or expressing their support.[23]

According to *Pământul strămoşesc*, the Legion was initially divided into four sections: (1) "Youth," including a subsection for members under nineteen years old called the Blood Brotherhood (Frăţie de Cruce), which had no connection to Amos Frâncu's organization of the same name; (2) "Protectors of the Legion," for older members dedicated to sustaining, encouraging, and protecting the Youth; (3) "[Women's] Aid," a female section performing auxiliary functions; and (4) "International," incorporating sympathetic Romanians living abroad. It was to be led by a council that included the presidents of each of the student centers, and by a senate with representatives from each county over the age of fifty.[24] Codreanu set a maximum number of legionaries at one hundred per county and three thousand in total. Those who joined were required to take an oath, to dedicate fifteen minutes each day to serving the Legion, to recruit five new members

21. "Mulţumiri," *Pământul strămoşesc*, 1/2 (15 Aug 1927): 15.

22. Gheorghe Clime, "Visuri. Nădejdi. Realitate." *Pământul strămoşesc*, 1/1 (1 Aug 1927): 13–14; Ioan Blănaru, "Speranţe," *Pământul strămoşesc*, 1/2 (15 Aug 1927): 6–7; "Cum e primită revistă noastra," *Pământul strămoşesc*, 1/2 (15 Aug 1927): 12–13; M. I. Lefter, "După mare 'ngrijorare, mare bucurie," *Pământul strămoşesc*, 1/4 (15 Sept 1927): 6–7; "Cum e primită revistă noastra," 1/4 (15 Sept 1927): 13; "Cum e primită revistă noastra," *Pământul strămoşesc*, 1/5 (1 Oct 1927): 12; Valer Danileanu, "Către soldaţii din Legiunea Arhanghelul Mihail," *Pământul strămoşesc*, 1/7 (1 Nov 1927): 13.

23. "Activitatea legiunii," *Pământul strămoşesc*, 1/3 (1 Sept 1927): 7; "Legiunea Arhanghelul Mihail," *Pământul strămoşesc*, 1/10 (15 Dec 1927): 7.

24. "Legiunea Arhanghelul Mihail," *Pământul strămoşesc*, 1/2 (15 Aug 1927): 3–4.

within five months, and to give help to other legionaries whenever they met them. With the exception of international members, legionaries in each section were organized into independent "nuclei" of three to thirteen people, later called *cuiburi* (nests).[25] *Pământul strămoșesc* dictated that married legionary women were to be mothers and to provide moral guidance, which included disapproving of excessive makeup, "Jewish" fashions, and immoral dancing. Single women were called "Sisters of the Legion" and were told to organize a craft exhibition to display legionary handiwork.[26]

A Legionary Home

The most immediate source of conflict between legionaries and Cuzists was a Cămin Cultural Creștin (Christian Cultural Center) that Codreanu and other LANC supporters had built in Iași. The idea for the *cămin* emerged immediately after the trial of the Văcăreșteni in March 1924. When he returned to Iași as a free man, Codreanu gathered university and high school students together in a garden that a noblewoman named Constanța Ghica made available to them as a meeting place. Here he spoke to them about the need for a building where students could meet together without being under the authority of the university.[27] Ultranationalist students had tried organizing within the dormitories, but the chancellor dismissed student leaders who used their authority to promote political groups within subsidized student accommodation.[28] Students had been protesting since 1922 against the overcrowded and underresourced conditions in the *cămine* (dormitories), but it was an uneven battle because the university authorities could revoke scholarships and deny students the right to live in the dormitories, measures that they regularly used to limit student activism.[29] One of Codreanu's goals was that the students build their own cămin, which they could not be thrown out of and that the university had no right to interfere in. More precisely, this was a *cămin cultural* (cultural center), meant to resemble the cultural centers being built in villages across the country by the Prince Carol Cultural Foundation.[30] The Royal Foundation intended its cultural centers to

25. "Organizarea Legiunii Arhanghelul Mihail," *Pământul strămoșesc*, 1/4 (15 Sept 1927): 3–4.

26. "Organizarea Legiunii Arhanghelul Mihail," *Pământul strămoșesc*, 1/5 (1 Oct 1927): 3–4.

27. Codreanu, *Pentru legionari*, 189; ACNSAS, Fond Penal, dosar 013207, vol. 1, f. 162.

28. Neagoe, *Triumful rațiunii*, 175–176; AN—Iași, Fond Universitatea A. I. Cuza, Rectorat, dosar 1021/1922, f. 263–264.

29. AN—Iași, Fond Universitatea A. I. Cuza, Rectorat, Reel #121, dosar 1025/1923, f. 2–3, dosar 1051/1924–1925, f 68–71.

30. ANIC, Fond Fundațiile Culturale Regale Centrală, dosar 13/1924, f. 1–6.

promote literate and "modern" Romanian culture within villages. The vision was that "a Cultural Center is every villager's second home. When it is ready, it should be the pride of the village, its ornament, a nest, a house of books."[31] Codreanu named his building a Cămin Cultural, but this was a "second home" for the ultranationalist students, not a means for the Royal Foundation to spread its version of national culture. By emphasizing that this was a "Christian" cămin, he identified it with the antisemitic student movement, which used the epithet "Christian" to contrast itself with Jewish and "Judaized" Romanian culture.

This was not the first ultranationalist building project in Iaşi. Several leading LANC members, including A. C. Cuza and the wealthy engineer Grigore Bejan, had already built a similar center in 1919. Anachronistically describing the Popular Athenaeum they established in the suburb of Tătăraşi as a cultural center similar to those built by the Royal Foundation, Bejan later wrote that "I, Ifrim, Cuza, and Father Mihăilescu, thought that it would be good to erect a *cămin cultural* in a part of the town where there are not so many Yids."[32] In 1924, Grigore Bejan donated some land next to his hotel on Elizabeth Boulevard at Râpa Galbena for Codreanu and his colleagues to build on. Ultranationalists already regularly met at the Hotel Bejan, which served as a de facto LANC headquarters in Iaşi. Members met here to relax together and students gathered on the veranda before moving off to commit acts of vandalism or assault.[33] Once they received the land, the students approached businesses asking them to provide the construction materials free of charge. Some responded positively. The Moruzzi family from Dorohoi gave one hundred thousand lei, General Gheorghe "Zizi" Cantacuzino provided three wagons of cement, and Romanians living in the United States sent four hundred thousand lei, not to mention smaller donations arriving from peasants scattered throughout the country.[34] Codreanu led roughly twenty-six students to a property in the village of Ungheni that had been offered to them by the businessman Olimpiu Lascăr, where they began making bricks.[35] They borrowed tools from the locals, and the village priest blessed the opening of the brickworks. Locals soon joined them and students, graduates, tradespeople, workers, and peasants all worked side by side. A convivial atmosphere developed

31. Gh. D. Mugur, *Căminul cultural: Îndreptar pentru conducătorii culturii la sate* (Bucharest: Fundaţia Culturală "Principele Carol," 1922), 18.

32. Asandului, *A. C. Cuza*, 85.

33. ACNSAS, Fond Penal, dosar 013207, vol. 1, f. 244–246, vol. 2, f. 269–271, vol. 3, f. 206–207; USHMM, Fond SRI Files, Reel #105, dosar 1151, f. 4323, 4514.

34. Codreanu, *Pentru legionari*, 238.

35. Ibid., 156. Other sources record that the land was provided by Zemstva Bălţi. ACNSAS, Fond Penal, dosar 013207, vol. 1, f. 52.

and Codreanu writes that the volunteers ended each day in the tavern "singing happy songs."[36]

The Cămin Cultural Creştin in Iaşi was the hub of legionary life for the first few years. Grigore Bejan allied himself with Cuza after the schism and he made several attempts to ensure his ownership of the cămin from August 1927 onward. Bejan asserted that his donation made him the proprietor of anything built on the property. Codreanu retorted that Ion Moţa had supplied over half of the building expenses (123,000 lei) and that therefore the cămin should remain under the exclusive administration of "the students," by which he meant the legionaries.[37] Legionaries managed to finish two-thirds of the roof and added a chapel on the third floor before they moved into the three completed rooms in September 1927.[38] Unmarried legionary women were entrusted with decorating the building.[39] The Legion held its first ball on 8 November 1927 to celebrate the saint's day of the archangel Michael. Legionaries sold 512 tickets and raised almost nine thousand lei, a quarter of which they put into the continued construction of the cămin.[40] That day the legionaries also held a requiem at St. Spiridon Church for Moldavian heroes such as Stephen the Great and Michael the Brave, after which they marched to their cămin singing "The Hymn of the Legion" ("Imnul Legiunii"). Back at the cămin they solemnly mixed soil that they had ordered from the graves and battlefields of those heroes whose souls they had just prayed for, and placed it in small sacks that all legionaries were to wear around their necks.[41]

As Christmas approached, legionaries everywhere were asked to hold their own balls or literary evenings, to organize choirs, to sell embroidery, or to organize caroling expeditions with *pluguşor* songs to raise money for the Legion.[42] Money was a genuine problem. In April 1928, only 836 of the 2,586 subscribers to *Pământul strămoşesc* paid their dues.[43] That October, Codreanu borrowed eighty-two thousand lei from a local bank to fund the movement but he did not manage to repay the loan until 1933.[44] The legionaries had to find money wherever they could, selling vegetables they had grown in Constanţa Ghica's garden

---

36. Codreanu, *Pentru legionari*, 191; Mihail Polihroniade, *Tabăra de muncă* (Bucharest: Tipografia Ziarului Universul, 1936), 3.

37. ANIC, Fond DGP, dosar 79/1927, f. 9; USHMM, Fond SRI Files, Reel #106, dosar 1151, f. 330.

38. "Căminul Cultural Creştin," *Pământul strămoşesc*, 1/2 (15 Aug 1927): 11–12; "Informaţiuni," *Pământul strămoşesc*, 1/5 (1 Oct 1927): 15.

39. "Organizarea Legiunii Arhanghelul Mihail," *Pământul strămoşesc*, 1/5 (1 Oct 1927): 4.

40. "Informaţiuni," *Pământul strămoşesc*, 1/7 (1 Nov 1927): 14; "Informaţiuni," *Pământul strămoşesc*, 1/8 (15 Nov 1927): 15.

41. "Ziua legiunii la Iaşi," *Pământul strămoşesc*, 1/8 (15 Nov 1927): 3–7.

42. "Ce trebuie să ştie şi să facă," *Pământul strămoşesc*, 1/10 (15 Dec 1927): 2.

43. Heinen, *Legiunea "Arhanghelul Mihail,"* 132.

44. ACNSAS, Fond Penal, dosar 011784, vol. 1, f. 139, 143. Codreanu's account gives a figure of 110,000 lei and says that it had still not been repaid in 1935. Codreanu, *Pentru legionari*, 324.

and eventually selling tiles they had put aside for the cămin. Radu Mironovici learned to drive a truck bought by the Legion and raised money transporting passengers from Iaşi to nearby cities and monasteries.[45] Legionaries asked supporters to sacrifice one hundred lei per month to help fund the Legion, and they gratefully publicized all donations in *Pământul strămoşesc.*[46] In August 1928, eight legionaries decided to give up smoking and to donate the money they saved to the Legion.[47] Others donated shares they owned in the LANC bank to fund legionary building projects.[48] Women's needlework was particularly useful in this regard. Ecaterina Constantinescu, a young woman from Cahul, managed to send three thousand lei in July 1928 after selling embroidery she had done for the Legion.[49] Others sent their handiwork directly to the cămin so that it could be displayed as part of an exhibition in Iaşi. This too was sold once the financial crisis struck in 1929.[50]

On November 14, 1927 Bejan used his position as "official administrator" of the property to post an eviction order issued by the Tribunal of Iaşi and he began court proceedings to officially expel the legionaries from the cămin.[51] Over the next eighteen months Teodor Mociulschi, a law student and an ardent Cuza supporter, wrote violent articles against Codreanu in *Cuvântul studenţesc* and threatened him with a revolver as the two sides quarreled over the building.[52] Bejan accused the legionaries of stealing tools from the cămin to use at Constanţa Ghica's garden in April 1928; Codreanu and six legionaries broke into Bejan's house at 7:30 a.m., beating him, splitting his head open, and disfiguring his face.[53]

As violence surrounding the cămin escalated, legionaries began work on a new building in June 1928. They dubbed it "Saint Michael's Castle," and individuals sent financial donations to pay for building supplies. Legionaries called the project "the first antisemitic university in Romania," because working on it was supposed to help "educate" them.[54] They made new members prove their

---

45. Codreanu, *Pentru legionari*, 324–325.

46. Heinen, *Legiunea "Arhanghelul Mihail,"* 133; "Comitetul de 100," *Pământul strămoşesc*, 2/14 (1, July 1928): 8; Corneliu Zelea Codreanu, "Dare de seamă rezumativă," *Pământul strămoşesc*, 2/21 (1 Nov 1928): 1–5.

47. "O hotărâre a Legiunii care se va întinde," *Pământul strămoşesc*, 2/16 (15 Aug 1928): 3.

48. Spiru Peceli, "Alte acţiuni," *Pământul strămoşesc*, 2/20 (15 Oct 1928): 3.

49. "Dela surorile noastre," *Pământul strămoşesc*, 2/14 (15 July 1928): 6.

50. "Dela surorile legiunii," *Pământul strămoşesc*, 2/24 (25 Dec 1928): 5; "Criza financiară, legiunea," *Pământul strămoşesc*, 3/1 (15 June 1929): 14–15.

51. "O nedreptate strigătoare la cer," *Pământul strămoşesc*, 1/9 (1 Dec 1927): 3–5; Corneliu Zelea Codreanu, "Răutatea omenească," *Pământul strămoşesc*, 2/18 (15 Sept 1928): 4–5.

52. ACNSAS, Fond Penal, dosar 000324, vol. 8, f. 134–138; Ion Banea, "Un sfârşit de an," *Pământul strămoşesc*, 4/8 (1 Jan 1931): 1.

53. ACNSAS, Fond Penal, dosar 011784, vol. 14, f. 130; "Atentatul contra d-lui ing. Gr. Bejan," *Apărarea naţională*, 6/9 (22 Apr 1928): 2.

54. "Situaţia la cărămidărie," *Pământul strămoşesc*, 2/14 (15 July 1928): 3.

worth by directing activities at the brickworks in Ungheni, as well as by undergoing a "theoretical" exam covering antisemitic doctrine and legionary ideology. A number of the so-called *muşchetari* (musketeers) in the Blood Brotherhood helped make bricks for the castle. Activity at the brickworks began at five o'clock each morning, and one boy rode his bicycle 185 miles from Galaţi to Ungheni so he could take part.[55] This burst of enthusiasm only lasted a few months, however, and legionaries soon went back to fighting over the cămin.

Conflict began again in September 1928 when legionaries forcefully evicted several Cuzists who were living in the cămin. Cuzists immediately began preparations to do the same to the legionaries who had taken their place.[56] A judge overturned Bejan's claims to legal ownership of the cămin in July 1929, but Cuzist students fought for de facto possession of the cămin for another twelve months.[57] As time passed, the Legion grew steadily in popularity among ultranationalist students in Iaşi, and more and more legionary students were gradually elected to the ASC in Iaşi. Now confident of their position, in March 1930 legionaries offered the cămin as a meeting place where the two sides could discuss further collaboration.[58] In addition to possessing a symbolic importance for the student movement, the cămin situated legionaries in a prominent position within the city's symbolic geography. The legionary cămin sat at the top of a large flight of stairs known as Râpa Galbenă, which was a popular location for leisure and relaxation during the interwar period. Until 1898, the park at the foot of the stairs had been quite extensive but erosion problems destabilized the soil and at the turn of the century Căile Ferate Române (the Romanian Railway Company, CFR) built several offices and a student dormitory on the property. Rather than displaying the rectangular, functional architecture of the CFR buildings, the legionary cămin was designed in an older, quintessentially Moldavian style that celebrated local culture and history. The cămin's design mattered because not only did the structure sit on a major junction, but also, located as it was at the top of a hill, it marked a boundary between the old city and newer districts around the railway station. Its visibility reinforced the character of Râpa Galbenă as a landmark, and the legionaries' architectural choices had the power to emphasize either the city's Moldavian heritage or the modernism of the age. In addition to dominating the park at Râpa Galbenă, its location on the main thoroughfare between the railway

---

55. "Veşti dela cărămidărie," *Pământul strămoşesc*, 2/15 (1 Aug 1928): 3; Corneliu Zelea Codreanu, "Situaţia la cărămidărie," *Pământul strămoşesc*, 2/16 (15 Aug 1928): 1; Corneliu Zelea Codreanu, "Dare de seamă rezumativă," *Pământul strămoşesc*, 2/21 (1 Nov 1928): 1–5.

56. USHMM, Fond MI-D, Reel #137, dosar 4/1929, f. 10.

57. Ibid., Reel #137, dosar 4/1929, f. 17.

58. Ibid., Reel #138, dosar 2/1930, f. 18–20, 42.

station and the city center, close to the university and Iaşi's historic churches, gave legionaries quick access to the city's key memorials and public buildings. Student gatherings on campus moved easily down the hill to the cămin and the building became a meeting place for groups planning marches or protests to the council chambers, the city center, or one of the city's many historic churches where legionaries regularly held religious services.[59]

The cămin fell into a state of disrepair during the three years that Bejan and Codreanu fought over it, but legionaries restored it during 1930 at a cost of two hundred thousand lei.[60] The Legion had an office in Bucharest as of November 1929, but Iaşi remained the hub of the movement until Codreanu himself moved to Bucharest in 1933. In addition to those who lived at the cămin, many legionaries and sympathizers used it as a place to socialize and relax. In an account from 2001, the legionary N. S. Govora said that going to the cămin regularly as a student at the Military High School in Iaşi was an important step towards his integration into the Legion. "There was an extremely friendly atmosphere," Govora writes; "some played chess, others wrote, drew pictures, or repaired their ripped clothing."[61] The cămin was not a particularly comfortable place to live, but everything in it testified to the legionaries' ingenuity. In his memoirs the legionary Dumitru Banea (1911–2000) writes about the building as "our *Cămin*," even though he himself was not one of the twenty legionaries who lived there in 1931. He says,

> We were so poor it was unbelievable. There was no *sobă* [a type of wood heater], and the inhabitants put several electrical wires on a tile and stuck them into a power socket to get some heat. They put one tile at their heads and another at their feet. We washed our clothes there. . . . When my brother could not pay his rent any more we made a room for him in the garage where we kept our truck, which we'd named "Căprioara" [Deer]. We found some planks in the attic and we laid floorboards down, we made him a table, a bookshelf,—I don't remember if we made him a bed—and we set them up like a tower. Not having enough money to put blue paper on the bookshelf, we decorated it with newspapers. He no longer had to worry about rent.[62]

---

59. Ovidiu Buruiană, "Incursiune în cotidianul Iaşului interbelic," in *Iaşi: Memoria unei capitale*, ed. Iacob Gheorghe (Iaşi: Editura Universităţii "Alexandru Ioan Cuza," 2008), 304–306.

60. "Cămin Cultural Creştin," *Pământul strămoşesc*, 4/8 (1 Jan 1931): 3.

61. N. S. Govora, "Corneliu Zelea Codreanu," in *Corneliu Zelea Codreanu*, ed. Stănescu, 106.

62. Dumitru Banea, *Acuzat, martor, apărător in procesul vieţii mele* (Sibiu: Puncte Cardinale, 1995), 10.

Despite the hardships associated with living in the cămin, the inhabitants remembered it as a center of their social life. In June 1932 they brought an icon of the archangel Michael that they had deposited at the St. Spiridon Church eight years earlier and hung it in the cămin.[63] Vera Totu and her husband, Nicolae, shared one of the upper stories with three other students during 1933. Seven years later she wrote,

> In the basement there was a canteen where for seven lei you'd receive a serving of food in a clay bowl and a spoonful of polenta that could satisfy a fully grown man. There was a large hall on the first floor that was whitewashed clean, swept and cared for with love. That was where the first legionary lectures were held, that was where student gatherings took unflinching decisions. On Sunday evenings the happiest and friendliest parties took place there, with young people coming in simple clothes, with nothing in their pockets, wanting only to meet with those they were close to, to dance a big *horă* and a crazy *sârbă*,[64] to listen to the judicious words of Ionică Banea and to cool off letting loose a lively song. Days passed this way at the *Cămin*, a week of work and study and an evening of good times.[65]

A medical student who already had his law degree, Ion Banea was well respected by the legionaries, but his were not the only "judicious words" that filled the hall at the cămin. Most legionary leaders lectured here at one time or another.[66] Lectures were a normal part of weekly meetings in nests, but they were also often used an excuse for large numbers of legionaries to gather together for a celebration or a routine inspection by their leaders.[67] Several hundred legionaries managed to fit in the room for these lectures, which sometimes ended with marches through the streets, taking oaths, or singing legionary songs.[68] In addition to speeches and dancing, they also held *parastase* (religious commemorations) here for legionaries who had been shot by the police, inviting curious students to come and honor martyrs of the student movement.[69]

---

63. ACNSAS, Fond Penal, dosar 011784, vol. 13, f. 124.
64. The *horă* and the *sârbă* are both well-known Romanian folk dances.
65. Vera Totu, "Jilava," *13 Jilava*, 7/1 (29 Nov 1940): 5.
66. ACNSAS, Fond Informativ, dosar 211932, vol. 1, f. 791–792.
67. Corneliu Zelea Codreanu, *Cărticia şefului de cuib* (Bucharest: Editura Bucovina, 1940), 15–18.
68. ACNSAS, Fond Penal, dosar 013206, vol. 2, f. 461; "O visită în Iaşiul naționalist," *Calendarul*, 2/489 (25 Oct 1933): 5.
69. AN—Iaşi, Fond Universitatea A. I. Cuza, Rectorat, Reel #266, dosar 1480/1934, f. 358–359.

Students

The process of recruiting students to Codreanu's cause was a slow one. In Bucharest it was a law student named Andrei Ionescu (1904–?) who did the most to sway ultranationalist students toward Codreanu's movement.[70] He had been involved in LANC organizing in Bucharest and Bârlad since 1925 and he established the first legionary nest in the capital in October 1927. In 1929 Ionescu founded the Stephen the Great Christian Students Association along the lines of the ASC in Iaşi. In November that year he was elected president of CSB, which gave him titular control over the most powerful ultranationalist student organization in Bucharest. Ionescu made a passionate plea for the Legion at the UNSCR congress in December 1929, influencing more students toward Codreanu's camp.[71] In Bucharest, CSB oscillated between the legionary and Cuzist factions for the next two years, until legionaries eventually had enough power to dismiss the Cuzist president in 1931 and replace him with the legionary Traian Cotigă (1910–1939).[72]

Once legionaries had enough support in Bucharest they began dominating student canteens and dormitories through intimidation and violence. An investigation of one dormitory in 1932 found that gangs of theology students were involved in "militant politics" and fought with students from other faculties in the dormitories. Many of those living there were overdue in passing their exams (*repetenţi*) or else had graduated. Legionaries held regular meetings in the building, and the student committee governing the dormitory had entirely lost control of the situation.[73] There is some evidence to suggest that ultranationalist dominance of student dormitories had been going on in other places for some time, although earlier victims did not explicitly identify the troublemakers as ultranationalists in their complaints. One student who worked at the canteen on Gutenberg Street in 1931—when Cuzists still met regularly there—said that "hooligans" had taken over the committee that ran the canteen and were feeding their friends for free, stealing from canteen funds, and distributing reduced-fare student train passes to nonstudents. When he objected they shouted him down at meetings and eventually replaced him with one of their own.[74] Another student

---

70. In memoir accounts and oral history interviews, several activists mention Andrei Ionescu's organizing and speeches as the reason why they joined the Legion. Horia Sima, "Cum am intrat în Legiune," in *Mărturii despre legiune: Patruzeci de ani dela întemeierea mişcării legionare (1927–1967)*, ed. Faust Brădescu (Rio de Janeiro: Dacia, 1967), 165–181; Lauric Filon, in *Ţara, Legiunea, Căpitanul: Mişcarea Legionară în documente de istorie orală*, eds. Mariana Conovici, Silvia Iliescu, and Octavian Silvestru (Bucharest: Humanitas, 2008), 37–38.

71. ACNSAS, Fond Penal, dosar 014005, vol. 11, f. 32–36, 39–45.

72. USHMM, SRI Files, Reel #106, dosar 1154, f. 22.

73. AN—Bucharest, Fond Universitatea din Bucureşti, Rectorat, dosar 11/1932, f. 32–33, 40.

74. Ibid., dosar 8/1931, f. 8–12; USHMM, Fond MI-D, Reel #136, dosar 6/1927, f. 95.

complained of being assaulted by the porter and a student when he tried to enter a different dormitory in July that year, but the president of the dormitory supported the porter's actions as if they were standard policy.[75]

Legionaries in Iaşi faced more sustained opposition from the Cuzist Teodor Mociulschi, who remained president of ASC until late 1933. The ASC headquarters at the Hotel Bejan was only 220 yards away from the legionary cămin, and violence escalated once LANC youth organized "Assault Battalions" in March 1933.[76] When elections for officeholders took place later that month the Cuzists changed the date at the last minute in order to prevent legionaries from voting. Legionaries challenged the Cuzists over this issue on March 26. When they agreed to meet a week later to hold new elections, Mociulski advised his followers to come armed with knives and pieces of wood.[77] Following a Cuzist meeting on the evening of March 28, one Cuzist student shouted, "Long live our Assault Battalions," while passing the legionary cămin on the way to the ASC headquarters. A legionary by the name of N. Arnăutu heard him and called back, "Where are your Assault Battalions?" Arnăutu whistled, and fifteen legionary students immediately appeared, armed and ready to fight. Only the presence of police officers prevented bloodshed.[78] The conflict continued into April, when eight legionaries and seven Cuzists were arrested after the groups clashed once again.[79] If the legionaries were to win over a student movement characterized by displays of violence, they had to do so violently.

That fall, both legionaries and Cuzists began terrorizing theaters and cinemas, demanding free entry to shows.[80] Legionaries stole an ASC flag when the building where it was hanging was evacuated by the police later that year, but then it went missing from a legionary's room where it was being held. Accusations of treachery immediately flew back and forth among legionaries, and Ion Banea promised to shoot anyone who had allowed their rivals' flag to be stolen.[81] The Cuzists responded by stealing a legionary flag from the cămin, and an open battle ensued. Both sides were armed with clubs and knives, and three of the combatants ended up in hospital with serious injuries.[82] Banea replaced Mociulski as ASC president later in 1933 and promptly announced, "The student movement has begun anew. It is led by the legionaries."[83]

---

75. AN—Bucharest, Fond Universitatea din Bucureşti, Rectorat, dosar 11/1931, f. 4.
76. USHMM, Fond MI-D, Reel #1, dosar 25.023M, f. 30.
77. AN—Iaşi, Fond Chestura de poliţie, dosar 52/1933, f. 106.
78. ACNSAS, Fond Documentar, dosar 012694, vol. 4, f. 310–312.
79. USHMM, Fond SRI Files, Reel #97, dosar 566, f. 332–334.
80. AN—Iaşi, Fond Universitatea A. I. Cuza, Rectorat, Reel #335, dosar 1722/1937, f. 48, 50.
81. AN—Iaşi, Fond Chestura de poliţie, dosar 52/1933, f. 123.
82. "Gravă încărcare între cuzişti şi codrenişti la Iaşi," *Dimineaţa* (25 Apr 1933).
83. AN—Iaşi, Fond Universitatea A. I. Cuza, Rectorat, Reel #335, dosar 1722/1937, f. 49; "Congresul studenţilor moldoveni," *Calendarul*, 473 (16 Sept 1933): 3.

Other student groups followed. In an oral history interview from 1999, Mircea Dimitriu (1913–2005) recalled that the earliest legionary nests in Timişoara were formed of students who had been affiliated with LANC.[84] By the end of 1933 both the Technical School at Timişoara and the Petru Maior Society in Cluj were firmly in legionary hands.[85] Isolated legionary cells appeared throughout the country during this period, among them the Blood Brotherhood formed at the Prince Nicolae High School in Sighişoară. Led by Stelian Stăncinel, some of the students established this Blood Brotherhood after a university student named Emil Stoenescu visited them from Iaşi in 1929. Stoenescu told them about Codreanu and the Legion, and after he left, the boys took the initiative and formed their own group. They were not in regular contact with Iaşi, but they still held weekly meetings while walking through the fields dressed as Boy Scouts, collected dues, sang "student songs," and avidly read antisemitic and anti-Masonic publications.[86] The nest formed in Sibiu by Nicu Iancu also initially ran without any connections with Iaşi. Iancu formed the group when he returned home after the first year of his law studies in Bucharest in 1931. He gathered together some colleagues from his old high school and a couple of lawyers who had been part of the student protests of 1922, all of whom had heard of the Legion and were eager to participate.[87] Even without immediate personal ties to the Legion, such small, isolated groups were able to sustain themselves by drawing on the literature and publicity produced by legionaries in Iaşi and Bucharest.

Peasants

In November 1928 twelve legionaries set out for villages in Moldova, Bucovina, and the Banat. As befitted an organization with no money, they went in pairs and on foot. Codreanu assigned each pair a region of between thirty and one hundred miles and asked them to report on their progress once every two weeks.[88] From this point onward, the Legion's presence in rural areas grew, and legionaries introduced a number of folk elements into their propaganda, including dressing up as *haiduci* (outlaws) and dancing with peasants. Siguranța agents wrote in February 1931 that although the Legion's rise was slow, the group was making

84. Mircea Dimitriu, "Istorie comentată a mişcării legionare, 1927–1999," in *Corneliu Zelea Codreanu*, ed. Stănescu, 69.

85. ANIC, Fond DGP, dosar 252/1939, f. 242; ACNSAS, Fond Documentar, dosar 012694, vol. 7, f. 1.

86. Stelian Stănicel, *Lângă Căpitan* (Buenos Aires: Pământul Stramoşec, 1978), 6–7.

87. Nicu Iancu, *Sub steagul lui Codreanu: Momente din trecutul legionar* (Madrid: Dacia, 1973), 11–13.

88. "O nouă campanie," *Pământul stramoşesc*, 2/21 (1 Nov 1928): 6.

steady gains in the countryside because "its leaders are teachers and priests scattered throughout the villages," where rural intellectuals enjoyed a disproportionate political influence.[89] But links between villages and towns were just as important as what was happening inside the villages themselves. The first legionary nests in Dolj County were established by three young peasants in the village of Mârşani on 23 April 1931. Three months later, each of them led a nest of his own and another nest had been established in the neighboring village of Damian. Students from the area who were studying in Bucharest learned of these nests that winter. They immediately organized propaganda pamphlets and a Blood Brotherhood in the county capital of Craiova, adding an urban dimension to the peasants' organizing and their eventual provocation of police retaliation.[90]

Propaganda tours among peasants began in earnest in December 1929, when Codreanu rode through villages in Bessarabia together with a crowd that eventually reached thirty to forty horse riders, all wearing turkey feathers in their hats. Gendarmes initially prevented them from holding a public meeting at the market in Bereşti but ignored them after the legionaries set out toward more isolated villages. Groups of legionaries ran ahead of the riders to announce their arrival, and villagers apparently received them with lighted candles and singing, after which Codreanu and others made speeches in the village church or the square.[91] The feathers were an ad hoc attempt by the legionaries to dress themselves as *haiduci*, which became a key image for legionaries during these years. *Haiduci* were outlaws who fought against local oppressors and were a popular theme of Romanian ballads during the nineteenth century.[92] Legionary songs of the early 1930s placed the Legion firmly in the *haiduc* tradition. Viorica Lăzărescu, a student from Iaşi, sang, "My ancestors were *haiduci* with muskets on their backs / Which gave justice to the poor."[93] Another student from Iaşi, Simion Lefter, promised in his music that "the time of the *haiduci* is coming," and called upon his listeners to "Leave the plow in the furrows / Abandon the scythe / The way of the forest and the gun / To embrace."[94]

Codreanu and small groups of legionaries continued mounted tours of remote areas during the winter of 1929–1930, traveling to villages in Transylvania and Bessarabia where they held impromptu meetings at marketplaces and were

89. USHMM, Fond MI-D, Reel #138, dosar 2/1930, f. 115.

90. "Istoricul redeşptării naţionale în Oltenia," *Garda Jiului*, 1/1 (4 Dec 1932): 1–2.

91. Codreanu, *Pentru legionari*, 340–353.

92. Gheorghe Vrabie, *Balada populară româna* (Bucharest: Editura Academiei Republicii Socialiste România, 1966), 362ff.

93. Viorica Lăzărescu, "Străbunii mei," April 1932, in USHMM, Fond SRI Files, Reel #102, dosar 700, f. 52.

94. Simon Lefter, "Hora legionarilor," in "Cântecele Gărzii de Fer," April 1932, USHMM, Fond SRI Files, Reel #102, dosar: 700, f. 49.

intermittently prevented from carrying out propaganda by local gendarmes. These self-styled "crusaders" called on the assembled peasants to "unite" and to "create a new destiny for our people."[95] They also helped with petty tasks to demonstrate their solidarity with the peasantry. According to Dumitru Banea, legionaries "went into the fields and, seeing someone filling a cart with hay, one of them took his place while the others spoke to him about our doctrine and our struggle."[96] Constantin Argetoianu (1871–1952), a prominent politician and outspoken critic of the Legion, saw such practices as cynical attempts to deceive peasants into thinking that Codreanu was a messianic figure or a saint:

> It was thus said that groups of students spread into villages, silently helped the peasants in their work, repaired roads and bridges, spaded channels for still waters and sprang wells in dry areas, then left announcing that in the following days "the One who had to come would come to the village." Indeed, "the Captain" came: riding a white horse, accompanied by several lads, he used to stop in the center of the village, get off the horse, kiss the earth, and then go away without a word. People watched with their eyes wide open, shook their heads and whispered: "Was this the Saint?" Some legionary agents then spread into the "visited" villages and, hiding their real identity under all kinds of pretexts, completed the action of conquering the souls.[97]

But the Legion's approach to propaganda was also a practical one that exploited older ultranationalist networks such as the Archers in Bucovina. In 1930 several Archers groups reorganized themselves along the lines of the Iron Guard's paramilitary structure. Over the next two years, Codreanu followed a deliberate policy of focusing on only six counties in order to make the most of the Legion's limited resources.[98] Teams of legionaries contested two by-elections in this manner, one in Neamţ County on 31 August 1931, when Codreanu won a seat in Parliament, and the other in Tutova County on 17 April 1932. The seat in Tutova went to Ion Zelea Codreanu.[99] Neamţ County consistently voted for

95. Secret Service Report on Codreanu's activities, June 1927–Jan 1930, reprinted in *Ideologie*, ed. Scurtu, vol. 2, 204–219.

96. Banea, *Acuzat*, 13.

97. Constantin Argetoianu, quoted in Constantin Iordachi, *Charisma, Politics, and Violence: The Legion of the "Archangel Michael" in Inter-war Romania* (Trondheim: Trondheim Studies on East European Cultures and Societies, 2004), 56. In an interrogation from 1938, Gheorghe Istrate confessed that "on the night of June 7, 1931, they were sent by the Legion through villages to announce to the peasants that the King, the Emperor had arrived." ACNSAS, Fond Penal, dosar 011784, vol. 5, f. 22.

98. USHMM, Fond MI-D, Reel #138, dosar 2/1930, f. 3–4.

99. Heinen, *Legiunea "Arhanghelul Mihail,"* 188–197.

whichever party stood the best chance of forming a government, but the ruling National Liberal Party did not contest the seat in 1931.[100] The lack of a government candidate in Neamţ County meant that the roughly one hundred legionary propagandists were relatively unmolested by the authorities. In 1932 they faced concerted opposition from the gendarmerie in Tutova County; legionaries were shot at by gendarmes and were trapped in abandoned buildings for up to forty-eight hours with no food or water. When one group of propagandists arrived at the village of Băcani, where other legionaries were losing a pitched battle with gendarmes for control of the gendarmerie post, Nicolae Totu ordered his followers to sound the bells of the church, calling out the villagers to support them as if during a popular uprising.[101]

Evoking the *haiduc* tradition in song and ringing church bells glamorized the Legion's political program and its violence. National-Peasantist politicians drove into rural areas in cars when they carried out electoral propaganda, and wore suits while speaking to prearranged crowds.[102] Coming on foot or on horseback and helping with the harvest implied that legionaries came from social backgrounds similar to those of the peasants and were thus able to better represent them than were urban politicians. Groups of legionaries ate and slept in the homes of local sympathizers at the beginning of their propaganda trips and when they were in new areas they begged hospitality and accepted it from anyone who was willing to give it to them. According to legionary memoirs, the peasants went out of their way to tend to wounded legionaries and were extremely generous with their food and their homes.[103] Enthusiastic peasants occasionally joined the propagandists, either recruiting other villagers or joining a team as it traveled around the countryside. In Vasile Coman's account of the electoral campaign in Neamţ County, one elderly woman told them that "from this day forward I will shout aloud all that I have learned from these gentlemen students. I will tell the women when we go to church, when I meet them at the well and wherever my path takes me."[104]

Expressions of sympathy did not necessarily mean that peasants were exclusively committed to the legionary movement. When questioned about their political affiliations in 1929, three police officers who joined the Legion in the Transylvanian village of Găneşti told their superiors that "before they became policemen,

100. Stelu Şerban, *Elite, partide şi spectru politic în România interbelică* (Bucharest: Paideia, 2006), 80–82.

101. Banea, *Acuzat*, 16–24; Codreanu, *Pentru legionari*, 378–380, 400–402; Tudor Bradu, "Printre legionarii muşchetari," in *Corneliu Zelea Codreanu*, ed. Stănescu, 26–30.

102. Vasile Coman, *Amintiri legionare*, vol. 1, AN—Cluj, Fond Personal Vasile Coman, dosar 1/1980, f. 40–48.

103. Ibid., dosar 1/1980, f. 40–48; Banea, *Acuzat*, 16–24.

104. Ibid., dosar 1/1980, f. 37.

back when they were civilians in the village, they were enrolled in the Legion of the Archangel Michael just as other villagers were—with or without their permission. They enthusiastically took part in the meetings of this League [*sic*] that were held in the village, but they also took part in the meetings of other parties when they were announced, especially on holidays, because like all villagers they were curious to see something new."[105] These men would have lost their jobs for being legionaries, so it is unlikely that they told the whole truth. Nonetheless, the picture they paint of peasants as swing voters intrigued by new political trends was confirmed by a sociological study of the village of Ghigoeşti in Neamţ County during the 1930s. This study found that just under half of the village's 250 inhabitants actively supported a political party and were divided among all the major political parties. These peasants were apparently interested only in personal gains that they hoped would materialize when their chosen party came to power. According to the researchers, ideology was completely irrelevant to voters in Ghigoeşti. Discussing the other half of the village, the sociologists commented that "more than 50 percent view such displays with apathy, and even irony. These people generally vote with the government, or under the sway of the moment, in which case they try new groups—not because they are swayed by the party's ideology but out of the desire to see something new, to see what others who have never been in power will do."[106]

As the Legion became more established, nests spread from village to village. An investigation carried out by the Securitate in Mehedinţi County in 1954 makes it possible to reconstruct how the Legion first spread through this region, showing how larger towns acted as organizational hubs for peasant legionaries. Securitate agents interviewed a number of peasant leaders in the south of the county, collecting enough information to reconcile various discrepancies between the accounts. Legionary organizing in villages around Cujmiru began in 1932, when Florea Odor (1893–?) met Sergiu Storjescu, a pharmacist from the town of Vânju Mare. Odor had been introduced to Storjescu by Alexandru Popescu, who was working as an administrator for an estate near the village of Gârla Mare.[107] Odor lived in Salcia, a small village near Vraţa, not far from the Danube River. He had finished five classes of primary school and inherited 3.5 hectares of land from his parents. Odor had fought in World War I, but when he met Torjescu and Popescu in 1932 he was engaged only in agricultural work.[108] Odor established the first legionary nest in Salcia, a group he named after Tudor Vladimirescu, a Romanian

105. USHMM, Fond MI-D, Reel #140, dosar 9/1930, f. 210, 215–217.

106. Gheorghe Mareş and Dumitru Mareş, *Monografia satului Ghigoeşti* (1938), quoted in Radu, *Electoratul din România*, 111.

107. ACNSAS, Fond Penal, dosar 014037, vol. 1, f. 23.

108. ACNSAS, Fond Informativ, dosar 257541, vol. 1, f. 28–29.

hero who had led an uprising against the Phanariots in 1821. One of his first recruits was Constantin I. Sfâru (1907–?), another farmer who had finished only four years of his education but who had slightly more land—4.85 hectares.[109] In 1935 Sfâru formed his own nest, named Constantin Brâncoveanu, after the Wallachian ruler who had died at the hands of the Turks. There were three nests in Salcia by the mid-1930s, but Sfâru had to dissolve his after only a couple of years, since he could not find enough people to join it. Ion Tâmbăluța (1912–?) also joined in 1932, and he became one of the region's most active legionaries after returning from military service in 1937.[110]

Legionaries in Salcia kept in touch with developments elsewhere through a theology student in Bucharest named Eugen Vladulescu. He brought news and instructions back to the nest leaders in Salcia, who then passed them on to the other members.[111] Florin Odor says that he also received instructions both from Sergiu Storjescu in Vânju Mare and from legionaries in the county capital of Turnu Severin.[112] In 1936 Odor and Storjescu began doing propaganda in Vrața, a slightly larger village than Salcia, where they managed to establish three nests.[113] Vrața also had connections with legionaries outside the village, in particular through Marin Iscru (1908–?), a carpenter who had temporarily moved to Brașov in Transylvania in 1935 looking for work. He discovered the Legion there and became a leader in Vrața when he returned in 1936.[114] Finally, another source from September 1937 mentions a sailor named Dumitru Săbău from the village of Gârla, 3.7 miles east of Vrața. Săbău lived at this time in Vienna, where he worked fueling Romanian vessels that passed through. It is not clear if he still had connections with his natal village, but he had established a legionary nucleus in Vienna that did propaganda among Romanian sailors whose vessels docked there.[115]

This account suggests that the first legionary nests in Salcia and Vrața were established by peasants of average means. They had enough education to cover basic literacy skills and owned enough arable land to support their families. The Legion's leaders in these villages had traveled for work or during military service, and both Ion Tâmbăluța and Marin Iscru became committed legionaries immediately after returning to their respective villages. In both Salcia and Vrața it was a pharmacist from a town twenty-three miles away who first convinced

109. Ibid., dosar 257541, vol. 2, f. 45–46.
110. Ibid., dosar 257541, vol. 2, f. 29–30, vol. 4, f. 11.
111. Ibid., dosar 257541, I.257541, vol. 2, f. 45.
112. ACNSAS, Fond Penal, dosar 014037, vol. 1, f. 23.
113. Ibid., dosar 014037, vol. 1, f. 25.
114. ACNSAS, Fond Informativ, dosar 257541, vol. 1, f. 23–25.
115. AN—Cluj, Fond Inspectoratul de Poliție, dosar 381/1937, f. 115.

the peasants to organize as legionaries, which is surprising given that the mayor of Drincea, a village near Punghina, only sixteen miles north of Salcia, was a legionary who ran three nests in his own village.[116] Establishing the Legion in this area was a slow process. Large nests did not form as soon as legionary propagandists appeared in a village but grew steadily thanks to the work of local peasants over several years. Connections with urban centers through students studying in Bucharest or carpenters traveling to Braşov were crucial for sustaining the movement and for inspiring young activists, but the nests themselves were run by local peasants. Moreover, Sfâru may have been able to establish a third nest in Salcia in 1937, but there were not enough people interested in legionary politics to be able to sustain three nests in such a small place. Whereas legionaries in cities had a seemingly inexhaustible pool of potential recruits, legionaries in rural areas had to move on to neighboring villages once they had approached all sympathetic inhabitants of their own village. Personal ties mattered a great deal in rural contexts, a factor intensified by the frequently illegal nature of legionary activity.[117]

As they became more involved in legionary activism, some people left their villages entirely and became itinerant propagandists. Vasile Coman (1912–?), for example, was born in Luduş, a village of 33,700 people in Transylvania's Turda County, where Romanians outnumbered Hungarians roughly nine to four.[118] He grew up reading Father Ion Moţa's *Libertatea*, and when Nicolae Totu murdered a Jewish high school student in Cernăuţi in 1926 his village took up a collection and sent it to Totu via Moţa's newspaper. A number of people from Luduş took out subscriptions to the Legion's first newspaper, *Pământul strămoşesc*, in 1927. Codreanu visited Luduş in 1928 to act as godfather at the baptism of Amos Horaţiu Pop's grandson, Codrenel. Pop was Coman's uncle, and as a publican he was well connected in the town. When Codreanu visited again during a propaganda tour a year later, Pop and other ultranationalists in Luduş hosted the legionaries and organized turkey feathers for them to wear. As a nineteen-year-old boy, Coman was eager to participate in the electoral campaign in Neamţ County in 1931, but his parents and his uncle considered him too young. Undeterred, Coman managed to get money for his travel expenses from a local schoolteacher and joined roughly one hundred other young people, who walked from village to village campaigning for Codreanu. Coman discovered a passion for public speaking and he sparred verbally with propagandists from other parties

116. ACNSAS, Fond Informativ, dosar 257541, vol. 1, f. 18–20.

117. Cf. Reichardt, *Faschistische Kampfbünde*, 406.

118. This account of Vasile Coman's life is based entirely on the first three volumes of his unpublished memoirs. These are found in AN—Cluj, Fond Personal Vasile Coman, dosar 1–3/1980, *Amintiri legionare*, vols. 1–3. On the population of Luduş in 1930, see Manuila, *Recensământul general din decemvrie 1930*, vol. 2, 484.

while haranguing onlookers to support him. He left home again three months after the Neamţ by-elections to help organize the Legion in neighboring Mureş County. Coman did two propaganda marches through Mureş County during 1931 and 1932, arguing with the Greek Catholic priests there and trying to convince local Hungarians that they were actually "Magyarized" Romanians.

When the Tutova by-elections took place in April 1932, Coman once again volunteered as a propagandist. Together with other legionaries, he marched long distances on foot, fought with gendarmes, and was eventually arrested. Coman campaigned in his home county of Turda during the general elections of July 1932, and in 1933 he was arrested after fighting with gendarmes during a propaganda campaign in Alba County. Despite being injured in these clashes, Coman traveled to Bucharest in August 1933 to help build Casa Legionarilor Răniţi (the House for Wounded Legionaries)—later Casa Verde (the Green House). Here he met legionaries from all over the country and participated in an official visit from the Italian diplomat Eugenio Coselschi. Coman was arrested together with nine other legionaries from Turda County when the government dissolved the Iron Guard on 10 December 1933, and then again following the assassination of the prime minister, Ion G. Duca, on 29 December 1933. The following year, Codreanu awarded him three White Crosses.

Coman remained in Jilava prison until April 1934, when he was conscripted and sent to Galaţi to do compulsory military service. Coman says that he was persecuted by his commanding officers because of his reputation as a legionary, but he did not react because he did not want to damage the "prestige" of the Legion. He kept in touch with changes in the movement by visiting legionaries whenever he had leave, and he met other legionaries who were also doing military service. He left the army in October 1936 and immediately went to agitate in Târgu Mureş, seven months after the student congress there during which legionaries had made death threats against leading public figures. Coman's activism in Mureş County left him no time to earn money, so he lived and ate at the houses of other legionaries.

Workers and Tradesmen

The Great Depression hurt both peasants and workers, but legionaries used economic despair as a way to appeal specifically to factory workers and tradesmen, just as they had used folk costumes and songs to attract peasants. In some places factory workers provided the key to legionary mobilization in areas that activists had previously been unable to penetrate. The legionary presence in Buhuşi increased rapidly in 1929, for example, when workers at the city's large textile factory joined the Legion en masse.[119] Similarly, the city of Piatra Neamţ was first organized in 1931 by a student, two carpenters, a factory worker, and a shoesmith, all of whom conducted propaganda both in the city and the surrounding villages.[120] Romania remained primarily agricultural until the 1950s, but industrialization increased significantly in Romania after 1887. Industrial expansion meant an increase in the size of factories more than in their number. Between 1900 and 1930 the number of industrial firms actually decreased, whereas the number of workers employed in industry more than doubled.[121] These changes transformed the lives of tens of thousands of people, but during the interwar period few had begun to think of themselves as "workers" in the Marxist sense. Living and working simultaneously in urban and rural settings caused interwar Romanians to group peasants together with industrial workers as part of the working poor. All categories of *muncitori* (workers) felt exploited by the wealthy financiers and landowners and often made little distinction between the different types of labor. Socialists tried to convince workers that they were being exploited by capitalists as a class, but ultranationalists lumped factory workers, tradesmen, artisans, and peasants together as exploited laborers and appealed to them as members of the Romanian nation. In the words of a legionary newspaper,

> Everyone who lives by the work of their hands is part of Corpul Muncitoresc Legionar [the Legionary Workers Corps, CML]: Factory workers, craftsmen, shop assistants, grocers, chauffeurs, servants, skilled and unskilled workers, waiters, taxi drivers, miners, and others. Small business owners with one or two employees who suffer the same hardships as workers are also part of CML.[122]

As happened elsewhere in Europe, the hardships of the Depression mobilized people behind political causes as never before. Harvests failed in the two years before the Depression hit, raising the price of agricultural goods to unaffordable levels for most workers.[123] The government mobilized the army against protesting peasants.[124] A number of Romanian banks failed in the wake of the 1929

---

119. ACNSAS, Fond Documentar, dosar 008912, vol. 23, f. 189.

120. Ibid., dosar 008912, vol. 23, f. 169–170.

121. Virgil N. Madgearu, *Evoluţia economiei româneşti după războiul mondial* (Bucharest: Editura Ştiinţifică, 1995), 105–106.

122. *Muncitorul legionar* (30 Jan 1937), quoted in Oliver Jens Schmitt, "'Zum Kampf, Arbeiter': Arbeiterfrage und Arbeiterschaft in der Legionärsbewegung (1919–1938)," in *Inszenierte Gegenmacht von rechts: Die "Legion Erzengel Michael" in Rumänien 1918–1938*, ed. Armin Heinen and Oliver Jens Schmitt (Munich: Oldenberg Verlag, 2013), 282.

123. Pearton, *Oil and the Romanian State*, 131.

124. Institutul de Studii Istorice şi Social-Politice de pe lănga C.C. al P.C.R., *1933: Luptele revoluţionare ale muncitorilor ceferişti şi petrolişti* (Bucharest: Editura Politica, 1971), 39.

stock market crash, and the oil industry suffered because international demand dropped significantly.[125] Peasants with small lots found themselves in a particularly precarious situation as the value of agricultural exports plummeted and the interest rates they had to pay on bank loans soared.[126] Unemployment skyrocketed. As the economic situation in Bukovina worsened, legionaries there began provoking peasants to attack Jewish houses. They threw rocks and sticks of dynamite through windows, and priests sympathetic to the Legion incited peasants to carry out pogroms against local Jews.[127] Street demonstrations increased in the major cities, involving not just factory workers but also students, teachers, pensioners, civil servants, and a range of individuals from other occupations.[128]

The ultranationalist press initially blamed foreign banks for the financial crisis, complaining that they were taking Romanian money down with them. Right-wing journalists were outraged when the Romanian government gave bailouts to banks and industrialists, and they called for prison terms for bank managers.[129] In their view, the economic crisis had clearly been caused by the "parasites" and yet it was hurting the "producers." They called on people to "buy Romanian" and demanded that business owners employ Romanian labor.[130] LANC was the first to call for the creation of a "new working class," in an article defending the rights of bus drivers in May 1931.[131] Ultranationalist students spoke about uniting with workers in early 1932, and the fascist mobilization of workers was under way in earnest by the beginning of 1933.[132] One article in *Pământul strămoşesc* from November 1932 mentions that thanks to particularly intense propaganda by a handful of workers in Bucharest's Blue III district, the Legion had "strong nests in the Lemaitre, Wolf, Bünger, and Griviţa factories, the National Culture factory, the match factory, and others."[133]

During 1933 gangs of twenty to thirty uniformed legionaries visited restaurants and coffee shops demanding that the owners employ people the gangs

---

125. Constantin C. Giurescu, *History of Bucharest* (Bucharest: Publishing House for Sports and Tourism, 1976), 86; Pearton, *Oil and the Romanian State*, 158.

126. Francisco Veiga, *Istoria Gărzii de Fier 1919–1941: Mistica ultranaţionalismului*, trans. Marian Ştefănescu (Bucharest: Humanitas, 1993), 138–145.

127. USHMM, Fond MI-D, Reel #138, dosar 4/1930, f. 14–16, 28–29, 132–134; "Cazul Borşa," *Biruinţa*, 1/1 (17 Oct 1930): 2.

128. Institutul de Studii Istorice, *1933*, 51.

129. N. Mucichescu-Tunari, "Falimentul Bancii Blank," *Cuvântul studenţesc*, 6/3 (20 Nov 1931): 3; Dragoş Protopopescu, "Malaxismul," *Calendarul*, 487 (2 Oct 1933): 1.

130. "Nici un ac de la jidani," *Cuvântul studenţesc*, 7/2 (1 Feb 1932): 5; "Pâine, pentru muncitorul român," *Cuvântul studenţesc*, 8/4 (16–30 Apr 1933): 5.

131. "Muncitorimea nouă," *Apărarea naţională*, 9/18 (17 May 1931): 3.

132. Şt. Iacobescu, "Studenţi, apropriaţi-vă la muncitori," *Cuvântul studenţesc*, 7/3 (15 Feb 1932): 1.

133. "Sectorul III Albastru, Seful Corpului Legionar: Dorul Belimace," *Pământul strămoşesc*, 4/1 (1 Nov 1932): 5.

recommended. They then organized boycotts of businesses that employed minority workers.[134] Recognizing the danger that organized ultranationalism posed, one Jewish-owned factory in Brăila instituted a policy of firing anyone who joined a right-wing movement.[135] In March 1933 LANC members formed their own union for fascist waiters.[136] Legionaries began to form workers' unions in April as part of a new plan to recruit workers.[137] According to an oral history interview with the legionary Dumitru Groza conducted in 1994, Groza lost his job at a factory in Cugir in 1932 and traveled to Bucharest, where he heard Aurel Serafim speak. Serafim was a chemical engineer who had joined the Legion in 1932 and within two years was put in charge of organizing the movement in Bucharest and Ilfov County.[138] Groza liked Serafim's message and enjoyed the legionaries' singing, so he too joined the Legion. He says that Serafim helped him find work by directing him to the legionary brickworks and building site, where legionaries were erecting a new headquarters.[139]

During the 1920s A. C. Cuza had called for "the harmonizing of the interests of capitalists and workers," with the final goal of overcoming the exploitation of *all* Romanians.[140] Early LANC propaganda distinguished between two types of industrialists: good ones, like Henry Ford, who made money through innovation and creativity, and Jewish ones, who did no work and lived only to make more money and did so primarily through speculation. According to Cuza, the entire capitalist system of exploitation, with its periodic crises and shortages, was a product of Jewish greed. One finds in Cuzist economic theory a hearty admiration for production and a sympathy for producers, whether they be industrialists, factory workers, or peasants. Rather than arguing that exploitation was intrinsic to the organization of production itself, ultranationalists accounted for economic inequalities by portraying unpopular industrialists as Jewish parasites living off Romanian workers.[141]

Fascist activists could convincingly frame labor conflicts in ethnic terms because the vast majority of factories operated under foreign ownership and

---

134. USHMM, Fond SRI Files, Reel #97, dosar 566, f. 22, 56.

135. "Muncitoreşti," *Axa*, 1/5 (Jan 1933): 3.

136. USHMM, Fond MI-D, Reel #1, dosar 25.023M, unnumbered.

137. R. Pavel, "Spre o nouă orientare a muncitorimei," *Axa*, 1/11 (30 Apr 1933): 1–2; USHMM, Fond SRI Files, Reel #97, dosar 566, f. 393.

138. USHMM, Fond SRI Files, Reel #68, dosar 23333, f. 7.

139. Dumitru Groza, in *Ţara, Legiunea, Căpitanul*, ed. Conovici, Iliescu, and Silvestru, 38–39.

140. A. C. Cuza, *Programul LANC*, quoted and trans. in Ioanid, *The Sword of the Archangel*, 169.

141. A. C. Cuza, "Henry Ford," *Apărarea naţională*, 1/7 (1 July 1922): 2–4; "Metodele jidoveşti," *Apărarea naţională*, 1/9 (1 Aug 1922): 9–12; "Jidanii capitaliştii," *Apărarea naţională*, 1/14 (15 Oct 1922): 17–18.

FIGURE 3.1 Legionary election poster, 26 September 1937. The text reads, "In the new country . . . the legionary movement will give workers more than a program, more than whiter bread, more than a better bed. It will give workers the right to feel that they are masters in their land, together with all Romanians. The worker will tread like a lord, not a slave, on streets full of light and luxuries, where today he does not even dare to lift his eyes. For the first time he will feel the pride and joy of being in control, of being the master of his country. Compared to this, all other things are insignificant. For the worker-lord will have laws, organization in the state, and the fate which he builds with his own masterful hands, head and conscience! SS. Corneliu Z. Codreanu." ACNSAS, Fond Penal, dosar 11784, vol. 10, f. 191.

management in the early 1920s.[142] The textile industry, for example, was run and managed entirely by English people.[143] Romanian industry was badly underdeveloped prior to 1920 and relied heavily on foreign imports for manufactured products even when Romanian factories were working at full capacity.[144] Successive Romanian governments reacted to this situation by attempting to nationalize

142. Madgearu, *Evoluția economiei românești*, 96.

143. Ralph M. Odell, *Cotton Goods in the Balkan States* (Washington, DC: Department of Commerce and Labor, 1912), 12–13.

144. Ibid., 5–6; Ștefan Zeletin, *Burghezia română: Origina și rolul ei istoric* (Bucharest: Cultură Națională, 1925), 130.

foreign-owned industry.[145] The mining law of 1924 stipulated that 75 percent of all categories of employees should be Romanian nationals.[146] This was sometimes a difficult quota to fill because foreign specialists were often the only people with the skills necessary to run certain plants. As factories failed to comply with these quotas, ultranationalist journalists complained constantly about the inability of successive governments to enforce this law.[147]

Legionary propaganda combined Cuza's insistence that economic injustice was an ethnic problem with antipoliticianism and the celebration of labor. One legionary poster from January 1933 addressed "the thousands, the tens of thousands of unemployed who have neither work nor bread and who, sadly, are all Romanian. Our brothers in blood and law: foreigners are privileged in our country. State-run institutions groan, they are crammed with foreign tradesmen and workers. Not to mention private enterprise, which is entirely in foreign hands."[148] Legionaries dismissed socialist and communist organizers as self-interested and impotent and declared that only a fascist approach that united workers and industrialists could guarantee rights for workers.[149] As one legionary book addressed specifically to workers made clear, "When legionaries fight against communism, they are not also fighting against the workers. . . . Communism is not a workers' movement, but a Jewish doctrine that exists only to serve a people without a fatherland."[150] Codreanu argued that work had value in itself, and he claimed that the brickworks at Ungheni had "generated a revolution in the thinking of the day" because it was the end of the idea that "it is shameful for an intellectual to work with his hands, particularly heavy labor, which in the past had been reserved for slaves or the lower classes."[151] Workers joined the Legion in especially large numbers after 1935, and by 1936 sailors joined the movement as well.[152] Internal legionary documents from 1937 report that in June there were 150 nests entirely made up of workers in Bucharest alone. In comparison, Bucharest's Răzleți corps had 112 legionary nests that August, made up of mostly intellectuals and middle-class professionals.[153]

---

145. Pearton, *Oil and the Romanian State*, 109.

146. Ibid., 117.

147. Ştefănescu, "Munca în viața economică," in *Enciclopedia României*, ed. Gusti, vol. 3, 78–79; A. C. Cusin, "Dl. Al. Vaida Voevod şi numerus clausus în industria națională: O nouă farsă a primului-minister," *Calendarul*, 441 (10 Aug 1933): 1; Gh. Ascenti-Justus, "Tragedia muncii româneşti," *Buna vestire*, 1/59 (1 May 1937): 13

148. USHMM, Fond SRI Files, Reel #97, dosar 566, f. 21.

149. Mihail Stelescu, "Cine apară pe muncitori?" *Axa*, 1/8 (5 Mar 1933): 1–2; R. Pavel, "Spre o nouă orientare a muncitorimei," *Axa*, 1/11 (30 Apr 1933): 1–2.

150. Traian Herseni, *Mişcarea legionară şi muncitorimea* (Bucharest: Tipografia Legionar, 1937), 6–7.

151. Codreanu, *Pentru legionari*, 191.

152. ANIC, Fond DGP, dosar 46/1936, f. 106; AN—Cluj, Fond Inspectoratul de Poliție, dosar 381/1937, f. 109.

153. ACNSAS, Fond Informativ, dosar 160181, f. 424; dosar 160182, vol. 1, f. 169. For a more detailed discussion of the size of CML, see Schmitt, "Zum Kampf, Arbeiter," 336.

Legionaries also explicitly targeted tradesmen (*meseriaşi*) in their propaganda, and legionary posters claimed to represent the needs of Romanian tradesmen alongside those of factory workers.[154] Ultranationalist newspapers complained that trained young people could not get jobs even though it was increasingly difficult to earn a trade qualification.[155] Toma Vlădescu wrote in *Buna vestire* that tradesmen "make up the largest part of our urban proletariat. The tradesman is the poor man from the city—he is the sad city, the city of the worker and the needy."[156] The poor suburbs where tradesmen lived were perfect recruiting grounds for communists, Vlădescu warned, and he said that the government needed to protect Romanian tradesmen to prevent a left-wing revolution. Tradesmen experienced poverty just as factory workers did, but unlike factory workers they could not hope that strikes or unions would better their situation. Each trade had its own problems, and no single strike could address the grievances of both shoesmiths and bricklayers. Tradesmen were thus a natural constituency for the Legion because their problems stemmed from corruption and nepotism at all levels of Romanian society.

Despite the similarities with the rhetoric of the student movement—Jews were apparently dominating industry just as they seemed to dominate the universities—ultranationalist workers did not express their grievances through violence. Whereas the students dominated the universities through their numbers, ultranationalist workers could not control labor relations and therefore relied on a political victory to resolve their problems. Once they joined, legionary workers were expected to put the Legion before class interests. CML is a good example of this. Codreanu formed CML on 26 October 1936, placing it under the leadership of Gheorghe Clime (1889–1939), a forestry engineer who had been a legionary since 1927.[157] Clime's first political involvement was in Nicolae Iorga's Nationalist Democratic Party, followed by A. C. Cuza's LANC and then Codreanu's Legion.[158] He had organized Muscel County in 1932, and he reorganized the Legion in Bessarabia in 1934. He went to Spain with Moţa and Marin later in 1936 and became president of Partidul Totul pentru Ţara (the Everything for the Fatherland Party) after General Cantacuzino died.[159] Placing Clime at the

154. USHMM, Fond SRI Files, Reel #97, dosar 566, f. 21.

155. Toma Vlădescu, "Revendicările meseriaşilor şi Asigurările Sociale," *Buna vestire*, 1/2 (24 Feb 1937): 5; V. Atanasiu, "Uneltirile ocultei iudeo-comunist," *Buna vestire*, 1/6 (28 Feb 1937): 5.

156. Toma Vlădescu, "Drama meseriaşul român," *Buna vestire*, 1/19 (14 Mar 1937): 1.

157. Corneliu Zelea Codreanu, *Circulări şi manifeste (1927–1938)* (Bucharest: Blassco, 2010), 97–99.

158. ACNSAS, Fond Penal, dosar 011784, vol. 5, f. 56.

159. USHMM, Fond SRI Files, Reel #68, dosar 23333, f. 10; ACNSAS, Fond Penal, dosar 011784, vol. 8, f. 181.

head of CML acknowledged the importance of workers to the Legion, but it also ensured that legionary workers did not organize around workers' issues. In Cluj the regional branch of CML was led by the student activists Roman Buzoianu and Gheorghe Vereş, once again keeping control of the organization out of the hands of workers.[160] CML members had their own special insignias, and workers figured prominent at legionary gatherings from that point on.[161] Codreanu offered a prize of two thousand lei to the person who could write the best lyrics to a "March of the Legionary Workers" and another two thousand lei for the best melody.[162] In December 1936 CML launched a new bimonthly newspaper called *Muncitorul legionar* (The legionary worker, 1936), the first issue of which was dedicated mostly to explaining how CML would be organized.[163] The organization grew rapidly.[164] Ion Victor Vojen (1906–?) took control of CML in August 1937, and at a meeting in Băcau he boasted:

> There was a need for another legionary corps which could work alongside the students to bring us victory. This second corps could not come from the peasantry, a class with strictly limited interests and horizons, nor from the bourgeoisie, a cowardly class interested in its wallet and its stomach. It had to be the workers, a chosen class, for it has been tested many times, counting 300 dead in a single day at Griviţa [during the 1933 strikes.] It has been on the barricades for a long time and has broad horizons, living next to one another in factories. . . . In Bucharest the legionary workers movement began with 47 nests, limping along so as to reach 300 nests today, while there are up to 1,200 nests throughout the country. A good number of the factories in Bucharest are in legionary hands. If we want to stop the trams, we stop them. If we want to blow up the Fireworks factory, we blow it up. If we want to stop the Malaxa or Bragadiru factories, we stop them.[165]

Vojen assumed that workers who had died fighting under left-wing banners during the 1933 strikes at Griviţa would be just as eager to die for the Legion, and his confidence that legionaries could paralyze the economy if they wanted to was

160. ACNSAS, Fond Penal, dosar 011784, vol. 10, f. 255–256.

161. Scurtu ed., *Ideologie*, vol. 4, 260–262; "O frumoasă manifestăţile a muncitorilor legionari," *Cuvântul* (24 Oct 1940);Vasile Posteuca, "Căpitanul şi muncitorii," *Cuvântul* (28 Oct 1940).

162. ACNSAS, Fond Penal, dosar 011784, vol. 11, f. 291.

163. *Muncitorul legionar*, 1/1 (1 Dec 1936): 1–6.

164. ACNSAS, Fond Penal, dosar 011784, vol. 11, f. 221; ACNSAS, Fond Informativ, dosar 160181, f. 424.

165. ACNSAS, Fond Informativ, dosar 160182, vol. 1, f. 162–164.

probably overstated, but his speech demonstrates how important workers were for the movement. By 1937, CML was both the largest and the most active of the Legion's divisions. Codreanu relied more and more heavily on them as time went on, but he never gave them the same leadership responsibilities as students or intellectuals.

Legionaries expected total obedience from their working-class colleagues. In another speech from July 1937 in Bucharest, Vojen told his audience that "wherever he might be, the legionary worker must spread the ideas of the Iron Guard and work for the Legion and for Corneliu Zelea Codreanu."[166] Few if any of legionary workers' tasks involved specifically working-class grievances. In spring 1937, tramway workers planted a new garden in front of the offices of the Everything for the Fatherland Party.[167] Similarly, members of CML were expected to stand guard outside the Legion's headquarters in Bucharest, and they were punished with extra duties if they failed to attend.[168] Large numbers of workers attended most legionary rallies in 1937, providing ready-made crowds that stood in formation for hours on end singing legionary songs.[169] Workers played a crucial role in the electoral campaign that year, doing propaganda on their worksites as well as throughout the country on motorbikes that the Legion had purchased specifically for this purpose.[170] In September 1937 Codreanu had a large placard printed up with a picture of a legionary worker giving the fascist salute while holding a hammer in his right hand and with his left hand grasping a cross to his chest. The placard was to be placed near major factories and worksites in Bucharest as the day of the elections approached.[171] Police reports from 1937 observed that legionaries in Cernăuţi were heavily recruiting workers, including workers with socialist and communist backgrounds, through friendship networks in factories. They put the ex-communists into special indoctrination groups before letting them join ordinary nests.[172]

Legionary pamphlets circulated at Griviţa railway factory in Bucharest during July 1937 spoke about the need for wage increases and declared that "legionaries are prepared to make any sacrifice in the fight against the exploitation of man

166. Ibid., dosar 160181, f. 218.

167. ACNSAS, Fond Penal, dosar 011784, vol. 9, f. 283.

168. Ibid., dosar 007215, vol. 2, f. 85, dosar 011784, vol. 9, f. 214.

169. Ibid., dosar 011784, vol. 10, f. 127, dosar 014005, vol. 10, f. 137.

170. Ibid., dosar 011784, vol. 10, f. 112, dosar 007215, vol. 2, f. 84, 87, 90–91; USHMM, Fond SRI Files, Reel #105, dosar 861, f. 17.

171. ACNSAS, Fond Penal, dosar 011784, vol. 9, f. 86.

172. USHMM, Fond SRI Files, Reel #105, dosar 863, f. 160; AN—Iaşi, Fond Chestura de Poliţie, dosar 7/1937, f. 305.

by man."[173] In 1938 legionary meetings sometimes involved discussion of workers' issues and the singing of workers songs.[174] Pro-legionary newspapers from the period carried frequent articles about the economic plight of workers, and Codreanu spoke on behalf of workers' rights in parliament.[175] But despite such rhetoric, CML rarely did anything that might help the working conditions of tradesmen or factory workers. In December 1937, Teodor Ioraş lost his job as a tramway worker because he had been trying to convince his colleagues to join the Legion. Vojen suggested approaching the tramway company to get Ioraş his job back. Legionaries had applied such pressure to businesses in 1933, but this time Codreanu vetoed Vojen's idea, declaring that "it is not now practical for us to focus on threats and persuasion. . . . We are in the midst of the decisive battle that we must win. And when we have won we will no longer make threats, but will put all those who have hurt us in various ways where they belong."[176] Instead, Codreanu suggested hiring Ioraş to work in the legionary cooperative, where he would earn a tiny wage but receive free food and housing.

The fact that legionaries promised so many different things to potential supporters suggests that for propagandists, building the movement took precedence over specific ideas or grievances. Opportunistic speakers offered land to peasants and jobs to workers, but only on the condition that they first help the Legion gain power. Legionaries recruited among students because their primary social relationships were with other students. Students were already connected to the ultranationalist movement and it was their protest repertoires that shaped legionary activities. Students were used to communal singing, listening to lectures, and reading antisemitic pamphlets, so these activities shaped legionary gatherings. When legionaries began reaching out to peasants, workers, tradesmen, and soldiers, they said that they could resolve the specific problems that these groups faced. Land redistribution, alcoholism, salaries, working conditions, corporatism, and the ethnic composition of businesses all entered the legionary agenda for the first time. But for propagandists, the Legion was a goal in itself and everything else took second place. Although legionaries spoke about poor wages, unemployment, and working conditions when they encouraged such people to join, they consistently postponed addressing any of these issues "until

173. USHMM, Fond SRI Files, Reel #105, dosar 861, f. 1.

174. "Sedințe legionare la Ploiesti," *Cuvântul* (7 Feb 1938).

175. Anton Davidescu, "Gânduri pentru muncitori," *Buna vestire*, 1/3 (24 Feb 1937): 5; P.T., "Ieftinarea vieții: Ințelegeri economice private şi monopoluri private," *Cuvântul* (25 Mar 1938): 8–9; Teban, "Corneliu Codreanu şi muncitorii," in *Corneliu Zelea Codreanu*, ed. Stănescu, 260, 263.

176. ACNSAS, Fond Penal, dosar 011784, vol. 12, f. 215.

the Legion is victorious." With the exception of CML and the preexisting student centers, Codreanu strictly opposed the formation of interest groups within the Legion. Discipline, vows of obedience, a hierarchical command structure, and an exhausting program of electoral campaigns and work camps ensured that rank-and-file legionaries could not question leadership decisions or agitate for short-term goals that might divert resources away from Codreanu's primary vision.

4

ELECTIONS, VIOLENCE, AND DISCIPLINE

I. C. Ghyka, the LANC president in Vlasca County, produced a particularly colorful account of electoral propaganda during the mid-1930s. LANC did not contest the local elections in the southern city of Giurgiu in 1934, leaving Ghyka free to write sarcastically about the behavior of the other parties as they competed for power:

> The most vulgar type of propaganda possible. An activist shouts as loud as his lungs can handle that whoever votes for this or that candidate, may his hands crack and his eyes fall out, or other things of that nature. In the town center the candidates from one list measure how high the tower is and how long and wide the footpaths are as if they were going to build some sort of Western boulevard, while at the same time on the edge of town you break your limbs navigating the holes in the road, which turn into lakes when it rains. In the midst of this electoral campaign, which reaches its noisy peak at 3–4 a.m. when drunk activists stagger out of the pubs waking you up with renditions of "Wake-Up Romanian" ending in "long live so-and-so," as if Andrei Mureşeanu had written the song especially for the future mayor of Giurgiu,—in the midst of this absurd campaign water does not run and you encounter filth at every turn. Accusations of stealing public money flow from both sides but the water does not flow at all.[1]

1. I. C. Gr. Ghyka, "Liga Apărarei Naţionale Creştină şi alegerile comunale din Giurgiu," *Svastica* 3/5 (15 Aug 1934): 2.

Such propaganda was effectively a continuation of the political culture of the nineteenth century, and interwar political commentators noted that the majority of voters viewed elections with disinterest.[2]

In contrast to the empty promises of mainstream politicians, legionaries embraced violence and "propaganda of the deed." Assassination and street violence became legionary trademarks during the early 1930s, telling voters that legionaries were serious about getting things done.[3] In December 1930 a high school student named Constantin Dumitrescu-Zăpadă walked into the offices of *Adevărul* and shot its editor, Emil Socor, wounding but not killing him. As Bucharest's largest center-left daily, *Adevărul* was highly critical of the Legion, and Socor had been disliked by ultranationalists since he had exposed A. C. Cuza's major work on political economy as plagiarism in 1911.[4] Dumitrescu refused to give any reason for trying to kill Socor and claimed that he was following the orders of A. C. Cuza's stepson, Gheorghe Lefter.[5] He did admit to being a legionary, but Codreanu did not take credit for ordering the assassination attempt. In the wake of Dumitrescu's crime, the National Peasant government led by Gheorghe Mironescu (1874–1949) dissolved and banned the Legion on 3 January 1931.[6] Even if they were not responsible, the attempted assassination identified Codreanu and his followers as people of action who cherished deeds, not words. In a political climate characterized by empty rhetoric and broken electoral promises, public exhibitions of a party's willingness to carry through on its threats were very attractive. Such actions earned respect from students who had grown up hearing about revolutionary heroes like Tudor Vladimirescu (1780–1821) and Avram Iancu (1824–1872), whose willingness to shun legality had made them national icons.

Codreanu wrote in 1932 that the Legion's goal was not win to elections—especially in an environment where votes were bought "with silver, with drink, with food"—but rather to ensure that Romania should "be led according to the will of the legionaries." Nonetheless, on the same page he conceded that "an electoral campaign is extremely important, because it is the only way that the law leaves open for us to impose any changes that we want in this country."[7] If legionaries hoped for electoral victories against the mainstream political parties then they had to extend their organization's reach beyond the

---

2. Radu, *Electoratul din România*, 92–111.

3. Radu Harald Dinu, *Faschismus, Religion und Gewalt in Südosteuopa: Die Legion Erzengel Michael und die Ustaša im historische Vergleich* (Wiesbaden: Harrassowitz, 2013), 86–92. Cf. Reichardt, *Faschistische Kampfbünde*, 133.

4. Asandului, *A. C. Cuza*, 63–67.

5. "Atentatul împotriva directorului nostru," *Dimineața*, 26/8629 (31 Dec 1930): 1; "Încercare de atentat împotriva directorului 'Adevărului,'" *Cuvântul*, 7/2045 (31 Dec 1930): 3.

6. "S'au emis mandate de arestare contra șefilor 'Gărzei de fier,'" *Curentul* (16 Jan 1931).

7. Codreanu, *Cărticica*, 45, 47.

university centers of Iaşi, Bucharest, and Cluj, and out of Moldova, Bessarabia, and Bukovina into the country's west and south. Carrying out electoral propaganda was especially difficult for small parties like the Legion because every Romanian election since the introduction of universal male suffrage in 1918 had been characterized by corruption and violence. The ultranationalist daily *Porunca vremii* (The dictate of the times, 1932–1943) reported that everyone who attended a National Liberal rally in a village in Oltenia during November 1936 received a quart of wine, a loaf of bread, half a pound of cheese, and thirty lei, all paid for with public money.[8] County prefects used the gendarmerie to intimidate opposition parties and to ensure that government candidates gained the maximum number of votes. Either because of intimidation, or thanks to a widespread conviction that a ruling party was more likely to be able to carry out its promises, the National Liberal Party won overwhelming majorities in elections when it was the incumbent in 1922 and 1927, but received only a handful of seats when it found itself in opposition before the 1926 elections.[9] *Apărarea națională* reported that in Moldova and Bessarabia, peasants sympathetic to LANC were systematically beaten and arrested during the elections of 1927.[10]

The millions of new voters enrolled after World War I changed the electoral balance in two important ways. First, a massive swing toward Partidul Național Român din Transilvania (the Romanian National Party of Transylvania) and Partidul Poporului (the People's Party) in the elections of 1919 demonstrated that dominating only part of the country—the National Liberal Party was strong in Wallachia and Moldova but not in the new provinces—was not enough to secure victory at the polls. Second, anticorruption, pro-peasant rhetoric now had genuine political appeal. The Romanian National Party of Transylvania and Partidul Țărănesc (the Peasant Party) merged in 1926 to form Partidul Național Țărănesc (the National Peasant Party, PNȚ) under the leadership of Iuliu Maniu (1873–1953) and Ion Mihalache (1882–1963). The new party held massive rallies in provincial capitals all over the country early in 1928, and it formed "civilian guards" to carry out propaganda trips prior to the elections that November.[11] Overseen by Maniu's interim government, these elections took place with minimal police interference, voter attendance was the highest of the interwar period, and PNȚ

8. C. N. Olteanu, "Cum se face la noi propaganda politică," *Porunca vremii*, 5/559 (1 Nov 1936).

9. Hitchins, *Rumania*, 380–381; Radu, *Electoratul din România*, 125–134.

10. "Alegerile dela Roman" *Apărarea națională*, 5/10 (27 June 1927): 2; "În jurul alegerile din Ismail," *Apărarea națională*, 5/10 (27 June 1927): 3.

11. Philip Vanhaelemeersch, *A Generation "without Beliefs" and the Idea of Experience in Romania (1927–1934)* (Boulder, CO: East European Monographs, 2006), 22.

won 77.76 percent of the vote. The National Liberal Party's era of unquestioned dominance was over.[12]

Iuliu Maniu's time in power came to an abrupt end when Prince Carol (1893–1953) unexpectedly returned to Romania in June 1930. The son of King Ferdinand I (1865–1927), Carol developed a reputation as an unreliable playboy during the 1920s. He married the daughter of a Romanian general in August 1918, only to have the marriage annulled seven months later. In 1921 he married Princess Elena of Greece and Denmark (1896–1982), but she divorced him in 1928. Carol began a very public affair with a commoner, Elena Lupescu (1895–1977), in 1925, and abdicated his right to the throne in order to keep Lupescu as his mistress. Carol's six-year-old son, Michael (1921–), was crowned king when Frederick died in 1927, and Carol's return in 1930 caused a constitutional crisis. Disagreements over whether to accept Carol as king split PNȚ in two, and Iuliu Maniu resigned as prime minister twice because he could not work with the new king. In April 1931 PNȚ was replaced by a government of technocrats from minor parties led by Nicolae Iorga, who now had the backing of the king.[13] The first national elections that legionaries contested were those of June 1931, in which the Legion won 29,900 votes (1.05 percent).[14] When Codreanu saw the list of legionary students who were to carry out propaganda in the provinces that year, he commented, "They are few, but they are fanatical."[15] Having few propagandists made contesting national elections difficult, but legionaries used small, roving electoral teams to great advantage during the by-elections in Neamț and Tutova counties in August 1931 and April 1932. Children in the Blood Brotherhoods acted as couriers between these teams and the central leadership.[16] Whereas PNȚ still used cars, celebrity speakers, and urban bands when it carried out propaganda in rural areas, the Legion's lack of resources forced its young propagandists to go on foot and to rely on local hospitality.

National elections were held again in July 1932 and once again involved violence and intimidation. Two people died in Buzău, one a Liberal and the other a Peasantist, and in Bacău the car of a Peasantist candidate exploded, killing his child and wounding three others.[17] Legionaries in Cluj were assaulted by groups of communists, those in Focșani were attacked by "thugs" allegedly working for

12. Hitchins, *Rumania*, 406–407, 414.

13. Ibid., 416–417.

14. Heinen, *Legiunea "Arhanghelul Mihail,"* 201, 464.

15. ANIC, Fond DGP, dosar 37/1931, f. 22.

16. Gheorghe Gh. Istrate, *Frăția de cruce* (Bucharest: Fundației Culturale "Buna Vestire," 2005), 21.

17. Nicolae Iorga, *Memorii: Sinuciderea partidelor (1932–8)*, vol. 7 (Bucharest: Tiparul Așezământului Tipografic "Datina Românească," 1939), 10, 12.

PNŢ, and LANC propagandists in Roman were arrested by the gendarmerie.[18] In Bârlad the head of the local PNŢ branch had one legionary candidate arrested and disputed the candidacy of another on the grounds that he was too young.[19] Despite being able to contest only forty counties because of lack of finances, the legionaries managed 68,700 votes (2.37 percent), which earned them five places in Parliament that year.[20]

Paramilitary Death Teams

Earlier in 1930, the legionaries had formed paramilitary "battalions" incorporated into a new organization called Garda de Fier (the Iron Guard).[21] Father Moţa's newspaper, *Libertatea*, described the Iron Guard as a group of "fighters for people and law, the bravest and most passionate members of the Legion of the Archangel Michael from Iaşi, organized into disciplined ranks as in the military."[22] These battalions served the Legion well once it began to seriously contest national elections. By 1933 the Legion was in a much stronger position than it had ever been before. In May, fifty counties had organized legionary cells, growing to sixty in July, and sixty-eight by the time of the general elections in December 1933. One police estimate put the number of legionaries at the end of 1933 as high as twenty-eight thousand.[23] Aware of the threat posed by the Legion, Alexandru Vaida-Voevod's National Peasant government banned the Iron Guard in April 1933. The government explained:

> These formations, based on principles of military discipline, dress people in uniforms, subject them to commands and to battle training, with the declared purpose of provoking violence and overturning the current legal political order. . . . They have recently gone beyond simple organizational activities so as to begin violent protests, disturbing the peace, and brutalizing peaceful citizens. In such conditions, all of these formations, some independent and others operating under the auspices of the "Iron Guard," "Hitlerists," or "LANC," have become a danger to the public.[24]

18. "Poliţia alegerilor la Cluj," *Calendarul*, 1/84 (2 July 1932): 5; "Terorarea electorală la Roman," *Calendarul*, 1/88 (6 July 1932): 5; "În jurul incidentelor electorale din Putna," *Calendarul*, 1/96 (14 July 1932): 5.

19. "Prigoana electorală la Bârlad," *Calendarul*, 1/91 (9 July 1932): 5.

20. Heinen, *Legiunea "Arhanghelul Mihail,"* 202, 465; "Candidaturile Gărzii de fer," *Calendarul*, 1/93 (11 July 1932): 5.

21. USHMM, Fond MI-D, Reel #138, dosar 2/1930, f. 35.

22. *Libertatea* (10 July 1930), quoted in Heinen, *Legiunea "Arhanghelului Mihail,"* 181–182.

23. Heinen, *Legiunea "Arhanghelul Mihail,"* 203.

24. Ministry of the Interior, Order 27.845/29, quoted in Beldiman, *Armata*, 56.

When they began their electoral campaign, legionaries relied primarily on the formula that had worked well for them in the past. Uniformed groups marched into villages singing nationalist songs and making short speeches to crowds attracted by the spectacle.[25] But this time they faced much more concerted opposition. For the legionaries, it was clear that the authorities were using violence to ensure a National Liberal victory.[26]

Aware that contesting the 1933 elections would not be an easy proposition, Codreanu formed disciplined *echipe morții* (death teams) who would use violence to ensure that their message was heard. Members of these teams told stories about prisons, high-speed police chases, and armed standoffs with gendarmes in front of crowds of peasants.[27] Ştefan Ionescu, an ultranationalist journalist who worked on a variety of right-wing periodicals during the 1930s, described election campaigns as "war in peacetime. War through discipline and through the style of fighting."[28] Ioan Victor Vojen argued in the pages of *Axa* that because the authorities had broken the law by introducing electoral violence, the only law that remained was that "of the fist, of the strongest." Given that the social contract forbidding violence had been broken, Vojen explained, "when legionaries are struck, they strike back."[29] When a police officer tried to stop legionaries from vandalizing the offices of a Jewish organization in Tighina in February 1933, the legionaries turned on him then broke the windows of other buildings in town.[30] Three months later local authorities attempted to close down the Legion's office in Cluj. Once they had broken in and confiscated important papers, the police were surprised by six legionaries, who threatened them with knives and sang legionary hymns. Intimidated, the police officers returned the Legion's confiscated papers and retreated from the scene.[31] In Alba County groups of legionaries supported by sympathetic peasants fought military units in a battle that lasted two hours.[32]

Vojen spoke about legionary propaganda from experience. He had joined the Legion in December 1932, and in early 1933 he began traveling through towns in Teleroman County dressed in traditional folk costume and speaking on behalf of the Legion. A failed actor, he and his comrades performed plays mocking the nepotism practiced by county prefects. In Alexandria they were heckled by local LANC representatives, and in Turnu-Măgurele they were interrogated by the

25. Heinen, *Legiunea "Arhanghelul Mihail,"* 232–233; Iancu, *Sub steagul*, 54–56.

26. Iancu, *Sub steagul*, 56.

27. N. Constantinescu, "Din carnetul unui Legionar," *Axa*, 1/16 (1 Aug 1933): 4.

28. Ştefan C. Ionescu, "Momentul electoral în luptă politică," *Axa*, 1/13 (31 May 1933): 3. On Ionescu's background, see ACNSAS, Fond Informativ, dosar 234303, vol. 2, f. 327.

29. Ioan Victor Vojen, "Cine îndeamnă la violența?" *Axa*, 1/14 (15 June 1933): 4.

30. "Scandal provocat de 'Garda de Fier' la Tighina," *Dimineața* (11 Feb 1933).

31. "Dizolvare a organizației "Garda de Fier" din Cluj," *Dimineața* (8 May 1933).

32. Veiga, *Istoria Gărzii de Fier*, 191.

police. When Vojen tried organizing Dâmboviţa County that spring he encountered widespread skepticism from the locals, but eventually he managed to gather supporters once workers in the petroleum industry began joining in large numbers, disaffected with the foreign management of their plants.[33] According to Vojen, harassment from the authorities greatly helped the propagandists because it generated sympathy for them among the local population.

Two incidents in particular enhanced the Legion's reputation during 1933. The first involved an attempt by legionaries led by Mihail Stelescu (1906–1936) to erect a cross on the grave of the unknown soldier. This monument had been erected in Carol Park amid much fanfare in May 1923 to commemorate Romanian soldiers who died during World War I, and in 1933 both ultranationalists and communists used the site to claim national legitimacy for their causes.[34] A delegation of students led by the president of the Bucharest Student Center, Traian Cotigă, visited the Orthodox patriarch and obtained his permission to erect the cross, and another delegation of legionary priests visited the prime minister, Alexandru Vaida-Voevod (1872–1950), to ask for his blessing.[35] The government explicitly warned the students that nonstate organizations were not allowed to erect plaques on the monument, but legionaries raised money for the cross nonetheless. They had it blessed at St. Anton Church, which was known as "the students' church" even though the official church of the university was now New St. Spiridon Church. The priest at St. Anton's was Father Georgescu-Edineţi (1891–?), who was a longtime supporter of the ultranationalist student movement. Legionaries embraced him as "the spiritual guide of the students."[36] On January 24, 1933, one thousand legionaries and ultranationalist students congregated at Carol Park. Georgescu-Edineţi and Father Dumitrescu-Borşa (1899–?) led them in prayer as the commemoration ceremony began. Dumitrescu-Borşa was also an active legionary and had been involved in stirring up antisemitic violence in Transylvanian villages together with a Roman Catholic priest in 1930.[37] Students threw rocks at the police and the police responded with bullets, wounding several students and Georgescu-Edineţi. Nine police officers were also injured in the clashes that followed.[38] The legionaries were quick to publicize official opposition to their plan as "the beginning of the battle of Christianity against the Antichrists and the

33. ACNSAS, Fond Informativ, dosar 160182, vol. 1, f. 425–427; N. Vlast, "Laudabilă încercări," *Axa*, 1/5 (30 Jan 1933); Victor Ioan Vojen, "Axa, Cuzismul şi Administraţie," *Axa*, 1/5 (30 Jan 1933).

34. Valeria Balescu, *Eroul Necunoscut* (Bucharest: Editura Militara, 2005), 110, 164.

35. Ibid., 164.

36. A. Vântu, "Duhovnicul studenţilor şi Patriarhia," *Axa*, 2/7 (19 Feb 1933): 2.

37. USHMM, Fond MI-D, Reel #138, dosar 4/1930, f. 3, 8–20, 54–55.

38. "Creştinismul în conflict cu francmasoneria," *Calendarul*, 280 (27 Jan 1933): 3; "Preotul Georgescu-Edineţi," *Axa*, 2/6 (5 Feb 1933): 2; Alexandru Serafim, in *Ţara, Legiunea, Căpitanul*, ed. Conovici, Iliescu, and Silvestru, 86–87.

ever more threatening atheism that grips our state under the influence of national and international masonry."[39] Public opinion sided with the Legion, and between seven thousand and eight thousand people turned out the next time legionaries tried to erect a cross at the monument.[40]

The second incident took place that summer, when Codreanu organized for two groups of five hundred legionary volunteers to build a levee to prevent the Buzău River from flooding fields near the village of Vişani every year. Legionary engineers had planned the dig but the county prefect denied them permission on the grounds that the Ministry of Public Works would build the levee once proper preparations had been made. The police intervened to stop the project. Roughly three hundred legionaries were arrested, locked in the local school, and beaten by the authorities on charges of rebellion, assault, and illegal possession of firearms.[41] For a student named Nicolae Constantinescu, this was the fourth time he had been injured in two months.[42] The local legionary newspaper from Buzău, *Vulturul* (the Vulture, 1933), dedicated a special issue to the conflict, emphasizing the noble goal of the legionaries and describing the oppression carried out by soldiers and gendarmes in great detail.[43]

Conflict between legionaries and the authorities increased during the election campaign that fall. *Calendarul* continued publishing scandalous articles about senior government and financial figures, and it was suspended again for fifteen days in November 1933.[44] On November 17, Codreanu issued a circular encouraging legionaries faced with opposition during the elections to "defend yourselves whenever you think it necessary."[45] Five days later a student named Virgil Teodorescu was shot by a gendarme while putting up propaganda posters in Constanţa. Legionaries in Iaşi immediately gathered at the cămin before moving to the city center to stage a protest together with other ultranationalist students from the university.[46] Ion Moţa claimed that Teodorescu had died "for the cross of Christ," and Alexandru Cantacuzino, a law student, used his death as proof that "we are not the aggressors, but the victims here."[47] Further scuffles

39. Mihail Stelescu, "Lupta pentru cruce," *Axa*, 2/6 (5 Feb 1933): 4.

40. Valentin Săndulescu, "Revolutionizing Romania from the Right: The Regenerative Project of the Romanian Legionary Movement and Its Failure (1927–1937)" (PhD diss., Central European University, 2011), 104.

41. "Mişcările Legionarilor Gărzii de fier în judeţul R.-Sarat," *Universul* (13 July 1933); Polihroniade, *Tabară de muncă*, 7; ACNSAS, Fond Documentar, dosar 008912, vol. 2, f. 19–20.

42. Codreanu, *Pentru legionari*, 435.

43. Ion Costea, *Presa legionară a Buzăului* (Buzău: Editura Vega, 2007), 12–18.

44. Mihail Polihroniade, "Cuvântul Justiţiei," *Calendarul*, 526 (1 Dec 1933): 1–2.

45. "'Garda de Fier' şi alegerile viitoare," *Ţara noastră* (17 Nov 1933).

46. AN—Iaşi, Universitatera A.I. Cuza, Rectoratul, Reel #266, dosar 1480/1934, f. 358–359.

47. Quoted in Dinu, *Faschismus, Religion und Gewalt*, 88.

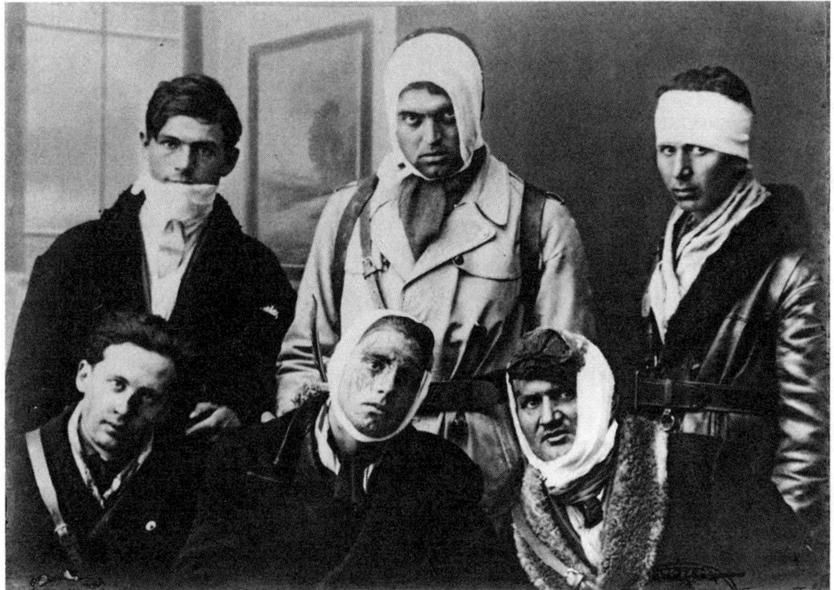

FIGURE 4.1 Legionaries injured during the 1933 election campaigns. Biblioteca Academiei Române, Secţia Manuscrise. Ref #35 A-B.

with police ensued and one of the legionaries shot a gendarme. The police raided the cămin in response to the shooting and the students held out for several days before they finally capitulated on November 27. Their friends outside supported them during the siege and a young worker named Constantin Niţa was shot by the police when he tried throwing bread up to the students.[48] The cămin was badly damaged during the siege, and the police sealed up the building after searching for weapons and evacuating the inhabitants.[49]

Assassination and Prison

The government dissolved the Legion on December 9, 1933, arresting thousands of legionaries prior to the elections of 20 December and then releasing many of them within a couple of weeks.[50] Students in Bucharest staged massive street

48. Totu, "Jilava," 5; Banea, *Acuzat*, 35–36.

49. ACNSAS, Fond Penal, dosar 015671, vol. 3, f. 176–177; ACNSAS, Fond Penal, dosar 011784, vol. 9, f. 375–377; AN—Iaşi, Fond Chestura de poliţie, dosar 52/1933, f. 250.

50. "După dizolvarea 'Gărzii de fer,'" *Universul* (13 Dec 1933); Iancu, *Sub steagul*, 57–61.

demonstrations in their support.[51] Legionaries protested against the conditions they were being kept in and hunger strikes began in prisons across the country. Nicolae Bălan (1882–1955), the metropolitan of Ardeal, intervened on behalf of arrested legionaries in Sibiu.[52] Only nine days after the elections, three legionaries shot and killed the prime minister, Ion G. Duca, at the train station in Sinaia. By February 1934 legionaries were selling photographs of the assassins for twenty lei each.[53] The man who pulled the trigger was the aforementioned Nicolae Constantinescu, a student propagandist who had been injured several times in scuffles with the police during the previous months and who had been arrested then released during the government repression of the Legion earlier that month.[54] He was accompanied by two Aromanian students, Ion Caranica (1907–1938) and Dorul Belimace (1910–1938).[55] Even more legionaries were arrested in the wake of Duca's assassination, four legionaries were killed during or after police interrogations, and the pro-legionary newspaper *Calendarul* was shut down permanently on 1 January 1934.[56]

Prison introduced many legionaries to each other for the first time. Arriving at Jilava after weeks spent in prisons at Arad and Lugoj, Nicu Iancu (1910–1984) says that when he entered his cell, "I found myself surrounded by comrades; they all crowded around to shake my hand and welcome me, even hugging me despite the fact that I did not know most of them."[57] Prison also helped create a legionary culture centered around discipline and poetic reflection on persecution. The journalist Nichifor Crainic was imprisoned together with the legionaries, and he writes in his memoirs that "the engineer [Gheorghe] Clime took command of the several hundred inmates, combining legionary and military discipline. He formed teams for cooking and cleaning, and divided the day up into periods of instruction, singing, discussions and leisure."[58] Legionaries sang to keep up

---

51. ACNSAS, Fond Documentar, dosar 012694, vol. 1, f. 10–12; "Sărbătoarea zilei 10 Decembrie," *Calendarul*, 536 (13 Dec 1933): 3.

52. "Cei 43 Legionari arestați la Iași în greva foamei," *Calendarul*, 536 (13 Dec 1933): 3; "Studenți gardiști internați la Someseni au declarat greva foamei," *Calendarul*, 538 (15 Dec 1933): 3; "Legionari arestați la Chișinău în greva foamei," *Calendarul*, 538 (15 Dec 1933): 3; "Legionarii închiși la Jilava au declarat greva foamei," *Calendarul*, 546 (24 Dec 1933): 2; "Legionarii deținuți la Sibiu atacați cu gaze lacrimogene," *Calendarul*, 550 (31 Dec 1933): 2; Iancu, *Sub steagul*, 73–75.

53. AN—Iași, Chestura de poliție, dosar 99/1935, f 37.

54. Heinen, *Legiunea "Arhanghelul Mihail,"* 235.

55. "Înstruirea asasinatului dela Sinaia," *Dimineața* (9 Jan 1934).

56. Nichifor Crainic, "Istoria 'Calendarului,'" *Sfarmă piatră* (24 Mar 1938): 2; ACNSAS, Fond Penal, dosar 014005, vol. 5, f. 221.

57. Iancu, *Sub steagul*, 117.

58. Nichifor Crainic, *Zile albe, zile negre: Memorii (I)* (Bucharest: Casa Editurială "Gândirea," 1991), 257. This is confirmed by police reports from the period. ACNSAS, Fond Penal, dosar 013206, vol. 3, f. 8.

their spirits.[59] One of the assassins who was in solitary confinement away from the others, Doru Belimache, wrote that when he heard his comrades singing, "I press[ed] my ear to the door and listen[ed], forgetting my chains."[60] The arrested legionaries even produced their own newspaper, called *13 Jilava*.[61] Radu Gyr (1905–1975), one of the Legion's most celebrated poets, began writing verses about the harsh conditions at Jilava prison, where he was being held. One of his poems from this period, "Ocnă Legionară" (The legionary prison), affirms not only the suffering of the legionaries but also their innocence and purity in the midst of persecution:

> No one mourns the humid prison.
> The mould on the walls turns sour.
> Silence flows, black, with the rats,
> And spiders, climbing the walls and fungi.
>
> And over wounds of gold and frankincense
> Through the bars of the dirty walls,
> A blue sky floods into the prison
> Pure as a legionary's soul.[62]

As poems like Gyr's circulated among the legionaries, the families, and the friends of those arrested, the image of the legionaries as persecuted heroes became more and more central to the movement's mythology. Vasile Marin's wife, Ana Maria, writes that visiting arrested legionaries was difficult, but nonetheless "families came with packets even if they did not have anyone locked up in the prison; they just hoped that their clothes and food would get to any of the legionaries inside."[63]

The assassination boosted the Legion's reputation, and a number of senior politicians came out in defense of the arrested legionaries. Alexandru Averescu, Constantin Argetoianu, Iuliu Maniu, Ion Mihalache, Gheorghe Brătianu, and Alexandru Vaida-Voevod all spoke in favor of legionaries at their trials. Intent on profiting from the legionaries' actions, King Carol II did not even go to Duca's funeral or visit the prime minister's widow.[64] Octavian Goga, a poet and anti-semitic politician who led the National Agrarian Party, made a gift of boots to all the prisoners in the hope of uniting the Legion with his own party.[65] As a

59. Crainic, *Zile albe*, 257.
60. Doru Belimache, "9 Mar 1934," *13 Jilava*, 7/1 (29 Nov 1940): 3.
61. "Poşta lui 13 . . ." *13 Jilava*, 7/1 (29 Nov 1940): 12.
62. Radu Gyr, "Ocnă Legionară," *Calendarul*, 547 (25 Dec 1933): 2.
63. Ana Maria Marin, *Poveste de dincolo* (Madrid: Editura Autorului, 1979), 117.
64. Heinen, *Legiunea "Arhanghelul Mihail,"* 237–240. For a description of the funeral, see Iorga, *Memorii*, 127–128.
65. Crainic, *Zile albe*, 261, 280.

reflection of the solidarity between the Legion and Mussolini's Fascists, Italian lawyers came to Romania to help defend the imprisoned legionaries.[66] There was clearly little stigma associated with Duca's murder. But the crackdown on the Legion nonetheless took its toll on the organization. In a circular from 1 January 1935, Codreanu gave a "balance sheet" for the past twelve months, listing "18,000 arrests, with 18,000 houses invaded by barbarians and filled with innocent blood: 300 sick in prisons, 16 dead, and 3 buried alive underground."[67] Sickness and death reduced the number of veteran legionaries available for future campaigns, but the "heroism" of prison inspired old and new recruits alike to be willing to make even greater sacrifices for the Legion.

Threatening Enemies and Friends

The Legion's willingness to engage in political violence attracted the attention of a new "convert" to ultranationalism—Istrate Micescu (1881–1951). Micescu had served as a deputy for the Liberal Party three times, in 1920, 1927, and 1931. He formed his own Liberal faction in 1925 and then temporarily joined Gheorghe I. Brătianu's dissident National Liberal Party (Partidul Național Liberal-Brătianu) after 1930.[68] Micescu invited the Legion to collaborate with his project to introduce a *numerus clausus* to the Bar Association of Ilfov County in February 1935. His brother was a committed legionary, and the movement's leaders hoped that he would follow his brother's example. The legionaries vacillated at first, and Micescu and Codreanu did not agree on a firm alliance until November 1935.[69] By that time it had become clear that what Micescu really wanted was to use legionary students to intimidate his political opponents in the bar association. Micescu called his group Asociația Avocaților Creștini Români (the Association of Romanian Christian Lawyers) and introduced a fascist-style oath that included the promise to boycott anyone who left the organization.[70] Within a short time the association had regional branches throughout the country.[71] Micescu proposed "Romanianizing" the bar in Ilfov County by excluding Jewish lawyers from membership. The existing council of the bar association rejected the idea, so Micescu and legionary lawyers introduced a vote of no confidence and successfully removed the council. They did so with the help of law students,

66. Ibid., 259.
67. Codreanu, *Circulări*, 32.
68. ACNSAS, Fond Penal, dosar 000324, vol. 7, f. 383.
69. Ibid., dosar 000324, vol. 9, f. 5, 6, 12, 14, 33; vol. 10, f. 9.
70. ACNSAS, Fond Penal, dosar 000324, vol. 9, f. 2.
71. ANIC, Fond DGP, dosar 107/1935, f. 115–116.

who guarded the entrances to the building and ensured that no one entered who might vote against the changes. Micescu's supporters telephoned potential opponents several days earlier, threatening to kill them if they tried to come to the meeting.[72] Ultimately, the Legion's alliance with Micescu lasted only as long as Micescu needed legionaries as thugs to ensure his own electoral victories. The following year Micescu switched his allegiance to the newly formed National Christian Party (Partidul Național Creştin, PNC) led by A. C. Cuza and Octavian Goga.[73] He turned against the legionary students as soon as his presidency of the Ilfov Bar Association was secure, leaving them bitter at having been manipulated by such an experienced politician.[74] Stung, Codreanu issued a circular in March 1937 that stated clearly that "people who have played an exceptional role in public life up until now can no longer join the legionary movement, even if they signify that they have understood this movement, even if they are ready to take the oath, and even if they seem to provide enough guarantees of their devotion."[75]

In April 1936, legionaries publicly stated that they would attack and kill prominent individuals who opposed them. Despite being warned not to by the government, UNSCR held its annual congress at Târgu Mureş that month. On the second day of the congress Alexandru Cantacuzino proposed forming "death teams" to avenge legionary martyrs. He identified potential targets as the king's mistress, Elena Lupescu (1895–1977); Bucharest's police prefect, Colonel Gabriel Marinescu (1886–1940); Mihail Stelescu; and a number of leading politicians. On the third day, the congress attendees, while making the fascist salute, vowed that "at the price of our blood we will ensure that the Nicadorii [Duca's assassins] no longer have to suffer." Gheorghe Furdui (1910–1939), UNSCR's president and a theology student in Bucharest, explained that these teams were actually "punishment teams" or "honor teams," that would regain the Legion's honor by demonstrating that it could take revenge on its enemies.[76]

In June 1936 Simion Toma (1913–?) formed a team to kill Grigore Graur (1884–1969), a left-wing journalist working for the newspapers *Adevărul* and *Dimineața*. Toma was a student at the Commercial Academy in Târgovişte who had become interested in the Legion after joining a student society, where some of his colleagues introduced him to legionary activism. He joined the Legion in March 1933, worked on the construction site at the Green House in Bucharest, took part in the 1933 electoral campaign in Târgovişte, and was arrested follow-

72. ACNSAS, Fond Penal, dosar 000324, vol. 9, f. 26; Vintilescu, "Biruința avocaților români creştini din baroul de Ilfov," *Porunca vremii* (29 Oct 1935); Scurtu ed., *Ideologie*, vol. 4, 138–140.

73. ACNSAS, Fond Penal, dosar 000324, vol. 7, f. 383, vol. 9, f. 1–33.

74. ANIC, Fond DGP, dosar 1/1938, f. 5–8.

75. Codreanu, *Circulări*, 129.

76. ANIC, Fond DGP, dosar 46/1936, f. 4–21.

ing Duca's murder. Toma failed most of his exams in 1933–1934 because he had been in prison, but there he met Gheorghe Clime, who he says became a significant mentor. The UNSCR congress at Târgu Mureş in 1936 was the first he had ever attended. *Adevărul* and *Dimineaţa* wrote very negative articles about the Târgu Mureş congress, and chemistry student Victor Dragomirescu (1912–1939) created several teams to "punish" the offending journalists. Toma's team was made up entirely of students, most from Târgovişte. They received their orders by telephone, and none of them knew what Graur looked like. They waited outside his house, but mistakenly attacked another man who lived in the same building, Iosif Störfer. The students struck Störfer with iron rods and Toma shot him three times in the abdomen. Toma was promoted for his actions and helped Ion Victor Vojen and Victor Dragomirescu organize CML in 1937.[77] Death threats continued despite such blunders, and the police immediately began looking to arrest Mihai Ianitschi after he threatened a number of influential people in his city of Storojineţ in October 1936.[78]

The only successful assassination of this period was of Mihail Stelescu, a prominent legionary who had formed his own rival organization. Upset at the sudden importance that Codreanu had started giving to Bucharest intellectuals, Stelescu tried to create his own personal faction within the Legion.[79] Codreanu expelled Stelescu from the organization in September 1934. It is unclear precisely what caused Codreanu to turn against Stelescu, but both ideological differences and a personal rivalry between Codreanu and Stelescu were probably involved.[80] Stelescu had written several of the Legion's most popular songs, led some of the most belligerent electoral teams during 1933, was a frequent contributor to the legionary newspaper *Axa*, had been a deputy for the Legion, and represented the Legion in negotiations with other ultranationalist groups. Stelescu then formed his own organization called Cruciada Românismului (the Crusade for Romanianism, 1935–1937). The crusaders denied that theirs was a new movement, claiming that "we are continuing, with the same creed, the same enthusiasm," the long-standing ultranationalist struggle.[81] The Crusade enjoyed generous funding from official circles hoping to undermine the Legion, and it managed to attract the formerly communist writer Panait Istrati (1884–1935) to its cause.[82] Stelescu

77. ACNSAS, Fond Penal, dosar 014005, vol. 4, f. 83–86, 102–120; vol. 5, f. 191–192; vol. 9, f. 96.

78. AN—Iaşi, Fond Chestura de Poliţie, dosar 7/1937, f. 11.

79. Iordachi, *Charisma*, 99–100. The story that Stelescu cultivated the Aromanians in particular is also found in Tudor V. Cucu, *Totul pentru ţară, nimic pentru noi* (Braşov: Editura Transilvania Expres, 1999), 172–175.

80. Veiga, *Istoria Gărzii de Fier*, 241; Heinen, *Legiunea "Arhanghelul Mihail,"* 300.

81. Mihail Stelescu, "Prefaţa," *Cruciada românismului*, 1/1 (22 Nov 1934): 1.

82. Heinen, *Legiunea "Arhanghelul Mihail,"* 250; Mircea Iorgulescu, "Panait Istrati şi Cruciada Românismului," *România literara*, 24/45 (7 Nov 1991): 4–5.

claimed that Codreanu's image as a virtuous and decisive leader was dishonest, and he questioned his suitability as a nationalist leader on the grounds that he had non-Romanian ancestors.[83]

In September 1934, after being informed by one of the conspirators that Stelescu was plotting to assassinate Codreanu, a group of legionaries that included Codreanu, General Cantacuzino, Nichifor Crainic, Virgil Ionescu, Gheorghe Clime, and Gheorghe Beza broke into the house of Luca Gheorghiade. Here they discovered two revolvers and a bottle of potassium cyanide, but a servant girl alerted Gheorghiade to their presence and a gun battle ensued. Codreanu took Gheorghiade and other Stelescu supporters to court, accusing them of plotting to kill him.[84] In a pamphlet titled *Demascarea trădării* (Unmasking treason, 1936), the legionaries claimed that Gheorghiade had obtained the poison from a chemical factory and was supposed to use it to kill Codreanu on Stelescu's behalf.[85]

Two months after the Târgu Mureş conference, ten legionaries approached Stelescu in a Bucharest hospital where he was recovering from an appendectomy. They shot roughly 120 bullets into his body and struck him repeatedly in the head with an axe. They sang legionary hymns while committing the murder, and then turned themselves into the police.[86] Rumors soon emerged that some of Stelescu's supporters were planning to get revenge on Codreanu. Hostility continued between the two camps; one of Stelescu's supporters was killed, others were assaulted, and the following year legionaries cut the nose off another when they found him alone one night.[87] Codreanu instituted a personal bodyguard for himself in October 1936.[88] Although it was never again practiced, the killing of legionaries who left the organization became official legionary policy in September 1936, when Codreanu created "punishment teams." He sent around a confidential circular ordering that "as soon as a comrade abandons the movement and begins to work together with our enemies, this team will present itself at his door and warn him that if he continues to work against the Legion he will have the same fate as Stelescu."[89]

---

83. Săndulescu, "Revolutionizing Romania," 139–141; "Polemica Mihail Stelescu—Corneliu Codreanu," *Lupta* (29 Mar 1935); reprinted in *Ideologie*, Scurtu ed., vol. 4, 92–93.

84. "Membrii fostei grupări "Garda de Fier" s-au despărţit în două tabere," *Dimineaţa* (9 Sept 1934); reprinted in *Ideologie*, Scurtu ed., vol. 4, 61–62.

85. ACNSAS, Fond Penal, dosar 011784, vol. 4, f. 168, vol. 8, f. 348–349.

86. Săndulescu, "Revolutionizing Romania," 141.

87. Heinen, *Legiunea "Arhanghelul Mihail,"* 290; ACNSAS, Fond Penal, dosar 011784, vol. 8, f. 249, vol. 13, f. 69; AN—Iaşi, Fond Chestura de Poliţie, dosar 119/1937, f. 43

88. AN—Iaşi, Chestura de Poliţie, dosar 93/1936, f. 237; ACNSAS, Fond Penal, dosar 011784, vol. 8, f. 199.

89. ANIC, Fond MI-D, dosar 10/1935, f. 164.

After almost a year of frequent legionary threats against public figures, would-be assassins stabbed the chancellor of the University of Iaşi, Traian Bratu (1875–1940), on 1 March 1937. According to Armand Călinescu (1893–1939), "Professor Traian Bratu was followed by several young students while he walked home from the university. They stopped him on a dark street, stabbed him in the back, and left him in a pile of blood."[90] Bratu did not recognize his assailants, but Călinescu blamed the Legion for the assassination attempt. Codreanu replied that "the legionary movement has no connection to the terrible incident," but he also reminded the authorities that professors such as Bratu had acted unjustly toward their students and that "every political movement . . . has its share of unbalanced people, who do not understand philosophy and who react in whatever way they like."[91] Bratu had opposed antisemitic students in Iaşi since the early 1920s, and this was not the first time he had been threatened by students.[92] An article censored out of *Buna vestire* from 3 March claimed that the assailants had been former servants of Bratu's who were upset about unpaid wages.[93] Several legionaries were charged with attacking Bratu but were acquitted for lack of evidence.[94] The day before the attempted assassination of Bratu, General Gabriel Marinescu (1886–1940), whom legionaries had targeted for assassination at the Târgu Mureş congress, and whom King Carol had just appointed minister of public order, drew up a list of thirty legionaries, including Codreanu, whom he wanted assassinated.[95] The government evacuated and reorganized all student dormitories in the country after the attack on Bratu—a move that they had already discussed a week before Bratu was stabbed—warned priests to stay out of politics, banned political uniforms, and closed down Masonic lodges.[96] Roughly four hundred police officers and gendarmes surrounded the legionary cămin in Iaşi, making forty-six arrests as they evacuated and sealed up the building.[97] Regardless of whether the Legion had actually orchestrated the attack on Bratu, its reputation for assassination and violence made it the ideal scapegoat. The government made very effective use of this attack to curtail legionary influence

90. Parliamentary debates, 2 March 1937, in *Ideologie*, Scurtu ed., vol. 4, 293.

91. Codreanu, *Circulări*, 125–126.

92. AN—Iaşi Fond Universitatea A.I. Cuza, Rectorat, Reel #121, dosar 1024/1923, f. 116–122; AN—Iaşi, Fond Chestura de Poliţie, dosar 95/1935, f. 11.

93. ACNSAS, Fond Documentar, dosar 012694, vol. 1, f. 88.

94. AN—Iaşi, Fond Chestura de Poliţie, dosar 91/1938, f. 234.

95. Rebecca Haynes, "Reluctant Allies? Iuliu Maniu and Corneliu Zelea Codreanu against King Carol II of Romania," *Slavonic and East European Review*, 85/1 (2007): 113.

96. "Desfiinţarea căminurilor studenţeşti," *Adevărul* (26 Feb 1937); Scurtu ed., *Ideologie*, vol. 4, 290–293.

97. "După monstruosul atentat din Iaşi," *Lupta* (3 Mar 1937).

in university dormitories and to demand that the hierarchy of the Orthodox Church prevent its clergy from participating in ultranationalist politics.

Obedient Legionaries

Codreanu's protestations that he could not control the "unbalanced people" in his organization sound disingenuous when one considers how strictly he disciplined those under his command. The violence and illegality associated with activism helped legionaries think of the Legion as a paramilitary organization with a strict hierarchy, discipline, and high expectations from members. After the violent electoral campaign of 1933, Codreanu began setting minimum standards for his followers and punishing legionaries who did not fulfill them. He introduced new membership requirements, distributed awards and honorary ranks, and regulated what happened during nest meetings. County leaders ranked their nests and fortresses according to how much they gave in donations, how far they marched, and how many new members they recruited. They expelled those who fell below a certain standard. Legionaries spoke about their movement as a school for creating "new men," and the fact that so many people committed themselves to Codreanu's strict and sometimes arbitrary regimen shows how committed legionaries were to shaping new, illiberal selves.

In a report to Codreanu dated 5 January 1935, an anonymous nest leader described the other inhabitants of his village. "Many defects," he wrote. "Excitable, but without stamina. I have not tried to convince them even for a moment; to increase their knowledge, promoting our cult, because it is impossible (they are mediocre and do not know anything outside their limited circles). . . . They do not know how to forgo poker or drunkenness for us. . . . They have no schooling, nor cultivation; far from it (and here I am even talking about some of the thirteen)." Despite such poor potential recruits, the writer had managed to enlist thirteen legionaries. He was equally negative about them, commenting that "we do not have enough forests around here to build stockyards to 'socialize' this agrammatical lot." The report dedicated twenty-eight pages to denigrating every social group in the village. The writer called working-class women "degenerates of the WORST kind" and complained that Jews were much better businesspeople than were the local Romanians. High school boys took sport to "irrational" extremes, building their muscles for only one or two years before tuberculosis or broken bones stopped them. Roughly 90 percent of the high school girls "have a disputable morality." His conclusion was that if the Legion was to become an effective social movement, "ABSOLUTELY ALL OF THEM MUST be passed through a legionary current—I will indicate the voltage myself, CAPTAIN, when the time comes. Essentially, the only way forward is a meaningful and relentless legionary school."[98]

For young people, legionary education began when they joined a Mânunchiu de Prieteni (Cluster of Friends—literally, a "*fasci* of friends") at the age of fourteen, and then a Frăţie de Cruce (Blood Brotherhood) at fifteen. Codreanu and Ion Moţa formed the first Blood Brotherhoods when they brought high school students to work at the brickworks at Ungheni, and these groups continued intermittently until they were reorganized in May 1935.[99] According to a manual written by Gheorghe Istrate, who led the Blood Brotherhoods from 1935 to 1938, the name came from two sources. First, Orthodox children baptized in the same water were called *fraţi de cruce* (literally "brothers of the cross"). Second, *haiduci* (outlaws) who swore an oath of loyalty to one another by carving a cross into the palms of their hands called themselves *fraţi de cruce* (hence: blood brothers). The Legion's Blood Brotherhoods drew on both of these ideas. Istrate described them as "new schools of heroism," based on "the power of sacrifice and friendship."[100]

Once male high school students reached the age of fourteen, older students began recruiting them to join a Cluster of Friends, which was a probationary organization that students joined before being allowed to join a Blood Brotherhood. Only the best students were supposed to be recruited, and oral histories affirm that members perceived themselves to be among the school's elite.[101] In his memoirs, Valeriu Anania (1921–2011), the future Orthodox metropolitan of Cluj, Alba, Crişana, and Maramureş, writes that when he was first recruited in 1936, "conversations happened almost daily, in the playground or the corridors of the dormitories. The more specific they became, the more discreet I was expected to be. I discovered that there was a secret, conspiratorial organization that had been active in the school for some time. Only those who are destined to become future legionaries of the Captain are called and accepted into it."[102] Potential recruits were told to read Codreanu's *Pentru legionari* and were tested on sincerity, love, will, ability to sacrifice, listening, and ability to make friends. During the testing phase, they were expected to give 2.5 percent of their time and

98. ANIC, Fond DGP, dosar 109/1934, f. 4–32.

99. Istrate, *Frăţia de cruce*, 9–32. Istrate's *Frăţia de cruce* was published in its current form in 1937, but the first, shorter version from May 1935 can be found in USHMM, Fond SRI Files, Reel #105, dosar 861, f. 92–120.

100. Istrate, *Frăţia de cruce*, 8.

101. Gheorghe Ungureanu in *Ţara, Legiunea, Căpitanul*, ed. Conovici, Iliescu, and Silivestru, 36.

102. Valeriu Anania, *Memorii* (Bucharest: Polirom, 2008), 11.

money to the Legion, keeping a daily record of their good deeds in a notebook.[103] According to a derogatory account written by Ion Victor Vojen in a communist prison many years later, "Several initiates who hoped to trap [the new recruit] 'helped' the chosen one in every situation: they brought him into their group when playing sports, they helped him with his homework, they permanently surrounded him with counterfeit warmth and calculated friendship. Older students from the same school gave him their attention, breaking the class barriers that are so rigid among school students."[104] Sometimes Brotherhoods operated quite openly and had the support of sympathetic teachers, which would have further increased the prestige associated with becoming a Blood Brother.[105]

The probationary period lasted forty to sixty days, after which students were initiated into a Cluster of Friends. Friends held their own meetings, which were a simplified version of those expected of Blood Brothers. Here they read legionary literature, learned to salute, gave short speeches on preselected themes, and learned legionary songs. Friends also kept a notebook of their good deeds, and they now began making financial contributions to the Legion. Regular attendance was required, and four unexplained absences resulted in a Friend being excluded from his Cluster.[106] Once a student had been a Friend for at least three months and had turned fifteen years old, he could take the oath to become a Blood Brother. Before taking the oath, Friends had to pass an exam on the Brotherhood's handbook and find some wormwood, preferably taken from a battlefield or from near the grave of a national hero. Initiates now received a flag and a symbol indicating their rank within the Brotherhood and were allowed to wear a green shirt for the first time.[107]

Blood Brothers met once a week, following a ritualized procedure that imitated the nest meetings of adult legionaries. They began by repeating the following formula after their leader:

> Let us pray. Let us raise our thoughts to the souls of the martyrs Moța and Marin, Stere Ciumeti, and all our other comrades who have fallen for the Legion or who died in the legionary faith. We believe in the resurrection of a legionary Romania and in breaking down the wall of hate and cowardice that surrounds it. I swear that I will never betray the Legion, the Captain, or my Blood Brothers.[108]

103. Istrate, *Frăția de cruce*, 32–47.

104. ACNSAS, Fond Informativ, Microfilm 5065, f. 219.

105. ACNSAS, Fond Penal, dosar 011784, vol. 5, f. 22.

106. Istrate, *Frăția de cruce*, 51–93.

107. Ibid., 96–99.

108. Prior to 1937, the formula read, "Let us turn our thoughts to God! Let us think of our Legionary brothers! Let us think about raising our country up through work and sacrifice! I will never

Everyone then saluted, and the "call of the dead" took place. This involved calling out the names of dead legionaries and collectively answering, "Present!" on their behalf. Then they opened the New Testament at random and read out a few verses before chanting the Lord's Prayer or "God is with us." Next came a minute of silence, during which Brothers handed over their financial contributions and meditated on the Legion's martyrs. After the moment of silence, physical instruction began, when Brothers learned military positions such as "at attention," "at ease," and "break ranks." Choir practice followed instruction, and then one of the Brothers gave a speech to his colleagues. The group read a page from Codreanu's *Pentru legionari*, and then each Brother reported on his area of responsibility—leader, secretary, treasurer—or on the activities of another Brotherhood that he had visited. Then Brothers confessed their struggles to one another, someone summarized which of the group's previous decisions had been carried out, new decisions were made, and the meeting closed with the singing of a legionary song.[109]

It is impossible to know how strictly most Brotherhoods followed this program, but memoir and oral history accounts do include a number of the elements mentioned in Istrate's handbook.[110] Valeriu Anania writes that although he belonged to a Brotherhood, he never took its activities very seriously. He preferred smoking, alcohol, sex, forbidden literature, and running away from boarding school to the puritanism of the Legion. He confessed his misdemeanors to his Brothers and gave himself punishments that he did not carry out.[111] Anania never became a legionary, but many Brothers did, becoming some of Codreanu's most reliable and committed followers.

Legionary instruction should also have taken place in weekly nest (*cuib*) meetings. According to Codreanu's *Cărticica şefului de cuib* (Little handbook for nest leaders), the meeting of an adult nest followed a similar program to that of the Blood Brotherhoods. Nests had between three and thirteen members and were run by a single leader, who was usually the founder. The leader began by greeting the group with "Comrades!" (Camarazi), at which signal everyone stood up and saluted. Those assembled repeated an oath after the nest leader, after which the leader passed on news and gave new orders. They read the newspaper *Pământul strămoşesc* at length and then held "educational" dis-

---

betray the Legion, the Captain, or my Blood Brothers. So help me God." USHMM, Fond SRI Files, Reel #105, dosar 861, f. 101–102.

109. Istrate, *Frăţia de cruce*, 109–113.

110. Ion Gavrilă Ogoranu, in *Ţara, Legiunea, Căpitanul*, ed. Conovici, Iliescu, and Silivestru, 58–63; Anania, *Memorii*, 11–13; Moise, *Sfântul închisorilor* (Alba Iulia: Asociaţia Synaxis, 2007); ACNSAS, Fond Penal, dosar 000160, vol. 1, f. 8–9, vol. 2, f. 262–263.

111. Anania, *Memorii*, 13.

FIGURE 4.2 Legionaries in uniform. ACNSAS, Fond Informativ, dosar 210821, vol. 3, f. 129.

cussions on political and social themes. Nests of younger legionaries could sing together, after which the group made decisions about future activities. At the end of the meeting everyone stood up and saluted, facing east, and repeated, "I swear that I will never betray the Legion."[112] There are few detailed descriptions of actual nest meetings, but those that we have conform to the formula laid out by Codreanu.[113]

Small women's groups, known as fortresses (*cetăţui*), followed a similar pattern. According to an article from April 1933 in the Bessarabian newspaper *Garda de Fier* (The Iron Guard, 1933), "the organization and function of a fortress is the same as that of a nest. The purpose of a fortress is:

a) The self-improvement of fortress members everywhere;
b) To support the Legion in every way possible;
c) To create and promote the morale of women;

112. Codreanu, *Cărticica*, 12–24.

113. Ion Roth Jelescu, *Şi cerul plângea: Amintiri din prigoana cea mare* (Madrid: Dacia, 1974), 58, 260; Bănică Dobre, *Crucificaţii: Zile trăite pe frontul spaniol* (Bucharest: I. N. Copuzeanu, 1937), 56; ACNSAS, Fond Informativ, dosar 234980, f. 73.

d) To develop and maintain an active life, the Christian traditions of our ancestors, consciousness and national solidarity among all Romanian women;
e) To give the new Romania a new woman, a seasoned and resolute warrior."[114]

At first glance, the ideology of the fortresses emphasized domestic skills. Codreanu's *Cărticica şefului de cuib* suggested that women discuss "how to serve a healthier meal to the family," "housework and care of children," and "how to sew entire sets of clothing at home."[115] But rather than engaging in cooking and sewing at home, members of fortresses used their talents publicly, in the service of the Legion. At times during the early 1930s, fortresses took part in sewing competitions to produce legionary insignias and collected dried flowers to sell for fund-raising purposes.[116] Even if their legionary work required many of the same skills that their domestic duties did, it was being used for political purposes.

Committed to the same ideal of creating a "new man" (*omul nou*) as male nests, legionary women also used oath taking, financial contributions, and discussions about self-improvement to create committed legionaries. In a circular from 1934, Nicoleta Nicolescu, who was responsible for reorganizing all fortresses at this time, said that in their fortresses legionary women were to listen to Codreanu's orders, attract new members, make financial donations, and write reports on their activities.[117] A sporting student named Maria Iordache joined Nicolescu's fortress in 1934, and according to her, the women in the fortress met weekly, paid dues, provided aid to imprisoned legionaries and their families, visited legionary graves, went to church, and volunteered at the legionary canteen and restaurant on Gutenberg Street in the center of Bucharest.[118] Iordache was a particularly devout Christian, and she entered a convent at the end of World War II. Her own piety might explain why she puts more emphasis on religious activities than do most male accounts of nest meetings, but it is not unlikely that the members of her fortress did frequently go to church together.

In recognition of service to the Legion, Codreanu instituted ranks and honors for legionaries who distinguished themselves. He distributed the first awards on 10 December 1932, making ten legionaries commanders (*comandanţi*

114. "Cum se constituie o Cetăţue," *Garda de Fier* (Bessarabia), 1/3 (1 Apr 1933): 3.

115. Codreanu, *Cărticica*, 16.

116. Valentin Măcrineanu, "Femei şi fete romănce," *Pămăntul strămoşesc*, 4/2 (1932): 14; "Ordin către suroriile legiuni, fraţiile de cruce şi tinerii legionari cari nu vor putea veni la dig," *Garda Râmnicului*, 2/6 (1 July 1933): 3.

117. Săndulescu, "Revolutionizing Romania," 173.

118. ACNSAS, Fond Penal, dosar 000160, vol. 3, f. 199.

legionari).[119] This was an honorary position and did not give the holder authority over a particular number or group of legionaries. Over the next two years, more and more legionaries who had collected large numbers of donations, recruited new members, or distinguished themselves in battles with the police became assistant commanders (*comandanţi ajutori*), instructors (*instructori legionari*) or assistant instructors (*instructori ajutori*).[120] Codreanu also introduced medals to be given for specific achievements, such as electoral campaigning or running a restaurant. The 114 people who swore an oath to the Legion in November 1927 wore sacks around their necks filled with soil from medieval battlefields. People who donated sums of money to the movement during its first few years received a Green Cross. In 1931, White Crosses were awarded to legionaries who displayed "faith and courage" during the electoral campaign in Neamţ County, and by 1938 roughly three thousand legionaries had earned this medal. As of 1933, commanders and legionaries who had already received a White Cross could be given a Rosetta White Cross, again for having undertaken risks on behalf of the Legion. Legionaries who fought in the Spanish Civil War were awarded an insignia engraved with the word "Majadahonda," the name of the battlefield in Spain where Ion Moţa and Vasile Marin died in 1937. And seventeen legionaries who helped establish the first legionary restaurant at Carmen Sylva received the Order of Legionary Commerce for their efforts.[121] Medals and honorary ranks made serving the Legion similar to serving in the military, which also awarded ranks and medals. Moreover, it reinforced the importance of the movement as an organization that deserved one's allegiance rather than being simply a means to an end.

As the Legion's membership expanded rapidly, Codreanu began to differentiate between long-standing members and new adherents. In May 1935 he ordered that "all those who enlisted after the persecution [of 1933–1934] are not legionaries, but members. Someone can only become a legionary after three years of probation."[122] In another circular issued on the same day, he said, "Everyone who attends a [work] camp earns the right to be a legionary."[123] Later instructions showed that new members had to fulfill both requirements and be recommended by two legionaries before the organization recognized them as "legionaries."[124] Despite such qualifications, police circulars and reports from interrogations

---

119. Ibid., dosar 014005, vol. 11, f. 32.

120. ACNSAS, Fond Penal, dosar 000160, vol. 9, f. 7–17; ACNSAS, Fond Informativ, dosar 262478, vol. 1, f. 234; ACNSAS, Fond Penal, dosar 014005, vol. 1, f. 85.

121. ACNSAS, Fond Penal, dosar 011784, vol. 10, f. 97.

122. Codreanu, *Circulări*, 42.

123. Ibid., 47.

124. ACNSAS, Fond Penal, dosar 011784, vol. 19, f. 6.

never mention "probationary members." The only categories that police knew were "legionary" and "sympathizer," and belonging to either category could get you into trouble.

In order to indoctrinate new members, in May 1935 Codreanu sent students into rural areas with instructions to teach anyone they found "less prepared" than they were. He told them to humbly hold "schools of legionary education," on issues such as "dress, saluting, presentation, good manners, honesty, trust in victory, respect for those who sacrificed, misunderstandings between legionaries, how the enemy fights: slander, lies, bribery, machinations, etc."[125] County leaders provided basic instruction for rural nest leaders under their command and put them in touch with seasoned legionaries in nearby villages who could continue their training.[126] Two years later, Ion Victor Vojen established the first "School for Cadres and Legionary Instruction" in Bucharest. Initially this school was for nest leaders, but it was quickly expanded to include all new recruits and assistant nest leaders.[127] Legionaries learned about the purpose of nests and legionary doctrine and participated in common rituals such as collective singing and oath taking.[128] Schools in Bucharest met once a week, while those in rural areas gathered for a single training session that lasted three or four days.[129] In January 1938, Codreanu launched a new school, this time for "county prefects and mayors," whom he trained personally so that they would be ready for promotions when the Legion came to power. When setting out the conditions for enrolling in this school, he specified that "a future prefect must be married, be moral, and be financially stable, so that he is not tempted to enrich himself."[130]

Discipline and Punishment

Beyond participating in rituals and giving, legionaries also had to obey rules and conform to a certain code of behavior. Writing in the legionary magazine *Însemnări sociologice* in 1937, Ion Covrig Nonea saw discipline as "an effective means of self-improvement." Legionary discipline taught you to structure your life and to orient yourself towards a goal, Nonea argued, allowing you to "*live*

125. Codreanu, *Circulări*, 46–47.

126. ACNSAS, Fond Penal, dosar 011784, vol. 8, f. 68–70; ACNSAS, Fond Penal, dosar 014745, vol. 1, f. 22; Vasile Iovin, "Momente din viața legionară," in *Corneliu Zelea Codreanu*, ed. Stănescu, 140.

127. ACNSAS, Fond Informativ, dosar 160181, f. 277, 279; ACNSAS, Fond Penal, dosar 007215, vol. 2, f. 82; Codreanu, *Cărticica*, 26–27.

128. ACNSAS, Fond Informativ, dosar 160181, f. 422.

129. ACNSAS, Fond Penal, dosar 011784, vol. 8, f. 65–67, vol. 10, f. 131–132.

130. Ibid., dosar 011784, vol. 12, f. 116.

your ideals."[131] Codreanu approached discipline as a means more for punishing mistakes than for orienting lives, however, and his disciplinary actions fundamentally shaped the Legion's practice of discipline. Codreanu established a Serviciul Legionar de Judecată (Legionary Court) in May 1935, explaining, "I want to use it to educate all Legionaries to know [how] . . . to recognize their mistakes and pay for them by being punished."[132] Legionaries disciplined people for a wide range of offenses, and in a number of ways. At the Carmen Sylva camp in 1936, some legionaries were caught stealing clothing, money, and a bag. Codreanu ordered four other legionaries to beat them as an example of what happens to thieves and then had them thrown out of the camp. Some of the other students there were not satisfied with the severity of the beating, and they followed them out of the camp to give them another beating.[133] At the other end of the spectrum, legionaries who failed to turn up to meetings or were late for work projects were chastised publicly or punished with extra work duties.[134] Some of Codreanu's punishments appear to have been quite arbitrary, such as the three-month suspension of three legionaries for failing to notice that Mihail Stelescu was going to betray Codreanu, or the two-year suspension of a legionary who joined a committee that also had Jews on it.[135] "Discipline," wrote Codreanu, "is our enclosure, helping us conform to ethical norms or to a leader's will."[136]

Codreanu set high standards for his followers and frequently disciplined people who failed to live up to them. In September 1936, he ordered county leaders to do a thorough inspection of the legionaries under their command and to expel "weak" elements. "As few legionaries and as many friends as possible," Codreanu explained. His new goal was that "for every twenty requests to join, nineteen will be rejected and one accepted. The best one."[137] In July 1937 Codreanu dissolved the Legion in Bălți County because the nests there were not of a high enough standard.[138] Legionaries who were not trustworthy with the organization's money were swiftly dealt with. Ghenadie Bulat, who ran a legionary kiosk in Tighina, was expelled in July 1937 when his superiors discovered that he had been stealing from the cash register.[139] Codreanu was concerned not only with theft but also with "insufficient care, order, scrupulousness, and strictness with

131. Ion Covrig Nonea, "Sensul disciplinei legionare," *Însemnări sociologice*, 3/8 (1937): 21–23.

132. Codreanu, *Circulări*, 36.

133. ANIC, Fond MI-D, dosar 3/1936, f. 4–5.

134. Codreanu, *Circulări*, 38; ACNSAS, Fond Penal, dosar 011784, vol. 9, f. 247.

135. Codreanu, *Circulări*, 27, 125.

136. Codreanu, *Pentru legionari*, 301.

137. Codreanu, *Circulări*, 91.

138. ACNSAS, Fond Penal, dosar 011784, vol. 9, f. 193.

139. Roth Jelescu, *Și cerul plângea*, 143.

money that is not theirs."[140] By carelessness he meant ordering legionary publications without paying for them, or taking pamphlets and failing to either sell or return them.

Insubordination was also a problem. Gheorghe Ratoi was expelled for having an "attitude that repeatedly fails to conform with the legionary way of doing things," and Gheorghe Ioniță was suspended for two months for being "insolent" toward one of his leaders, who would not let him hit a Jew living near the legionary work camp they were at.[141] Failing to follow orders properly was another reason for discipline, as the legionaries in the village of Cudalbi (Covorlui County) discovered when General Cantacuzino dissolved their nests after they held a march during a period when Codreanu had forbidden marching.[142] Similarly, five legionaries threatened the National Peasantist politician Virgil Madgearu (1887–1940) after he closed a work camp they were attending. Codreanu had ordered that legionaries maintain peaceful relationships with the authorities that year, and he punished the camp leader, Ion Dobre (1906–1942), as well as the five guilty legionaries.[143] Disciplining leaders often had implications for their subordinates as well. In February 1936, Codreanu suspended Nicoleta Nicolescu for three months after she had a fight with two other leaders over whether they should hold a church service in a cemetery during a legionary funeral. Not only was Nicolescu punished, but all fortresses in the capital were dissolved for three months as well.[144]

Discipline was an effective means of demonstrating Codreanu's control over his subordinates, and the more arbitrary the punishments seemed, the more complete Codreanu's authority was. The legionary Grigore Manoilescu writes that Codreanu punished the editor of *Buna vestire*, Mihail Polihroniade, in 1937, by removing him from the newspaper and suspending him from his leadership position in the Legion. The next time that they saw each other, Codreanu asked Polihroniade, "Do you know why I punished you?" Polihroniade said that he did not. "Neither do I," replied Codreanu, "because you were not punished, just tested. I wanted to see how you would react to an injustice that came from the head of the Legion."[145] This policy permeated the entire legionary educational system—legionaries were expected to do something because they were told to,

140. Codreanu, *Circulări*, 105.

141. ACNSAS, Fond Penal, dosar 011784, vol. 9, f. 193, vol. 18, f. 125.

142. Ibid., dosar 011784, vol. 12, f. 224–225.

143. Ibid., dosar 011784, vol. 8, f. 159, 224–225, 227.

144. Ibid., dosar 011784, vol. 8, f. 356.

145. Grigore Manoilescu, "Un om din altă plămadă: Corneliu Codreanu," in *Corneliu Zelea Codreanu*, ed. Stănescu, 161–162.

not because it was the right thing to do. Discipline emphasized subordination to authority and taught legionaries to follow orders without questioning them. Virtues such as honesty, chivalry, sacrifice, and service were commanded, not cultivated, inside legionary schools, where subordination to Codreanu was paramount. Ion Moța wrote to a friend abroad who had heard about Mihail Stelescu's expulsion that "there is no intrigue inside our movement, we are all grouped in a single spiritual bloc around our Captain, ready to die for the Legion or to avenge it."[146]

The election campaign of 1933 may have been traumatic for legionaries, but it helped galvanize those who remained in the movement into becoming committed activists. The distinction that Codreanu and others made between those who joined the Legion before and after 1933 was not merely honorific. It distinguished those who had sacrificed and suffered for the Legion when it had little hope of success from those who joined a rapidly growing social movement on the ascendency. The "schools," rituals, and discipline introduced during the mid-1930s helped prepare newcomers for the next wave of violence and to establish the absolute authority of Codreanu against dissenters such as Mihail Stelescu and Istrate Micescu. State violence and imprisonment gave the legionaries much-needed publicity as determined opponents of corrupt politicians. It also solidified the bonds between legionaries and their leader. Suffering together as a group, legionaries learned to trust and rely on one another, and the more one suffered for the Legion, the more invested one became in it. When government persecution eased up after 1934, the movement's leaders either had to attract conflict, as they did at the Târgu Mureş conference and in battles with Stelescu's followers, or else find other ways to ensure the unquestioning loyalty of new legionaries. It is no coincidence that Codreanu's emphasis on hierarchy and discipline increased after 1934, or that the expectations placed on legionaries who joined during this time were so high. If government oppression was not going to test the loyalty of rank-and-file legionaries, Codreanu would have to do it himself.

---

146. Moța, *Corespondența cu Welt-Dienst*, 43.

5

THE POWER OF PRINT

In his book *Pentru legionari* (For my legionaries, 1935), Codreanu described the establishment of the newspaper *Pământul strămoşesc* in 1927 as the Legion's "first battle."[1] Whereas only those in Iaşi could hear lectures and participate in rituals at the Cămin Cultural Creştin, newspapers connected legionaries with a diffuse network of supporters around the country. They publicized legionary activities and promoted the movement's symbols and slogans. As legionaries began producing posters, pamphlets, postcards, and books, the writing process forced them to articulate their positions on a wide variety of issues. From 1932 onward, legionaries gave increasing importance to intellectuals and journalists who could write clearly about economics, art, literature, politics, violence, and European fascism. This meant not only the ascendency of intellectuals within the Legion but also a blurring of boundaries between legionary writers and ultranationalist publicists who were sympathetic to the legionary cause. Printing and distributing propaganda materials were also specialist occupations. In the early 1930s legionaries learned how to run printing presses, sold newspapers on the streets, and organized their own distribution networks using their own couriers and the Romanian postal service. Printed propaganda helped express what legionarism meant on an intellectual level, but it also made printing and distribution a common part of legionary everyday life.

1. Codreanu, *Pentru legionari*, 302.

Political Broadsheets

Despite the poverty of their movement's early years, legionaries made newspapers and propaganda pamphlets a priority. When a new law against political agitation landed fourteen legionaries and scores of sympathetic peasants in prison in autumn 1930, the Legion's first action was to launch *Garda de Fer* (The Iron Guard, Bucharest, 1930), an intermittent, single-sheet newspaper aimed at a Bucharest audience. It attacked the government and portrayed the Legion as a persecuted group of patriots.[2] At the same time legionaries in Galaţi began another newspaper, titled *Biruinţa* (The victory, 1930–1933). The editors of *Biruinţa* also said that they began their newspaper in reaction to the persecution of legionaries. When the second issue appeared during the Neamţ by-elections, *Biruinţa*'s tone became more militant, bitterly attacking Jews just as LANC publications had during the 1920s.[3] Elections were another reason to establish new newspapers. Just before the general elections of June 1931 Ion Moţa used his father's press to print a single issue of another newspaper, also called *Garda de Fier* (The Iron Guard, Oraştie, 1931). This was a broadsheet dedicated entirely to introducing potential voters to the "Corneliu Z. Codreanu Group."[4]

As soon as they were able, the legionaries acquired their own press, which they operated from the basement of their cămin in Iaşi. Dumitru Banea writes that in 1931, "we bought ourselves, on credit, a small hand-operated printing press, [and] we all set about learning the art of printing. We made ourselves business cards, but not knowing what titles to give ourselves we wrote things like 'Mitu Banea, musketeer [*muşchetar*].'"[5] The legionaries found the press through their connections in Focşani, where support for the Legion was relatively strong.[6] Most legionary pamphlets were printed here for the next few years, as were *Pământul strămoşesc* and *Garda Moldovei* (The guard of Moldavia, 1930–1933), the latter a newspaper aimed at peasants and workers living in and around Iaşi.[7] Perhaps because of the legionaries' printing press, the Cuzist Teodor Mociulschi, who was president of ASC in Iaşi, spent an enormous three hundred thousand lei of student contributions that year to buy his organization its own press.[8] The legionaries were proud of their press. When the ultranationalist publicist Nichifor Crainic (1889–1972) visited Iaşi in March 1932, they surrounded him after his lecture at the university

2. *Garda de Fer* (Bucharest), 1/1 (1 Sept 1930).
3. "Români!" *Biruinţa*, 1/1 (17 Oct 1930): 1; "Două note," *Biruinţa*, 2/2 (19 July 1931): 1.
4. *Garda de Fier* (Oraştie), 1/1 (20 May 1931).
5. Banea, *Acuzat*, 10.
6. ACNSAS, Fond Penal, dosar 011784, vol. 2, f. 99.
7. AN—Iaşi, Fond Chestura de Poliţie, dosar 52/1933, f. 50; ACNSAS, Fond Informativ, dosar 211932, vol. 2, f. 22, dosar 259143, vol. 1, f. 119.
8. ACNSAS, Fond Documentar, dosar 012694, vol. 3, f. 66.

and led him down the hill so that they could show it to him. Crainic gave another speech when they reached the cămin, praising the Legion and promising to support it through his Bucharest daily, *Calendarul* (The calendar, 1932–1933). But the Iron Guard was declared illegal on 26 March 1932 and a police raid forced *Calendarul* to temporarily cease publication.[9] The Legion was still allowed to function even if its paramilitary battalions had been outlawed, and legionaries staged public rallies in support of *Calendarul* that month. In June it became a legionary newspaper, employing legionaries as editors at Codreanu's request.[10]

Crainic was a well-known poet and a theologian, and *Calendarul* presented itself as a Christian newspaper that many priests subscribed to and supported.[11] The first issue, from 25 January 1932, addressed itself to a broad ultranationalist audience, announcing that the newspaper would be dedicated to exposing political and economic corruption.[12] *Pământul strămoşesc* was out of print at the time that Crainic transformed *Calendarul* into a legionary newspaper, although the press at the cămin continued to produce *Garda Moldovei*. In Galaţi *Biruinţa* appeared only intermittently, and in Brăila another newspaper called *Garda de Fer* (The Iron Guard, 1932) appears to have died a quick death.[13] *Calendarul* was thus a major coup for the Legion. Legionaries received much-needed press coverage, and *Calendarul* carried cultural elements that the Legion's political broadsheets had lacked, such as book and film reviews, women's columns, and celebrity gossip. Accurate circulation figures are not available, but it is clear that even while *Calendarul* never became one of the country's largest newspapers, it was certainly read by many people who were not members of Codreanu's Legion.[14] This was not a one-way partnership, and Crainic needed the legionaries just as much as

---

9. Heinen, *Legiunea "Arhanghelul Mihail,"* 199; Nichifor Crainic, "Reîncepem!" *Calendarul* (9 June 1932): 1.

10. ACNSAS, Fond Penal, dosar 013206, vol. 2, f. 346, 362, 364.

11. "Căminul Soc. Preotesc 'Renaştera' din Oltenia," *Calendarul* (20 Aug 1933): 1; "Manifestaţie religioasă dela Carpineni-Bucovina," *Calendarul* (2 Sept 1933): 3.

12. Nichifor Crainic, "Începem," *Calendarul* (25 Jan 1932): 1.

13. *Garda de Fer*, 1/1 (1 Jan 1932). Only one issue of the newspaper exists in the Biblioteca Centrală Universitară in Cluj-Napoca.

14. Crainic claims that "in only several months *Calendarul* had left *Cuvântul* and *Curentul* far behind, becoming the newspaper with the third largest print run in the country." Crainic, *Zile albe*, 232. Zigu Ornea disputes this, writing that *Calendarul* "could not go beyond 10,000 copies . . . [and] could not equal the performances of Şeicaru (*Curentul*) and Nae Ionescu (*Cuvântul*)." Zigu Ornea, *Anii treizeci: Extrema dreaptă românească* (Bucharest: Fundaţiei Culturale Române, 1995), 244. Neither man cites his sources. *Calendarul's* balance sheet from 12 February 1934 may give some clue about the reality. It records 492,510 lei in sales from Bucharest and 1,671,553.75 lei in sales from the provinces. The time period is unclear, but presumably refers to the financial year 1933. Assuming that *Calendarul* received 1.25 lei for every newspaper sold (the newstand price was 2 lei), this adds up to 1,732,251 copies—an average of 4,949 copies for each of the 350 days it was printed that year. "Raport de expertiză," 12 Feb 1934. ACNSAS, Fond Penal, dosar 013206, vol. 1, f. 34.

they needed him. *Calendarul* had had difficulties from the outset. Crainic priced it at two lei in order to undercut his rivals, who then banded together and convinced newspaper stands to refuse to sell it.[15] Crainic therefore needed legionaries to sell his newspaper on the streets of Bucharest, and he also sought help from LANC students in Iaşi.[16]

Crainic spent months convincing some of the younger editors and contributors at *Calendarul* to join the Legion, and several of them became the Legion's most prominent ideologues.[17] The importance of Crainic's patronage for young journalists can be seen in a letter written by Nicolae V. Iliescu to his parents on 1 December 1933. Iliescu apologized that he had not followed his uncle's wishes and joined LANC, but he explained:

> In Bucharest I was able to set my business in order: I have been entrusted with running the newspaper *Calendarul* in Ardeal, and especially in Cluj. For this I will be paid a fixed salary every month from the central office in Bucharest. . . . But luck has been even kinder to me: after I did a job for Dr. Zaharia Boilă on behalf of my boss from *Calendarul*, Mr. Nichifor Crainic, . . . this Mr. Boilă offered me a job in his newspaper [*România nouă*] as press secretary (this means a big responsibility—the second most important man after the director), which I accepted."[18]

Iliescu went on to explain that he owed his job with Zaharia Boilă (1892–1976)—one of Transylvania's most important publicists and a prominent member of Iuliu Maniu's National Peasant Party—to Crainic's recommendation and that now he could not abandon his legionary politics because his livelihood was irrevocably bound up with the Legion's success.

Almost all political parties in the 1930s distributed their own political broadsheets in the capital and most also had regional publications in their strongest counties. These newspapers carried speeches by party leaders, policy statements and manifestos, and slanderous attacks on political opponents. In 1934—the only year for which reliable statistics exist—the print runs of regional newspapers representing the major parties such as the National Liberal Party or the National Peasant Party ranged from one thousand to five thousand copies an

15. Nichifor Crainic, "Coaliţia zialelor împotriva ieftenirii vieţii," *Calendarul* (31 Jan 1932): 1.

16. ACNSAS, Fond Penal, dosar 013206, vol. 2, f. 343.

17. *Calendarul* writers who became legionaries in 1932–1933 thanks to Crainic's influence include Mihail Polihroniade, Dragoş Protopopescu, Ioan Victor Vojen, Nicolae V. Iliescu, and Nicolae Crevedia. Others, such as Toma Vlădescu, Al. Gregorian, Alexandru Cusin, and Gib. Mihaescu, remained convinced ultranationalists but avoided aligning themselves with the Legion. Crainic, *Zile albe*, 237; Heinen, *Legiunea "Arhanghelul Mihail,"* 169.

18. ACNSAS, Fond Penal, dosar 013206, vol. 3, f. 17–18.

issue, whereas smaller parties like LANC managed only between five hundred and fifteen hundred copies, depending on the county.[19] In autumn 1932 the Legion launched a regional press of its own, publishing such original titles as *Garda* (Brăila, 1932; Muscel, 1932–1933), *Garda Bucovinei* (Rădăuți, 1932–1933), *Garda Jiului* (Dolj, 1932–1933), *Garda Prahovei* (Ploiești, 1932–1933), and *Garda Râmnicului* (Râmnicul Sarat, 1932–1933). By February 1933 it could boast seventeen regional broadsheets.[20] Usually selling for only one leu, regional legionary broadsheets of the early 1930s reported on local gendarmes who were facing disciplinary action for assaulting legionaries during election campaigns, speeches made by local legionary leaders, new nests that were established, and rallies held in the vicinity. They also contained articles on legionary doctrine, photos of Codreanu, lyrics to legionary songs, and advertisements for *Calendarul*.

Intellectuals

Alongside *Pământul strămoșec* and *Calendarul*, the other major legionary periodical of 1932–1933 was known as *Axa* (The axis, 1932–1933, 1940–1941), which came out in print runs of between one thousand and two thousand copies.[21] *Axa* was launched in October 1932 by Mihail Polihroniade (1907–1939) and Ioan Victor Vojen, two journalists who had worked on *Calendarul* for most of that year. A student named Nicoleta Nicolescu (1911–1939) was responsible for distribution. Legionary couriers sent it to each of Bucharest's six districts and Nicolescu either mailed it to legionaries in the provinces or else transported it together with copies of the center-right newspaper *Universul*.[22] *Axa* was not originally a legionary newspaper and even had collaborators with left-wing and moderate sympathies—Eugen Ionescu (a playwright) and Octav Șuluțiu (a writer) wrote the newspaper's first literary columns. The decisive issue driving *Axa*, Nichifor Crainic explained in the opening editorial, was the desire for an "anti-democratic revolution." This revolution might be corporatist or communist, he said, but it should be corporatist because only the former "completely corresponds with the spirit of this people."[23] *Axa* grew out of the cultural circles of the "Criterionists" and the "Young Generation"—students and young intellectuals based in

19. ANIC, Fond Ministerul Propagandei Nationale, vol. 1, Presa internă, dosare 251/1934—280/1934, 295/1934—308/1934, 316/1934—318/1934.

20. Heinen, *Legiunea "Arhanghelul Mihail,"* 203.

21. Veiga, *Istoria Gărzii de Fier*, 159.

22. ACNSAS, Fond Informativ, dosar 160182, vol. 1, f. 426.

23. Nichifor Crainic, "Spre stângă sau spre dreaptă," *Axa*, 1/1 (20 Oct 1932): 1.

Bucharest who held lectures on controversial topics and saw themselves as the unaligned yet revolutionary vanguard of the Romanian intelligentsia.[24]

Valentin Săndulescu notes that whereas the contributors to *Axa* were originally most impressed with the idea of a stable, authoritarian state such as Fascist Italy, by March 1933, when *Axa* had fallen firmly under the influence of the Legion and included regular contributions from long-standing activists such as Ion Moța and Mihail Stelescu, the emphasis shifted to celebrating revolutionary movements such as Hitler's newly ascendant Nazi Party in Germany.[25] As a legionary newspaper with a literary focus, *Axa* published work by intellectuals such as the poet Radu Gyr, the painter George Zlotescu, the historian Vasile Cristescu, and the economist Alexandru Constant. In addition to being committed legionaries, all these men were accomplished in their respective fields and used *Axa* to speak about issues such as economics, politics, and literature, on which no official legionary policies existed. As Constantin Iordachi notes, *Axa* "systematized the Legion's ideas into a comprehensive ideology" for the first time, taking the hooliganism and hatreds of the 1920s and transforming them into an intellectually respectable worldview.[26]

Polihroniade and Vojen had both studied at the prestigious Spiru Haret High School in Bucharest together with Mircea Eliade (1907–1986), the acknowledged leader of the Young Generation, and under Crainic's influence first Polihroniade and then Vojen joined the Legion in December 1932.[27] In a confession from January 1934 Vojen told the police that he became interested in legionary politics after he returned from studying theater abroad and discovered that he could not work in the Romanian theater world because it was corrupted by political interest groups. "I realized," he said, "that a reform of the theater and of national art was impossible without a total reform of politics. Then I became involved in politics myself."[28] The intellectual circles that Polihroniade and Vojen belonged to embraced intellectuals with both left- and right-wing leanings, and once they joined the Legion these two men immediately began recruiting others for their cause. Intellectuals associated with the Young Generation often spoke of themselves as "spiritual youth" who were breathing new life into Romanian culture, and this rhetoric blended easily with the Legion's self-image as a youth movement

24. Săndulescu, "Revolutionizing Romania," 105–128; Vanhaelemeersch, *A Generation*, 252–274; Cristina Adriana Bejan, "The Criterion Association: Friendship, Culture, and Fascism in Interwar Bucharest" (PhD diss., University of Oxford, 2009).

25. Săndulescu, "Revolutionizing Romania," 127–128.

26. Iordachi, *Charisma*, 63.

27. ACNSAS, Fond Informativ, dosar 160181, f. 414–415.

28. Ibid., dosar 160182, vol. 1, f. 426.

with spiritual values.[29] Polihroniade and his wife held gatherings of intellectuals sympathetic to the Legion in their home, and within a couple of years they were joined by Mircea Eliade and his wife, Nina; the writer Haig Acterian and his wife, Marieta Sadova; the sociologist Mircea Vulcănescu; Petrişor Viforeanu; the philosophers Constantin Noica and Emil Cioran; and a veteran legionary named Ion Belgea, who worked at the library of the Romanian Academy.[30] Eliade and Vulcănescu were both protégés of the philosopher Nae Ionescu (1890–1940). After several months of negotiations Ionescu also became a supporter of Codreanu in late 1933 and influenced many of his students to get involved in right-wing politics. Ionescu preached a variation of existentialism he called *trăirism*, a philosophy of experience (understood as *Erlebnis*), or of "living in the moment." His lectures and his personality fascinated his students, who formed a cultlike following around him.[31] Some of these rising stars of Bucharest's intellectual and literary elite formally joined the Legion, while others contributed to legionary publications and praised the movement in the press.

The world of theater, art, and literature was not one that the Legion's early leaders were all familiar with. In the words of Francisco Veiga, these intellectuals had "an unequalled glamour, refinement, and chic. They brought the leadership of the Legion an intellectual sophistication and a big-city style, which contrasted with the provincial and sometimes coarse image that the movement had had up until 1931."[32] When Marieta Sadova (1897–1981)—a famous actress turned legionary—met Codreanu for the first time she was shocked to discover that he had never heard of her.[33] The participation of the Young Generation in the gatherings at the Polihroniade home and their published writings opened up a new social group to legionary politics, one that would prove to be particularly fruitful in terms of its contribution to written propaganda.

It also created tensions within the movement. One police report from 1934 stated that many of the Legion's early leaders resented the influence of the *Axa* journalists. They thought of the newcomers as "opportunistic intruders" and worried that this small group from Bucharest was taking control of the Legion.[34] Indeed, the abil-

---

29. Mircea Eliade, "Linii de orientare," *Cuvântul*, 3/857 (6 Sept 1927): 1; Sorin Pavel, Ion Nestor, and Petre Marcu-Balş, "Manifestul 'Crinului Alb,'" *Gândirea*, 8/8–9 (1928): 311–317; Mircea Vulcănescu, "Tânară generaţie": crize vechi în haine noi (Bucharest: Compania, 2004). Cf. Bejan, "The Criterion Association," 34–54.

30. ACNSAS, Fond Informativ, dosar 209489, vol. 2, f. 2–6.

31. Mircea Eliade, "Un cuvânt al editorului," in Nae Ionescu, *Roza vânturilor* (Bucharest: Roza Vânturilor, 1990), 421–444; Mihail Sebastian, *Cum am devenit hooligan* (Bucharest: Humanitas, 2006), 48–55; Ornea, *Anii treizeci*, 221–241.

32. Veiga, *Istoria Gărzii de Fier*, 160.

33. Mihail Sebastian, *Jurnal, 1935–1944* (Bucharest: Humanitas, 2005), 90.

34. Quoted in Săndulescu, "Revolutionizing Romania," 135.

ity of this literate elite to produce high-quality journalism and propaganda texts promoted them ahead of activists who had been members of the Legion for much longer and gave them a disproportionate influence over the Bucharest-based leadership. Legionary intellectuals proved ambivalent toward the notion of "intellectuals" as a social group, and they condemned philosophizing that was not accompanied by immediate political action.[35] When the young philosopher Emil Cioran (1911–1995) sent a copy of his book *Schimbarea la față a României* (The transfiguration of Romania, 1936) to Codreanu, the latter responded ambivalently by contrasting his own actions as a "fighter" with Cioran's efforts as a mere "writer."[36]

The government closed most of the Legion's periodicals and arrested many of its leaders after Duca's assassination in December 1933. Although the three assassins received life sentences, the other fifty arrested legionaries were released in April 1934. After prison, the legionaries quickly set about reviving their press and within a short time had established more newspapers than ever before.[37] Legionaries were sometimes forced to look beyond their own membership for money to finance these publications, and in November 1934 the president of UNSCR, a legionary named Traian Cotiga (1910–1939), began negotiations with both Stelian Popescu and Mihail Manoilescu for money to run *Cuvântul studențesc*. Neither Popescu nor Manoilescu was a legionary, and although both men were sympathetic, each had his own, nonlegionary, conditions for any money that might be forthcoming.[38]

A police report from 1935 described the most important of the Legion's new publications:

> *România creștină* [Christian Romania], in Chişinău, is the organization's propaganda organ for Bessarabia and has a print-run of 10,000 copies; *Brațul de fier* [The arm of iron, 1935–1937] in Focşani, is an unflinching defender of the Legionary spirit; *Glasul strămoşesc* [The ancestral voice, 1934–1935] appears in Iaşi [*sic*] and is the oldest phalanx carrying the Legionary creed; *Biruința legionară* [The legionary victory] appears in Brăila as the propaganda organ for that region and is funded from contributions and donations of local Legionaries; *Românul de mâine* [The Romanian of tomorrow], a magazine of Christian nationalist propaganda appearing in Bălți, in Bessarabia, since fall 1935.[39]

35. Nicolae Roşu, "Situația intelectualilor," *Axa*, 2/5 (Jan 1933): 1–2; Ioan Victor Vojen, "Parazitismul intelectualilor," *Axa*, 2/9 (19 Mar 1933): 2; Ernest Bernea, *Tineretul și politică* (Bucharest: Rânduiala, 1936), 26.

36. Joanne Roberts, "The City of Bucharest, 1918–1940" (PhD diss., University College London, 2009), 73.

37. Heinen, *Legiunea "Arhanghelul Mihail,"* 263.

38. ACNSAS, Fond Documentar, dosar 012694, vol. 3, f. 60.

39. Scurtu ed., *Ideologie*, vol. 4, 151.

The variety and number of legionary newspapers is one indication of just how many people were writing legionary news and ideology by the mid-1930s. Far from being the exclusive domain of a handful of leaders, the Legion's written corpus was produced by individuals with diverse perspectives and interests. Each publication catered specifically to the needs of its readers. *Glasul strămoșesc*, for example, spoke to an urban audience in Cluj, where it was printed, and carried a regular women's column as well as news about student politics within the university. *Brațul de Fier*, on the other hand, was a more general publication suitable to a middle-class audience in Focșani, who could read about legionary ideology and national politics in its pages. Smaller local newspapers, such as *Buletinul legionar* (The legionary bulletin, 1937–1938) in Buzău printed mostly circulars from Codreanu and reprints of articles from more important newspapers, as well as announcements about local meetings and activities.[40] Finally, legionary magazines such as *Orientări* (Orientations, 1931–1938), which was published in Moinești in Bacău County, carried almost exclusively long ideological articles and short reviews of books and magazines. Most legionary periodicals were subject to censorship. Every issue of *Glasul strămoșesc* had blank spaces where articles had been censored, and *Brațul de fier* wrote in 1935 that "the pages of *Cuvântul studențesc* appear empty, empty—and as clean as our hearts, purified like this country will soon be."[41] The police became so accustomed to confiscating prohibited legionary newspapers that occasionally they even confiscated publications from vendors that had been approved by the censors.[42] Not all these newspapers were officially legionary publications. When a group of legionaries in Brăila asked permission to launch a newspaper in January 1935, Codreanu gave his permission on the conditions that they did not use "the name of the Archangel" and that they immediately resign from the Legion. He had ordered a temporary pause in publishing and thought that the Brăila initiative ignored these orders.[43]

As they appeared less frequently, carried longer articles, and were written by more prestigious figures, magazines were a popular medium for printing ideological articles. *Însemnări sociologice* (Sociological notes, 1935–1941), for example, blended sociological writings with legionary propaganda. It was run by a professor of ethics, sociology, and political science at the University of Cernăuți, Traian Brăileanu (1882–1947), who had been involved in LANC in the early 1920s before joining the Legion in 1930.[44] Brăileanu's pre-legionary writings called the

40. Costea, *Presa legionară*, 26–38.

41. "Polemici, știri, și poșta noastră," *Brațul de fier*, 1/2 (1 July 1935): 4.

42. AN—Iași, Fond Chestura de Poliție, dosar 8/1938, f. 312

43. Codreanu, *Circulări*, 33–34.

44. Heinen, *Legiunea "Arhanghelul Mihail,"* 116, 168.

nation a "moral community," by which he meant that the political organization of a state must flow out of family organization and local circumstances. Brăileanu argued in favor of a strong leader who could shape and defend the nation because of his absolute hold on power.[45] During the 1930s he created a circle of young Bucovinian intellectuals around *Însemnări sociologice* and promoted the Legion through lectures, dances, and cultural evenings.[46]

Brăilescu was not the only sociologist who contributed significantly to printed legionary propaganda. Several legionaries took part in the famous monographic teams organized by Dimitrie Gusti (1880–1955), who sent out small groups of students to survey village life and compile detailed reports on peasant customs and lifestyles in specific areas.[47] One of Gusti's students, the legionary Dimitrie Bejan (1909–1995), spent five years in Bessarabia, after which he wrote a detailed account of his research experiences, hoping to demonstrate that Bessarabia was culturally and socially a Romanian territory.[48] Another of Gusti's protégées, Traian Herseni (1907–1980), also became a legionary in 1936. Like Haig Acterian and Ion Victor Vojen, Herseni had embraced left-wing politics during the early 1930s and quarreled with other legionary sociologists over methodological approaches in their discipline.[49] A prominent sociologist in his own right, he decided to join the Legion after being refused a job at the University of Cluj because—he believed—he did not have the proper political connections and had declined to join the National Liberal Party. According to a declaration he wrote in July 1944, Herseni chose the Legion because "it seemed to be the most revolutionary political group at the time," and he wanted to "protest against the political parties, the state authorities, and the Romanian university."[50]

Other young sociologists, including Ion I. Ionică (1907–1944), Dumitru Cristian Amzăr (1906–1999), Ernest Bernea (1905–1990), and Ion Samarineanu, were all active legionaries during the 1930s. They also set out to create their own current within Romanian sociology through the journal *Rânduiala* (Order, 1935, 1937–1938).[51] Influenced by both Marcel Mauss and Dimitrie Gusti but coming

45. Traian Brăileanu, *Politica* (Bucharest: Albatros, 2003).

46. Scurtu ed., *Ideologie*, vol. 4, 165; Lauric Filon, in *Ţara, Legiunea, Căpitanul*, ed. Conovici, Iliescu, and Silvestru, 37–38. On Gusti, see Mircea Vulcăncescu, *Şcoala sociologica a lui Dimitrie Gusti* (Bucharest: Editura Eminescu, 1998); Antonio Momoc, *Capcanele politice ale sociologiei interbelice* (Bucharest: Curtea Veche, 2012).

47. Many of these studies were published in *Sociologie românească* (Romanian sociology, 1936–1942).

48. Dimitrie Bejan, *Hotarul cu cetăţi* (Bucharest: Editura Tehnica, 1995).

49. Momoc, *Capcanele politice*, 270–275.

50. ACNSAS, Fond Informativ, dosar163318, vol. 2, f. 99–105.

51. The other members of the "*Rânduiala* circle" were Nicolae Brânzău, Ion Conea, Mac Constantinescu, Ion Creangă, Nicolae Crişan, Constantin Floru, Eugen I. Ionică, Mihail Orleanu, Valeriu Papahagi, Victor I. Rădulescu-Pogoneanu, Emil Turdeanu, and Haralambie Ungureanu.

increasingly to see the ultranationalist philosopher Nae Ionescu as their intellectual mentor, these graduate students examined regional trends rather than doing village-level studies.[52] Feeling stifled by their elders, they distanced themselves from Gusti's Romanian Sociological Institute but had few strong criticisms to make of its approach.[53] Their research focused heavily on peasant ritual, folklore, art, and religion, which they argued was intimately related to how peasants worked the land and organized their lives.[54] Early editions of *Rânduiala* chronicled and discussed Romanian peasant culture. Describing the magazine as an "archive," the editors printed "research on Romanian life and thought of the past and the present; . . . [and] reflections on people and places where our the spirit of our lives is embodied in images and icons as an enduring recognition and guide for future generations."[55] The content of the magazine changed when it began printing explicit legionary articles in 1937, but it still maintained a mostly academic tone and discussed issues of general interest to sociologists as well as to legionaries.

According to Dan Dungaciu, Ionică joined the Legion out of a sense of obligation after his brother—also a legionary—was shot.[56] Perhaps because the Legion was not their primary commitment, Ionică and Samarineanu wrote little legionary propaganda. Amzăr produced only one short booklet and several articles supporting Romanian ultranationalism, but Ernest Bernea was a prolific legionary publicist.[57] Bernea worked with both Dimitrie Gusti and Nae Ionescu before joining the Legion and establishing *Rânduiala* in 1935.[58] His legionary writings located Codreanu within a long tradition of brave Romanian leaders, emphasized the importance of young people for effective social change, and claimed that the

52. Calin Cotoi, "The Imagining of National Spaces in Interwar Romania: Nationalist Regionalism and Ethnology," in *New Europe College Yearbook 2006–2007*, ed. Vlad Russo (Bucharest: New Europe College, 2008), 129–156.

53. Ernest Bernea's critique of Gusti, Stahl, and Herseni failed to identify any strong methodological disagreements with the Gustian school and focused instead on "emphases." Ernest Bernea, "Monografia sociologică," *Rânduiala*, 1/1 (Jan–Mar 1935): 60–71. Cf. Momoc, *Capcanele politice*, 216–220.

54. Ion I. Ionică, *Dealul Mohului: Cermonia agrară în cununii în ţară Oltului* (Bucharest: Minerva, 1996), 6. Cf. Ion I. Ionică, *Manifestările spirituale în cercetarea sociologică* (Bucharest: n.p., 1940); Dumitru Cristian Amzăr, *Rânduiala* (Bucharest: România Press, 2006); Ernest Bernea, *Sociologie şi etnografie româneasca: Ordinea spirituală* (Bucharest: Vremea, 2009).

55. "O arhivă de gând şi faptă românească," *Rânduiala*, 1/1 (Jan–Mar 1935): 3–4.

56. Dan Dungaciu, *Elita interbelică: Sociologie românească în context european* (Bucharest: Mica Valahie, 2003), 40.

57. Dumitru Cristian Amzăr, *Naţionalismul tineretului* (Bucharest: Rânduiala, 1936). For an analysis of Amzăr's legionary writings, see Momoc, *Capcanele politice*, 249–261.

58. ACNSAS, Fond Informativ, dosar 15702, vol. 1, f. 1–2, 11, 101; Manuela Gheorghe, "Bernea, Ernest," in *Dicţionar de sociologie rurală*, ed. Ilie Bădescu and Ozana Cucu-Oancea (Bucharest: Editura Mica Valahie, 2004), 50–54.

Legion was an organic product of Romanian history and culture.[59] Using their journals as a pretext for running printing presses, Brăileanu, Bernea, and the others published and distributed numerous legionary pamphlets and booklets through *Rânduiala* and *Însemnări sociologice*. In doing so they spread legionary culture within their own academic circles as well as producing printed materials that were used by legionary propagandists throughout the country.

Although academics did join the Legion, they rarely created a "legionary" approach to their subjects in the way that Marxist or neoliberal scholars have. One example of how far legionary scholars were from pioneering a "legionary history" is the historian Petre P. Panaitescu (1900–1967), who contributed to *Rânduiala* and *Însemnări sociologice* and was a regular speaker at legionary events. Panaitescu joined the PNŢ in 1926 and the National Liberal Party in 1930 and—depending on which police report one reads—became a legionary sympathizer at some stage between 1933 and 1936. Panaitescu officially joined the Legion in November 1937 and immediately attached himself to a nest of intellectuals, publishing in legionary newspapers and working together with Nae Ionescu and others to promote the Legion within academic circles. His true reasons for joining will probably never be known, but several police informers suggested that Panaitescu joined on the urging of his wife, Silvia, a painter, who pointed out that all the bright young historians of his generation had begun promising political careers and told him to join the Legion so that he could "do something important as well."[60] He was part of a circle of young historians grouped around *Revista istorică română* (Journal of Romanian history, 1931–1947) who, rejecting the Romanian historiography dominated by Nicolae Iorga, hoped to bring a new level of professionalism to Romanian history writing, exploring social, economic, and cultural aspects of the past instead of writing straightforward nationalist narratives as earlier Romanian historians had done.[61] For Panaitescu, academic rigor, not ultranationalist politics, mattered when he wrote history.

During the mid-1930s the contributions of the former "Axa" group were represented by *Ideea românească* (The Romanian idea, 1935–1936). This magazine was edited by Pavel Costin Deleanu, who had worked under Nae Ionescu at *Cuvântul* and had been one of the directors of *Axa* in 1933.[62] Deleanu presented ultranationalism as the logical conclusion of the Young Generation's evolution, which he said had passed through a spiritual, Orthodox phase in 1922–1923, followed by the discovery of "experientialism" (*trăirism*) under Nae Ionescu

59. Ernest Bernea, *Cartea Căpitanilor* (Bucharest: Serviciul Propagandei Scrise, 1940); Ernest Bernea, *Tineretul şi politică*; Ernest Bernea, *Stil legionar* (Bucharest: Serviciul Propagandei Legionare, 1940).

60. ACNSAS, Fond Informativ, dosar 234303, vol. 1, f. 2, 74, vol. 2, f. 164–165.

61. Alexandru Zub, *Istorie şi istorici în România interbelică* (Iaşi: Junimea, 2003), 222–230.

62. Fond Informativ, dosar 234303, vol. 2, f. 328.

from 1926 to 1930, before embracing ultranationalism from 1930 onward.[63] *Ideea românească* explored questions that the Young Generation were interested in—such as Orthodoxy, mysticism, art, literature, philosophy, and culture—but presented them in a light that resonated with the legionary worldview. Although left-wing writers such as Eugen Ionescu (1909–1994) also contributed to the magazine, it was a far cry from the broad cosmopolitanism that had characterized the Young Generation in 1932.[64]

In Cluj, legionary literature and culture was represented in *Revista mea* (My magazine, 1935–1937), edited by Marta Rădulescu (1912–1959), who was a writer of short stories and comic novels and the daughter of Dan Rădulescu (1884–1969), a professor of chemistry at the University of Cluj.[65] Rădulescu advertised her magazine as being full of "the clearest and most readable literature, honest reviews, [and] social and literary journalism, . . . [as well as essays on] sociology, economics, psychology, science, etc."[66] But she made her legionary sympathies clear from the opening article, which blamed a Jewish conspiracy for the fact that her most recent novels had been rejected by the Adevărul publishing house—according to Rădulescu, because of her father's support for the Legion.[67] *Revista mea* maintained its literary focus, including frequent contributions from legionaries such as Ion Banea, Ion Moța, and Emil Cioran. The magazine also printed frequent reflections on the relationship between ultranationalism and culture, asserting that good art "must be nationalist art."[68]

With encouragement from Traian Brăileanu, a group of young writers and poets from Cernăuți led by Mircea Streinul (1910–1945) and Iulian Vesper (1908–1986) decided "to imprint an accelerated rhythm onto the literary movement of the young generation," through the literary magazine *Iconar* (Iconographer, 1935–1938).[69] They also shared legionary sympathies and in the words of the National Liberal politician Ion Nistor (1876–1962), they used the magazine "to develop a lively national[ist] propaganda clothed in literary form."[70] In an interview for *Iconar* in 1936 the legionary poet Radu Gyr answered the question

63. Pavel Costin Deleanu, "Clipă de față a tineretului românesc," *Ideea românească*, 1/2–4 (June–Aug 1935): 92–94.

64. On the Criterion symposium, which was the clearest expression of this generation's early cosmopolitanism, see Bejan, "The Criterion Association," 67–160.

65. Mariana Vartic, "Rădulescu, Marta D.," in *Dicționarul scriitorilor români: R–Z*, ed. Mircea Zaciu, Marian Papahagi, and Aurel Sasu (Bucharest: Editura Albatros, 2002), 32–33.

66. "De vorbă cu d-ra Marta Rădulescu," *Glasul strămoșesc*, 2/3 (20 Jan 1935): 3.

67. Săndulescu, "Revolutionizing Romania," 178.

68. Traian Brăileanu, "Arta pentru artă," *Revista mea*, 1/7–8 (1936), quoted in Ornea, *Anii treizeci*, 423–424.

69. Mircea A. Diaconu, *Mișcarea "Iconar": Literatură și politică în Bucovina anilor '30* (Iași: Editura Timpul, 1999), 44.

70. Ion Nistor, quoted in ibid., 71.

"Can poetry serve a political idea?" by declaring, "Serve an idea, no! Politicianism is synonymous with a quagmire, vermin, putrification. . . . [But] in the service of the national idea, in the service of a new, productive ethnic soul, *yes*! In the service of legionarism, which is itself as pure as a ballad that melts into our historic national destiny."[71] *Iconar* published legionary poetry, recollections, and ideology, and its reviews of books, music, and magazines celebrated ultranationalist themes. Speaking about "national rebirth" and the seeking to introduce fresh ideas into Romanian culture, the editors of *Iconar* pushed this legionary publication to the forefront of Bucovina's literary scene.

An Antimodern Revolt?

When intellectuals joined the Legion they brought with them debates about Romanian society that had troubled Romanian writers since the mid-nineteenth century. Scholars writing under the influence of the modernization theories of the 1960s and 1970s argue that legionary intellectuals were rejecting "modernity," by which they mean the technological, institutionalized, rational, secular world of Western Europe.[72] Radu Florian, for example, argues that at the heart of the Legion's program lay "the preservation of the traditionalism of rural civilization, of its spirituality, the sole channel of Romanianness, which cannot exist in a modern capitalist society."[73] Some legionaries, mostly Bucharest intellectuals influenced by Nae Ionescu, did express such views. The writer Arşavir Acterian (1907–1997) wrote in *Ideea româneasca* in 1935 that "the city does not characterize Romania. There has never been an urban style that was quintessentially Romanian. The city represents our efforts at civilizing, Westernizing, modernizing. The city is borrowed, influenced, compromised."[74] Two years later the essayist Dan Botta (1907–1958) argued against educating Romanian peasants because "ignorance . . . guarantees a mysticism of wisdom, power and victory."[75] Legionary intellectuals criticized anything that they thought threatened the "organic"

71. Radu Gyr in *Iconar*, 1/7 (1936): 4, quoted in Ornea, *Anii treizeci*, 425.

72. Andrew C. Janos, "Modernization and Decay in Historical Perspective: The Case of Romania," in *Social Change in Romania, 1860–1940: A Debate on Development in a European Nation*, ed. Kenneth Jowitt (Berkeley: Institute of International Studies, University of California, 1978), 74.

73. Radu Florian, "Ideologia fascistă—o expresie a crizelor civilizației moderne," in *Ideea care ucide: Dimensiunile ideologiei legionare*, ed. Insitutul de Teorie Socială al Academiei Române (Bucharest: Editura Noua Alternativă, 1994), 30.

74. Arşavir Acterian, "Gânduri în 'luna Bucureştilor' şi despre urbanistică româneasca," *Ideea româneasca*, 1/2–4 (June–Aug 1935): 136.

75. Dan Botta, "Țara analfabetă," *Buna vestire*, 1/7 (28 Feb 1937): 1.

unity of the nation.[76] Nichifor Crainic, one of the pioneers of this way of thinking in Romania, argued in 1929 that "traditionalism desires a culture created with autochthonous values."[77] According to Crainic's logic, peasants most truly represented the nation and therefore they had to form the basis of the ideal fascist state.[78] Any political development that ruptured the "natural" development of the nation was suspect. Thus Nicolae Roşu condemned the revolutionaries of 1848 because "they went from the outside in: they studied abroad, they did not know the historical conditions [of Romania] and knew nothing of ethnic autochthony."[79] For his part, Vasile Marin rejected democracy because it "falsified the historic sense of this nation."[80] As the patron of these legionary intellectuals, Nae Ionescu pointed out that what mattered most was not the peasants themselves, but their "mentality," which he summarized as realistic, concrete, and spiritual.[81] His disciple, Mircea Vulcănescu (1904–1952), described this intellectual program as "expressing this Romanian spirit in universal forms."[82] This meant that legionaries could effectively ignore real peasants while still building a nation-state based on imagined peasant values.

The anti-Enlightenment writings of this group are an example of what Jeffrey Herf calls "reactionary modernism," an intellectual current widespread in interwar Europe that "turned the romantic anti-capitalism of the German Right away from backward-looking pastoralism, pointing instead to the outlines of a beautiful new order replacing the formless chaos due to capitalism in a united, technologically advanced nation."[83] Reactionary modernists romanticized the peasantry while still embracing technology and rationality. Codreanu's wedding in 1925 illustrates how legionaries imagined the peasantry: He rode a horse from the town to the wedding site, while his bride followed in a cart drawn by six oxen. Both wore peasant costumes.[84] Prince Ferdinand and his wife had also used ox-drawn carriages in 1893 when they acted as godparents to thirty-two couples in

76. On organicist metaphors in European nationalism, see Pheng Cheah, *Spectral Nationality: Passages of Freedom from Kant to Postcolonial Literatures of Liberation* (New York: Columbia University Press, 2003), 17–60.

77. Nichifor Crainic, "Sensul tradiţiei," *Gândirea*, 9/1–2 (1929): 2.

78. Angela Harre, *Wege in die Moderne: Entwicklungsstrategien rumänischer Ökonomen im 19. und 20. Jahrhundert* (Wiesbaden: Harrassowitz, 2009), 167–185.

79. Nicolae Roşu, "Democraţie şi cultură," 1936, quoted in Ornea, *Anii treizeci*, 29.

80. V. Marin, *Crez de generaţie*, 49.

81. Vanhaelemeersch, *A Generation*, 225–228.

82. Mircea Vulănescu, "Generaţie," *Criterion* (1934): 6, quoted in Marta Petreu, *De la Junimea la Noica: Studii de cultură românească* (Iaşi: Polirom, 2011), 256.

83. Jeffrey Herf, *Reactionary Modernism: Technology, Culture, and Politics in Weimar and the Third Reich* (Cambridge, UK: Cambridge University Press, 1984), 3.

84. Codreanu, *Pentru legionari*, 236.

Bucharest.[85] Neither couple was actually pretending to be peasants. The royal nuptials took place in the middle of the capital city and Codreanu filmed his wedding, whose guests arrived by cars and trains. Codreanu welcomed the material and technological achievements of the modern era while reminding onlookers that he also cherished peasant customs. When legionaries promoted "tradition," it was one that had been carefully molded for a twentieth-century nation-state. What worried Codreanu was not telephones, automobiles, or literacy, but the idea that Jews were dominating Romania because they were the ones who controlled access to technology and education.[86] Instead of seeing Romanians as active participants in the creation of their own culture, Codreanu maintained that foreigners had imported the institutions, ideas, and technology of modern Romania. His rural utopia had been invented by a group of intellectuals led by Nicolae Iorga in the 1890s. Iorga's "Sămănătorists" (Sowerists) cultivated an anti-liberal nationalism by promoting folk values in art and arguing against the free circulation of foreign literature and the recognition of foreign degrees.[87] They also romanticized the peasantry, nostalgically hoping to return to an imagined age before Romania was "corrupted" by capitalism, industrialization, and other foreign imports.[88]

Despite their intellectual fame, Sămănătorist rhetoric had little impact on everyday legionary practices. We see a glimpse of how rank-and-file legionaries experienced "modernity" if we compare cooking recipes recommended in two publications from the 1930s, one a mainstream peasant magazine and the other a fascist newspaper. *Femeia satelor* (The village woman, 1935) was a nonpartisan magazine aimed at rural housewives. It suggested traditional peasant dishes such as dill soup (*ciorbă de mărar*), lamb *borş*, and custard (*lapte de pasăre*).[89] In contrast, the recipes in Nae Ionescu's *Cuvântul* (The word, 1924–1933, 1938, 1940–41), a fascist daily newspaper that was very popular among legionaries, used less traditional ingredients and reflected French cuisine more than traditional Romanian cooking. A recipe for peas and rice called *rizi-bizi*, for example, recommended using canned peas, which were not part of a traditional rural diet.[90] Other recipes included orange jelly (*gelatin de portocale*), fried brains with dressing, and goose liver with aspic.[91] Cooking was presented as a "living art, which evolves, transforms and adapts" and that must be learned anew when new ideas

85. Regina României Maria, *Povestea vieţii mele*, vol. 2 (Iaşi: Editura Moldova, 1991), 21.
86. Codreanu, *Pentru legionari*, 285.
87. Zigu Ornea, *Sămănătorismul* (Bucharest: Editura Minerva, 1971), 167–188.
88. Ibid., 128–164.
89. *Femeia satelor* (1935), issues 1/2, 1/3–4, and 1/5.
90. M. M. L., "Poftiţi la masă!" *Cuvântul* (30 Jan 1938).
91. M. M. L., "Poftiţi la masă!" in various issues of *Cuvântul* (1938).

appear.[92] *Cuvântul* introduced women to recent European fashions and beauty treatments while maintaining a strict code of modesty in what it suggested.[93] Instead of encouraging that one manicure one's hands, which makes them useless for practical work, the newspaper instructed women to use polenta and lemon peel to produce healthy nails and skin.[94] Beauty, according to *Cuvântul*, must be practical, aesthetic, and moral.[95] Whereas articles in *Femeia satelor* taught peasant women to dust their homes, *Cuvântul* assumed that urban lodgings were clean, and it showed girls how to profit socially from good presentation.[96] Rather than rejecting modern culture outright, *Cuvântul* tried to control it, teaching legionaries how to adapt to contemporary conditions without offending old-fashioned morality.

If legionaries were not trying to turn back the clock, were they nonetheless revolting against the culture of their era? Modernism was a literary and artistic movement that swept Europe between 1890 and 1930, and a number of modernists found themselves drawn to fascist politics. In the words of George Mosse, "Both fascism and expressionism share the urge to recapture the 'whole man' who seemed atomized and alienated by society, and both attempt to reassert individuality by looking inwards, towards instinct or the soul, rather than outwards to a solution in those positivist, pragmatic terms which bourgeois society prized."[97] Modernism was a passionate reaction against the increasingly rationalist and mechanistic nature of European society in the early twentieth century. By the late nineteenth century German philosophy had demonstrated the limits of rationalism, and writers such as Friedrich Nietzsche were arguing that reason, morality, and European hierarchies of power, all of which had been tied to Christian notions of God, were dead.[98] As the idea of the rational God of the early nineteenth century became less and less convincing, modernists became increasingly frustrated with people who continued to follow outdated moral and social codes. Extending further Nietzsche's metaphor of the death of God, modernism can be seen as a revolt against widespread apathy in the face of the death of God and an attempt to imagine a new world with creative possibilities.[99] Modernist

92. M. M. L., "Feluri noi," *Cuvântul* (3 Feb 1938).

93. M. M. L., "Pălăriile de seară," *Cuvântul* (23 Jan 1938); M. M. L., "Moda: Efecte cromatice," *Cuvântul* (2 Feb 1938); M. M. L., "Tinereţe fără bântrâneţe," *Cuvântul* (2 Mar 1938).

94. M. M. L., "Cum să ne îngrijim mâinile?" *Cuvântul* (29 Jan 1938).

95. Trandafir Lucia, "Legionara şi disciplina," *Cuvântul* (16 Nov 1940).

96. Maria Pârvulescu, "Ordinea şi curăţenia," *Femeia satelor* 1/2 (1935): 16; M. L. M., "Despre politeţa şi buna cuviinţă," *Cuvântul* (1 Jan 1938).

97. Mosse, "Introduction," 15.

98. Friedrich Nietzsche, *On the Genealogy of Morals*, trans. Douglas Smith (Oxford: Oxford University Press, 1996) III.24, p. 127.

99. Roland Clark, "Lev Shestov and the Crisis of Modernity," *Archaevs*, 11–12 (2007–2008): 240.

writers, poets, and artists celebrated chaos, violence, mysticism, and nihilism as they struggled to find freedom and meaning in a world whose forms and values they found shallow, hypocritical, and oppressive.[100] Seeking a political expression of their philosophical and artistic ideas, some modernists turned to fascism because it celebrated power, irrationality, and the promise to create a new, utopian order.[101]

Legionary intellectuals were no exception. In his cultural periodical, *Gândirea* (Thought, 1923–1944), Nichifor Crainic combined literary and artistic modernism with an antidemocratic, racist, and authoritarian agenda.[102] In 1933, when he was most closely associated with the Legion, Crainic wrote that "our era is the era of the youth. An old world is collapsing, a new one seeks its form. Its pulse seethes in the arteries of the youth. A pulse quickened by disquiet, bated by insecurity, lashed by enigmas. . . . Fascist Italy and Soviet Russia have bound their destinies to the young generation. Germany depends on its youth for victory."[103] When he argued for the "transfiguration of Romania" through revolution and war, Emil Cioran wrote that "the affirmation of a historically young people must take the form of barbarism on the outside, but the explosion of energy that flows out of it hides the seed of an idea, the passion of spiritual individualization."[104] In 1937 Mircea Eliade spoke of a "war between two worlds: on one hand the old world that believed in its stomach (in the primacy of economics and politicianism), and on the other the new world, which dares to believe in Spirit (in the primacy of the spiritual)." He identified this new world with Codreanu's "new man," who according to Eliade rejected individualism for the collective, the nation, and Eastern Orthodox Christianity.[105]

Roger Griffin has made the influential argument that fascism was simply an expression of a modernist "matrix" involving "the search for transcendence and regeneration, whether confined to a personal quest for ephemeral moments of enlightenment or expanded to take the form of a cultural, social, or political movement for the renewal of the nation or the whole of Western civilization."[106]

---

100. Malcolm Bradbury and James McFarlane eds., *Modernism, 1890–1930* (Harmondsworth: Penguin, 1976); Catriona Kelly ed., *Russian Literature, Modernism, and the Visual Arts* (New York: Cambridge University Press, 2000).

101. Antliff, *Avant-Garde Fascism*; Ruth Ben-Ghiat, *Fascist Modernities in Italy, 1922–1945* (Berkeley: University of California Press, 2001); Emilio Gentile, *The Struggle for Modernity: Nationalism, Futurism, and Fascism* (Westport, CT: Praeger, 2003).

102. Irina Livezeanu, "After the Great Union: Generational Tensions, Intellectuals, Modernism, and Ethnicity in Interwar Romania," in *Nation and National Ideology: Past, Present and Prospects*, ed. Irina Vainovski-Mihai (Bucharest: New Europe College, 2002), 110–127.

103. Nichifor Crainic, "Tinereul şi creştinismul," *Gândirea*, 13/3 (1933): 65.

104. Emil Cioran, *Schimbarea la faţă a României* (Bucharest: Humanitas, 1990), 58.

105. Mircea Eliade, "Revoluţie creştină," *Buna vestire*, 1/100 (27 June 1937): 3.

106. Griffin, *Modernism and Fascism*, 39.

How many people embraced modernism in the interwar period? Griffin admits that "until 1914 . . . [modernists] were vastly outnumbered by millions of apparently ontologically secure human beings, who . . . heard no trumpets summoning them on a 'truly awesome journey' whose destination could only be designated as 'away from here.'"[107] Modernism was an elite, and elitist, movement that was primarily limited to writers, poets, and artists with sophisticated philosophical educations. But World War I may have changed this. War intensified a process that George Mosse has termed "the nationalization of the masses," meaning the increased acceptance of and identification with the symbols and rhetoric of nation-states.[108] In other words, mobilization for total war allowed Germans to think of themselves as members of a national community rather than as subjects of the kaiser.[109] Moreover, as the war progressed Europeans began talking about the war as a "purifying" moment, when old structures were being swept away and a new world created.[110] War gave a sense of urgency to modernist writers and artists in particular, who struggled to come to terms with the carnage and chaos around them.[111]

Griffin argues that the war transformed "modernist" impulses toward communal regeneration already found in movements such as theosophy, socialism, and the life reform movement (*Lebensreform*) in Switzerland into popular visions of national regeneration, or palingenesis.[112] Modernist intellectuals now suddenly "recognized" fascism as the political equivalent of their earlier cultural projects.[113] This chronology was quite different in Romania. Here the transition from antisemitism to ultranationalism and eventually to fascism was a slow, evolutionary process. Nineteenth-century antisemites and twentieth-century ultranationalists sought to impose the authority of ethnic Romanians within a Romanian nation-state. Despite the country's suffering an unusually high death toll, World War I was not transformative for Romania in the same ways that it changed Germany or England. The Romanian state was unable to mobilize its citizens for total war, its elites were divided, and Romania's war lasted only two years. The political system changed very little after the war, and the majority of people still felt alienated from their leaders. When the state tried to unite Romanians in national rituals of mourning for the war dead, many rejected the official narrative of the war for

107. Ibid., 67.

108. Mosse, *The Nationalization of the Masses.*

109. Peter Fritzsche, *Germans into Nazis* (Cambridge, MA: Harvard University Press, 1998).

110. Griffin, *Modernism and Fascism*, 153–159, 164–167.

111. Robert Wohl, *The Generation of 1914* (Cambridge, MA: Harvard University Press, 1979); Morris Eksteins, *Rites of Spring: The Great War and the Birth of the Modern Age* (Boston: Houghton Mifflin, 1989).

112. Griffin, *Modernism and Fascism*, 130–146, 167–175.

113. Ibid., 216–218, 357.

more meaningful, personal rites.[114] Among ultranationalists, talk of nationalism as a spiritual endeavor first appeared in 1927 when Codreanu and his friends had to justify breaking away from LANC to form their own movement. Early references to the Legion as a spiritual movement also lacked the apocalyptic overtones that characterized Italian Fascism and German Nazism, and modernist apocalypticism first entered legionary publications in 1933 through the writings of the young Bucharest intellectuals influenced by Nae Ionescu and Nichifor Crainic. While legionary illiberal identities did involve cultivating "new men" through discipline, obedience, suffering, and sacrifice, they emerged through the practice of social movement activism under a hostile regime, not in the libraries and lecture halls of the universities. As long as Codreanu ran the Legion, modernist ideas took second place to promises about excluding Jews from universities, abolishing political corruption, bringing justice to poor peasants, achieving fair wages for workers, and addressing other political grievances. Rank-and-file legionaries fought against the government, Jews, and foreign influences on their society, but they did so by engaging in specific battles with concrete foes, not in the name of abstract principles or metaphysical revolts.

Books

Beyond the newspapers and magazines dominated by Bucharest intellectuals, legionaries issued circulars, books, pamphlets, calendars, photographs, and posters, a number of which made it into public libraries.[115] In his memoirs, the legionary Ion Bozoşan (1905–1991) says that he first became convinced of "how much spirituality, purity and healthy teachings the Captain [Codreanu] was giving to youth and to our whole people," after reading Codreanu's *Pentru legionari* in 1936.[116] According to a eulogy from November 1940, the peasant Ilie Giulan "was not very educated," but he too joined after reading legionary literature.[117] Legionaries were supposed to read and discuss books when they met together in their nests, and books were some of the most commonly confiscated items when police raided legionaries' homes.

The Legion's most widely distributed works were those written by Codreanu. His shortest writings were circulars of one or two paragraphs addressing urgent issues. They were sent to legionaries throughout the country, and Codreanu

114. Bucur, *Heroes and Victims*, 49–143.
115. AN—Iaşi, Fond Chestura de Poliţie, dosar 115/1939, f. 116.
116. Ion Bozoşan, "Căpitanul," in *Corneliu Zelea Codreanu*, ed. Stănescu, 18–20.
117. Petru Galiş, "Ilie Giulan," *Cuvântul* (22 Nov 1940).

expected each person who received one to send one leu to Bucharest to pay for printing costs.[118] In July 1933 he collected some of his earlier writings into *Cărticica şefului de cuib* (The little handbook of the nest leader), which was reissued several times during the 1930s.[119] It outlined basic legionary doctrine and explained the regulations for establishing and running a nest.[120] His next attempt at writing was *Însemnări* (Daily reflections), a diary that he kept in prison during February and March 1934. It contained fragments of the Legion's history as well as reflections on political alliances, international fascism, lucky and unlucky days or weeks, and the value of ascetic practices such as fasting.[121] This diary was never published, but Codreanu included fragments of it in the first volume of his memoirs, *Pentru legionari* (For my legionaries, 1936). This was a history of his political activities from 1919 until 1933, interspersed with newspaper clippings and discussions of the Jewish peril.[122] The first edition of *Pentru legionari* came out in ten thousand copies, of which twenty-five hundred were distributed for free to members who did not have the financial resources to buy it themselves. It sold out within a week, and in September 1936 Codreanu turned to Stelian Popescu (1874–1954), the editor of *Universul*, in the hope that Popescu would print the book on credit.[123] Popescu eventually gave him a discount of one hundred thousand lei for printing another ten thousand copies, including a "luxury edition" that sold for 180 lei.[124] *Pentru legionari* was translated into Italian in 1938 and into German in 1939.[125] Codreanu's works were extremely popular among legionaries, and in 1936 the leader Vasile Iaşinschi (1892–1978) issued a circular requiring all legionaries to carry a copy of *Cărticica şefului de cuib* with them whenever they were doing propaganda.[126]

Codreanu's were not the only writings that came to define the Legion. In a meeting in March 1937, Codreanu explained what his priorities were in terms of printed materials. In addition to promoting *Pentru legionari* and *Cărticica şefului de cuib*, he instructed his followers to distribute two books by Ion Moţa; photographs of legionaries; an album with photographs of legionary work camps; the magazines *Însemnări sociologice*, *Rânduiala*, and *Ideea românească*; and the news-

---

118. Codreanu, *Circulări*, 43–44.

119. Heinen, *Legiunea "Arhanghelul Mihail,"* 211.

120. Codreanu, *Cărticica*.

121. Codreanu, *Însemnari*.

122. Codreanu, *Pentru legionari*.

123. ACNSAS, Fond Penal, dosar 011784, vol. 8, f. 200–201, 220; Heinen, *Legiunea "Arhanghelul Mihail,"* 263.

124. ACNSAS, Fond Penal, dosar 011784, vol. 9, f. 65, vol. 11, f. 182–183.

125. Corneliu Zelea Codreanu, *Guardia di ferro* (Roma-Torino: SA Casa Editrice Nazionale, 1938); Corneliu Zelea Codreanu, *Eiserne Garde* (Berlin: Brunnen, Willi Bischoff, 1939).

126. ANIC, Fond MI-D, dosar 10/1935, f. 87.

papers *Libertatea* and *Cuvântul Argeşului.*[127] Codreanu wanted propagandists to take these publications to legionaries in isolated areas, who were supposed to buy them at full price.

Ion Moţa and Vasile Marin died fighting in the Spanish Civil War in January 1937, and their works immediately became best-sellers among legionaries. Moţa's major journalistic works since 1922 were collected into a volume titled *Cranii de lemn* (Wooden skulls, 1937). Taken from an article Moţa had written in 1933 to commemorate the death of Virgil Teodorescu at the hands of the police, the title referred to the way in which bureaucrats hid the tragedy of legionary deaths by burying broken skulls under piles of paperwork written in "wooden" language (*un limbaj de lemn*). This volume pontificated on issues from the League of Nations to Orthodox Christianity, effectively creating a handbook of legionary ideology.[128] Moţa's letters and articles written from the front were also collected and published as quickly as possible.[129] Vasile Marin (1904–1937) had been involved in the student movement while a law student in Bucharest during the early 1920s. He studied under Ion Lugoşianu (1890–1957), a lawyer and politician who encouraged him to join Iuliu Maniu's National Peasant Party. Marin wrote his doctoral thesis on Italian Fascism in 1932, a text that portrayed Mussolini's party as a revolutionary force establishing a new social order to replace the anarchism and individualism that he said had resulted from the style of democracy instituted by the French Revolution.[130] Maniu suggested sending him to Rome as a cultural attaché, but Marin turned down the offer in order to join the Legion and become a journalist.[131] Marin had first encountered legionaries during the election campaign in Neamţ County in 1931, and he joined them in 1933, working first at Nae Ionescu's *Cuvântul* and then at *Axa* before starting his own newspaper, *Vestitorul* (The herald, 1934). Marin was well respected inside the Legion, and Codreanu made him a commander (*comandant*) in July 1935.[132] His collected works were published as *Crez de generaţie* (Creed of a generation, 1937). Whereas Moţa's writings focused on legionary mysticism and nationalism as a cultural phenomenon, Marin discussed economics, democracy, and revolu-

127. ACNSAS, Fond Penal, dosar 011784, vol. 9, f. 332–333.

128. Ion Moţa, *Cranii de lemn*, 4th ed. (Bucharest: Editura Mişcării Legionare, 1940).

129. Ion Moţa, *Prezent* (Bucharest: Tipografia "Bucovina" I.E. Toroutiu, 1937); Ion Moţa, *Testamentul lui Ion I. Moţa* (Bucharest: Editua Sânziana, 2007).

130. Vasile Marin, *Fascismul: Organizarea constituţională a statului corporativ Italian* (Bucharest: Serviciul şi Editura Colportajului Legionar, n.d.), 8–9.

131. Ana Maria Marin, in *Ţara, Legiunea, Căpitanul*, ed. Conovici, Iliescu, and Silvestru, 39–40, 82.

132. A. M. Marin, *Poveste de dincolo*, 106–123; Mihail Polihroniade, "Vasile Marin, biografie," *Cuvântul studenţesc*, 12/1–4 (Jan–Feb 1937): 28–34.

tion from the perspective of a political scientist.[133] Between them, these two men expressed the Legion's "official" positions on most issues of interest to ultranationalists.

Propaganda

Photographs were another particularly important form of propaganda. Mihail Polihroniade's *Tabăra de Muncă* (The work camp, 1936) was the most elaborate of the legionary photo albums and sold for 120 lei. It contained pictures and short commentaries on forty-three of the Legion's major building projects to emphasize what Polihroniade called "a great Romanian and legionary achievement"[134] More often, photographs or postcards were sold separately as a way of raising money for the Legion. In 1934 legionaries sold photographs of Duca's assassins for twenty lei each, and in 1936 they circulated a postcard featuring Codreanu, General Cantacuzino, and George Clime alongside King Carol II to show their loyalty to the monarch.[135] Students hung photos of legionaries on the walls in their dormitories and it was not uncommon for the police to find photographs when they raided the homes of legionaries.[136] Other propaganda material included fliers with the lyrics to legionary songs, antisemitic cartoons, or lists of Jewish businesses. As did most political parties, legionaries produced their own wall calendars listing religious holidays and saint's days and picturing legionary symbols. One calendar for the year 1937 included pictures of the legionaries who had gone to Spain and an image of communists shooting bullets into a statue of Christ. It was not submitted to the censors. This particular calendar sold for three lei and was printed in fifty thousand copies.[137]

Electoral posters were less heavily illustrated and usually contained legionary symbols, a photograph of Codreanu or of the local candidate, and text announcing a meeting or explaining the Legion's views on a specific issue. Posters and fliers were often designed for specific regions. One letter from Alexandru Hogoş to Nicolae Totu written during the election campaign of November 1933 asks for another one thousand fliers "similar to those already printed for Ismail county," but with several more position statements added from a pamphlet that had

133. V. Marin, *Crez de generație.*

134. Polihroniade, *Tabăra de muncă*, 1. On other legionary photo albums, see AN—Iaşi, Fond Chestura de Poliție, dosar 93/1936, f.200

135. AN—Iaşi, Fond Chestura de Poliție, dosar 99/1935, f. 37, dosar 93/1936, f. 14.

136. ACNSAS, Fond Documentar, dosar 012694, vol. 12, f. 22; ACNSAS, Fond Penal, dosar 000324, vol. 11, f. 243.

137. ANIC, Fond MI-D, dosar 3/1936, f. 382.

been prepared for Brăila County, including "support for the death penalty, the inspection of politicians, ministerial responsibility, and the destruction of Freemasonry." Hogoş needed these urgently, and he promised to support the costs himself.[138]

Legionary books, photographs, and fliers were distributed by legionaries themselves while on propaganda trips, as well as being posted on fences and walls by local activists.[139] In August 1937 Alexandra Russo and Fr. Gheorghe Tudorache were caught distributing two short booklets—Traian Herseni's *Mişcarea legionară şi muncitorimea* (Workers and the legionary movement) and Alexandru Cantacuzino's *Pentru Christos* (For Christ)—in the small Bessarabian city of Orhei.[140] Russo was a wealthy landowner who spearheaded the Legion's recruitment of university students in Chişinău, and Tudorache had become a legionary while training to be a priest there in 1934.[141] Neither of the booklets had been censored, and Russo and Tudorache were giving them out for free in an attempt to spread the Legion's influence beyond Chişinău and into other Bessarabian cities.

Neamţ County provides a particularly clear example of how legionary fliers were printed and distributed in rural areas. According to a history of legionary activism in the region written by a Siguranţa agent in 1942, police identified 896 members in the county scattered across fourteen different villages after the by-elections of 1931. In July 1932 legionaries in Iaşi began posting copies of *Pământul strămoşesc* and fliers specifically addressing Neamţ County to activists living in the region. Enthusiasm for the Legion waned after the by-election, and there were only 702 members left by 1933. Legionary propaganda in the area was more subdued during 1934, being coordinated by a student from the county capital of Piatra Neamţ named Ion Herghelegiu, and another from the nearby town of Roznov named Ion Gaucan. Herghelegiu was the region's most active propagandist between 1931 and 1935, organizing workers, peasants, and high school students in Piatra Neamţ and its hinterland. Herghelegiu formed Blood Brotherhoods in town in 1931 but did not manage to establish any in rural areas until 1935. He and a handful of other legionaries faced court in 1936 for holding meetings illegally but were acquitted. Later that year a team of sixty legionaries led by Codreanu visited the region to erect crosses in a cemetery in the village of Vânători and a stone cross in Slobozia and to finish building a student dormitory at Rarău Hermitage near the village of Crucea. Ion Herghelegiu and Gheorghe Clime organized a propaganda march through

138. ACNSAS, Fond Penal, dosar 015671, vol. 1, f. 27.

139. ACNSAS, Fond Informativ, dosar 257541, vol. 1, f. 18–20.

140. ACNSAS, Fond Penal, dosar 014083, vol. 2, f. 14.

141. On Alexandra Russo, see Colesnic, *Basarabia necunoscută*, vol. 4, 196–209. Gheorghe Tudorache's involvement in the Legion as a theology student in Chişinău is described in ACNSAS, Fond Penal, dosar 013206, vol. 3, f. 36.

Neamţ County in October 1937, but in April 1938 Herghelegiu was arrested for illegally distributing legionary fliers. He spent the next seventeen months in prison before he was killed by police on 22 September 1939.[142]

A law student in Iaşi named Constantin Fulger (1911–1941) took over responsibility for Neamţ County after Herghelegiu's arrest. He had been a legionary since 1932 and made use of his connections in Iaşi to guide the movement from Piatra Neamţ, where he grew up.[143] Without work, Fulger relied on another student, Moldoveanu, to support him while in Iaşi on the understanding that he would become financially independent "when the Legion came to power."[144] Moldoveanu organized fliers and circulars for Neamţ County, and he would write to Fulger whenever it was time for him to go to Iaşi to pick them up. Fulger's travel expenses came by money order or directly from two high school students, who collected it from supporters in the nearby town of Târgu Buhuşi. He was assisted by the son of his landlady, Gheorghe Creţu, who had graduated from an industrial high school in Bucharest. Creţu brought a hectograph to Piatra Neamţ when he came back from school and they used it to copy fliers for distribution. Fulger and Creţu gave some of these to the students in Târgu Buhuşi, some Fulger posted directly to legionaries in the surrounding towns, and others they threw into the front yards of specific individuals or on the busiest streets of Piatra Neamţ.[145]

As with publishing a newspaper or a magazine, distributing posters or fliers required the cooperation of a whole team of people. Leaders like Herghelegiu and Fulger depended on their contacts in Iaşi to produce fliers; they needed their own equipment to reproduce them, money from local legionaries to pay for them, and key people who could distribute them in the right places. Distributing legionary propaganda was not a safe operation, and every step of the process had to be kept secret, even when legionaries relied on the postal system to transmit their materials.

Sympathetic Newspapers

Alongside newspapers such as *Pământul Strămoşesc* and *Axa*, legionaries read some of the successful ultranationalist dailies including *Calendarul*, *Buna vestire*, *Porunca vremii*, and *Cuvântul*. None of these were official legionary organs, but

142. ACNSAS, Fond Documentar, dosar 008912, vol. 23, f. 161–165, 169–170, 191–194.
143. ACNSAS, Fond Informativ, dosar 047321, vol. 2, f. 2, dosar 259143, vol. 1, f. 191.
144. Ibid., dosar 262481, f. 6
145. Ibid., f. 6; ACNSAS, Fond Documentar, dosar 008912, vol. 23, f. 293–294.

all carried legionary news, were edited and written by legionaries, and in several cases were also distributed by the Legion. For example, when Nae Ionescu's *Cuvântul* reappeared in January 1938 after having been out of print since Duca's assassination in December 1933, it had a number of legionaries on the editorial board and as contributors.[146] Codreanu visited the editorial offices as soon as the first issue came out, and Nae Ionescu's editorials frequently defended the Legion on *Cuvântul*'s front page.[147]

Jewish vendors were sometimes reluctant to sell ultranationalist newspapers, which often had to establish their own distribution networks through smaller vendors who specialized in ultranationalist publications.[148] Legionaries were pragmatic about how to best make use of their resources. They maintained connections with less extremist newspapers and sometimes cooperated with other ultranationalists. The Mirescu brothers worked at Stelian Popescu's *Universul*, where they acted as intermediaries between Popescu and the Legion.[149] Similarly, the legionary Cezar Giugiovanu worked at *Tempo* (Tempo, 1933–1941), a daily newspaper that specialized in exotic and sensationalist reporting, giving equal space to parties from across the political spectrum. *Tempo*'s director Vasile Canarache (1896–1969) had reported for the center-left dailies *Adevărul* and *Dimineața* before starting out on his own. Giugiovanu also worked for *Monitorul Oficial* (The official monitor, 1832–present), a government publication that reported new legislation and reprinted parliamentary speeches. Whereas at his job at *Tempo* he had acted as an intermediary between the newspaper and the Legion, at *Monitorul Oficial* Giugiovanu limited himself to passing on news of interest to the movement's leadership.[150] Despite ongoing conflict between the Legion and LANC, in March 1935 the Eminescu printing press, owned by the legionary leader Bartolomeu Livezeanu, agreed to print a newspaper for the Cuzist Alexandru Gregorian (1909–1987) titled *Studentul național ist* (The nationalist student). Gregorian printed antilegionary articles in his newspaper, but Livezeanu's press was probably happier to do business with another ultranationalist—even a rival—than with other types of newspapers.[151]

Ultranationalists who were not legionaries were generally sympathetic to the movement even when they were not willing to join it themselves. The daily news-

146. Including Petre P. Panaitescu, Pavel Costin Deleanu, Mircea Duțescu, Ioan T. Angelescu, and Ștefan Ionescu.

147. Ornea, *Anii treizeci*, 235–236.

148. ACNSAS, Fond Documentar, dosar 008912, vol. 23, f. 53; ANIC, Fond DGP, dosar 252/1939, f. 215–217; Costea, *Presa legionară*, 30–31.

149. ACNSAS, Fond Informativ, dosar 234303, vol. 2, f. 330.

150. Ibid., dosar 234303, vol. 2, f. 333.

151. ANIC, Fond DGP, dosar 107/1935, f. 39; ACNSAS, Fond Documentar, dosar 008909, vol. 4, f. 89–92; "Barbăriile gardiste," *Studentul naționalist*, 1/1 (15 Mar 1935): 3.

paper *Porunca vremii* had supported ultranationalist movements in general since it appeared in 1932, and in 1935 the director, Ilie Rădulescu, established an Association of Christian Journalists in Romania (Asociaţia Ziariştilor Creştini din România) based at *Porunca vremii*'s editorial offices. The association included members of LANC and PNŢ alongside other ultranationalists, but Rădulescu named the legionary Dragoş Protopopescu as one of the organization's vice presidents, and other legionaries were on the leadership committee.[152] Nonetheless, Codreanu distanced himself from the newspaper in November 1935, sending out a circular that explained that although "*Porunca vremii* is a good antisemitic newspaper," its journalists were recent converts to the ultranationalist cause. "Therefore," Codreanu wrote, "be cautious of every article and every word, for it is not ours. . . . You should all read *Porunca vremii*, but do not believe everything that is written in it."[153] When circulation figures for *Porunca vremii* dropped and police began harassing children selling the newspaper in September 1936, Rădulescu turned to the Legion for help.[154] He offered to supply a dormitory with thirty beds, lighting, and heating for legionaries if they helped with distribution and sales. Codreanu agreed, forming two teams of fifteen legionaries each, one of which would be responsible for the newspaper stands and the other for protecting children selling the newspaper on the streets.[155] The newspaper hired more legionary journalists at this point and consistently published pro-legionary news and editorials throughout 1937.[156]

Similarly, nine days after *Buna vestire* (The annunciation, 1937–1938, 1940–1941) was established on 23 February 1937, Codreanu issued another circular, explaining that "this newspaper is not legionary. We are friends and we support it. But I would not want legionaries to confuse the point of view of this newspaper with that of the legionary movement."[157] He needed to clarify this because *Buna vestire* presented itself as pro-legionary. Its opening editorial was a eulogy to "the legionary sacrifice" of Ion Moţa and Vasile Marin, and the front page of the second issue featured a large photograph of legionaries saluting at the funeral.[158] The newspaper was funded by the economist Mihail Manoilescu (1891–1950), who was sympathetic to the Legion but ran Liga Naţional Corporatistă (the National Corporatist League), which was not subject to

152. ANIC, Fond DGP, dosar 66/1935, f. 9–10.

153. Codreanu, *Circulări*, 73–74.

154. V. Lovinaru, "Teroarea poliţiei contră ziarului nostru," *Porunca vremii*, 5/521 (24 Sept 1936).

155. ANIC, Fond MI-D, dosar 3/1936, f. 150.

156. Legionaries who worked at *Porunca vremii* include Ilie Ciutescu, Ion Diaconescu, and Ştefan Ionescu.

157. Codreanu, *Circulări*, 128–129.

158. Dragoş Protopopescu, "Contemporanii lui Isus . . ." *Buna vestire*, 1/1 (23 Feb 1937): 1.

Codreanu's leadership.[159] Codreanu and Manoilescu had cooperated since 1934, but the Legion had always resisted Manoilescu's requests for a merger.[160] Legionaries nonetheless embraced *Buna vestire* and used its pages to promote a number of legionary causes. *Buna vestire* was directed by Dragoş Protopopescu (1892–1948) and Toma Vlădescu (1903–?). As well as being a novelist and a professor of English literature, Protopopescu had been one of the Legion's staunchest supporters at *Calendarul* and a frequent contributor to *Axa*. He was arrested together with other legionaries in the wake of Duca's assassination in 1933 and afterward wrote a novel based on his prison experiences called *Fortul 13* (Fort no. 13).[161] Vlădescu had also worked at *Calendarul*, but afterward he contributed to Crainic's next project, *Sfarmă piatra* (The rock crusher, 1936–1941), which initially supported the National Christian Party of A. C. Cuza and Octavian Goga, and then became a means for Crainic to promote a new party he was trying to form called Partidul Muncitoresc Creştin (the Christian Workers' Party).[162] Vlădescu left *Sfarmă piatra* after fighting with Crainic over money, but Codreanu still considered his past affiliations suspect.[163] Popescu and Vlădescu quarreled in December 1937 as a result of the latter's sympathies for Istrate Micescu (1881–1951), who had been subsidizing the newspaper through Vlădescu. It is likely that Micescu withdrew his financial support for *Buna vestire* at this time because soon after Vlădescu resigned as director the newspaper published a plea to any of its readers who were willing to lend it five hundred thousand lei for a year.[164] Codreanu had little sympathy for Micescu at this point. Micescu had turned his back on Codreanu after legionary students helped him gain control of the Ilfov Bar Association in 1935, he had made denigrating remarks about Codreanu's electoral alliances earlier in 1937, and in December 1937 Codreanu had just lost a libel suit against him.[165]

Once Protopopescu was firmly in control of *Buna vestire*, the newspaper took on an even firmer legionary tone. Virgil Gheorghiu (1916–1992) writes in his memoirs of visiting *Buna vestire*'s editorial offices when he was a young journalist in early 1938. "All newspaper offices have the same smell of paper, printers ink, and melted lead that the linotype machine turns into letters," Gheorghiu recalls. "The offices of *Buna vestire* had none of these smells. Instead, there was a

159. Ornea, *Anii treizeci*, 275.

160. ACNSAS, Fond Penal, dosar 011784, vol. 11, f. 265–266.

161. Anania, *Memorii*, 63.

162. ACNSAS, Fond Penal, dosar 013206, vol. 3, f. 255–258, 275.

163. Horia Roman, "Reflecţii în jurul unei . . . polemici" *Adevarul* (29 May 1937).

164. ACNSAS, Fond Documentar, dosar 008909, vol. 5, f. 1.

165. Istrate N. Micescu, "Pactul de neagreiune Maniu-Codreanu şi procesul de calomnie Codreanu-Micescu," *Ţara noastră* (2 Mar 1937); "D. Istrate Micescu ia act de procesul pe care i l-a intentat d. Corneliu Zelea Codreanu," *Curentul* (2 Dec 1937).

very strong smell of leather. Everyone was dressed in leather. They had overcoats, boots, belts, and shoulder straps of leather. It is the legionary uniform."[166] Legionaries not only dominated the content of the newspaper; they also transformed its culture into one that demanded conformity with legionary ways of dressing and behaving.

The ways in which legionaries infiltrated the ultranationalist press suggests that the boundaries between legionary and not-legionary publications were sometimes vague. In the case of political broadsheets, the newspaper's affiliation was clearly printed on the front page. But this was not the case with other periodicals. *Calendarul* was a legionary newspaper, and yet its director never joined a legionary nest. Codreanu emphasized that *Buna vestire* was not a legionary newspaper, yet its orientation was entirely pro-legionary. Journals and magazines such as *Însemnări sociologice* or *Ideea românească* were ostensibly sociological or literary publications, yet they were run by legionaries and were distributed as examples of legionary propaganda material. Codreanu struggled to define which publications were legionary and which were not, and yet he had to approach the nonlegionary publicist Stelian Popescu for help publishing a second edition of *Pentru legionari*. The complex relationships formed between legionaries and other ultranationalists helped situate the Legion firmly within a context of local ultranationalist activism even as it drew closer in style and substance to fascist parties and regimes elsewhere in Europe. Moreover, gaining the support of well-known intellectuals and major daily newspapers significantly reinforced the respectability of legionaries. It also changed the Legion itself. Putting a legionary message in print transformed a group of antisemitic thugs into a respectable social movement with a coherent ideology and clearly articulated positions on important social issues. However they felt about having their organization run by Bucharest intellectuals, legionaries and potential activists read and distributed these publications and believed what they found there. Nonetheless, the situational and occasionally contradictory nature of legionary ideology suggests that the fact that printed propaganda existed was sometimes more important than what the pamphlets said. There are no records of rank-and-file members questioning anything they read. Instead they treated pamphlets, books, and newspapers as reliable sources of doctrine and considered themselves duty bound to make them as widely available as possible.

---

166. Virgil Gheorghiu, *Memorii: Martorul Orei 25.* Translated by Sanda Mihaescu-Carsteanu (Bucharest: 1001 Gramar, 1999), 389.

6

IRON-CLAD BREASTS AND LILY-WHITE SOULS

Even while some legionaries continued to use gang violence, intimidation, and assassination, Codreanu increasingly preferred peaceful methods that gave the Legion the high moral ground in its contest with Romania's major political parties. In stark contrast to their celebration of violence during the early 1930s, between 1934 and 1938 legionaries spoke constantly about cultivating themselves, educating their fellow Romanians, and creating a new moral elite. Legionary education, they argued, was the key element that attracted "many young Christians" to the movement.[1] Whereas antisemitism had been the central focus of the student movement and of A. C. Cuza's LANC, legionary propaganda emphasized workers' rights, anti-Masonry, and antipoliticianism during the Great Depression. In the years that followed, the idea emerged that legionaries had to be honest, selfless, and hardworking if they were to replace Romania's corrupt leaders. One of the Legion's most popular songs was "Imnul tinereții legionare" (Hymn of the legionary youth), written in the summer of 1936. A professional songwriter, Ion Mânzatu, had only just joined the Legion at the time, and he says, "I thought to try and compose a march in a more modern and simplified spirit; a eulogy to legionary youth."[2] Radu Gyr's lyrics celebrated youth, virility, and strength as virtues that would allow legionaries to mold the blood and soil of their ancestors into a holy new land established by God and the archangel Michael.

1. Barbu Slușanschi, "Școala tineretului de azi și țelurile ei," *Însemnări sociologice*, 1/8 (1935): 20.
2. Ion Mânzatu, "Imnul tinereții legionare," in *Corneliu Zelea Codreanu*, ed. Stănescu, 165–168.

Holy legionary youth
With iron-clad breasts and lily-white souls,
The bold assault of springtime
Brows tranquil as the lakes of the Carpathians.
Under the sun our arms raise
An iconostasis for the ages.
We build from rocks, from fire, from oceans,
And bind it together with Dacian blood.

Chorus: The Guard, the Captain,
We become hawks of iron,
The country, the Capitan,
And the Archangel from heaven.[3]

Legionaries had used rhetoric about honor and purity since 1927, when they contrasted their youthful innocence with A. C. Cuza's political cynicism. But the idea of creating "new men" (*oameni noi*) structured legionary speech and activism between 1933 and 1938.[4] Codreanu wrote in 1936, "This country is dying because it lacks *men*, not because it lacks [political] programs. That is our belief. Therefore we do not need to build programs, but *men, new men*. Because people as they are today—*raised on politicianism* and *infected* by the Jewish influence—will compromise even the best programs." He concluded that "the Legion of the Archangel Michael will be . . . more a school and an army than a political party. . . . Everything that our minds can imagine that is nobler in the soul, everything that can make our race prouder, higher, more righteous, stronger, wiser, purer, harder working, and more courageous—that is what the legionary school must produce!"[5]

Legionaries found that promising to create "new men" had strong appeal to the population at large. Thanks to peaceful propaganda through community events, marches, work camps, and businesses, the period from 1935 to 1937 was one of unparalleled growth for the Legion. Much of this growth took place during 1937 itself. In Tighina County, for example, the Legion had 17 nests and a total of 230 legionaries in July 1937. Three months later, after a rigorous propaganda campaign through rural villages, there were 60 nests and roughly 600 legionaries. Legionaries also formed roughly 30 "sympathizers' nests" during this campaign,

---

3. Radu Gyr and Ion Mânzatu, "Sfântă tinerețe," in *Cântece legionare*, by Anonymous (Bucharest: I. E. Torouțiu, 1940), 37–38.

4. I translate the Romanian *omul nou* as "new man" to emphasize that this is the same phrase used by fascist groups all over Europe, but it should be noted that the Romanian noun is neutral, not masculine. Literally, *omul nou* means "new person."

5. Codreanu, *Pentru legionari*, 286.

TABLE 6.1 Ethnic groups in Romania in 1930

DATE	NESTS	MEMBERS
December 1933	3,495	28,000
May 1935	4,200	24,000
August 1936		70,000*
January 1937	12,000	96,000
December 1937	34,000	272,000

Source: Armin Heinen, *Legiunea "Arhanghelul Mihail": mişcare socială şi organizaţie politică*, translated by Cornelia and Delia Esianu (Bucharest: Humanitas, 2006), 357.

Note: These numbers are estimates based on various sources. The starred estimate from August 1936 was not given by Heinen but comes from a speech by General Cantacuzino in August 1936 (ANIC, Fond MI-D, dosar 3/1936, f. 81).

with a total of 340 sympathizers.[6] Data compiled by Armin Heinen shows how rapidly the Legion expanded in only a short period of time (table 6.1).

The Everything for the Fatherland Party won 478,378 votes (15.58 percent) in the elections of 20 December 1937, making it the third-largest party in the country after the National Liberal Party (PNL) and the National Peasant Party (PNŢ).[7] As Traian Sandu notes, these election results were still surprisingly low given the number of legionary propagandists. Whereas Cuza's National Christian Party won 12 votes for every party member, the Legion achieved only 1.75 votes per legionary.[8] Ordinary political parties could count on a large number of voters who were sympathetic but not enthusiastic enough to join the party. By 1937, as the organ of a social movement, the Legion had managed to transform most sympathizers into members, giving it a strong public presence but not guaranteeing electoral success.

One police report from October 1935 said that "in the towns [legionaries conduct] propaganda through members of different sporting associations; in the countryside by erecting crosses [*troiţe*], making roads, by putting up fences around cemeteries, . . . Guardists help peasants harvest their fields, pick grapes, build houses, [and] even help them with money."[9] The following year Vasile Iaşinschi (1892–1978)—a pharmacist from Rădăuţi and an important leader ordered that legionaries also compile reports on the regions they visited while doing propaganda. They were to discover how many Jews lived in an area, whether non-Orthodox sects were active, what level of schooling was available, what

6. Roth Jelescu, *Şi cerul plângea*, 260.

7. Heinen, *Legiunea "Arhanghelul Mihail,"* 466.

8. Traian Sandu, "Der Ertrag der Militanz und der regionale Erfolg der Eisernen Garde. Eine Analyse des Wahlverhaltens und die Folgerungen für die Theorie," in *Inszenierte Gegenmacht von rechts: Die "Legion Erzengel Michael" in Rumänien 1918–1938*, ed. Armin Heinen and Oliver Jens Schmitt (Munich: Oldenberg Verlag, 2013), 177.

9. ACNSAS, Fond Informativ, dosar 160181, f. 394.

occupations most people practiced, and what the material needs of the locals were. If there were legionaries in the area then the propagandists were to compile a list of nest members and to help indoctrinate them. All this was to be done in the most disciplined manner possible, with a copy of *Cărticiă şefului de cuib* at hand.[10]

Work Camps

Legionaries affirmed the importance of self-improvement and contributing to social progress by instituting a vast system of work camps and rest camps during the mid-1930s. The scale of the legionary camp system was unparalleled anywhere in Europe, but the idea was not new. The International Voluntary Service had organized similar camps throughout the continent during the early 1920s to help with reconstruction after World War I.[11] In Germany, Nazi adults and youth attended camps that helped the nation through physical labor.[12] In both France and Italy, fascists ran holiday camps for young people that taught leadership skills and emphasized the importance of practical work for the nation.[13] Across the English Channel, Sir Oswald Mosely's British Union of Fascists ran annual holiday camps where families relaxed together at the seaside.[14] Inside Romania, UNSCR, ethnic German groups, and Jewish youth groups ran voluntary labor camps during the summer.[15] Once legionary camps were well established, Cuzists, groups of apprentices, and state-run youth groups also began organizing their own work camps.[16] Camping, charitable labor, and regimented activities were common in ultranationalist groups all over Europe, situating the Legion of the Archangel Michael within the mainstream of European fascism.

Legionaries had helped with petty jobs in villages during the election campaigns of 1931 and 1932, they had attempted to build a levee on the banks of the Danube

10. ANIC, Fond MI-D, dosar 10/1935, f. 87–88.

11. Veiga, *Istoria Gărzii de Fier*, 219.

12. Michael Kater, *Hitler Youth* (Cambridge, MA: Harvard University Press, 2004), 13–69; Kiran Klaus Patel, *Soldiers of Labor: Labor Service in Nazi Germany and New Deal America, 1933–1945* (New York: Cambridge University Press, 2005).

13. Laura Downs, "'Each and Every One of You Must Become a *Chef*': Toward a Social Politics of Working-Class Childhood on the Extreme Right in 1930s France," *Journal of Modern History*, 81/1 (2009): 1–44; Tracy Koon, *Believe, Obey, Fight: Political Socialization of Youth in Fascist Italy, 1922–1943* (Chapel Hill: University of North Carolina Press, 1985), 101–102.

14. Spurr, "Living the Blackshirt Life," 316–317.

15. N.A., "O tabară studenţească la mare," *Calendarul*, 439 (7 Aug 1933); Nicolae Bogdon, "Progresul taberelor de muncă în Ardeal," *Calendarul*, 453 (24 Aug 1933); ACNSAS, Fond Penal, dosar 011784, vol. 14, f. 221.

16. Petriceanu, "Tabăra de muncă a lăncierilor sătmăreni," *Porunca vremii*, 5/554 (27 Oct 1936); ANIC, Fond DGP, dosar 254/1937, f. 16; ANIC, Fond MI-D, dosar 3/1936, f. 138; AN—Braşov, Fond Inspectoratul Muncii, dosar 90/1935, f. 37.

River at Vişan in 1933, and they ran their own farm at Giuleşti in Ilfov County, but the first organized work camps began during the summer of 1934.[17] The work camps were based on the Legion's two major building projects to date—the Cămin Cultural Creştin in Iaşi and Casa Verde (the Green House) in Bucharest. Work first began on the Green House in August 1933, after police arrested and beat three hundred legionaries working on the levee in Vişani. The idea was to build Casa Legionarilor Răniţi (the House for Wounded Legionaries), where legionaries who had been injured while doing legionary business could stay. Most of the money was raised through small donations, but the project did receive support from wealthy patrons. A Mrs. Anghel donated the land, the law student Alexandru Cantacuzino gave five thousand lei to help begin construction, and an architect named Mr. Ioţu drew up the plans.[18] The engineer Virgil Ionescu (1892–1966) donated all the timber for one level of the building.[19] Others gave their time and their energy. A team of eighty legionaries led by the lawyer Victor Silaghi (?–1941)—a legionary since 1927 who had led small groups of activists in battles against the gendarmerie in the 1933 elections—worked for three months making bricks for the building.[20] Visitors arrived almost immediately, and the first contact many of the intellectuals from *Calendarul* and *Axa* had with other legionaries happened while they worked side by side at the construction site.[21] Building continued sporadically for the next few years, and legionaries continued to make financial contributions to a special fund for the Green House.[22] Legionary women cooked and served lunch for the volunteer workers each day.[23] They planted a vegetable garden and added a roof in 1936, so that the "Legionary Palace" was eventually completed in September 1937.[24] Such projects provided opportunities for introducing sympathetic observers to the Legion, and in 1937 an Italian law student named Lorenzo Baracchi Tua traveled to Romania as a representative of the Anti-Bolshevik Front (UMON). Tua helped on a building site at the legionary headquarters in Gutenberg Street and then wrote a book praising Codreanu and the Legion.[25]

---

17. On the farm at Giuleşti, see ACNSAS, Fond Penal, dosar 014005, vol. 5, f. 191–192, dosar 011784, vol. 11, f. 265–266.

18. Al. M. Savonarioia, "Casa Legionarilor răniţi," *Calendarul*, 1/480 (24 Sept 1933): 1; "Patronul Gărzii de Fier," *Calendarul*, 1/520 (10 Nov 1933).

19. "Săptămâna contribuţile legionare," *Calendarul*, 2/512 (1 Nov 1933): 3.

20. Polihroniade, *Tabăra de muncă*, 7. On Victor Silaghi, see "La moartea lui Victor Silaghi," *Axa*, 10/64 (23 Jan 1941): 7; Fănică Anastasescu, "Comandantul Legionar Victor Silaghi," *Cuvântul*, 18/98 (23 Jan 1941).

21. "Casa Legionarilor răniţi," *Axa*, 1/19 (1 Oct 1933).

22. "Pentru Casa Verde," *Porunca vremii*, 5/531 (4 Oct 1936).

23. ACNSAS, Fond Penal, dosar 011784, vol. 10, f. 291.

24. Polihroniade, *Tabăra de muncă*, 11.

25. Tua, *Garda de Fier*.

Organized camps began in 1934. Codreanu led the largest work camp in the Rarău Mountains, and Mihail Stelescu organized a rest camp—also called a sporting camp—at the seaside.[26] The number of camps increased dramatically during 1935 and 1936, as legionaries embarked on hundreds, if not thousands, of construction projects.[27] The difference between these and earlier building projects was that building was no longer the main reason legionaries ran their camps from 1934 onward. As an article from *Libertatea* in April 1936 explained, work camps were schools for molding legionary character:

> This legionary host does not publicize itself loudly, it does not bluster in the alleyways, it does not promise the world, but it works silently to build a new life. This new life must be created and led by new men, who do not seek riches and gold squeezed out of the helpless worker, but who must be used to living only from hard and sober work. That is why the Captain of the legionaries has filled the country with work camps where churches are built, houses are erected for the poor, things are built for the public good. Because by working arduously here, intellectuals and city folk—the future leaders of a legionary country—will become used to another life, difficult and hard, and will no longer long for a life of luxury based on theft.[28]

Building projects were a welcome by-product of the camps system, but the main goal of the work camps was to create the sorts of legionary heroes depicted in the movement's songs and artworks. In contrast to their reputation for violence and terrorism in the early 1930s, legionaries now used the camps to present the Legion as a "constructive" movement contributing to national renewal.[29] As volunteers worked, propagandists would often speak to onlookers, explaining how the project fitted into legionary ideology.[30] Whenever a work camp coincided with a national holiday, legionaries used the opportunity to hold festive events for the locals.[31] After they built a *cămin cultural* (cultural hearth) in the village of Lazu in Alba County, legionaries held a dance and performed Corneliu Georgescu's play *Vremuri de restrişte* (Hard times) about official corruption, Jewish treason, and

26. ACNSAS, Fond Penal, dosar 000160, vol. 9, f. 45–50.

27. Based on a report in *Însemnări sociologice* from October 1936, Armin Heinen writes that "the number of work camps grew from 4 in 1934, to 50 in 1936, and there were another 500 smaller work-sites that year." Heinen, *Legiunea "Arhanghelul Mihail,"* 261. Rebecca Haynes draws on Horia Sima's history of the Legion—a much later and less reliable source—when she says that in 1936 "there were seventy-one camps throughout the country, as well as thousands of smaller work sites throughout Romania." Rebecca Haynes, "Work Camps, Commerce, and the Education of the 'New Man' in the Romanian Legionary Movement," *Historical Journal*, 51/4 (2008): 947.

28. "Tace şi munceşte la temeliile unei vieţi noi," *Libertatea*, 33/1 (5 Apr 1936): 4.

29. Valentin Săndulescu, "'Taming the Body': Preliminary Considerations Concerning the Legionary Work Camps System (1933–1937)," *Historical Yearbook* 5 (2008): 87.

30. ACNSAS, Fond Penal, dosar 011784, vol. 8, f. 228.

31. Ion Ţurcan, "Tabere şi şantiere," *Însemnări sociologice*, 2/9 (1936): 16.

the heroism of the antisemitic movement.[32] In other places legionaries followed their building projects with choral performances for the local population.[33] Horia Sima, Codreanu's successor as leader of the movement, writes in his history that meetings at the legionary work camp at Carmen Sylva always "ended in singing, a chorus of hundreds of young voices: sad songs, heroic songs, songs which eloquently evoked ancestral glories, songs which seemed to transfigure them."[34]

In his close study of a work camp at Rarău Mountain in Bukovina—one of the four camps held in 1934—Valentin Săndulescu shows how much effort legionaries put into activities that were not directly related to the building process. The day started with tea at 6:00 a.m., followed by two hours of group exercises before work began on what was to be a summer house for legionary students. Food was scarce, the daily program was rigorous, and once a week legionaries hiked up the mountain barefoot as a training exercise. In the evenings Codreanu spoke to the roughly one hundred students present, instructing them about legionary politics, treason, and the differences between the Legion and other political parties.[35] During moments of relaxation, legionaries made use of the nearby hermitage to pray and to mingle with the local population.[36] A similar schedule governed the largest of the work camps, which took place near the Carmen Sylva tourist resort on the Black Sea—today known as Eforie Sud. Here hundreds of legionaries worked over two summers to build a large camping ground, including a number of stone buildings, kitchens, cellars, roads, wells, drainage canals, flower gardens, picnic tables, and a hen house.[37]

A police officer observing the camp in 1936 wrote:

> The wake-up call sounds at 6 am, after which Codreanu receives the [morning] report; orders are given to break ranks and legionaries begin their activities. Some do manual labor, other military training, continuing until 11:30 when it is time for [another] report and for lunch. Military training takes place in the morning three times a week. . . . Manual labor and other theoretical instruction continues on the other days, ending in the evening with a report in front of Zelea in irreproachable dress and discipline. From time to time a national celebration is held, which is attended by crowds of tourists from the resort.[38]

---

32. ANIC, Fond MI-D, dosar 3/1936, f. 111–112.

33. ACNSAS, Fond Penal, dosar 011784, vol. 10, f. 290.

34. Horia Sima, *Histoire du movement legionnaire* (Rio de Janeiro: Editôra Dacia, 1972), 248.

35. Săndulescu, "Revolutionizing Romania," 153–158.

36. Nicolae Nicu Păun, *Un soldat pe baricadă idealului legionar: "Audiatur et altera pars"* (Braşov: n.p., n.d.), 118.

37. Haynes, "Work Camps," 959.

38. ANIC, Fond MI-D, dosar 3/1936, f. 181–182. Cf. the detailed programs given in George Macrin, "O nouă şcoală românească: Taberele de muncă," *Însemnări sociologice*, 1/4 (1935): 19, and Ţurcan, "Tabere şi şantiere," 12–13.

FIGURE 6.1 Legionaries at the Carmen Sylva work camp. Mihail Polihroniade, *Tabăra de muncă* (Bucharest : Tipografia Ziarului Universul, 1936), 34.

Military training appears to have been a common feature of work camps.[39] Legionaries building a road up to the Arnota Monastery in Vâlcea County in 1935 and 1936 deposited firearms at the monastery and practiced target shooting during the camp.[40] At the Carmen Sylva work camp in 1936, one legionary shot himself in the arm.[41]

Work camps provided opportunities for people living nearby to contribute to legionary projects. Women cooked food for the camp; at Carmen Sylva food was supplied by legionary groups from fourteen different cities.[42] Local peasants also provided food for the legionaries.[43] Some of the food at Carmen Sylva was sold to tourists at low prices, encouraging more people to visit the camp

39. Legionaries also practiced target shooting on other occasions. I. C. Crişan, "Amintiri despre Corneliu Zelea Codreanu," in *Corneliu Zelea Codreanu*, ed. Stănescu, 59; ACNSAS, Fond Penal, dosar 011784, vol. 13, f. 68.

40. ACNSAS, Fond Informativ, dosar 260639, vol. 1, f. 302.

41. ANIC, Fond MI-D, dosar 3/1936, f. 4–5.

42. Marin, *Poveste de dincolo*, 124; ACNSAS, Fond Informativ, dosar 184933, vol. 1, f. 189; Codreanu, *Circulări*, 44–45.

43. ANIC, Fond DGP, dosar 4/1936, f. 105–107.

and see what the legionaries had achieved.[44] Sales of food and donations from visitors to the Carmen Sylva camp totaled seventy-three thousand lei in 1935 alone.[45] How much food was available at legionary camps varied considerably, and sometimes having anything to eat at all seemed miraculous to those who were there. Writing about the work camp at Nicoreşti in Tecuci County during 1935, Vasile Popa claimed that "just when our provisions were running out, God did not abandon us, but someone with a good heart would come and place their gift and their soul on our poor camp table."[46] According to Popa, peasants from nearby villages came during the night, when gendarmes would not see them, offering flour, chicken, beans, potatoes, cheese, and other food to the legionaries so that they could keep working. Local peasants often helped with the construction work as well.[47] Occasionally unemployed tradesmen found paid employment on legionary worksites, but this was rare.[48] In Bistriţa, the local council was so supportive of the legionaries that it donated land in a local park for them to raise a cross (*troiţa*).[49]

Local residents were not always friendly to the legionaries. In 1934 Codreanu had trouble buying land to build on because owners of a nearby tourist resort worried that the presence of too many legionaries in the region would hurt tourism.[50] Two years later, the newspaper *Libertatea* recounted two stories of local vandals cutting down wooden memorial crosses erected by legionaries. The vandals were apprehended in one of these instances, and the criminal was identified as the son of the National Liberal mayor in the village.[51] Most accounts of legionary camps suggest that visitors and locals welcomed the work that the legionaries were doing, however, and the outcry against the vandalism of legionary memorials reported by *Libertatea* also suggests that the majority of people in the village liked having the crosses there.

Taking advantage of their nationwide organization, legionaries were able to implicate nonlegionaries from the other side of the country in their work camps. In 1936, legionaries invited fifty children aged between seven and fifteen years old from mining families to the Carmen Sylva camp, where female students fed

44. Păun, *Un soldat pe baricada*, 138–139.

45. ACNSAS, Fond Penal, dosar 011784, vol. 8, f. 443–444.

46. Vasile Popa, "Tabără din Nicoreşti," *Braţul de fier*, 1/7 (Dec 1935): 3.

47. ANIC, Fond MI-D, dosar 3/1936, f. 151–152.

48. ANIC, Fond DGP, dosar 252/1939, f. 318–319; ACNSAS, Fond Penal, dosar 011784, vol. 12, f. 215.

49. ACNSAS, Fond Penal, dosar 011784, vol. 11, f. 230.

50. Ibid., dosar 011784, vol. 2, f. 195.

51. "Sfinte cruci batjocorite şi tăiate cu şecurea de către slujitorii Diavolului," *Libertatea*, 33/3 (26 Apr 1936): 4.

and cared for them all summer.[52] At the Green House in Bucharest, the legionaries Nicoleta Nicolescu and Bartolomeu Livezeanu "adopted" seventy orphans. Nicolescu put them in a legionary group home and told them that "from now on, I am your mother."[53] When they were old enough, these children were given jobs in the legionary restaurants and cooperatives.

Legionaries also mixed with outsiders through baptisms and weddings at the summer camps. Codreanu acted as godfather for a child baptized at the Carmen Sylva work camp in August 1936. The child was named Mihai, presumably in honor of the Legion of the Archangel Michael (Romanian: Arhanghelul Mihail).[54] General Cantacuzino also acted as godfather for the children of poor peasants who were baptized at various legionary camps in rural areas.[55] Weddings also took place at work camps, away from the couple's natal homes but with their legionary friends in attendance.[56] Legionaries saw such occasions not only as a way to deepen ties within the community but also as opportunities for propaganda.[57] It is tempting to read these weddings as an example of the party overwhelming family ties, but that would be to misunderstand the importance of nuclear families to the legionary movement. Legionaries recruited heavily among their own family members, and they relied on their families for material support during difficult times. The Legion's success lay in its ability to gain access to preexisting kinship networks, affirming them and inscribing them as apparently natural elements of the movement. Instead of replacing the family with the party, legionaries made the family fascist.

As the Legion grew, it generated its own social world; incorporating important ritual occasions such as weddings, providing leisure activities, and inventing its own songs and folklore. Codreanu issued circulars during 1936 dictating how his followers would spend their vacation time.[58] Most were expected to attend work camps for substantial periods and to spend the rest of their time doing propaganda for the Legion. One police report from August 1936 confirmed that "almost all of the Aromanian students in the capital are away at colonies and work camps in diverse locations."[59] The same could probably have been said for most legionary

52. ACNSAS, Fond Penal, dosar 011784, vol. 8, f. 251–252; ANIC, Fond MI D, dosar 3/1936, f. 4–5.

53. Ilie Tudor, *Un an lângă Căpitan* (Bucharest: Sânziana, 2007), 24, 45–47; Codreanu, *Circulări*, 141.

54. ANIC, Fond MI-D, dosar 3/1936, f. 4–5.

55. ACNSAS, Fond Penal, dosar 011784, vol. 11, f. 218–237.

56. Polihroniade, *Tabară de muncă*, 51; Coman, *Amintiri legionare*, vol. 4, in AN—Cluj, Fond Personal Vasile Coman, dosar 4/1980, f. 100.

57. ACNSAS, Fond Documentar, dosar 012694, vol. 12, f. 19.

58. ANIC, Fond MI-D, dosar 10/1935, f. 68, 92.

59. ACNSAS, Fond Penal, dosar 011784, vol. 8, f. 252.

students that summer. Work camps such as Carmen Sylva were carefully organized, requiring participants to register beforehand, while others were ad hoc projects organized by legionaries in their local areas.[60] Some traveled for long distances to attend camps. In 1936 three legionaries from Orhei County marched three hundred miles over eight days in order to attend the camp at Carmen Sylva.[61]

A number of priests profited from the work camps to get their churches built. Father Teofil Băliban, who ran as a candidate for the Legion in the 1937 elections, told Securitate interrogators in 1948 that he first approached legionaries because he wanted their help building a church.[62] Both the local council and the church authorities had turned down his requests for funding, so he turned to the legionaries. He claims to have had misgivings about the Legion's violence but was willing to overcome them to get his church built.[63] Father Ştefan Palaghiţă also managed to convince legionaries to do construction work on his church in the Bucharest suburb of Pantelimon, and he led a large crowd of legionaries in a religious ceremony blessing the church after the work was completed.[64] In the village of Ştefan cel Mare, in Romanaţi County, Father Ştefan Smarandescu organized his own work camp, mobilizing legionaries from the local area to build a cultural center and a parsonage for him to live in.[65] Priests who were less involved in legionary activism took part in blessing crosses, churches, cultural centers, and work camps that took part in their parishes, often preaching pro-legionary sermons appropriate to the occasion.[66]

Although legionaries often spoke about the charitable nature of their work camps, many building projects actually helped legionaries more than anyone else. The house at Rarău, for example, was destined for the use of legionaries alone, as was the Green House in Bucharest. Legionaries rebuilt the house of George Cosma in the village of Gura Humorului (Suceava County) after it had burned down, but they did so because they used it for legionary meetings.[67] Similarly, many of the crosses or memorials raised during summer camps were to honor legionary martyrs rather than to help the local population.[68] Legionaries named

---

60. On the organization of Carmen Sylva, see ibid., dosar 011784, vol. 8, f. 276. For much smaller projects, see "O fântână legionară," *Libertatea*, 33/2 (12 Apr 1936): 1; ANIC, Fond MI-D, dosar 3/1936, f. 92, 151.

61. ACNSAS, Fond Penal, dosar 011784, vol. 8, f. 65–67.

62. On Father Băliban's candidacy, see USHMM, Fond SRI Files, Reel #105, dosar 859, f. 195.

63. ACNSAS, Fond Penal, dosar 490, vol. 1, f. 85.

64. ANIC, Fond MI-D, dosar 10/1936, f. 93–94.

65. Ibid., dosar 3/1936, f. 92.

66. Ibid., dosar 3/1936, f. 93, 110–112, 119; ACNSAS, Fond Informativ, dosar160181, f. 393.

67. ACNSAS, Fond Penal, dosar 011784, vol. 10, 290.

68. ACNSAS, Fond Informativ, dosar 257488, f. 32; dosar 234687, vol. 3, f. 56–57; Polihroniade, *Tabară de muncă*, 47, 60.

many of the fountains that they erected after heroes of the movement.[69] Nicu Iancu tells an illuminating story in his memoirs about a fountain in the village of Sadu, in Sibiu County. He says that the legionaries placed an icon of the archangel Michael on the fountain once they had finished building it but that gendarmes confiscated the icon because it was a political symbol. Miraculously, the fountain immediately dried up. The water did not begin to flow again until gendarmes replaced the icon at the insistent requests of the villagers.[70] Iancu's story suggests that the building project became worthless the moment an icon representing the Legion was removed. Legionary work camps made valuable contributions to many villages, but their main purpose was to celebrate the Legion itself. From the ideological discussions of an evening to the symbols erected by legionaries, the publicity and educational value of the camps far outweighed any charitable goals that might have been achieved.

Cooperatives and Restaurants

Alongside the work camps, legionaries established restaurants, cooperatives, and specialty shops. The businessman Constantin Cristescu (1900–?) joined the Legion because he was impressed by these businesses, which he says "aimed at the complete socialization [of legionaries] so as to give the oppressed a better standard of living, and to create honest men."[71] The most common of these businesses were cooperatives, where customers could buy a wide variety of goods at low prices. The first cooperative was established next to the legionary headquarters on Gutenberg Street in Bucharest in September 1935.[72] Everything was as cheap as possible to attract customers and to suggest that prices at Jewish-owned shops were unfairly inflated.[73] When legionaries held a special exhibition of their fruit in November 1937, they claimed that they paid higher prices for fruit to the producers and sold it for less than their competitors.[74] Codreanu explained, "Legionary commerce means a new phase in the history of commerce, which has been corrupted by the Jewish spirit of dishonesty: it is called Christian commerce and is based on love for our fellow human beings, not on stealing from

69. Polihroniade, *Tabară de muncă*, 16, 53.
70. Iancu, *Sub steagul*, 131–133.
71. ACNSAS, Fond Penal, dosar 014005, vol. 1, f. 207–208.
72. Codreanu, *Circulări*, 54–57, 88.
73. The prices of goods sold at one cooperative are listed in ACNSAS, Fond Penal, dosar 011784, vol. 10, f. 242.
74. ACNSAS, Fond Penal, dosar 011784, vol. 10, f. 101.

them; a commerce based on honor."[75] Codreanu spoke about self-improvement and sacrificial labor to encourage his volunteers, but he used the language of economic antisemitism when explaining the importance of legionary commerce in general. He said, "Victory Road and Lipscani Street, places of glory in the history of Romanian business, are today in the hands of Yids. There are probably only one or two Romanian shops left. . . . The legionary comes to the aid of Romanian business once again. The legionary has everything necessary for victory, and he will defeat Yid business, crowning Romanian business in this country."[76] Legionaries expanded into the timber industry, establishing a lumber yard in Bucharest right next to two existing yards owned by Jews to drive them out of business. They also bought textiles from a factory in Sibiu and sold them in a quarter of Bucharest known for its Jewish-owned textile shops.[77] Legionary kiosks sold newspapers, magazines, and cigarettes, making a quick profit for the movement while also helping distribute legionary propaganda.[78] Some legionary leaders frowned on smoking as immoral, but apparently this did not prevent them selling cigarettes.[79] Legionaries encouraged Romanians to buy from them as a patriotic duty, suggesting that "otherwise your money pays for the foreigner's bread and for his fight against your nation."[80]

Alongside cooperatives, kiosks, and other businesses, legionaries established their own restaurants. The canteen at the Carmen Sylva work camp provided a model for legionary restaurants, which gradually spread throughout the country. The first was established next to the legionary cooperative on Gutenberg Street in Bucharest.[81] The walls were covered with pictures of Codreanu, Ion Moța, and Vasile Marin, and food was served by female legionary students.[82] Working at the restaurant took a lot of free time from volunteers. Maria Iordache (1914–1963) told Securitate interrogators in 1955 that when she volunteered at a legionary restaurant during the mid-1930s, "I worked in the kitchen at night together with lots of other female students, and during the day I went to classes."[83] Advertisements emphasized that different social groups mixed in the restaurants and that all the staff were unpaid volunteers.[84] Former legionaries recalled the surprise on customers' faces when they discovered that they were being served their soup by

75. "Căpitanul despre economia legionară," *Cuvântul*, 17/1 (14 Oct 1940).
76. ACNSAS, Fond Penal, dosar 011784, vol. 10, f. 16.
77. Ibid., dosar 011784, vol. 10, f. 187–188.
78. Roth Jelescu, *Şi cerul plângea*, 260; Costea, *Presa legionară*, 30–31.
79. Anania, *Memorii*, 17; ACNSAS, Fond Penal, dosar 011784, vol. 8, f. 72–74.
80. Codranu, *Circulări*, 88.
81. ACNSAS, Fond Penal, dosar 011784, vol. 11, f. 9; Codreanu, *Circulări*, 58–61.
82. Ibid., dosar 011784, vol. 10, f. 291.
83. Ibid., dosar 000160, vol. 3, f. 186–195, 244.
84. ANIC, Fond DGP, dosar 254/1937, f. 5.

lawyers who refused to accept tips.[85] Serving lower-class customers must have been equally uncomfortable for some of the lawyers, making this a powerful exercise for molding legionary character.

In August 1937, Codreanu announced, "We will organize canteens [*cooperative de consum*] next to every county office of the Everything for the Fatherland Party; we will open a wine cellar in Bucharest on Griviței Road, and a legionary restaurant in Sinaia."[86] When it opened two months later, the "wine cellar" included a restaurant; a shop selling tea, coffee, and spices; and a bar (*bodegă*).[87] Some of these restaurants were deliberately located near factories in order to attract workers to the movement.[88] A restaurant next to the Grivița factory in Bucharest ran at a 50 percent loss because its propaganda value was more important than any profits it might make.[89] Legionaries did not receive special discounts, but the prices were already quite affordable.[90]

Sacrificial Giving

Writing to inactive nests in villages surrounding the Bessarabian city of Orhei in October 1936, Alexandra Russo (1892–1941), the head of the Legion in Orhei County, chastised her legionaries for failing to send her regular reports and financial contributions (*cotizații*). "We need contributions so that we can have an office in Orhei with legionary newspapers," she wrote. "If we want to print materials, contributions are the first sacrifice." Several lines later, Russo explained that "the Legion must create a new man, punctual, good, and ready to sacrifice for his people and for the Legion. How can one demonstrate punctuality and sacrifice? Through meetings and reports, through financial contributions and work."[91]

Running a large movement cost money, so legionaries had to sacrifice both time and money. Some would work a week or ten days and then donate their wages to the Legion. Others held fund-raising balls or went door to door collecting money.[92] When legionaries needed large sums of money to buy Codreanu a car or to send a team to fight in the Spanish Civil War, they issued special appeals

85. Tudor, *Un an lângă Căpitan*, 33–37.

86. ACNSAS, Fond Penal, dosar 011784, vol. 10, f. 209.

87. Ibid., dosar 011784, vol. 10, f. 172.

88. Veiga, *Istoria Gărzii de Fier*, 225–226.

89. ACNSAS, Fond Penal, dosar 011784, vol. 10, f. 187–188.

90. Dumitru Funda, in *Țara, Legiunea, Căpitanul*, ed. Conovici, Iliescu, and Silivestru, 93–95. Restaurant prices can be found in ANIC, Fond DGP, dosar 254/1937, f. 5.

91. ACNSAS, Fond Penal, dosar 011784, vol. 8, f. 74–75.

92. Roth Jelescu, *Și cerul plângea*, 261; Viorica Nicolenco, *Extrema dreaptă în Basarabia* (Chișinău: Civitas, 1999), 93–94; ACNSAS, Fond Penal, dosar 014005, vol. 1, f. 85–88.

to their members.[93] At one stage during 1937, the Legion borrowed money from its members while offering interest rates that favored the organization rather than the lenders.[94] Sympathizers who could not become legionaries because they had public service jobs that prohibited them from joining political parties could take part in a "Committee of One Hundred," the only requirement being that they donate one hundred lei per month to the Legion.[95] One of the most ingenious means of raising revenue was the "Battle for Scrap Metal," which Codreanu launched in September 1937. Legionaries opened a scrap metal depot next to their headquarters on Gutenberg Street in Bucharest, and Codreanu asked legionaries throughout Romania to collect scrap metal.[96] His circulars gave detailed instructions about which sorts of metal were the most valuable and how it should be sorted.[97] Codreanu turned to children aged between five and seventeen in particular, offering legionary books, photographs, and songbooks as prizes to the children who collected the most.[98] Scrap metal sold for three lei per kilogram at the time, and Codreanu even began buying some from factories so that the Legion could resell it for a profit.[99] By late January 1938, legionaries had collected one hundred truckloads, which they sold for roughly five hundred thousand lei.[100] Scrap metal proved to be a very successful fund-raiser, and legionaries continued collecting it throughout the first half of 1938.[101]

Most often, individual legionaries donated a portion of their income on a regular basis, which is what Russo meant when she spoke about financial contributions. Amounts varied widely. One police report mentioned that the historian Petre P. Panaitescu gave five hundred lei every nest meeting, but most legionaries did not achieve anything close to this.[102] Regional leaders ranked the nests under their command according to how many meetings they held, what projects they were involved in, and how much they gave in contributions. The reports used to rank nests provide particularly useful data on how much legionaries sacrificed in their contributions. Over the space of a month, three fortresses in the city of Târgu Neamț met three times each during February 1937 and collected 1,017 lei

93. For an appeal for money to pay for Codreanu's car, see "Pentru automobilul Capitănului," *Libertatea*, 33/27 (11 Oct 1936): 3. On the campaign to raise money for the Spanish expedition, see AN—Iași, Fond Chestura de Poliție, dosar 93/1936, f. 311.

94. USHMM, Fond SRI Files, Reel #105, dosar 861, f. 34; ACNSAS, Fond Penal, dosar 011784, vol. 13, f. 103.

95. Roth Jelescu, *Și cerul plângea*, 261.

96. ACNSAS, Fond Informativ, dosar 234687, vol. 1, f. 6.

97. Codreanu, *Circulări*, 169–171.

98. ACNSAS, Fond Penal, dosar 011784, vol. 10, f. 113–114.

99. Ibid., dosar 011784, vol. 10, f. 82, vol. 13, f. 95.

100. Ibid., dosar 011784, vol. 14, f. 149.

101. AN—Iași, Fond Chestura de Poliție, dosar 8/1938, f. 2, dosar 91/1938, f. 154.

102. ACNSAS, Fond Informativ, dosar 234303, vol. 1, f. 27.

from the 687 women who attended meetings—an average of 1.48 lei per person.[103] That month male legionaries in the nearby village of Zăneşti gave an average of 1.35 lei per person.[104] Legionaries in the capital did much better, because salaries and the cost of living in general were much higher in Bucharest than anywhere else in the country.[105] According to reports on the Central region of Bucharest, legionaries there gave an average of 24.60 lei per person in December 1935 and 18.49 lei per person in January 1936.[106] As Russo suggested, these contributions were proof of an individual's commitment to the movement, teaching virtues such as sacrificial giving, but they were also the Legion's major source of regular income.

In addition to members' contributions, the Legion received significant sums of money from businesspeople and aristocrats. Codreanu recognized some of these donors in November 1936 by calling them "honorary members" and "protectors of the Legion." Some of the benefactors identified by Codreanu included the Bolintineanu brothers, wholesalers from Bucharest; an industrialist named Mr. Mociornița and his son; and the director of the center-right newspaper *Universul*, Stelian Popescu.[107] Other wealthy contributors formed an organization called the Friends of the Legion. Codreanu first floated the idea of such a group in September 1936, when a banking official named Grigore T. Coandă donated a large sum of money to defray building costs at the Green House.[108] It took on its final form in October 1937, with Corneliu Şumuleanu, the princess Zoe Sturza, Maria Beiu Palade, and Father Duminica Ionescu on the organizing committee.[109] Şumuleanu and Father Ionescu had been involved with the Legion since the late 1920s, while the women were both prominent members of Romanian high society. Among the Legion's major benefactors were a number of engineers or industrialists. Corneliu Cassasovici (1886–1961), a chemical engineer and former National Liberal politician who made his fortune developing the Romanian textile industry, became a "friend of the Legion" in 1937.[110] The engineer Virgil Ionescu gave hundreds of thousands of

103. ACNSAS, Fond Documentar, dosar 008912, vol. 23, f. 268–277. Târgu Neamț was industrially and commercially underdeveloped during the 1930s. It had few factories or banks, and its major industries were timber, firewood, cereals, and livestock. Gusti ed., *Enciclopedia României*, vol. 2, 312.

104. ACNSAS, Fond Documentar, dosar 008912, vol. 23, f. 283–285.

105. N. Georgescu-Roegen, "Veniturile individuale" and "Costul vieții," in Gusti ed., *Enciclopedia României*, vol. 4, 891–903, 935.

106. ACNSAS, Fond Penal, dosar 011784, vol. 4, 152–156.

107. Ibid., dosar 011784, vol. 8, f. 139.

108. Ibid., dosar 011784, vol. 8, f. 141.

109. AN—Iași, Fond Chestura de Poliție, dosar 7/1937, f. 362.

110. ACNSAS, Fond Informativ, dosar 160182, vol. 2, f. 1–5.

lei to the Legion in 1933 and was quickly promoted to lead the movement first in Constanța and then throughout Dobrogea.[111]

Not everyone gave voluntarily. According to oral history interviews and memoir accounts, industrialists such as Nicolae Malaxa (1884–1969), Max Auschnit (1888–1959), Mr. Kaufmann, and Mr. Shapiro also made large contributions to the Legion.[112] Malaxa was an anglophile, but he made donations to a vast number of causes, including nationalist ones.[113] His armaments business became deeply implicated in ultranationalist politics from 1938 onward, and he allied himself successively with King Carol, the Legion, General Ion Antonescu, and then the Romanian Communist Party.[114] Ausnit, Kaufmann, and Shapiro, on the other hand, were all Jewish, and it is likely that they contributed to the Legion to guarantee the safety of their businesses.

One suggestive but unreliable source on such donors comes from Petre Pandrea (1904–1968). During the 1930s, Pandrea was a lawyer and essayist whose left-wing, philosemitic views often put him at odds with the Legion. He drew closer to his former opponents once the Romanian Communist Party gained power in 1946 and spent years together with legionaries in various communist prisons. He wrote about the Legion while in Aiud prison in 1964, drawing on conversations he had with legionaries there. Some of his information is certainly accurate, but—like many of the histories of the Legion that emerged from Aiud in the early 1960s—he shamelessly slandered legionaries to satisfy his communist jailers. According to Pandrea, most of the goods for legionary businesses came from two businessmen in Craiova, Ion P. Gigurtu (1886–1959) and Ștefan Barbu Drugă (1881–1969). Neither man was a legionary. Gigurtu was a member of A. C. Cuza's National Christian Party, and Barbu Drugă was a National Liberal. Pandrea claims that these men sent goods from their factories to legionary shops and restaurants because they feared legionary violence against their businesses. Pandrea did not know how these relationships were first established and says that the managers of the legionary businesses that received goods from Gigurtu and Barbu Drugă were baffled when they first began receiving goods from Craiova.[115]

Legionaries argued that how much money someone gave to the movement was evidence of how dedicated they were to the cause. Of course, poor legion-

111. USHMM, Fond SRI Files, Reel #68, dosar 23333, f. 6–7.

112. Veiga, *Istoria Gărzii de Fier*, 222.

113. AN—Bucharest, Fond N. Malaxa, dosar 5/1932, f. 1–252, dosar 6/1936, f. 25.

114. Ausnit-Berry Correspondence, Burton Yost Berry Collection, Lilly Library, Indiana University, Bloomington, Indiana. I am grateful to Justin Classen for sharing these documents with me. Cf. Florentina Țone and Ciprian Stoleru, "Malaxa contra Auschnitt," *Historia*, 12/121 (2012): 14–35.

115. Petre Pandrea, *Garda de Fier: Jurnal de filosofie politică, memorii penitenciare* (Bucharest: Vremea, 2001), 117–120.

aries were not expected to give as much as the rich, but when individuals like Virgil Ionescu gave large amounts of money they were handsomely rewarded. Financial contributions from members were the primary source of income for the movement, and the Legion could not have functioned without them. Fund-raising activities took up a lot of time and energy, and the sacrifices involved reinforced the idea that the Legion was deserving of such efforts. Furthermore, the fact that giving was obligatory for all members meant that every legionary effectively "owned" the movement—implying that they had all contributed to its success, not that they all had decision-making powers.

Fascist Displays

Legionaries opened a weeklong exhibition at the Green House celebrating their achievements on 26 September 1937.[116] They hung an enormous Romanian flag on the front of the building, with a picture of the archangel Michael in front of it.[117] The artistic and literary works on view at the Green House portrayed legionary heroes alongside examples of legionary commerce and building projects. Legionary aesthetics included fewer folk themes between 1933 and 1938, and there was almost no mention of Jews, Communists, or Freemasons at the Green House this week. Rather, the focus was on "new men" who were building a new, rejuvenated Romania. Images of strong, handsome men and modest women embodying universal virtues replaced the Romanian peasantry as legionary ideals.

A police report discussed activities at the Green House the week before the exhibition opened:

> Numerous spectators watch daily as the building rises on the worksite; sympathizers bring their relatives, children, and friends to show them legionary work, organization, and charity. These occasions boost the organization's reputation. Afterward people visit the cooperative, followed by the restaurant. Thus the turnover of both the restaurant and the cooperative increase daily. From here, visitors move to the legionary store, where they can buy books, magazines, legionary newspapers, etc., and get information about other products of legionary labor.[118]

---

116. USHMM, Fond SRI Files, Reel #105, dosar 683, f. 18.
117. ACNSAS, Fond Penal, dosar 011784, vol. 9, f. 56–58.
118. Ibid., dosar 011784, vol. 9, f. 56.

The building was designed to be functional, with the cooperative's office and a legionary store carrying goods produced by legionary businesses on the ground floor. The first floor had a large auditorium, and the second floor housed offices for the Everything for the Fatherland Party. Legionaries working in the cooperative and permanent staff at the Green House lived in the attic.[119]

The basement of the Green House served as a storeroom for the legionary cooperative, but during the exhibition it became a temporary art gallery. Decorated with garlands, the display in the basement featured numerous oil paintings and ink and pencil drawings by legionary artists such as Alexandru Basarab (1907–1941) and George Zlotescu (1906–1983). These and other artworks carried a price tag of between two thousand and three thousand lei each.[120] The ground floor was filled with carpets, embroidery, and handmade ornaments created by legionaries.[121] Legionary women had their own workshop in Bucharest, where they wove carpets on looms, sewed clothes on sewing machines, and crocheted doilies and tablecloths or for sale.[122] Overall, the exhibition was a commercial success. Sales from the restaurant, the cooperative, and the shop during the first six days totaled an impressive three hundred thousand lei.[123]

The first floor of the Green House was a large auditorium, where legionaries made speeches, held meetings, and gathered for a ball and dancing. Legionaries regularly held dances and balls as fund-raisers and as a way to attract young people to the movement.[124] During the exhibition legionaries placed a plaster statue of a Roman athlete throwing a discus in the middle of the room, together with special luxury editions of legionary books. Large paintings of Codreanu and other leaders hung on the walls alongside architectural drawings of the Green House and photographs from various legionary worksites. In one corner stood a display by the Legionary Workers Corps, with pictures of legionary martyrs, diagrams about the movement's growth, and tables listing membership numbers and donations. Another two tables displayed legionary articles and publications, as well as the letters, books, and photographs of Ion Moța and Vasile Marin. Finally, the Bucharest Student Center arranged a display in another corner with photographs from the student congress in Târgu Mureș in 1936 and a picture declaring that "students become brothers through struggle."[125] All the art, handicrafts, and displays at the Green House focused on the Legion as a movement of

119. Ibid., dosar 011784, vol. 11, f. 50.
120. Ibid., dosar 011784, vol. 9, f. 56–58, vol. 11, f. 50.
121. Ibid., dosar 011784, vol. 9, f. 56–58.
122. Polihroniade, *Tabăra de muncă*, 30.
123. USHMM, Fond SRI Files, Reel #105, dosar 683, f. 51.
124. Ibid., Reel #102, dosar 722, f. 186; ACNSAS, Fond Penal, dosar 011784, vol. 11, f. 218–237.
125. ACNSAS, Fond Penal, dosar 011784, vol. 9, f. 56–58.

heroes and martyrs fighting valiantly for a nation they loved and whose virtues they embodied.

The first thing that contemporary observers noticed about legionaries was that they *looked like fascists.* In an antifascist pamphlet from the mid-1930s, the budding young writer Maria Arsene (1907–1975) mocked the legionaries:

> Friend, when you passed by me today, towering,—with your head proudly erect, your chest stuck out to show off the swastika blatantly stuck on your buttonhole,—I trembled. . . . I have seen you parading with [the swastika], friend dressed in the colored shirt, singing battle hymns. You march four abreast, one after another, joyful and full of life. You, the intellectual youth of the country, from whom we expect love and light. You preach hatred and darkness instead through your gestures and your songs. Hatred toward your neighbor. Darkness, which covers the light of justice. But you have a firm step. You bravely strike your foot against the ground. A brusque command. You stop short, military-like. An about-face before the commander then, all at once, two hundred arms raised in front. Palms down: the Roman salute.[126]

Distinctive clothing made fascists stand out in a crowd, transforming individuals into walking advertisements for their parties. The earliest legionary uniforms were Romanian folk costumes, often adorned with a swastika lapel badge.[127] This was a tradition begun by Ion Zelea Codreanu before World War I.[128] Mihail Stelescu introduced green shirts as part of the legionary uniform in 1933, soon after Hitler's rise to power in Germany.[129] LANC Assault Battalions began wearing military-style uniforms at the same time.[130] Codreanu wrote in *Cărticica şefului de cuib* that "there exists a current all over Europe in favor of introducing military virtues into public life." Legionaries should wear uniforms, he said, "because behind it lie all these great *military virtues*, which raise nations up and make them *victorious* over all difficulties."[131]

At a minimum, *Cărticica* defined the legionary uniform as "a green shirt and a shoulder belt," but there were a number of variations on this theme.[132] During the winter of 1936, legionaries introduced an overcoat (*suman*) resembling

126. Maria Arsene, *Iuda . . .* (Bucharest: Atelierele "Adevărul," 1936), 22–23.
127. ACNSAS, Fond Informativ, dosar 211932, vol. 2, f. 12; Codreanu, *Însemnări*, 31–46.
128. Banea, *Acuzat*, 17.
129. Crainic, *Zile albe*, 237.
130. ACNSAS, Fond Informativ, dosar 211932, vol. 2, f. 12.
131. Codreanu, *Cărticica*, 40–41.
132. Ibid., 41.

those worn by peasants in cold weather.[133] A police report from the following year noted that legionaries in Chişinău usually added a black ribbon and a dagger or revolver to this costume.[134] By 1938, legionaries had begun exhibiting their rank within the organization through slight variations in their uniforms.[135] When they were first introduced, some legionaries made their own uniforms, while others organized for everyone in their nest to buy their uniforms from the same supplier to ensure consistency.[136] Others had their mothers sew their uniforms for them.[137] One legionary was arrested in 1938 after he had walked all over his village asking people if they would dye his shirt green for him. The police confiscated the shirt in question and were able to verify his guilt because the shirt was still white under the label.[138]

When the National Liberal government abolished political uniforms in March 1937, the newspaper *Tempo* commented that nine different colored shirts were now illegal. Six of them belonged to ultranationalist parties. Law-abiding citizens were no longer allowed to wear black (Romanian Front), blue (National Christian Party), green (Legion of the Archangel Michael), white (Archers, Group H), yellow (People's Party), purple (Swastika of Fire), violet (National Guard), cherry (Crusade of Romanianism), or red (Communists).[139] This was not the first time that officials had attempted to curb the use of political uniforms. On 28 January 1936, the Ministry of the Interior introduced a law that prohibited "civilians from wearing any uniform in public. The elements of a uniform include: shirts, ties, belts, shoulder belts, epaulettes, insignias, armbands, distinctive symbols, etc., which can serve as propaganda for extremist activities."[140] New regulations in October 1936 identified green and blue shirts in particular as illegal.[141] The swastika itself was allowed; some police circulars considered it to be a recognized electoral symbol, while others classified it as a religious symbol.[142]

Uniforms often caused the authorities to arrest legionaries, so Codreanu was careful to limit their use. From 1936 onward, legionaries were allowed to wear

133. ACNSAS, Fond Penal, dosar 011784, vol. 11, f. 282.

134. Ibid., dosar 011784, vol. 10, f. 104.

135. Ibid., dosar 011784, vol. 14, f. 207.

136. Ibid., dosar 011784, vol. 2, f. 139; Fond Informativ, dosar 234980, f. 73.

137. USHMM, Fond Odessa Oblast Archives, Izmail Branch, RG-31.014M, Reel #2, 7525/1c/68, f. 305–306.

138. ACNSAS, Fond Penal, dosar 011784, vol. 14, f. 207. I do not understand how you can dye (*vopsi*) a shirt green while keeping the part under the label white, but this is what the police report said.

139. ACNSAS, Fond Documentar, dosar 012694, vol. 1, f. 108.

140. ANIC, Fond MI-D, dosar 10/1935, f. 6.

141. AN—Braşov, Fond Chestura de Poliţie, Serviciul Exterioare, dosar 216/1936, f. 14

142. ANIC, Fond MI-D, dosar 10/1935, f. 6; AN—Iaşi, Fond Chestura de Poliţie, dosar 7/1937, f. 150.

uniforms only at home, or on special occasions indicated by Codreanu.[143] He forbade legionaries to wear uniforms at the official opening of the Green House on 8 November 1936—a day celebrating the archangels Michael and Gabriel in the Romanian Orthodox calendar—"in order to avoid incidents with the [Cuzist] National Christians or the authorities."[144] But legionaries who attended the funeral of Ion Moța and Vasile Marin in February 1937 were under strict orders to arrive in full legionary dress.[145] As long as legionaries wore their uniforms under conditions approved by Codreanu, the movement had a number of lawyers available who would defend them if they were arrested.[146]

Legionaries also displayed their political affiliations through insignias and jewelry. In 1936 they made crucifixes from enamel or mother-of-pearl shells that they attached to their clothing with green string. The words "By sacrificing our lives we will escape from thieves" were written below the crosses, which were sold for two hundred lei each.[147] A year later they began selling white crosses with a swastika in the middle and small icons showing the archangel Michael with a Jew in chains.[148] Some of the most popular objects sold by legionaries were *mărțișoare*, decorative white-and-red amulets given to women on 1 March to celebrate the beginning of spring. Legionary *mărțișoare* included pictures of Ion Moța and Vasile Marin and used green and gold coloring, adding politics to their usual meaning of friendship or love.[149] Women could apparently wear these without being legionaries. Several girls who were interrogated by the police for legionary involvement claimed that they had no interest in politics but had taken part in legionary activities only because their boyfriends were legionaries.[150] Police confiscated forty-nine hundred legionary *mărțișoare* when they arrested the engraver Georgescu in February 1938. This was a substantial loss for the legionaries, who had been planning to sell them for twenty lei each.[151]

Legionaries displayed their distinctive image during long marches that they made through cities or from village to village. The goal of marching was both to attract new members and to serve as a form of physical exercise.[152] Legionaries marched very long distances during election campaigns, sometimes lasting one

143. ACNSAS, Fond Penal, dosar 011784, vol. 8, f. 171; Codreanu, *Cărticica*, 27.

144. ACNSAS, Fond Penal, dosar 011784, vol. 8, f. 132–133.

145. Ibid., dosar 011784, vol. 8, f. 9, 38.

146. Costea, *Presa legionară*, 30.

147. ANIC, Fond MI-D, dosar 3/1936, f. 10, dosar 10/1936, f. 46.

148. AN—Iași, Fond Chestura de Poliție, dosar 7/1937, f. 125.

149. Ibid., dosar 7/1937, f 107; Valeriu Olaniu, "Mărțișoare," *Buna vestire* 1/7 (28 Feb 1937): 1.

150. USHMM, SRI Files, Reel #102, dosar 723, f. 276–284; ANIC, Fond DGP, dosar 252/1939, f. 119–121.

151. ACNSAS, Fond Penal, dosar 011784, vol. 12, f. 17–18, 22.

152. USHMM, Fond SRI Files, Reel #97, dosar 566, f. 321.

or two weeks.[153] These could be physically demanding ventures, and participants were expected to come prepared with boots, loose trousers, long socks, shirts, and tuques.[154] Ion Victor Vojen led a typical propaganda march on 6 February 1938, from the legionary headquarters in Bucharest to the village of Budeşti, where marchers held a meeting for legionaries and sympathizers, speaking about the Legion and the virtues of Corneliu Zelea Codreanu and singing legionary hymns. They returned to Bucharest via the village of Brăneşti, where gendarmes stopped them to check their identity cards. At 4:30 in the afternoon the team held an electoral meeting at the house of Father Popescu in Brăneşti before marching back to their headquarters in Bucharest. In total, Vojen's team walked roughly sixty miles.[155]

More often, legionaries marched in large groups through the middle of cities. The march in Târgu Neamţ on 15 September 1936 is quite normal in this regard. General Cantacuzino and Nicolae Totu arrived in town at 12:00 noon, and they immediately made their way to St. George's Church, where they were met by Father Ionescu and a crowd of roughly five hundred people. The crowd marched out of the city singing legionary hymns until it reached Neamţ citadel, situated on a hill outside town. The whole distance was little over a mile, but it took them straight through the city center. When they arrived at the citadel, Father Ionescu blessed a cross that had been erected by a local pensioner named Tudoraş in memory of legionaries fallen in the line of duty. Several people gave speeches after the ceremony had ended, and then the crowd dispersed quietly.[156]

Marching allowed legionaries to travel cheaply to less accessible areas such as Budeşti, or to announce their presence in a locality by marching through the center of a city like Târgu Neamţ. These were opportunities to practice singing, to ensure that legionaries were physically fit, and to develop a sense of solidarity through time spent together in difficult circumstances. They were also propaganda events, whether this meant blessing a cross or giving electoral speeches. Going on foot allowed legionaries to gather a crowd of interested bystanders more easily because people saw them passing by their houses on the way to the church or square where meetings were held.

Legionaries often combined meetings with marches, in that once a rally finished it was not unusual for some of the participants to continue the gathering outside. After Father Grigore Cristescu gave a speech about the Legion to a

153. ACNSAS, Fond Informativ, dosar 259143, vol. 1, f. 222.

154. ACNSAS, Fond Documentar, dosar 008912, vol. 3, f. 492.

155. ACNSAS, Fond Penal, dosar 007215, vol. 2, f. 95. The police report suggests that they completed this entire journey in one day. If so, Vojen's team must have walked very quickly.

156. ANIC, Fond MI-D, dosar 3/1936, f. 76.

crowd of four hundred students in the auditorium of the University of Cernăuți in May 1935, the audience left the building and danced a *hora* in front of the university, singing legionary songs.[157] Father Cristescu used his position as an academic to arrange public lectures that he turned into political rallies. When he gave a lecture on "Christianity and social problems" in a theater in Bazargic, in Caliacra County, Cristescu was introduced by a student wearing a legionary uniform. The crowd sang legionary hymns before he began speaking, and most of his lecture was about why Aromanians should join the Legion. After his talk, part of the audience marched three abreast to the local park, where they had lunch. They were joined by Father Dobrescu, the county protopope for the Orthodox Church, and afterward they marched to the cathedral in the center of town before dispersing.[158]

Other legionary rallies were much larger affairs. When all the legionaries from Caliacra and Constanța counties gathered on the football field in front of the town hall in Bazargic on 24 October 1937, Codreanu, Cristescu, and other prominent legionaries spoke to a crowd of between fifteen hundred and two thousand people. Those present assembled in a military formation and saluted their leaders, and then local leaders stepped forward to report that "Captain, the Legionaries from the village of . . . are ready and await your command." These reports were noted down by a scribe, and the crowd sang "Imnul Legiunii" (The hymn of the Legion). Next Father Ilie Imbrescu (1909–1949) led the crowd in taking the legionary oath, and the leader of the Legion in Dobruja, Nicolae Bujin, called out the names of the dead legionaries as the crowd stood to attention, saluting, and answered, "Present!" More speeches and singing followed, and the rally ended a little under two hours after it had begun.[159]

Military-style marches and parades, fascist salutes, uniforms, oath taking, calling out the names of the dead, and singing were trademarks of most self-styled fascist groups in interwar Europe. They alerted onlookers that there was something distinctive about the Legion, showing that legionaries valued hierarchy, order, discipline, and physical fitness. The speeches and songs communicated legionary ideology, and the size of the crowds gave the impression that this was indeed a mass movement. Such behavior gave legionaries a distinctively fascist image, demonstrating that a gathering in small regional cities like Târgu Neamț or Bazargic were not only local affairs; they were part of a political trend that was sweeping across all of Europe.

---

157. ACNSAS, Fond Informativ, dosar 258626, f. 109.

158. Ibid., dosar 258626, f. 91–92.

159. ACNSAS, Fond Penal, dosar 014083, vol. 2, f. 44.

Muscular Masculinity

One striking element of writings about the Legion after 1938 is how often they describe legionaries as handsome and manly. Dumitru Leontieş writes that he immediately recognized Codreanu when he saw him for the first time in 1929, because "he was the most imposing and handsomest of all the young men."[160] Nicolae Teban remembers seeing Corneliu Georgescu and Ion Moţa drinking beer with some friends in 1927 and says, "I suddenly felt my heart beat faster. In their national costumes, they looked like heroes out of a children's story [*păreau nişte Feţi-Frumoşi din poveste*]."[161] Nicolae Păun describes another legionary, Sebastian Erhan, as "a man built like an athlete; one would think he was one of the archers of Ştefan Vodă."[162] Pavel Onciu says that what attracted him to legionaries was that "they were honorable, committed to raising the nation up to its proper place despite the risks to their personal safety. They believed in the movement, listened to Corneliu Codreanu's orders, helped each other, respected each other."[163] Eleven of the twenty-eight biographies of dead legionaries published in *Cuvântul* in October and November 1940 talk about how strong, healthy, and handsome individual legionaries were. Twenty describe the departed as having had a noble and hardworking character. Five mention an extraordinary capacity for suffering. Almost all mention dedication to the cause.[164] In addition to their uniforms, their marches, and their songs, these characteristics contributed to an image of legionaries as handsome, strong, and decisive men.

Nationalists all over interwar Europe celebrated the same masculine ideal cherished by the legionaries. Nazi groups in Germany drew on Greek models of manly beauty as ideals for young boys to aspire to.[165] Zionists encouraged gymnastics and body-building for Jewish men who would become warriors and colonists in a future Zionist state.[166] Austrians, Czechs, and other ethnic groups saw cultivating the male body through gymnastics as part of perfecting their nations.[167] Members of the Faisceau trained boys physically so that they could be

---

160. Dumitru Leontieş, "Cum l-am cunoscut pe Căpitan," in *Corneliu Zelea Codreanu*, ed. Stănescu, 145.

161. Nicolae Teban, "Corneliu Codreanu şi muncitorii," in *Corneliu Zelea Codreanu*, ed. Stănescu, 261.

162. Păun, *Un soldat pe baricada*, 117.

163. Pavel Onciu, "Întâlnirea cu Căpitanul şi legiunea lui," in *Corneliu Zelea Codreanu*, ed. Stănescu, 210.

164. *Cuvântul* (Nov–Dec 1940).

165. Mosse, *Nationalism and Sexuality*.

166. Todd Samuel Presner, *Muscular Judaism: The Jewish Body and the Politics of Regeneration* (London: Routledge, 2007).

167. Claire Nolte, "'Every Czech a Sokol!': Feminism and Nationalism in the Czech Sokol," *Austrian History Yearbook*, 24 (1993): 79–100; Wolfgang Weber and Paula Black, "Muscular *Anchsluss*:

the future leaders of the French nation.[168] Interwar Europeans generally associated muscular masculinity with patriotism and virtue, and this image was not exclusively fascist.[169] The "new fascist man," Mosse argued, "was not so new after all. Most of his basic traits were shared with normative masculinity, but he extended them, giving them an aggressive and uncompromising cast as an essential tool in the struggle for dominance."[170] Ultranationalist newspapers in Romania printed pictures of German Nazis or Italian Fascists that emphasized how closely they resembled the image of an ideal man. These same qualities were also prominent when they published photographs of legionary work camps. Photographs from work camps frequently showed half-naked young men working in the sun. Pictures of overweight or undernourished legionaries were only ever distributed if the people involved were important legionary heroes.[171]

Several legionaries established sporting societies as part of their contribution to the movement. Ion Găvănescu, a professor of pedagogy at the University of Iaşi, founded the Legion's first sporting society in 1929, focusing especially on boxing, fencing, and target shooting "to teach the use of arms and to cultivate feelings of honor."[172] Legiunea sportivă (the Sporting Legion) was established in 1932, and legionaries held a sporting competition to celebrate the work done on the Green House that year.[173] Later, individual legionaries joined sporting societies as a way to carry out propaganda among potential recruits.[174] Sport helped transform male bodies into the ideal cherished by legionaries, but it was primarily an activity for students. The legionary Alexandru Băncescu observed in an oral history interview from 1998 that although he did do military training exercises in the Legion, he and his colleagues ignored strength training because "we were all farm boys and harvested with our parents at home, which is the most complex sport possible and trains all your muscles."[175]

German Bodies and Austrian Imitators," in *Superman Supreme: Fascist Body as Political Icon*, ed. J. A. Mangan (London: Frank Cass, 2000), 62–81.

168. Samuel Kalman, "Faisceau Visions of Physical and Moral Transformation and the Cult of Youth in Inter-war France," *European History Quarterly*, 33/3 (2003): 343–366.

169. Ina Zweiniger-Bargielowska, "Building a British Superman: Physical Culture in Interwar Britain," *Journal of Contemporary History* 41/4 (2006): 595–610.

170. George Mosse, *The Image of Man: The Creation of Modern Masculinity* (New York: Oxford University Press, 1996), 180.

171. The most obvious exception to this rule was the stout Father Ion Dumitrescu-Borşa, whose role as a priest perhaps allowed him to embody virtue in other ways.

172. USHMM, Fond MI-D, Reel #137, dosar 4/1929, f. 33.

173. Săndulescu, "'Taming the Body,'" 85; "Serbarea înalţărei zidelor a Gărzei de Fier," *Calendarul*, 483 (28 Sept 1933): 2.

174. ACNSAS, Fond Informativ, dosar 160181, f. 394; AN—Cluj, Universitatea Ferdinand I, Facultatea de Ştiinţe, dosar 308/1937, f. 1–7.

175. Alexandru Băncescu, in *Ţara, Legiunea, Căpitanul*, ed. Conovici, Iliescu and Silvestru, 76.

The centrality of the male figure in legionary iconography can be seen most clearly in legionaries' artworks. An anonymous poster depicts a uniformed legionary holding a guard—the symbol of the legionary movement and a play on words likening the Iron Guard (Garda de Fier) to an iron fence (*un gard de fier*) (fig. 6.2). His bulging muscles and defiant glare protect Romania against demonic enemies, including communists, apocalyptic horsemen, and a winged angel of death. Sheltering behind the legionary guard are peasants sowing seeds, weaving cloth, attending church, plowing fields, and dancing a *hora* in front of a factory. The church and the plowman are overshadowed—but not overwhelmed—by the towering industrial complex in the background. Both the legionary and those he protects are colored green, in contrast to their black enemies. The poster follows a pattern typical of apocalyptic paintings on the walls of Romanian churches, where demons drag people down into hell and angels raise pious Christians to heaven. The difference is that here Romanians build their nation up through their own strength, and that—thanks to the legionary—demons cannot approach vulnerable people. The poster relies on a strong contrast of dark and light, and masculine strength and power dominate the image.

The Legion had a number of talented artists, including Simion Lefter (1909–1993), a lawyer and activist who also wrote many of the movement's early songs. Lefter painted portraits of noble-looking legionary leaders, sometimes surrounded by the archangels Michael and Gabriel.[176] Andrei Cantacuzino Andronic, who had studied at the Parisian École nationale supérieure des Beaux-Arts, and Vasile Chipariş (1911–1942) were also active legionary painters.[177] A graduate of the Chişinău School of Painting and a teacher with his own workshop, Chipariş painted mostly on a commission basis for local buyers. He joined the Legion in 1933, serving several prison sentences and doing propaganda tours through Bessarabian villages until he was executed by the People's Commissariat for Internal Affairs (NKVD) in 1941.[178] N. S. Govora mentions another, anonymous painter in 1933 who presented Codreanu with a collection of drawings depicting the suffering of Romanians during World War I.[179] All these men were committed legionaries, and they are known today more for their legionary activism than for any artistic talents they may have possessed.

The Legion's two most accomplished painters were Alexandru Basarab (1907–1941) and George Zlotescu (1906–1983). Basarab joined the Legion in 1932, and

176. ACNSAS, Fond Informativ, dosar 259143, vol. 1, f. 119, 198.

177. On Andrei Cantacuzino Andronic, see Gheorghe Buzatu, Corneliu Ciucanu, and Cristian Sandache, *Radiografia dreptei româneşti 1927–1941* (Bucharest: FF Press, 1996), 78.

178. Colesnic, *Basarabia necunoscută*, vol. 1, 136–139.

179. N. S. Govora, "Corneliu Zelea Codreanu," in *Corneliu Zelea Codreanu*, ed. Stănescu, 106.

FIGURE 6.2 Legionary propaganda poster, c. 1937. ANIC, Fond MI-D, dosar 10/1933, vol 2. I would like to thank Oliver Jens Schmitt and Justin Classen for providing me with this image.

most of his best-known woodcuts depicted legionary themes.[180] He had studied under Ion Teodorescu-Sion (1882–1939), an influential professor at Bucharest's Academy of Fine Arts, and then perfected his skills through private lessons from Constantin Vlădescu (1890–1951). Zlotescu also studied under Ion Teodorescu-Sion, whose work legionary art critics such as Dinu Buzdugan wrote positively about.[181] He then moved to Paris to learn from André Lhote (1885–1962) and Othon Friesz (1879–1949), both of whom achieved fame as Fauvists—adherents of a painting style characterized by its vivid, arbitrary, and emotional use of color.[182]

Neither Ion Teodorescu-Sion nor Constantin Vlădescu were legionaries, but both were well known in Romania as Traditionalist artists.[183] Seeking to create a specifically Romanian art form, Traditionalists painted Romanian peasants and scenes from rural life. Traditionalist artists used the peasantry to embody all that they loved about the Romanian nation. Unlike the realist, passive peasants of nineteenth-century artists such as Nicolae Grigorescu (1835–1907), peasants portrayed by Traditionalists were active, heroic figures who embodied Romanian strength and virility.[184] In a seminal article from 1924, the Traditionalist painter Francisc Şirato (1877–1953) wrote that "Romanian personality is revealed not through a servile copy of nature, but by emphasizing its physical, general character to reflect the mysteries of the Romanian soil and its people. Free and unconditional Romanian nature and being is shown by reducing [the artist's subject] to its essence, by spiritualizing its formal elements."[185] George Zlotescu was an art critic as well as an artist, and he wrote very positive reviews of established Traditionalist artists, including Francisc Şirato, Ion Theodorescu-Sion, and Dumitru Ghiaţa (1888–1972).[186] Other legionaries affirmed the importance of the rural elements in Traditionalist art, adding that Orthodoxy was just as important as the peasantry for bringing a "spiritual" dimension to a work of art.[187] Echoing this school of thought, the ultranationalist newspaper *Calea nouă* (The new way,

---

180. ACNSAS, Fond Informativ, dosar 260632, f. 1.

181. Dinu Buzdugan, "Însemnări," *Rânduiala*, 1/1 (Jan–Mar 1935): 106–107.

182. Michel Laclotte ed., *Petit Larousse de la Peinture*, vol. 1 (Paris: Libraire Larousse, 1979), 665, 1024.

183. On Ion Theodorescu-Sion and Constantin Vlădescu, see Mircea Deac and Tudor Octavian, *300 de pictori români: Dicţionar de pictură românească modernă* (Bucharest: Noi Media Print, 2007), 66, 72.

184. Erwin Kessler, "Retro-garde," in Erwin Kessler ed., *Culorile avantgardei: Arta în România 1910–1950* (Bucharest and Sibiu: Institutul Cultural Român and Muzeul Naţional Brukenthal, 2007), 15.

185. Francisc Şirato, "Artă plastică românească," *Gândirea*, 4/1 (1924): 4.

186. Petre Oprea, *Critici de artă în presa bucureşteană a anilor 1931—1937* (Bucharest: Editura Tehnică Agricolă, 1997), 84–87.

187. Haig Acterian, "Arta şi naţiunea," *Rânduiala*, 2/2 (1937): 75–80.

1936–1937) described Alexandru Basarab's work as a "guide" for the next generation and as expressing "a Christian and purely Romanian structure."[188]

A legionary article from 1940 argued that "Basarab is the apologist of a type of Tracian obstinacy, a fixed orientation toward the eternal and the spiritual. . . . The ability to portray eternal values of the soul in the lines of a face makes Basarab into more than a painter. [He is] the chronicler of a destiny."[189] Even though they obviously appreciated the Traditionalist fascination with rural themes, the legionary works of Basarab and Zlotescu focus almost entirely on heroic images of legionary men. Zlotescu's political cartoons for *Axa* starkly portrayed communism as an anti-Christian force opposed by strong, valiant warriors.[190] Work by Basarab and Zlotescu featured prominently in the exhibit at the Green House in September 1937. Both artists used prominent contours and evocative contrasts between light and darkness to portray their subjects as dynamic, virile, and decisive.

Contemporaries did not speak about "legionary art" as a recognized category, but the exhibit at the Green House collected legionary artists together in a way that brought out their common values. Most art critics ignored the exhibition, but the magazine *Iconar* held it up as evidence that themes of victory and heroism—flowing out of the country's mountains and plains—had finally returned to Romanian literature and art.[191] Groupings of artists in interwar Romania were small and generally lasted only a short time. Moreover, the high cost of putting together an exhibition usually prevented more than five artists—at the most—from displaying their works.[192] The artists who contributed to this exhibit all had their own unique styles, but the works on display here used portraits of legionary heroes and key moments in the Legion's history to create a clearly recognizable set of images that represented the Legion.

Basarab produced a number of woodcuts on legionary themes. The popularity of woodcuts increased significantly in the first half of the twentieth century because they were cheap and easy to reproduce, features that made them particularly suitable for use in magazines or for political purposes.[193] Almost all

188. I. A. V., "Expoziția pictorului Basarab," *Calea nouă*, 1/5 (10 Feb 1936): 7.

189. Ion Frunzetti, "Grupul grafic. Sala Dalles," Universul literar, 28 (1940): 4, quoted in Corina Teacă, "Artă și ideologie: Expoziția *Munca legionară*," *Studii și Cercetării în Istoria de Artă Plastică*, 1/45 (2011): 200.

190. George Zlotescu, "Paradisul roșu," *Axa*, 1/5 (Jan 1933); George Zlotescu, "A două râstignire," *Axa*, 1/9 (19 Mar 1933).

191. Gabriel Bălănescu, "Literatură și revoluție," *Iconar*, 3/3 (1937): 6.

192. Amelia Pavel, *Pictura românească interbelică: Un capitol de artă europeana* (Bucharest: Editura Meridiane, 1996), 59.

193. Christine Javid ed., *Color Woodcut International: Japan, Britain, and America in the Early Twentieth Century* (Madison, WI: Chazen Museum of Art, 2006). I would like to thank Cristina Albu for bringing this to my attention.

FIGURE 6.3 Alexandru Basarab, *The Archangel Michael*, 1935. Mihail Polihroniade, *Tabară de muncă* (Bucharest : Tipografia Ziarului Universul, 1936), cover.

of Basarab's woodcuts portrayed male legionaries in stalwart, uncompromising poses, often carrying weapons or accompanied by archangels. The sharp, decisive lines of his woodcuts project steadfastness and intransigence. In contrast, Zlotescu's drawings in *Axa* relied on blurry outlines and obscure images. The legionaries in Zlotescu's works were usually anonymous figures whose qualities were conveyed by their activities in the picture, or in their defiant gazes. Images depicting women are almost completely missing from legionary artworks, and photographs of men far outnumber those of women. Male portraits appear so often in legionary iconography because heroic, "new men" epitomized the movement's ideal; women, machines, nature, or peasants received a distant second place.

Good art, according to legionary writers, reflected something intrinsic and essential to reality. A number of influential interwar Romanian critics—not only legionaries—argued that art revealed virtue; the spirit of a place, person, or epoch; or the mystery of a divine-human encounter.[194] This theme reappears frequently in legionary writings and speeches of a more philosophical bent. In a sermon titled "The Gospel and Art" from August 1939, the legionary priest Ilie Imbrescu argued that "there is no artistic current in which it is impossible to establish this essential sense of things, which raises the visionary and creator up to the ceiling of inspiration and truth, which the Holy Spirit gives to those whose mission is godmanhood." Imbrescu quoted the French musicologist Adolphe Boschot (1871–1955) to the effect that "music is a direct revelation of the 'thing in itself,' [and] the laws of music uncover for us the mysterious laws of the 'substratum' of the world."[195] Legionaries mattered because through their devotion to the land they exhibited its beauty, as Christians loyal to the faith of their ancestors they embodied virtue, and as men who cultivated their minds and bodies they realized ideal masculinity. For legionaries beauty, virtue, and manhood were things, not abstract ideas, and they believed in them because they incarnated them in their work camps, their training exercises, and their artworks.

The virtues depicted in paintings and drawings of legionary men and celebrated in marches and rallies were the cardinal virtues of interwar European fascism: strength, virility, courage, manly beauty, and decisiveness. Legionaries cultivated these virtues in their schools—work camps, restaurants, businesses, and nest meetings—and claimed that assassinations and electoral violence were expressions of these same ideals. All these virtues were intrinsically linked to the

---

194. Cf. Lucian Blaga, "Fragment despre Agia Sofia," *Gândirea*, 13/6 (1934): 215–219; Nichifor Crainic, *Nostalgia paradisului* (Iaşi: Editura Moldova, 1994).

195. Ilie Imbrescu, "Evanghelia şi artă sau Schimbarea la faţa ca Temei evanghelic al Teologiei estetice," 9 Aug 1939, in ACNSAS, Fond Penal, dosar 000324, vol. 12, f. 224–233.

Legion itself. The heroes described in songs and paintings were leaders of the movement, and they were praiseworthy precisely because they were legionaries. Legionary images promoted the movement as a place where "new men" proved themselves; yet their primary focus was on the Legion, not on the virtues that it was supposed to produce.

7

SALVATION AND SACRIFICE

When the theologian and publicist Nichifor Crainic was arrested for his legionary activities in the wake of I. G. Duca's assassination in 1933, Father Grigore Cristescu (1895–1961) took over Crainic's theology courses at the University of Bucharest. Already sympathetic to the Legion, Cristescu led the students in singing legionary hymns in class.[1] Student leaders in the theology faculty, including Gheorghe Furdui, Florian Constantinescu, and Sica Popescu, rallied the student body in support of Crainic.[2] Earlier that year, Nicolae Bălan (1882–1955), the metropolitan of Ardeal, had intervened on behalf of arrested legionary priests and theology students and managed to organize their release.[3] More theology students were either arrested or hunted by the police following Duca's murder, and sympathetic professors and priests hid the fugitives for several months.[4] Father Dumitru Stăniloae (1903–1993) blamed the assassination on the "catastrophic influence [of secular democracy] on the soul of contemporary youth."[5]

1. Crainic, *Zile albe*, 283; ACNSAS, Fond Informativ, dosar 258626, f. 13.

2. ACNSAS, Fond Penal, dosar 013206, vol. 3, f. 4, 25.

3. "Cei 43 Legionari arestați la Iași în greva foamei," *Calendarul*, 536 (13 Dec 1933): 3; "Studenți gardiști internați la Someșeni au declarat greva foamei," *Calendarul*, 538 (15 Dec 1933): 3; "Legionari arestați la Chișinău în greva foamei," *Calendarul*, 538 (15 Dec 1933): 3; "Legionarii închiși la Jilava au declarat greva foamei," *Calendarul*, 546 (24 Dec 1933): 2; "Legionarii detinuți la Sibiu atacați cu gaze lacrimogene," *Calendarul*, 550 (31 Dec 1933): 2; Iancu, *Sub steagul*, 73–75.

4. ACNSAS, Fond Informativ, 257158, f. 11–13.

5. Quoted in Hans-Christian Maner, "Aspects of Modernisation and the Orthodox Church in Romania," in *Romania and Europe: Modernisation as Temptation, Modernisation as Threat*, ed. Bogdan Murgescu (Sibiu: German-Romanian Academy, 1999), 77.

Writing frequently in *Telegraful român* (The Romanian telegraph, 1904–present), an Orthodox newspaper he edited, Stăniloae publicly supported Crainic. He also urged greater instruction in morality and religion in secondary schools.[6]

Cristescu became heavily involved in the Legion from this point on, traveling around the country making speeches on Codreanu's behalf.[7] He also took a personal interest in the academic work of legionary students, mentoring those among them who wanted to pursue careers in theology.[8] When in 1936 Father Popescu-Malăeşti tried to wipe out the Legion's influence in the theology faculty at the University of Bucharest, Cristescu was his first target.[9] Student leaders rallied to Cristescu's defense, but Popescu-Malăeşti closed down their societies.[10] The campaign to remove Cristescu from his teaching post lasted two years and was successful only when the ultranationalist journalist Niţa Mihai proved that Cristescu had plagiarized some of his academic work.[11]

Cristescu's teachings resonated with legionary ideas, even in the years prior to his joining the Legion. His writings from the 1920s argued that the state should supervise public morality, that teachers should be missionaries in their schools, and that journalists should publish only Christian messages.[12] He taught students to place Jesus Christ at the center of their activities and to resist idols of the prevailing culture such as sport, sex, fashion, and alcohol.[13] Finally, he called for "vibrant, steady, and fulfilling deeds" in place of empty rhetoric.[14] Such actions, he wrote, would involve sacrifice:

> First, the times call on us to sacrifice that individualism which atomizes the social organism and the selfishness which nourishes it. Second, we must sacrifice our materialism, which becomes more and more aggressive as it is fed by the belligerent tendencies in our society. And third, we

---

6. Dumitru Stăniloae, "Religia şi filosofia în şcoala secundara," *Telegraful român*, 82/7 (1934): 1–2; Dumitru Stăniloae, "Un atlet al naţionalismuli creştin," *Telegraful român*, 82/14 (1934): 1. Both are reprinted in *Naţiune şi Creştinism*, ed. Constantin Schifirneţ (Bucharest: Elion, 2004), 25–29, 33–35.

7. "Informaţii," *Cuvântul studenţesc*, 11/2 (15 Feb 1936); ACNSAS, Fond Informativ, dosar 258626, f. 23, 26, 33, 55–56, 86.

8. ACNSAS, Fond Informativ, dosar 258626, f. 25.

9. According to Ion V. Georgescu, also a legionary, Popescu-Malăeşti was simply a strong disciplinarian who demanded high standards—something that would have frustrated many legionary students who were more interested in politics than in scholarship. Haralambie Roventa and Ion V. Georgescu, *Ioan Popescu-Malăeşti: Activitatea sa ca preot şi profesor* (Bucharest: n.p., 1939), 11–12.

10. ANIC, Fond MI-D, dosar 10/1936, f. 103–105.

11. ACNSAS, Fond Informativ, dosar 258626, f. 106, 116, 121, 122.

12. Grigore Cristescu, *Isus în viaţa modernă* (Sibiu: Tiparul Tipografiei Arhidiecezane, 1927).

13. Grigore Cristescu, *Semănături de primavara: Gânduri inchinate tineretului* (Sibiu: Tip. "Dacia Traiana," 1927).

14. Grigore Cristescu, *Jertfe, datorii şi răspunderi de ieri, de azi şi de mâine* (Sibiu: Tiparul Institutului de Arte Grafice "Dacia Traiana," 1929), 12.

> must sacrifice the politicianism that bewitches society and turns its profound ethnic energies sterile; politicianism that is unfortunately served by mutated individualism and an excess of materialism.[15]

Cristescu's rhetoric about sacrifice, individualism, the corruption of society, the power of the deed, and the importance of strong, moralistic government resonated perfectly with legionary teachings, and his sermons of the 1930s endeavored to show how Codreanu's Legion embodied all the changes he wished to see in Romanian society.[16]

Religious Nationalism

As legionaries emphasized traditional Orthodox themes like virtue, sacrifice, and regeneration, more and more priests affiliated themselves with the movement. Priests were often the most highly educated people that many peasants knew and their religious role gave them unique prestige within Romanian society, making them a very important group for legionaries to cultivate. One police report from 1937 estimated that 1.2 percent of legionaries were ordained priests.[17] Priests did undoubtedly join the Legion in large numbers. Francisco Veiga estimates that by January 1937 roughly two thousand of the ten thousand Orthodox priests in the country were legionaries.[18] At the very least, extant archival documents give the names of several hundred.[19]

Theologians wrote in support of the Legion, and priests and other clergy helped legitimize fascist groups by blessing their flags or by attending political funerals. Priests joined the Legion because their religious views resonated with a political platform that they also agreed with. They had religious views and political views, not a secular religion.[20] Moreover, legionaries had a diverse range

15. Ibid., 11.

16. For some of Cristescu's sermons from the 1930s, see ACNSAS, Fond Informativ, dosar 258626, f. 2–5, 13, 109; Grigorie Cristescu, "Înapoi la Molitfelnic," *Predania*, 1/1 (15 Feb 1937): 7.

17. ANIC, Fond Inspectoratul General de Jandarmerie, dosar 41/1937, f. 1–4. This report listed all known legionaries, Cuzists, communists, and socialists in every county in Romania and categorized all activists as intellectuals, priests, teachers, or workers. It is difficult to know how the various police officers who compiled this data understood those categories. Moreover, this report determined the number of legionaries at 16,499, whereas more recent estimates suggest that the Legion was up to sixteen times larger. For a detailed discussion of legionary demographics, see Sandu, "Der Ertrag der Militanz," 155–192.

18. Veiga, *Istoria Gărzii de Fier*, 231.

19. The longest lists naming legionary priests come from 1955 and can be found at ANIC, Fond MI-D, dosar 10/1936, f. 74–75.

20. Historians who interpret fascism as a secular religion include Emilio Gentile, *Politics as Religion* (Princeton: Princeton University Press, 2006); Roger Griffin, "Introduction: God's Counterfeiters?

of religious views—some were committed Orthodox believers, whereas others cared little about organized religion. Some legionaries were even prominent Roman Catholics, among them the theologian Iosif Frollo (1886–1966) and the Franciscan historian Father Ioan Mărtinaş (1900–1986).[21] Romanian Orthodoxy certainly had nationalist tendencies in the interwar period, and these tendencies encouraged people like Metropolitan Nicolae Bălan to support the Legion and other ultranationalist causes when appropriate occasions arose.[22] Parish priests participated in the Legion just as other activists did, although as priests their prestige made them more likely to take leadership roles. The fact that they gave legionaries access to their churches and performed religious rituals on behalf of the Legion puts them in a special category that deserves to be explored in its own right and helps us understand why the Legion was so often associated with the Church.

Ultranationalism and religion had not always been comfortable bedfellows in Romania. In the 1870s the philosopher Vasile Conta (1845–1882) celebrated "the principles of modern science" as the basis for his antisemitic nationalism.[23] Twenty years later Ion D. Protopopescu wrote in the *Jewish Peril* that "I have no type of religious faith, being a complete atheist. I am guided only by national sentiment, by love for my people."[24] It was a physiologist by the name of Nicolae Paulescu (1869–1931) who first linked Romanian antisemitism, Christianity, and ultranationalism in the early twentieth century. Paulescu deduced philosophical laws about "social instincts" and "human conflicts" from the study of biology and used them to argue that Christian morality was based on ethical principles derived from nature.[25] "The opposition between science and religion is a shameless lie," Paulescu wrote in 1910, arguing that antisemitism was a Christian duty.[26] In a popular book from 1913, Paulescu wrote that "Yids, who have inherited the teachings of the Pharisees—transmitted through the Talmud—dare to strangle

---

Investigating the Triad of Fascism, Totalitarianism, and (Political) Religion," *Totalitarian Movements and Political Religions* 5/3 (2004): 291–325; and Michael Burleigh, *The Third Reich: A New History* (New York: Hill and Wang, 2000). Cf. the idea of clerical fascism, Matthew Feldman, Marius Turda, and Tudor Georgescu, eds. *Clerical Fascism in Interwar Europe* (London: Routledge, 2008).

21. R. Chris Davis, "Certifiably Romanian: National Identity and Contested Identity of the Moldavian Csangos, 1923–85" (PhD diss., St. Anthony's College, University of Oxford, 2012), 61.

22. On the relationship between the Legion and the Romanian Orthodox Church, see Iordachi, *Charisma,* 104–110; Paul A. Shapiro, "Faith, Murder, Resurrection: The Iron Guard and the Romanian Orthodox Church," in Kevin P. Spicer, C.S.C., ed. *Antisemitism, Christian Ambivalence, and the Holocaust* (Bloomington: Indiana University Press, 2007), 136–170; and Mirel Bănică, *Biserica ortodoxă română: Stat şi societate în anii '30* (Bucharest: Polirom, 2007).

23. Volovici, *Nationalist Ideology*, 14.

24. Ion D. Protopopescu, *Pericolul Ovreesc* (Craiova: Editura Ramura, n.d.), 4.

25. See Paulescu's articles in *Dascălul*, 1/1–5 (Nov 1909–June 1910).

26. Nicolae Paulescu, "Prefaţa," in Toma P. Chiricuţa, *Religia omului de ştiinţă (Răspuns dat liber-cugetătorilor)* (Bucharest: Tipografia Gutenberg, 1910), 3.

the divine religion, just as their ancestors 2,000 years ago had the unthinkable audacity to crucify God himself."[27] Paulescu collaborated with A. C. Cuza in forming UNC and LANC. When he died in 1931, legionaries claimed him as one of their heroes.[28] A. C. Cuza suddenly adopted religious antisemitism in 1922 after having been a convinced atheist for many years. Like Paulescu, Cuza rejected the Old Testament as the work of a vengeful God who had nothing in common with the Christian deity.[29] Jews have no homeland, Cuza said, only "a doctrine of greed and hate" that constituted the core of their religious beliefs.[30]

Despite their efforts, the combination of religion and antisemitism promoted by Paulescu and Cuza did not become popular among ultranationalists during the 1920s. LANC activists tried to attract priests by distributing pamphlets at the gates of the metropolitan residence in Iaşi in 1922. But the attempt backfired when the patriarch himself read in one of Cuza's pamphlets that Romanian Orthodoxy had been "Judaized" because it used the Old Testament. The patriarch promised to issue a circular warning priests not to associate themselves with the movement.[31] Undeterred, LANC continued to criticize the Church hierarchy's ties to the major political parties and its refusal to align itself with ultranationalist politics.[32] LANC first started gaining support from prominent clergy in the early 1930s, when theologians such as Father Ioan Gheorghe Savin (1885–1973) in Chişinău and Metropolitan Irineu Mihălcescu (1874–1948) in Bucharest encouraged their students and colleagues to support LANC.[33] Neither Savin nor Mihălcescu were impressed by the hooliganism or revolutionary rhetoric of the legionaries, but both were passionate antisemites and influential educators. Their support, together with Cuza's political clout, accounts for the greater part of clerical involvement in LANC.

Ultimately it was not LANC but the Legion that successfully blended religion and ultranationalism in Romania. Nichifor Crainic, who taught mystical theology at the University of Chişinău between 1926 and 1932, became enamored with French integral nationalism in 1930 and offered courses on Nicolae Paulescu's philosophy. In 1932, after transferring to the University of Bucharest from Chişinău, Crainic launched his daily newspaper, *Calendarul*, which explicitly cultivated a clerical audience. He wrote that "teachers and priests are . . . agents of the light, missionaries of the eternal truth, pillars of the moral order, antennas of the national consciousness, sentinels of the ideas of the Romanian

27. Paulescu, *Spitalul*, 134.
28. "Morală cuzista," *Axa*, 1/17 (6 Sept 1933): 2.
29. Paulescu, *Spitalul*, 34–35.
30. A. C. Cuza, "Uniunea Naţională Creştină," *Apărarea naţională*, 1/1 (1 April 1922): 4.
31. USHMM, Fond Ministerul de Interne—Diverse, Reel #133, dosar 2/1922, f. 57.
32. "Neorânuielile în Biserică," *Naţionalistul*, 13/4 (21 Jan 1926): 2.
33. ANIC, Fond DGP, vol. 2, dosar 1/1938, f. 17–18; ACNSAS, Fond Penal, dosar 011784, vol. 8, f. 202.

state."[34] When Adolf Hitler came to power in Germany, Crainic proclaimed that "the political German Right is creating a Christian spiritual front against the Jewish anarchy of socialism and communism."[35] Crainic wrote numerous essays over the next ten years linking his version of Romanian Orthodoxy with antisemitism and ultranationalism, providing a crucial intellectual foundation for the Legion's religious nationalism.[36] According to Crainic, Christian spirituality is realized when it is *lived* in the temporal world, which is in turn *transfigured* when Christians infuse it with the grace of God. The Romanian national heroes Mircea cel Bătrân, Ştefan Vodă, Vasile Lupu, and Mihai Viteazu were all simultaneously heroes of the Orthodox Church thanks to Crainic's habit of conflating church and nation. All that is temporal about the Romanian nation "participates in the divine life according to how close or how far away it is from God," and although "spirituality is not a product of race, . . . race itself is transfigured from generation to generation by the energy of the divine light."[37] Even though Crainic abandoned the Legion for LANC in 1934, his ideas remained highly influential among ultranationalists in the decade leading up to World War II.

Clerical writings from the interwar period repeatedly claimed that the Romanian nation had emerged the moment the ancient Dacians converted to Christianity and that Romanian nationalism emerged out of Orthodoxy.[38] Teodor Farcaş, for example, argued in *Lumina tineretului* (The light of the youth, 1933–1938) that "the Church introduced the principle of nationality into the soul of the people, thanks to which we could build the Romania of today."[39] Nationalism and morality were closely related concepts for these priests. According to Father Marin S. Diaconescu, "To be able to have a true national consciousness that identifies with the serious and vital aspirations of your people, you must first have an unquestionably moral life, a personal life full of virtue. Because the mind is human, a sinner, a slave of vice, and is permanently buffeted by all sorts of temptations, it *cannot* have pure national feelings."[40] Ultranationalist clergy

34. Nichifor Crainic, "Spre blocul preoţilor şi învăţătorilor," *Calendarul*, 1/56 (20 Mar 1932): 1.

35. Nichifor Crainic, "In Germania şi la noi," *Calendarul*, 1 (4 Feb 1933); reprinted in Nichifor Crainic, *Lupta pentru spiritul nou: Germania şi Italia în scrisul meu dela 1932 încoace* (Bucharest: Editura Cugetarea, 1941), 32–34.

36. Roland Clark, "Orthodoxy and Nation-Building: Nichifor Crainic and Religious Nationalism in 1920s Romania," *Nationalities Papers*, 40/4 (2012): 538–538; Roland Clark, "Nationalism and Orthodoxy: Nichifor Crainic and the Political Culture of the Extreme Right in 1930s Romania," *Nationalities Papers*, 40/1 (2012): 111–116.

37. Nichifor Crainic, "Spiritualitate şi românism," *Gândirea*, 15/8 (1936): 377–383.

38. Lucian Boia, *History and Myth in Romanian Consciousness*, trans. James Christian Brown (Budapest: Central European University Press, 1997), 100.

39. Teodor Farcaş, "Biserica şi neamul românesc," *Lumina tineretului*, 1/8 (1 Aug 1933): 1–2.

40. Marin S. Diaconescu, "Nevoia unei lamuriri," *Păstorul ortodox*, 18/1 (1937): 14–15.

also complained that Orthodoxy was not sufficiently shaping Romanian public life. In the words of Stăniloae:

> We are living at a crossroads. Our social and political life has come to an impasse which forces us to discern that the path we have traveled up to now was wrong, and that to continue in that direction would involve national ruin. The politicians of our state have to date lacked the most essential element for consolidating a country, for its spiritual and technical strengthening: religious faith.[41]

Other influential clerical publicists agreed. Father Dumitru Iliescu-Palanca (1903–1963) wrote in his independent Christian newspaper, *Păstorul creştin ortodox* (The Christian Orthodox shepherd, 1933–1943) in support of priests engaging in politics and about the "revolution" that Romanian youth were bringing about.[42] The newspaper never mentioned the Legion, yet it consistently echoed legionary messages. Beginning in 1936, students at Iliescu-Palanca's seminary in Curtea de Argeş formed legionary cells. He was arrested at least five times for legionary activities between 1939 and 1948.[43]

Clerical Activism

In part because of the political leanings of their professors, theology students were at the forefront of antisemitic agitation in the early 1920s. In Cernăuţi, the theology student Teodosie Popescu played a key role in organizing the National Romanian Fascists in 1922.[44] Less than two years later he joined Codreanu, Moţa, and others in the plot of the Văcăreşteni.[45] Another leading agitator during the student rioting in 1922 was Paraschiv Anghelescu (1901–?), who became president of the Bucharest Student Center in 1926.[46] He engineered an attempt to reconcile Cuza and Codreanu in 1933. The following year he was appointed parish priest at St. Sava, a church in central Bucharest with close ties to the student movement.[47]

---

41. Dumitru Stăniloae, "Spre statul român creştin," *Telegraful român*, 84/18 (1936): 1; reprinted in Schifirneţ ed., *Naţiune şi creştinism*, 40.

42. Dem. I. Iliescu-Palanca, "Biserica şi viaţa socială," *Păstorul creştin ortodox*, 2/12 (Sept 1934): 1; Dem. I. Iliescu-Palanca, "Tineretul," *Păstorul creştin ortodox*, 3/22–23 (July–Aug 1935): 1, 3; Dem. I. Iliescu-Palanca, "Clerul şi politică," *Păstorul creştin ortodox*, 3/22–23 (July–Aug 1935): 1, 3.

43. Fabian Seiche, *Martiri şi mărturisitori români din secolul XX. Închisorile comuniste din România* (Făgăraş: Agaton, 2010), 399–401; ACNSAS, Fond Informativ, dosar 233835, vol. 2, f. 38.

44. ANIC, Fond DGP, dosar 36/1923, f. 18–21; ACNSAS, Fond Penal, dosar 013207, vol. 1, f. 2.

45. Livezeanu, *Cultural Politics*, 245–297.

46. Paraschiv Angelescu, "Înainte!" *Sfarmă piatră*, 2/55 (10 Dec 1936): 8.

47. ACNSAS, Fond Informativ, dosar 261893, f. 3.

Another student church in Bucharest was St. Anton's, where Father Nicolae Georgescu-Ediniți became known as the "students' confessor" because of his patronage of the antisemitic students. The students appreciated him as a mentor because he did not charge them for performing religious services and because he gave money to poor students.[48] He joined the Legion in 1928, making his church available for legionary meetings and religious services. While dressed in his priestly robes, Georgescu-Ediniți led crowds of ultranationalist students in clashes with gendarmes.[49] His superiors rebuked him for leading a riot in Carol Park in 1933, and three years later he faced trial for the same incident.[50] He was arrested again in 1938 and 1939, but he continued to serve at the altar and rose to prominence again when the Legion came to power in 1940.[51] Georgescu-Ediniți was just one of a number of priests who abandoned Cuza for Codreanu. Prominent Christian writers such as Toma Chiricuța (1887–1971) also joined the Legion in 1928; Chiricuța put his reputation as a clerical publicist behind the young movement.[52] Soon another leading LANC activist, the deacon Ion Popescu-Mozăceni (1900–?), was ordained as a priest and became a nest leader in the Legion.[53]

A new generation of theology students joined the Legion between 1928 and 1932. For some of these young men—such as George Racoveanu and Fathers Vasile Boldeanu and Ștefan Marcu—their legionary commitments would shape the nature of their ministries for years to come. Racoveanu (1900–1967), a theologian and journalist under the influence of Nae Ionescu, edited pro-legionary publications during the 1930s before becoming an influential voice within the legionary diaspora after World War II.[54] In 1935 Father Vasile Boldeanu (1902–1991) wrote in legionary newspapers, comparing the Legion's struggles to the Roman persecution of the early Christians. He became a key figure in the schismatic Romanian Orthodox Church when he settled in Paris at the end of the 1940s.[55] After graduation, Father Ștefan Marcu (1906–1989) became a parish priest in the village of Nistorești in Putna County. He carried out intensive legionary propaganda in the region, organized marches and celebrations,

48. A. Vântu, "Duhovnicul studenților și Patriarhia," *Axa*, 1/7 (19 Feb 1933).

49. USHMM, Fond SRI Files, Reel #68, dosar 233.33, f. 510–517.

50. Vântu, "Duhovnicul studenților"; Ilie Imbrescu, "Procesul crucii," *Porunca vremii*, 5/331 (21 Feb 1936): 2.

51. ACNSAS, Fond Penal, dosar 000751, vol. 12, f. 147; "Sărbătorirea zilei de 10 Decembrie," *Universul*, 12 Dec 1940.

52. ACNSAS, Fond Documentar, dosar 012694, vol. 1, f. 10–11.

53. ACNSAS, Fond Penal, dosar 000324, vol. 7, f. 377.

54. ACNSAS, Fond Informativ, dosar 234879, vol. 1, f. 55, 62, 90.

55. Vasile Boldeanu, "Ideia nu moare!" *Brațul de fier*, 1/2 (1 July 1935): 1; Shapiro, "Faith, Murder, Resurrection," 163.

collected financial donations, erected a memorial cross in the village, and trained high school students as propagandists.[56] He also carried out memorial services for dead legionaries. Marcu was named a regional leader in 1938 and became head of the Legion in Putna County during the National Legionary State. He was arrested for his legionary activism in 1933 and 1938, and his rivals in the village used his political affiliations against him whenever petty conflicts arose. Despite complaints that he was often absent from his post on legionary business, a petition from December 1938 signed by 413 of his parishioners claimed that Marcu was an excellent priest who never discriminated against any of his flock on political grounds.[57] Although these three men all joined the Legion during its early years, their political careers varied greatly over the next decade. Marcu committed himself to grassroots activism in rural areas; Boldeanu wrote articles for a regional legionary broadsheet in Focşani; and George Racoveanu joined Bucharest's intellectual elite, writing and editing highbrow publications with legionary sympathies.

Having fascist connections could be helpful for priests who came into conflict with their superiors, and legionary lawyers defended Father Suşnea from Huşi when his bishop took him to court for calumny.[58] When the metropolitan of Bessarabia, Gurie Grosu (1877–1943), was removed from office on corruption charges, legionaries and other ultranationalists flew to his defense.[59] Gurie had patronized legionary events in the past, and when he faced disciplinary action Codreanu publically petitioned King Carol II on his behalf.[60] Although there probably was some substance to the charges, behind the corruption scandal lay the metropolitan's long-standing feud with the king because Gurie demanded that he abandon his mistress, Elena Lupescu. Legionaries were also outspoken in their criticism of Lupescu, whom they particularly despised because she was Jewish. As far as the legionaries were concerned, if Metropolitan Gurie was an enemy of Elena Lupescu, then he was their friend. Others were not so lucky. According to one legionary newspaper, Father Ioan Grigoraş from the parish of Ciurbeşti, near

56. ACNSAS, Fond Informativ, dosar 259455, f. 11, 28, 46–47.

57. Ibid., dosar 259455, f. 1–4, 10, 15–19, 31–34.

58. ANIC, Fond DGP, vol. 2, dosar 44/1938, f. 22. Ion Zelea Codreanu was also involved in this calumny case but was not brought to trial. "Scandalul din Eparhia," *Porunca vremii*, 5/534 (7 Oct 1936): 5.

59. Grigore Fortu, "Mitropollile noastre," *Calea nouă*, 1/7 (24 Feb 1936): 1–2; Lorin Popescu, "'Cazul Gurie' se apropie de clarificare," *Curentul* (22 Oct 1936): 5; G. C., "Mitropolitul Gurie poate fi judecat în Casaţie?" *Porunca vremii*, 5/559 (1 Nov 1936): 3; "Informaţiuni," *Predania*, 1/1 (15 Feb 1937): 8.

60. ANIC, Fond DGP, vol. 2, dosar 49/1936, f. 28; Nicolenco, *Extrema dreaptă*, 84. For Gurie's own account of the charges, see Gurie Grosu, *Denunţarea complotului apocaliptic* (Bucharest: Tipografia ABC, 1937).

Iaşi, was suspended from his post and then driven out of his village by National Liberal sympathizers afraid he would expose their corruption.[61]

Becoming a legionary did not guarantee a successful career within the Romanian Orthodox Church, but neither did it exclude one. The theologian Ion V. Georgescu (1909–1976) was a legionary activist from his student days, yet he still managed to build a successful career within Bucharest's theological faculty. He ran nest meetings and helped turn the dormitories into a legionary stronghold while remaining a careful Old Testament scholar who avoided the polemical press of the day.[62] The closest Georgescu came to writing a political tract was his book *Actualitatea profetilor* (The contemporaneity of the prophets, 1934), in which he argued that Romanians would be able to take back their country from foreigners only if they underwent "a total, massive reawakening, one based on our foundational beliefs about life and human society."[63] He held the Old Testament prophets up as radical social critics whose example should be followed by Romanians seeking to renew their own society.

Priests supported the Legion in a number of other ways. During the 1930s Petre Chirica from the Barnovschi Church in Iaşi wrote a number of plays attacking sects, "Yids," and Freemasons. The plays themselves were never performed, but he did circulate the texts among most of the Legion's local leadership.[64] Documents from 1933 mention Father Vasile Jigau from Buhuşi blessing legionary flags, erecting a memorial cross in a nearby village, and displaying legionary posters on the walls of his church.[65] In November 1936 villages from Iacobeni, near Botoşani, complained that Father Moldoveanu added the words "long live the legionaries and their Captain" into the liturgy, conducted legionary propaganda within the village, and worked on Sundays. He also removed the icon of the Virgin Mary from the front of the church, replacing it with an icon of the archangel Michael. Below this he placed another icon displaying a Jew lying on the ground underneath a green curtain, tied up with a bloody chain.[66] In Buzău, Father Ion Frăsineanu removed the icon of the archangel Michael from his church to hang it in the town's legionary offices.[67]

---

61. "Un procedeu ingenios," *Calendarul*, 2/547 (25 Dec 1933): 9.

62. On Ion Georgescu's legionary activities, see ACNSAS, Fond Informativ, dosar 233849, f. 4, 5, 8, dosar 233835, vol. 2, f. 224–230, vol. 3, f. 13–15. An example of Georgescu's early scholarship can be found in his doctoral thesis, Ion V. Georgescu, *Demonologia Vechiului Testament: Satan in profeția lui Zaharia* (Bucharest: Tipografia Cărților Bisericeşti, 1938).

63. Ion V. Georgescu, *Actualitatea profetilor* (Bucharest: Tiparul Academic, 1934), 6.

64. ANIC, Fond Teatrul National, dosar 10/1940, f. 147–149.

65. ACNSAS, Fond Penal, dosar 013206, vol. 2, f. 381; Fond Documentar, dosar 008912, vol. 23, f. 192.

66. ANIC, Fond DGP, dosar 43/1935, vol. 2, f. 58.

67. ACNSAS, Fond Informativ, dosar 252842, vol. 1, f. 5–7.

Sacrifice

Legionaries spoke constantly about sacrifice and regeneration, a theme which was also found frequently in church newspapers. In 1936, for example, *Lumina tineretului* proclaimed that "Romania's youth must relive moments [in Romanian history] of complete sacrifice and perfect victory so as to be ready at any time to make its own contribution and to receive the reward for its sacrifices."[68] One of the most famous Romanian folk ballads, the "Mioriţă" (The little ewe), is a story about a shepherd who is killed by other shepherds, who then steal his sheep. Warned by a lamb of his impending death, the shepherd accepts his fate and says to tell people that he has "gone to marry a princess," by which he means that he has wedded himself to nature.[69] Interwar nationalist poets frequently used this story as an expression of how Romanians made suffering into a virtue. The legionary poet and songwriter Radu Gyr used this motif to explain why legionary death has no sting. His "Hymn of the Legionary Youth" intoned:

> Death, only Legionary death,
> For us, the dearest wedding of all,
> For the holy cross, for the country,
> We cover forests and subdue mountains.
>
> No prison frightens us,
> Nor torture, nor the enemy's storm,
> We fall together from blows to the head,
> Death for the Captain is dear to us.[70]

When Codreanu established *echipele morţii* (death teams) in May 1933, he explained that these propaganda teams must be ready to suffer violence at the hands of the police. In Codreanu's words, they were "*to receive death.* They decided to move forward, passing through death," in the spirit of the shepherd from the "Miroiţă."[71] Legionaries equated heroism with suffering. Imprisonment, torture, or death made someone into a hero.[72] At every nest meeting they spent time remembering those who had died, and their oaths and songs were filled with promises to lay down their lives for the movement. In 1937, when talk

68. "Jertfă şi biruinţă," *Lumina tineretului*, 3/18 (1 Apr 1936): 1–2.

69. "Mioriţa," in the version collected by Vasile Alecsandri. From http://ro.wikisource.org/wiki/Miori%C5%A3a. Accessed 7 July 2014.

70. Gyr and Mânzatu, "Sfântă tinereţe," in *Cântece legionare*, by Anonymous, 37–38.

71. Corneliu Zelea Codreanu, "Echipa morţii," May 1933; reprinted in Scurtu ed., *Ideologie*, vol. 3, 185. His italics.

72. "Legionari dela Chişinău suferinzi," *Calendarul*, 539 (16 Dec 1933): 4; Vasile Marin, "Răboj," *Axa*, 1/18 (19 Sept 1933); Ştefan Ion Gheorghe, "Modul eroic al istoriei," *Buna vestire*, 1/17 (12 Mar 1937): 1.

about heroic suffering and death had reached its peak, the legionary sociologist Dumitru C. Amzăr wrote, "The first legionaries started out from in front of the icon, under the sign of the cross—the sign of victory through sacrifice. They understood that suffering is the road to glory. . . . They sought it in work, fasting and prayer, in solitary thought, in respectfulness and in obedience. They did not avoid it in times of persecution; they sought it out in battle."[73] Legionaries could accept that they needed to suffer because they heard talk about sacrifice and heroism so often within legionary circles. Moments of reflection during nest meetings, difficult conditions at work camps, and frequent commemorations of the dead helped reinforce this idea.

Honoring the courage and sacrifice of people who had died for their country was an important legionary activity. Writing about the soldiers who died during World War I, Grigore Cristescu said, "We are called to interpret the profound meaning of the sacrifices of yesterday in order to make ourselves worthy of carrying out all the sacrifices that are required of us today."[74] One of the Legion's defining moments in 1933 was an attempt to erect a cross at the grave of the unknown soldier, and legionaries continued to erect similar monuments for the next few years.[75] They also remembered the war dead by celebrating 15 August—the date when Romania entered World War I—through religious commemorations, dances, and rallies.[76] Legionaries insisted that they were part of a struggle that had been carried on by Romanian patriots for centuries. "The fight of the youth," Ernest Bernea said in 1937, "is nothing other than continuing the good traditions and all the virtues of our people in conformity with the current historical moment."[77] Legionaries drew on nationalist and Orthodox ideas about the nation and the church as eternal communities that were quite common in this era. As did prominent Orthodox theologians, legionaries conflated the national community with the Christian community, honoring national heroes as champions of the faith and religious figures as if they had been fighting for the nation.[78] What was remarkable about legionary attitudes to the past was not the content of their beliefs but the lengths they took them to.

73. Dumitru C. Amzăr, "Destin legionar," *Rânduială*, 2/2 (1937): 51.

74. Cristescu, *Jertfe, datorii și răspunderi*, 9.

75. ANIC, Fond MI-D, dosar 3/1936, f. 119.

76. ACNSAS, Fond Penal, dosar 011784, vol. 8, f. 237–238.

77. Bernea, *Stil legionar*, 9.

78. Romanian Orthodox theologians and historians who honored religious heroes as national heroes and vice versa include Dumitru Stănescu, *Din trecutul nostru politic și bisericesc* (Bucharest: Tipografia Curții Regale F. Göbl Fii, 1921); Dumitru Stăniloae, *Viața și activitatea patriarhului Dosoftei al Ierusalimului și legaturile lui cu țările românești* (Cernăuți: Editura Autorului, 1929); Alexandru Lapedatu, "Statul și Biserica ortodoxă," *Biserica și școala* 59/44 (1935): 2–3.

Modern nationalists frequently assume that the dead and the living are bound together in an organic community. Ancestors are important for imagining national communities, first, because they affirm the supposed continuity of the nation from time immemorial and, second, because important individuals can stand as surrogates for the nation as a whole. Many of the people who legionaries honored were also remembered in state-sponsored commemorations.[79] Claiming national heroes as *legionary* heroes let legionaries equate their movement with the nation itself, something that other nationalists occasionally objected to. When Cuzists and legionaries turned a commemoration of the poet Mihai Eminescu into a fascist rally in June 1934, the writer Mihail Sadoveanu (1880–1961) very conspicuously stood up, pushed his hat onto his head, and stormed out.[80]

Legionaries honored rulers such as Petru Muşat (?–1391), Stephen the Great (1433–1504), and Ion Vodă the Terrible (1521–1574).[81] These were all medieval princes who nineteenth-century historians had portrayed as Romanian heroes. Legionaries revered them as saints. When the monks at Putna Monastery refused to bless their flag in 1929, legionaries left it on Stephen the Great's tomb for three days, believing that this would sanctify it.[82] Codreanu tried to buy the house of the country's first ruler, Alexandru Ion Cuza (1820–1873), when it came up for sale in 1936, because this was effectively a sacred site for the Romanian nation.[83]

In *Pentru legionari*, Codreanu defined the nation (*neam*) as "(1) All Romanians found, at present, alive; (2) All the souls of the dead and the graves of the ancestors; (3) All those who will be born Romanian."[84] He claimed that the final goal of a nation was not life but "the resurrection of peoples in the name of the savior Jesus Christ." In heaven, Codreanu said, "every nation will have its place before the throne of God," for "nations are realities in the world to come, not just in this world."[85] Orthodox theologians argue that the church unites all believers, both living and dead, into one living, organic community—the body of Christ. Church rituals reinforce this community through prayers to the saints, holy days remembering spiritual heroes, and icons that allow believers to venerate the saints

---

79. Bucur, *Heroes and Victims*, 98–143.

80. AN—Iaşi, Fond Inspectoratul de Poliţie Iasi, dosar 14/1934, f. 157.

81. "Sfinţirea crucii în amintirea lui Ion Vodă cel Cumplit la Roşcani-Corvului," *Calendarul*, 454 (25 Aug 1933); ANIC, Fond DGP, dosar 104/1928, f. 11, dosar 109/1934, f. 33–34; ACNSAS, Fond Penal, dosar 011784, vol. 11, f. 230.

82. Codreanu, *Însemnări*, 23.

83. "La 29 septembrie se vinde la licitatie casa lui Cuza Vodă," *Porunca vremii*, 5/521 (24 Sept 1936).

84. Codreanu, *Pentru legionari*, 396.

85. Ibid., 397–398.

by reflecting on their images.[86] Orthodox Christians remember the dead in two ways. Most often, the souls of the dead are prayed for or commemorated during a part of the weekly liturgy known as the Proskomide. The officiating priest performs the Proskomide behind the iconostasis, where he reads out the names of those to be prayed for and prepares the bread and wine for the Eucharist.[87] Special services known as *parastase* can also be held especially for commemorating the dead.[88] These are a way of showing that the living stand alongside the dead, praying that God would forgive their sins. A *parastas* is usually held after forty days, after one year, and then again after seven years, whereas praying for the dead during the Proskomide takes place whenever it seems appropriate.

Legionaries used both forms of Orthodox commemoration, holding *parastase* for medieval heroes and nineteenth-century nationalists as well as for fallen legionaries. They held *parastase* for their colleagues who had died as legionary martyrs or from natural causes.[89] They did so both to show their solidarity with the dead and their families and because this was one common legionary gathering that the authorities were unlikely or unable to prevent. Legionaries used such events as excuses to hold meetings or to communicate important information to one another.[90] At other times they held "days of prayer and mourning," during which Codreanu forbade public gatherings and even *parastase*.[91] Erecting crosses was another common way legionaries honored their dead, but this was one custom that the authorities sometimes restricted.[92] Unlike the students of the 1920s, legionaries refrained from holding public celebrations on 10 December from 1935 onward, hoping to avoid further conflicts with the police. Instead, several hundred students would gather in a church for a *parastas* in honor of "students who died for the national ideal."[93]

When legionaries died they were buried using words and symbols that showed that they were a part of the Legion. In May 1935 the body of Ioan Ilinoi,

---

86. John Meyendorff, *Byzantine Theology: Historical Trends and Doctrinal Themes* (New York: Fordham University Press, 1987), 221–222; Georgij Fedotov, *The Russian Religion Mind: Kievan Christianity from the Tenth to the Thirteenth Centuries* (New York: Harper and Row, 1963), 16–17.

87. John Anthony McGuckin, *The Orthodox Church: An Introduction to its History, Doctrine, and Spiritual Culture* (Oxford: Blackwell, 2008), 296.

88. For a description of *parastase*, see Gheorghe Enache, *Călătoria cu roua-n picioare, cu ceața-n spinare: Studiu asupra ceremonialului de cult funebru la români* (Bucharest: Paideia, 2006), 274–284.

89. ANIC, Fond MI-D, dosar 10/1935, f. 143; AN—Iaşi, Fond Universitatea A. I. Cuza, Rectoratul, Reel #226, dosar 1480/1934, f. 358–359; ACNSAS, Fond Informativ, dosar 257488, f. 32; Fond Penal, dosar 007215, vol. 2, f. 92.

90. ACNSAS, Fond Penal, dosar 011784, vol. 11, f. 52; Fond Informativ, dosar 210821, vol. 1, f. 49.

91. "Ziua de doliu a Garzii de Fier," *Calendarul*, 534 (8 Dec 1933): 2.

92. ANIC, Fond MI-D, dosar 10/1935, f. 143.

93. ACNSAS, Fond Documentar, dosar 012694, vol. 3, f. 138, 290; AN—Iaşi, Universitatea A. I. Cuza, Rectoratul, Reel #335, dosar 1722/1937, f. 12.

Codreanu's brother-in-law, was transported using a cart covered in pine branches and swastikas and pulled along by oxen. A crowd of legionaries followed the coffin, transforming the funeral into a distinctively legionary spectacle.[94] When the theology student Gheorghe Grigor died in August 1936, over eight thousand people—most of them legionaries—came to his funeral in Cernăuţi.[95] At the funeral of Iarca Davidescu in April 1937, Father T. Bratu said in his eulogy that "Iarca served God (he was a theology student) and the Nation (he was a legionary) because 'it is only possible to fulfill the call of our times and our lives through the Legion.'" Bratu was the leader of the Legion in Buzău County, and the dead student's father, Father Ioan Davidescu, was also a well-known legionary.[96] Funerals and commemorations made death a regular part of legionary life. They helped confuse the family, the nation, and the church with the Legion, and they provided numerous examples of heroism that legionaries could aspire to.

Legionaries claimed that they fought on behalf of their dead compatriots, who had aided them in their struggle. A front-page article in the first issue of *Pământul strămoşesc* suggested that they had a sacred duty to the dead:

> No one hears [the testimony of the soil] on this troubled and enslaved earth, neither in the melancholy folk song [*doina*] about the eternal sufferings of the ancestors, nor in the powerful battle melody, nor in the song warning of glory, which is hummed by the depths of the earth: the archers with Stephen [the Great] in front, Michael [the Brave] in the field of Turda, and Tudor and Horia and Iancu. O, soil of our ancestors! We cry in pity for you. Speak! We listened to you once and we swore faith to you: either we will rescue you from slavery or we shall die in the fight.[97]

According to this article, Romanians have a moral responsibility to rule the territories where their ancestors were buried. If that land was under foreign occupation or exploited by foreigners such as Jews it would dishonor the sacrifices of those buried there. Later legionary writers argued that the spirits of the dead could continue to aid the living. Codreanu's *Cărticica şefului de cuib* said that "the battle will be won by those who know how to attract through the spirit, from the heavens, the mysterious forces of the invisible world and assure themselves support from them. These mysterious forces are the spirits of the dead, the

94. ACNSAS, Fond Penal, dosar 013206, vol. 3, f. 141–143.
95. ANIC, Fond DGP, dosar 4/1936, f. 56.
96. Costea, *Presa legionară*, 32.
97. Corneliu Zelea Codreanu, Ilie Gâneaţă, Ion Moţa and Corneliu Georgescu, "Pământul stămoşesc," *Pământul strămoşesc*, 1/1 (1 Aug 1927): 1.

spirits of our ancestors."[98] In 1936, Vasile Marin glorified "the spirits of our dead, which are one with the soil, who have overcome matter [*materia*] once again and brought victory to us, trampling down death by death [*cu moartea pe moarte călcând*]."[99] Marin took this last phrase from the "Paschal Troparion," a hymn sung by Orthodox Christians during the Easter service to remember how Jesus Christ overcame death by dying on the cross.[100] Marin implied that Romanian heroes also defeated death because they were buried in soil that sustained future generations of Romanians.

The Spanish Civil War

The outbreak of the Spanish Civil War on 17 July 1936 gave a small group of legionaries the opportunity to become fascist heroes by fighting communism in a modern war. Throughout the conflict, ultranationalist newspapers were full of stories about atrocities committed by left-wing forces against priests, women, and children.[101] As did the Nazis, legionaries used stories about attacks on churches and clergy and women to recruit priests to their cause.[102] In 1936 a team of eight legionaries traveled to Spain to present a sword to General José Moscardo (1878–1956), the military governor of the province of Toledo and a leader of the nationalist forces in Spain. Legionaries were asked to donate twenty lei each to fund the expedition, and Nae Ionescu contributed fifty thousand lei alone.[103] Several of the team members sent regular letters back to Romania to be published in sympathetic newspapers. Both these letters and the books written by survivors afterward presented the Spanish expedition as an example of legionary heroism. In his book *Crucificații* (The crucified, 1937), one of the legionaries

98. Codreanu, *Cărticica*, 23.

99. Vasile Marin, "Morții noștri," *Cuvântul Argeșului* (20 Mar 1936).

100. Alexander Schmemann, *For the Life of the World: Sacraments and Orthodoxy* (Crestwood, NY: St. Vladimir's Seminary Press, 1973), 104–106.

101. A. de Grijalba, "Sunt un evadat!" *Sfarmă piatră*, 2/40 (27 Aug 1936): 4; Paul Mihail, "Mersul războiului Spaniol," *Buna vestire*, 1/17 (28 Feb 1937): 6; Ion Victor Vojen, "Politică Vaticanului," *Buna vestire*, 1/116 (17 July 1937). Cf. Fascist speeches about the Spanish Civil War in ANIC, Fond DGP, dosar 45/1937, f. 20–21, 57–58.

102. ANIC, Fond MI-D, dosar 3/1936, f. 160. On the German case, see Beth A. Griech-Polelle, "The Impact of the Spanish Civil War on Roman Catholic Clergy in Nazi Germany," in *Antisemitism, Christian Ambivalence, and the Holocaust*, ed. Kevin P. Spicer (Bloomington: Indiana University Press, 2007), 121–135. Romanian theologians also argued that priests should be ready to face death in the battle against anti-Christian forces in Spain and Russia. Dumitru Stăniloae, "Eroismul preotesc," *Telegraful român*, 85/4 (24 Jan 1937): 1–2.

103. ACNSAS, Fond Penal, dosar 011784, vol. 8, f. 50–53; AN—Iași, Fond Chestura de poliție, dosar 93/1936, f. 311; Dumitrescu-Borșa, *Cea mai mare jertfă*, 13.

who went to Spain, Bănică Dobre (1908–1939), showed how between them, the team combined all the legionary virtues:

> General [Cantacuzino] is honorable, aristocratic in his gestures, pure in his thoughts, and sublime in his actions. [Ion] Moţa is idealistic, seemingly detached from worldly things, overflowing with goodness, and sometimes as rigid and calm as an Englishman. Vasile Marin is spiritual; scornful and impatient to taste battle. The prince [Alexandru Cantacuzino] is isolated and proud. [Nicolae] Totu is sometimes childish, at other times paternally serious, and always looking for souvenirs to bring back home. . . . Mr. [Gheorghe] Clime . . . never worries about what could happen. He looks for maps, makes plans, teaches himself Spanish, and is always busy thinking about those at home. The priest [Ion Borşa-]Dumitrescu seems to me a true stoic martyr, separate from all that is of the flesh. It is like he would be disappointed if fate brought him back home. For him the Cross and Christ are the only reasons to be alive.[104]

These men all came from diverse backgrounds, but each was deeply committed to the Legion. The fact that the team included an aristocrat, an engineer, a priest, a lawyer, a journalist, and an unemployed activist, Traian Brăileanu argued, proved that the Legion was overthrowing the old social order to create a genuine "aristocracy of merit."[105] According to the propaganda accounts written by the participants, the first thing any of them did before leaving the country was to go to confession and to say good-bye to their families as dutiful sons.[106] Their friends gave them small icons, prayer books, and lucky amulets to carry with them on the journey.[107] Recording such incidents reinforced the idea that these legionary heroes were pious and obedient as well as courageous. They traveled through Poland and Germany by train, stopping at Berlin to do some sightseeing. They were disgusted with the number of Jews they saw in Poland but awed by German efficiently, cleanliness, and prosperity.[108] In Hamburg they boarded a boat named *Monte Olivio* (The Mount of Olives) that took them to Lisbon in Portugal, from where they caught more trains to Toledo via Salamanca.[109] On the boat the

104. Dobre, *Crucificaţii*, 9–10.

105. Traian Brăileanu, "Desăvârşirea structurii elitei legionare," *Însemnări sociologice*, 2/9 (1936): 1.

106. Dumitrescu-Borşa, *Cea mai mare jertfă*, 20–21, 25; Moţa, *Testamentul*, 19–22.

107. Dumitrescu-Borşa, *Cea mai mare jertfă*, 26.

108. Dobre, *Crucificaţii*, 7–8; Marin, *Crez de generaţie*, 19–22.

109. In the biblical accounts Jesus visited the Mount of Olives the night before he was crucified. The fact that the legionaries caught this boat to Spain might have been serendipitous, but the biblical allusions would not have been lost on contemporaries.

legionaries said that they kept themselves separate from other tourists, displaying legionary discipline by not dancing, laughing, or joking in public.[110]

As they traveled, the legionaries reflected on how closely they identified with fascists abroad. Ion Ţurcan, the leader of the Legion in Suceava, wrote that for these men "the Yid problem was global. Not only the Romanian nation is in danger, but all of Christianity. Judaism is an international force—the most powerful that has ever existed—which seeks to dominate through two means: Freemasonry and Communism."[111] As far as they were concerned, the fight in Spain was the same battle that they had been fighting for years in Romania. Legionary accounts frequently mention coming into contact with other European fascist groups. They saw "a team of young nationalists" in Lwów who gave them the fascist salute.[112] When they arrived in Lisbon, Marin discovered that the Carlists and the Falangists were "perfectly informed" about the Legion. He felt a deep solidarity with them based on "the common battle we are fighting against diabolic Masonic-Marxism."[113] They were impressed by the number of flags with swastikas, representing both German Nazis and Portuguese nationalists, that they saw.[114] Nicolae Totu taught young Spanish nationalists to salute like legionaries and to shout, "Long live the Legion!" in Romanian.[115] For his part, Moţa taught the Spaniards legionary hymns.[116] The team apparently got along well with the other foreign volunteers—"though they were foreigners, Turks, Germans, Italians, Portuguese, Romanians, etc., it seemed like Spain united us all and made us part of the same people [*neam*]."[117]

Several accounts mentioned favorable omens, such as finding the symbol of the Iron Guard embroidered on a tablecloth in Lisbon or noticing pictures and statues of the archangel Michael on public buildings.[118] The legionaries took this to mean that God was on their side and was guiding them forward. They reported holding frequent church services and prayer meetings while on the trip.[119] Moţa tried divining their fortunes through cards, which showed that they would have success.[120] Fortunetelling proved to be an ambiguous lacuna in the Legion's moral

110. Dumitrescu-Borşa, *Cea mai mare jertfă*, 34, 38.

111. Ion Ţurcan, *Ion I. Moţa şi Vasile Marin în lumina scrisului şi faptei lor* (Cernăuţi: Insemnări Sociologice, 1937), 32.

112. Dumitrescu-Borşa, *Cea mai mare jertfă*, 29.

113. Marin, *Crez de generaţie*, 26.

114. Ion Moţa, "Cei din urma articole," *Libertatea*, 34/15 (8 Apr 1937): 1.

115. Marin, *Crez de generaţie*, 24.

116. Dobre, *Crucificaţii*, 15; Dumitrescu-Borşa, *Cea mai mare jertfă*, 78.

117. Dumitrescu-Borşa, *Cea mai mare jertfă*, 100.

118. Marin, *Crez de generaţie*, 25, 27; Moţa, "Cei din urma articole"; Dumitrescu-Borşa, *Cea mai mare jertfă*, 31, 49–50, 74–75, 96.

119. Dumitrescu-Borşa, *Cea mai mare jertfă*, 20, 53–54, 66, 95–96, 112, 122.

120. Alexandru Cantacuzino, *Opere complete* (Prahova: Antet XX, n.d.), 80.

teaching. Clime frowned on Moța's card tricks because he felt that they were un-Christian. But as Vasile Marin pointed out, their heroism outweighed any wrongdoing involved. He commented that "if Nicoleta [Nicolescu] saw us with cards like this, with ugly and almost naked women on them, she would throw them in the fire and turn her back on us. But if I (who made them) or Ionel [Moța] (who told our fortunes with them) were to die in Spain and someone were to show these cards to Nicoleta, she would put them in a museum."[121]

When they arrived in Salamanca, General Cantacuzino presented General Moscardo with a sword engraved with a picture of the archangel Michael. The official part of their mission completed, Ion Moța convinced the others to enlist to fight in the war. They joined as foreign volunteers, although General Cantacuzino returned to Romania because the Spanish would not let him fight because of his advanced age. Some of them apparently found military drills difficult despite all the marching they had done in Romania, and it took a while for them to learn how to use their weapons and to get into shape.[122] They complained bitterly about the cold, and three of them fell ill with the flu.[123] Accounts of their first days on the front expressed horror at the desolated churches and villages that they passed through, but also jubilation over their initial victories.[124] In crisp, short sentences that retold the story like an action movie, Totu described how "we advanced rapidly. Our speed overwhelmed them. We caught several communists who did not have time to retreat. They were killed immediately. That is the law."[125] Bănică Dobre was shot in the shoulder soon after the fighting began, and he was taken to a field hospital behind the lines. Ion Moța and Vasile Marin died on 13 January 1937, killed by the same grenade. Alexandru Cantacuzino covered Moța with a flag bearing the image of the archangel Michael, and the Romanians slowly retreated.[126] They left the front as soon as they were able and accompanied Moța's and Marin's bodies back to Romania.

All those who wrote about Moța and Marin's deaths discussed them in terms of sacrifice. Before he left Romania, Ion Moța had written to his parents that "*this is how I have understood my life's duty. I have loved Christ and gone happily to die for Him!* Why worry yourselves too much, when my soul is saved, [and] in the Kingdom of God?"[127] After their deaths, Nae Ionescu said that "Ion Moța went

121. Dumitrescu-Borșa, *Cea mai mare jertfă*, 142.

122. Dobre, *Crucificații*, 35. Cf. Dumitrescu-Borșa, *Cea mai mare jertfă*, 106, 108–109.

123. Marin, *Crez de generație*, 38.

124. Dobre, *Crucificații*, 41–66; cf. Nicolae Totu, "Însemnări de pe front," serialized in *Buna vestire* during February and March 1937.

125. Nicolae Totu, "Însemnări de pe front," *Buna vestire*, 1/3 (24 Feb 1937) 1–2.

126. Dobre, *Crucificații*, 94–95.

127. Scurtu ed., *Ideologie*, vol. 4, 225. His italics.

to die. He believed deeply that the salvation of our people needed the sacrifice of his physical body. . . . He did not go to fight, but so that he might overcome death for us. . . . But Vasile Marin did not have to die. He went to face the enemy of his faith and to battle him."[128] Nicolae Totu wrote of his awe at having had the privilege to live together with these "great saints" despite his own shortcomings.[129] Hagiographic writings about the pair appeared in a number of fascist periodicals in the following months.[130]

The deaths had a great impact on observers, and the journalist Mircea Eliade wrote that he became involved in Legion as a result of Moța and Marin's "sacrifice for Christianity."[131] Spanish Catholics also defined death in the Civil War as a form of martyrdom.[132] Deliberately confusing dying for the nation with dying for the Church proved very effective in both countries. In Romania, a number of church magazines and newspapers praised Moța and Marin, "whose fight for the victory of the Cross over God's enemies was holy and glorious."[133] They affirmed that the deaths of these "martyrs" would produce much spiritual fruit in Romania. *Predania* wrote that "from now on we believe—all our intuition tells us—that churches will not be blown up in our country, the bones of the saints will not be profaned, and the unanimous conscience of an entire people will not allow the chaos of communism to enter the spiritual and physical borders of Romania. . . . Men fell, but the archangels in them triumphed over Lucifer."[134]

Burying the Martyrs

Using the bodies of the two dead men, the assembled mourners, the Romanian rail system, and the streets of Bucharest, legionaries transformed their mourning rituals into an enormous propaganda exercise. Funerary rites began almost

---

128. Nae Ionescu, "Prefața," in Marin, *Crez de generație*, xii.

129. Scurtu ed., *Ideologie*, vol. 4, 258–259.

130. See especially the special edition of *Cuvântul studențesc*, 12/1–4 (1937).

131. Mircea Eliade, "Ion Moța și Vasile Marin," *Vremea*, 10/472 (1937): 3. Much of Eliade's scholarly work between 1938 and 1943 dwelled on the notion of sacrificial death as a creative action. Eugen Ciurtin, "Raffaele Pettazonni et Mircea Eliade: Historiens des religions généralistes devant les fascismes (1933–1945)," in *The Study of Religion under the Impact of Fascism*, ed. Horst Junginger (Leiden: Brill, 2008) 356.

132. Brian D. Bunk, *Ghosts of Passion: Martyrdom, Gender, and the Origins of the Spanish Civil War* (Durham: Duke University Press, 2007), 36, 40.

133. "Cronica internă," *Luminătorul*, 70/2 (Feb 1937): 126. Cf. "Crucea Martirilor," *Lumina tineretului*, 4/24 (1 Feb 1937): 3; "Cronica internă," *Păstorul ortodox*, 18/1 (Jan 1937): 33; Coriolan Dragan, "Lacrimi în amintirea eroului Ionel Moța," *Telegraful român*, 85/5 (31 Jan 1937): 1; and several articles in *Lumina satelor* from 24 January to 28 February 1937.

134. "Ion Moța și Vasile Marin," *Predania*, 1/1 (15 Feb 1937): 8.

as soon as news of Moța and Marin's deaths reached Romania.[135] On 17 January, the Legion held a commemoration service at a "student church" in Bucharest.[136] The police reported fifteen hundred to two thousand participants in all. The religious service was carried out by a group of priests (a *sobor*) led by the vicar of Bucharest, Veniamin Pocitan (1870–1955). Afterward the priests, together with Codreanu, led a parade of mourners into the public square, where they held another religious service. Two priests gave short speeches at the end of the service, stressing the need for sacrifices such as Moța's and Marin's and explaining that these men had died "for the cross of Christ." Then the crowd sang "Imnul legionarilor căzuți" (The hymn of the fallen legionaries).[137] The centrality of the Orthodox priests and liturgy in this spectacle, together with the solemn singing and disciplined organization, emphasized how important both political power and religious ritual were to the Legion.

Father Zosim Oancea expressed sentiments often found in church publications that month when he wrote in *Lumina satelor* (The light of the villages, 1922–1952):

> For our souls, bound so tightly to this earth and to these times, the icon of sacrifice is overwhelming. We tremble before the face of the Archangel in Ion Moța, the only son of the old priest from Orăştie who, in the fullness of his youth, leaving his wife and two small children, two dewdrops—Michael and Gabriela—went to die for the *Cross*. Yet for him the moment when he died with the word "*Christ*" on his lips was certainly one of unimaginable joy, a leap into the joy of all martyrs. Let their sacrifice raise us up, awaken us to the spirit of selflessness, to knowledge of the truth, for only through martyrdom can we escape the Bolshevik hell which seeks to enter the country of Avram Iancu, Tudor Vladimirescu, Ion Moța and Vasile Marin.[138]

Representatives from every ultranationalist student organization were in attendance at the initial commemoration, as were LANC members and Spanish and German diplomats. Community groups that were not able to attend quickly sent telegrams expressing sympathy and support.[139] Student leaders and

---

135. Codreanu announced the deaths in a circular on 15 January 1937. Codreanu, *Circulări*, 119.

136. The *pomenirea* was initially meant to be held at Sf. Gorgani-Ilie Church, but it was moved to Sf. Anton at the last minute. Legionaries regularly held services in both churches. ACNSAS, Fond Penal, dosar 011784, vol. 8, f. 54.

137. Scurtu ed., *Ideologie*, vol. 4, 261–262; Codreanu, *Circulări*, 119–120.

138. Zosim Oancea, "Ion Moța şi Vasile Marin," *Lumina satelor*, 16/4 (24 Jan 1937): 1–2.

139. ACNSAS, Fond Penal, dosar 011784, vol. 8, f. 15, 18; Zinaida Vintan, "La moartea unui erou," *Telegraful român*, 85/5 (31 Jan 1937): 3.

representatives of the Legionary Workers Corps (CML) were in the forefront of these groups, highlighting those sections of the population that the Legion was targeting in 1937. Flags emphasized that this was a *legionary* event, and the presence of specially invited foreign diplomats showed that even if the Romanian government did not care about these two young men, the Legion was recognized as a political force by foreign powers. A number of Romanian public figures associated with the Legion also took part, although no prominent members of the government appeared. Having LANC members in attendance demonstrated, first, that the two competing fascist groups could cooperate on matters of importance and, second, that in becoming martyrs, the legionaries had outdone the Lancieri (LANC members) in their willingness to sacrifice themselves for the nation. No members of either of the dead men's families were mentioned amongst the multitude of names contained in the police report.[140] Other services were held throughout the country in late January, often run by organizations not officially associated with the Legion.[141]

When it came to the preparations for the actual funeral, the Romanian government was consistently on the back foot. Rather than taking the bodies of Moța and Marin across the country, where thousands of people could see them, the government had requested that the bodies be brought directly to Bucharest. This suggestion was overruled by the Legion's supporters in Parliament.[142] The bodies were brought back to Romania via Germany and Poland, a journey that took twenty-six days. When they reached Berlin, the coffins of Moța and Marin were greeted with a military parade that included SS and SA members, Hitler's personal bodyguard, and diplomatic representatives from Germany, Spain, and Italy.[143] When the bodies entered Romania, Codreanu and the families of the dead met the train at the Polish border. The train then took seven more days to transport Moța and Marin to Bucharest. It stopped at major cities as well as at places where Ion Moța had spent time during his childhood.[144] The train bypassed cities such as Iași and Galați, where the Legion was particularly strong, but zigzagged through Transylvania, where legionaries needed to gain more supporters. The cathedral at Cernăuți—the city closest to the border—overflowed with mourners when the train stopped there for an entire day.

---

140. Scurtu ed., *Ideologie*, vol. 4, 261–262.

141. "Legionarii Moța și Marin," *Ardealul* (24 Jan 1937); AN—Iași, Fond Inspectoratul de Poliție, dosar 7/1938, f. 91.

142. Ion Modreanu, G. Urziceanu, and Adam Ionescu all spoke in favor of allowing the mortuary train its choice of route. Scurtu ed., *Ideologie*, vol. 4, 264.

143. "Salutul dat la Berlin," *Curentul*, 10/3241 (9 Feb 1937).

144. Sima, *Histoire*, 305–313.

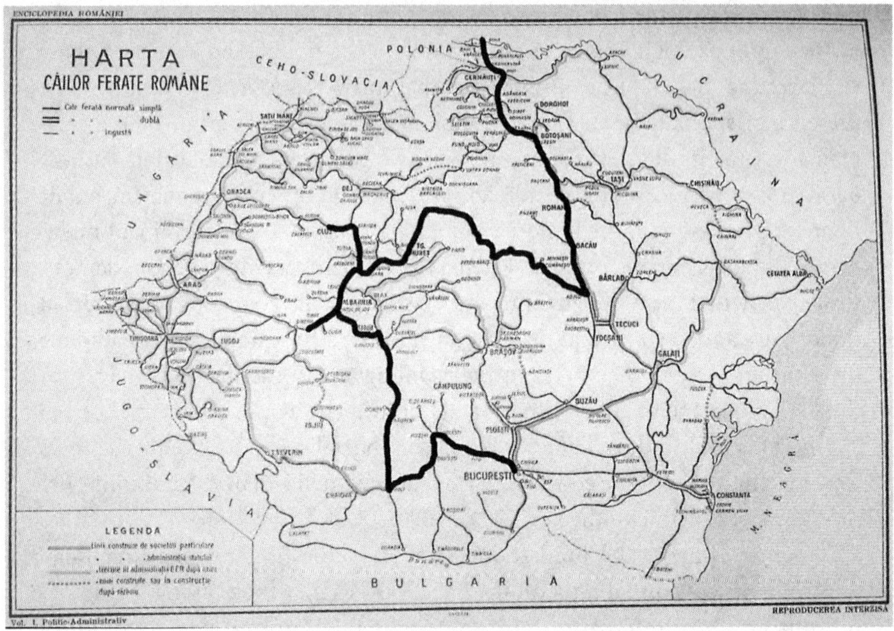

FIGURE 7.1 A map of the Romanian rail system showing the route taken by the train carrying Moţa and Marin. The original map is taken from Dimitrie Gusti ed., *Enciclopedia României*, vol. 4 (Bucharest: Asociaţiunea Ştiinţifică pentru Enciclopedia României, 1936–1940), 52.

According to Bănică Dobre, "the main road looked like a black snake, undulating and climbing [toward the Cathedral.] Everyone was in national costume or green shirts; women, children, and old men came together to weep and to hope."[145] Religious activities accompanied the train wherever it went.[146] A crowd of over five thousand peasants fell to its knees when the bodies arrived in Paşcani. The train station at Băcau smelled of incense and myrrh thanks to the religious service carried out on the platform in front of the train. High officials from both the Orthodox and Uniate churches made speeches in front of the coffins in Cluj.[147] Olimpiu Borzea, who was a high school student in 1937, said that his entire class except for two students went to see the train when it passed through

145. Dobre, *Crucificaţii*, 109.

146. "Trenul cu rămăşiţele lui Moţa şi Marin, spre Capitală," *Curentul*, 10/3245 (13 Feb 1937): 9.

147. Valentin Săndulescu, "Sacralised Politics in Action: The February 1937 Burial of the Romanian Legionary Leaders Ion Moţa and Vasile Marin," *Totalitarian Movements and Political Religions*, 8/2 (2007): 264.

Sibiu, where a *sobor* of thirty-two priests carried out commemorative services at the train station.[148]

Using a train to allow as many people as possible to see the bodies imitated the funeral of the Swiss Nazi leader Wilhelm Gustloff (1895–1936) in northern Germany in 1936. Constantin Iordachi writes that "the journey of Gustloff's coffin had taken fifteen hours, with the train stopping in every station for religious-liturgical commemorations."[149] A welcoming committee of over 180 priests and roughly 3,000 people met Moța and Marin's train on the platform when it arrived in Bucharest, with another 15,000 to 20,000 people waiting outside the station. Despite the snow, legionaries were all dressed in their green shirts—instead of the black dress customary at funerals—carrying flags and with their knives clearly visible. The coffins themselves were also painted green.[150] Silence was maintained the whole time, in keeping with the somber occasion.[151]

Students demanded that their classes be canceled to allow them to mourn properly, and the university authorities were too intimidated to refuse. The government was also outmaneuvered when Codreanu invited diplomatic representatives from Spain, Italy, Germany, and Poland to attend the funeral. This made it look like this was a state funeral, but the government allowed the foreigners to come anyway, using the excuse that they did not wish to offend the foreign governments involved.[152] Rejecting the foreign ambassadors would have been a particularly charged move considering that the bodies had already received a warm welcome from German, Spanish, and Italian officials when they arrived in Berlin on the way to Romania.[153]

The funeral procession of 13 February 1937 filled the main streets of Bucharest with legionaries marching in formation, demonstrating their discipline and their numbers. The pallbearers marched in the shape of a cross. Such "living crosses" became a regular feature of legionary funerals under the National Legionary State in 1940–1941.[154] Nicolae Iorga complained that "Codreanu followed the funeral car like a sovereign, with everyone falling to their knees and bowing before him."[155] Codreanu's behavior belied the purely memorial nature of the occasion, demonstrating that the purpose of this funeral was to assert

148. Olimpiu Borzea, in *Țara, Legiunea, Căpitanul*, ed. Conovici, Iliescu and Silvestru, 55–57.

149. Iordachi, *Charisma, Politics, and Violence*, 102.

150. Scurtu ed., *Ideologie*, vol. 4, 266–267.

151. Lorin Popescu, " Înmormântarea lui Ion Moța și Vasile Marin," *Curentul*, 10/3247 (15 Feb 1937): 11.

152. Scurtu ed., *Ideologie*, vol. 4, 270–274. Cf. ACNSAS, Fond Penal, dosar 011784, vol. 8, f. 44–45; Pamfil Șeicaru, "În greu impas," *Curentul*, 10/3251 (19 Feb 1937): 12.

153. "Salutul dat la Berlin," *Curentul*, 10/3241 (9 Feb 1937): 1.

154. "Înmormântarea Legionare Dr. Elena Petela," *Cuvântul* (14 Oct 1940).

155. Iorga, *Memorii*, vol. 7, 398.

FIGURE 7.2 A "living cross" of legionaries at the funeral of Ion Moţa and Vasile Marin. Secţia Manuscrise. Biblioteca Academiei Române.

Codreanu's importance and his power vis-à-vis the government. The Romanian Orthodox Church was also well represented by two metropolitans, a bishop, and between two hundred and four hundred priests in full robes.[156] At the funeral, the metropolitan of Ardeal, Nicolae Bălan, prayed, "We praise you, Father, that You send the light of the exemplary sacrifices of Your chosen ones, Ioan and Vasile, so that we might escape from the darkness of ambivalence, of doubt and of any quelling of the soul in the face of our destiny. . . . May their names be written in your Book of Life and may they remain in the memory of our people forever and ever."[157]

After the funeral ceremony, those present took an oath, saying, "I swear before God, and before your holy sacrifice for Christ and for the Legion, to separate myself from all worldly pleasures, to renounce worldly love, and to be

156. Bănică, *Biserica ortodoxă română*, 150.

157. Nicolae Bălan, "Fă Doamne să rodeasca jertfa robilor tai Ioan si Vasile, pe pământul ţării noastre . . ." *Lumina satelor*, 16/8 (21 Feb 1937): 1.

always ready to die for the resurrection of my people."[158] Mircea Eliade reflected upon the uniqueness of this oath, writing that "Christianity has never appeared so robust in the history of modern Romania as it does in these days, when tens of thousands of people swore before God to tear themselves from earthly joys. Romanian nature has never before been willing to be so tragic, so substantial—in a word, so Christian."[159] Rather than collectively chanting the Orthodox liturgy, mourners were expected to repeat words that bound them to the Legion in the same way that they might have bound themselves to God in a different context.

Romanian funerary rituals and beliefs about the dead vary dramatically from place to place. Ion Moța came from Transylvania, and Vasile Marin from Bucharest, meaning that no one funeral held for both men could reflect the practices of their natal communities. This created a problem for any movement seeking to embody traditional Romanian peasant practices on a national scale. In Transylvania, where Moța grew up, only the deceased's closest relatives dug the grave, whereas in Marin's birthplace of Bucharest, the priest was supposed to move the first soil. In Moldavia, where the Legion first took root, only villagers who were not related to the deceased could dig the hole.[160] In this case a team of legionaries, including Codreanu, did the work. This burial was about the Legion, not about the two men's families. Uniformed legionaries guarded the mausoleum near the Green House in Bucharest, where Moța and Marin were buried. Legionaries were scandalized when lightning struck the mausoleum later in 1937, occasioning a fresh pilgrimage to the site.[161]

At Codreanu's request, Radu Gyr and Ion Mânzatu wrote "Cântecul eroilor Moța-Marin" (Song of the heroes Moța and Marin).[162] This song was not sung at the funeral. Instead, they sang "Imnul Legionarilor căzuți" (The hymn of the fallen legionaries). This was a slow, plodding dirge that emphasized the irrevocability of death and the fact that even though everyone else—even their families—had forgotten the fallen legionaries, the singers will never forget. "Cântecul eroilor Moța-Marin" introduced a different theme, which was that death itself would give birth to life and victory. Mânzatu says that the song was deliberately split into two distinct aspects: the verses would carry the accentuated march of a solemn funeral dirge, and the chorus would end in the "apotheosis" of the fallen heroes. The lyrics of the second chorus capture the apotheosis quite succinctly by quoting Moța

158. Sima, *Histoire*, 313.

159. Mircea Eliade, "Comentarii la un jurământ," *Vremea*, 10/476 (1937): 2.

160. Simeon Florin Marian, *Înmormântarea la români: Studiu etnografic* (Bucharest: Grai și Suflet—Cultura Națională, 1995), 207.

161. "Mausoleul Legionarilor Moța și Marin a fost lovit de trăznet," *Ardealul*, 20 June 1937.

162. "Imnul tinereții legionare," in *Corneliu Zelea Codreanu*, ed. Stănescu, 169.

himself, albeit in a more romanticized context than when he had originally written the words:

> Moța, in the trench, covered in blood
> Whispers, dying, the prayer:
> "Death calls us to its bosom
> To make the Legion even prouder;
> Captain, create a country
> Like the holy sun in the sky."[163]

In this song, Gyr and Mânzatu associated the heroic acceptance of suffering and death with regeneration and new life. Legionaries could die, they said, confident in the knowledge that their sacrifices would make the Legion stronger. Relating movement, nation, and Christianity to one another, the song suggested that the country would become holier as the Legion became prouder. Legionaries not only stated that church and nation were identical communities that were represented most perfectly by their movement; they enacted these relationships by using Orthodox funerary rituals to commemorate legionaries as national heroes. Legionary nationalism did not replace religious communities with national communities. Through ritual commemorations it reinforced the Orthodox Church as national, and the nation as Orthodox.

Electoral Success

Together with the public sympathy legionaries won from their work camps and charity projects, the publicity surrounding the deaths of Ion Moța and Vasile Marin translated directly into electoral success in the elections of December 1937. Nonetheless, legionaries could not have done well at the polls had the balance of power in Romanian politics not shifted significantly over the past ten years. The dominance of PNL during the early 1920s was challenged when PNȚ won a landslide victory in the elections of 1928. PNȚ had more support in the newly incorporated provinces and promised to support peasant farmers against the industrial elites. PNȚ's popularity did not last long, however, as its agricultural policies proved just as exploitative as those of earlier governments. Both parties practiced what Angela Harre calls "authoritarian liberalism." Power rested in the hands of the party's leadership, whose policies subordinated regional concerns to the needs of Bucharest and made the villages serve the interests of a handful of

163. ACNSAS, Fond Penal, dosar 011784, vol. 21, f. 42–50.

industrialists.[164] The Great Depression brought to a head growing social tensions and further alienated peasants and workers from the political system. Coupled with King Carol II's return in 1930, it effectively ended any chance that PNL and PNȚ had of managing a workable democracy.

Royal influence over Romanian politics had declined significantly during the 1920s, but from 1930 onward King Carol worked to undermine the dominance of the already fractured and unpopular parties by replacing governments seemingly at will. Romania had twenty-five cabinets and eighteen different premiers in only ten years. For the first three years of his rule Carol governed through coalitions led by figures with personal ties to the king. Between 1933 and 1937, he formed a camarilla of his friends, powerful personalities, and industrialists, which constituted an alternative center of power undermining that of Gheorghe Tătărescu's PNL government.[165] Tătărescu's PNL was already split between older, protectionist liberals and a younger generation that tolerated the Legion and welcomed foreign investment.[166] As the major parties proved unable to function because of the influence of Carol's camarilla and the rhetoric of the numerous minor parties became increasingly authoritarian, extremists such as Codreanu's Everything for the Fatherland Party were able to perform well in the elections of December 1937.

Electoral campaigning overshadowed legionary activism for most of 1937. In March, the central leadership appealed to rural priests and schoolteachers in particular, asking them to organize marches, singing, and rallies in their villages.[167] The legionary Mihail Sturdza (1886–1980) writes that legionaries marched into villages during this campaign "in formation, with manly steps," and then knelt down and prayed in front of the church before making speeches so that the peasants could see their love for God and country.[168] Another of the Legion's leaders, Gheorghe Clime, specified that instead of marching in formation, legionaries should "crowd together" when entering a village so that no one could start a fight with individuals on the periphery of the group.[169] The government banned legionary marches from 19 September 1937 onward, and this time Codreanu ordered his followers to submit so that the Romanian people could see "the spirit of legality and righteousness that animates them."[170] In place of marches, Ion

164. Harre, *Wege in die Moderne*, 100–101.

165. Dylan J. Riley, *The Civic Foundations of Fascism in Europe: Italy, Spain, and Romania, 1870–1945* (Baltimore: Johns Hopkins University Press, 2010), 131–132.

166. Hitchins, *Rumania*, 418.

167. AN—Iași, Fond Chestura de Poliție, dosar 7/1937, f. 95.

168. Mihail Sturdza, *România și sfârșitul Europei: Amintiri din țara pierdută* (Paris: Fronde, 1994), 124.

169. ACNSAS, Fond Documentar, dosar 008912, vol. 3, f. 482.

170. Codreanu, *Circulări*, 175–178.

Victor Vojen organized teams of legionaries to ride through Alba, Argeş, and Maramureş counties on motorbikes spreading legionary propaganda.[171]

Electoral meetings in regional capitals involved speeches by local and national representatives, but also singing of legionary hymns.[172] State functionaries and railway workers featured prominently as propagandists because their free rail passes allowed them to travel extensively.[173] Codreanu deliberately appointed legionary candidates to counties where they had no friends or relatives. Ion Roth, for example, grew up in Horeza (Vâlcea County) and studied in Cluj, but he was put in charge of Tighina County, on the other side of the country.[174] Codreanu explained, "I want to destroy the mentality that a county is the political property of a county chief, in which he invests money so as to recuperate it at a later date through travel expenses, backroom deals, and business arrangements."[175]

A police report describing legionary meetings in three counties on 26 September 1937 shows how careful legionaries now were when doing propaganda. Bănică Dobre (1908–1939) was a candidate for Codreanu's Everything for the Fatherland Party in Muscel County, but on 26 September he was in the neighboring county of Argeş, where all he did was attend a church service together with 100–120 legionaries from the village of Valea Danului. Elsewhere in Argeş County a group of legionaries that included twenty-one nest leaders followed the river north from Boreşti toward Valea Danului, hoping to rendezvous with Dobre's group. To the southeast, seventy to eighty legionaries met in the village of Teiu before spreading out in small groups to distribute fliers through neighboring communities. In the city of Sântana, in Arad County, over three thousand legionaries gathered for a rally that began with a service in an Orthodox church. Alexandru Cantacuzino, a candidate in Arad County, arrived and speeches were planned but the authorities stepped in and prevented him from speaking. Ion Zelea Codreanu ran in Covurlui County in 1937, and on 26 September he held a meeting in the garden of one of his supporters in the village of Găneşti.[176] None of these meetings involved violent clashes with police, no one incited attacks on Jews, and none of the legionaries dressed up as *haiduci*. Isolated individuals were arrested for wearing legionary uniforms during 1937, but Codreanu had forbidden

171. ACNSAS, Fond Penal, dosar 007215, vol. 2, f. 90–91.

172. "Întâlnirea partidului 'Totul pentru ţară' la Braşov," *Ardealul*, 14 Dec 1937.

173. ACNSAS, Fond Penal, dosar 011784, vol. 12, f. 162.

174. ACNSAS, Fond Informativ, dosar 260633, f. 1.

175. Scurtu ed., *Ideologie*, vol. 4, 355.

176. USHMM, Fond SRI Files, Reel #105, dosar 863, f. 27–28. For a list of which legionaries ran in which counties, see ibid., Reel #105, dosar 859, f. 189–204.

legionaries to wear them in public, and clothing was rarely an issue during this campaign.[177]

Legionaries exploited existing social networks during these elections. On 10 October 1937 they held a ball in Bucharest as a way to publicize the movement through a festive occasion.[178] That month student leaders also organized a campaign aimed at students from Ardeal who were living in Bucharest. Students generally identified strongly with the region that they had come from, and legionaries used regional solidarities to promote the Legion.[179] Some propagandists focused specifically on factory workers, and the Legion produced fliers picturing workers carrying their tools while doing a legionary salute.[180] Once the elections were over the movement's leadership praised legionary workers for their contribution to the campaign, which was apparently the most significant of any group within the Legion.[181]

Individual testimonies suggest that sometimes the most effective propaganda took place not during large public rallies but from person to person. Chirilă Ciuntu, for example, writes in his memoirs that he became a legionary because of one-on-one testimony by a propagandist during 1933.[182] Similar accounts by former legionaries mention that it was discussions with family and friends that convinced them to join the Legion.[183] For others, such as the veterinarian Tudor Cicală or the Cuzist medical student Şerban Milcoveanu (1911–2009), a personal meeting with Codreanu convinced them to join.[184] A declaration given to the Securitate by the publican Dumitru Ionescu in 1948 said that he became a legionary at the time of the 1937 elections when a lawyer named Vasile Teodorescu from the nearby village of Moviliţa came to Roşiori, a village in Ilfov County where Ionescu lived. A number of parties had held electoral rallies in Roşiori earlier in the year, but when the legionaries arrived, Ionescu recognized Teodorescu. Ionescu said that his late father had been a friend of the National Peasantist politician Dr. Nicolae Lupu and that he also voted PNŢ for the same reason. Teodorescu told him that PNŢ had no chance of winning the upcoming

177. Ibid., Reel #105, dosar 863, f. 95.

178. Ibid., Reel #105, dosar 863, f. 76.

179. Ibid., Reel #105, dosar 863, f. 50.

180. Ibid., Reel #105, dosar 863, f. 7.

181. ACNSAS, Fond Penal, dosar 007215, vol. 2, f. 87, 90–91.

182. Chirilă Ciuntu, *Din Bucovina pe Oder (amintirile unui legionar)* (Constanţa: Metafora, 2004), 10.

183. Stănescu ed., *Corneliu Zelea Codreanu*, 36–48, 62–82, 89–116, 165–174; Păun, *Un soldat pe baricada*; Sofia Cristescu Dinescu, "Cetăţui sfărâmate," in *Lacrima prigoanei: Din lupta legionarelor române*, ed. Nistor Chioreanu (Timişoara: Gorian, 1994), 7–16; Horia Sima, "Cum am intrat în Legiune," in *Mărturii despre legiune*, ed. Brădescu, 165–181.

184. Stănescu ed., *Corneliu Zelea Codreanu*, 49–50, 179.

elections and pointed out that the Legion had prominent supporters in a number of villages in the area. Convinced by Teodorescu's personal approach, Ionescu joined a legionary nest.[185]

Rules governing propaganda tightened as the day of the elections approached. No party was allowed to enlist minors or students in its campaign, marching in paramilitary formation was forbidden, political uniforms were banned, guns were not allowed near voting booths, and pubs were closed for several days before and after the elections.[186] Police in Cluj County searched for hidden stockpiles of wine that they believed might be used to bribe voters.[187] But these measures did not prevent electoral violence, which was subdued but not eradicated during these elections. A former LANC senator named Mumuianu was attacked by peasants while campaigning. He suffered broken bones and was left unconscious in a ditch. A former PNŢ senator, the mathematics professor Cezar Spineanu, was stabbed during a visit to another village. The Legion's office in Constanţa was destroyed by vandals and the building's owner, Mr. Slăvescu, was badly beaten. In Bucharest a group of legionaries fought with council workers who were tearing down legionary propaganda posters. One legionary and four of the council workers were taken to hospital.[188] By and large legionaries followed Codreanu's orders to avoid conflict, but when the mayor of Moreni, in Prahova County, slapped the legionary Traian Ioniţă, Codreanu told his followers to "demand satisfaction and wash the offense away as quickly as possible," even if this meant losing the elections.[189]

One factor that significantly reduced the violence surrounding the Legion was an electoral pact signed by Codreanu and the PNŢ politician Iuliu Maniu on 26 November 1937. Codreanu had approached both Maniu and Gheorghe Brătianu, a leader of a dissident PNL faction, in April 1937 to discuss forming a united front against King Carol. Maniu's response was positive but noncommittal, while Brătianu strongly supported the idea. In November, Maniu publicly offered to form an electoral alliance with Codreanu and Brătianu, and both accepted.[190] The pact scandalized legionaries, PNŢ, and PNL supporters alike, but their leaders remained firm.[191] All three parties ran independent candidates and did not endorse each other's policies, but they did commit to ensuring free elections

185. ACNSAS, Fond Informativ, dosar 160161, vol. 3, f. 64–76.
186. AN—Cluj, Fond Inspectoratul de Poliţie, dosar 675/1937, f. 6, 21, 24, 78.
187. Ibid., dosar 675/1937, f. 40.
188. "Incidente electorale," *Ardealul*, 19 Dec 1937.
189. Codreanu, *Circulări*, 207.
190. Haynes, "Reluctant Allies?" 114–117.
191. In the days that followed Codreanu repeatedly defended the pact in his circulars and press releases. Codreanu, *Circulări*, 208–216.

with minimal fraud or violence. This pact significantly reduced the violence that legionaries faced—or caused—during the election campaign, though legionaries still clashed with Cuzist militants associated with PNC.[192] The pact did not erase the Legion's problems completely, however. On 11 December members of Gheorghe Tătărescu's PNL, supported by PNC's Istrate Micescu, successfully contested the legality of any list that included legionaries who had fought in the Spanish Civil War. They said that the legionaries were no longer Romanian citizens because they had fought under a foreign flag. This last-minute challenge disqualified the Legion from contesting eighteen counties.[193]

Even though Codreanu did not gain power, the movement's growth during the mid-1930s was remarkable. Contemporaries consistently attributed this success to the publicity created by the Legion's work camps, businesses, and marches rather than to the assassination attempts and gang violence practiced by some members. Codreanu's new commitment to peaceful propaganda translated the goal of creating "new men" into practical legionary activities. Ideology and practice coincided in the work camps and businesses, presenting the Legion as a movement that fulfilled its promises and had the country's best interests at heart. Issues such as antisemitism, which had been a core legionary platform in the late-1920s, no longer attracted votes for the Legion because antisemitism had become a standard policy for a number of parties. Nor were legionaries simply profiting from protest votes against the major parties, as they had in the elections of the early 1930s. Instead, legionaries gained votes in regions where they did the most intensive campaigning and where the electoral apparatuses of the major parties were weakest.[194] Opposing the clientalism and corruption of the major parties, legionaries mobilized new social groups for the first time, channeling their votes into what Dylan Riley has called "fascist authoritarian democracy."[195] The celebrity gained through Moța and Marin's funeral and the system of work camps and businesses that proclaimed the Legion's commitment to replacing politicianism and corruption with honest labor became central to legionary propaganda and rapidly increased the political clout of legionaries.

---

192. Paul A. Shapiro, "Prelude to Dictatorship in Romania: The National Christian Party in Power, December 1937–February 1938," *Canadian-American Slavic Studies*, 8/1 (1974): 56.

193. Scurtu ed., *Ideologie*, vol. 4, 366–367; Codreanu, *Circulări*, 222.

194. Armin Heinen, "Wahl-Maschine. Die Legion "Erzengel Mchael," die Wahlen 1931–1937 und die Integrationskriese des rumänischen Staates," in *Inszenierte Gegenmacht von rechts: Die "Legion Erzengel Michael" in Rumänien 1918–1938*, ed. Armin Heinen and Oliver Jens Schmitt (Munich: R. Oldenbourg Verlag, 2013), 130–154.

195. Riley, *Civic Foundations*, 147.

8

RISE AND FALL

The elections of 1937 produced a hung Parliament. For the first time in Romanian history, the incumbent party failed to win the election. Gheorghe Tătărescu's governing coalition won only 35.92 percent of the vote. Iuliu Maniu's PNŢ won 20.40 percent, and Codreanu's Everything for the Fatherland Party won 15.58 percent.[1] With PNL obviously lacking public support, and disinclined to give power to either Maniu or Codreanu, the king asked the fourth-largest party—PNC, led by A. C. Cuza and Octavian Goga, which won 9.15 percent of the vote—to form a cabinet. It was composed of five PNC deputies; three PNŢ members; and two independents, including Istrate Micescu as the minister for foreign affairs and Armand Călinescu (1893–1939), a committed enemy of the Legion, as the minister of the interior. This alliance was shaky from the beginning, and Cuzist supporters even assaulted one of Călinescu's appointees in the courtyard of the Ministry of the Interior so that he could not take his oath of office.[2]

The new Goga-Cuza government immediately began instituting antisemitic measures. It appointed commissars to oversee businesses owned by non-Romanians; revoked Jews' rights to sell alcohol, tobacco, cigarettes, matches, and other goods that fell under a state monopoly; banned Jewish newspapers; dictated that only ethnic Romanians were allowed to work as journalists; closed down Jewish

1. C. Enescu, "Semnificaţia alegerilor din Decemvrie 1937 în evoluţia politică a neamului românesc," *Sociologie românească*, 2/11–12 (1937): 521.

2. Shapiro, "Prelude to Dictatorship," 66–72.

publishing houses, cinemas, and theaters; and began the process of taking citizenship away from Jews. These steps paralyzed the economy and boosted fears among Romania's mostly pro-French allies that Cuza and Goga were planning an alliance with Nazi Germany.[3] Codreanu was not convinced that this antisemitic legislation made him a friend of the government, and he reminded legionaries that Călinescu and Cuza had attacked them in the past.[4] Cuza and Goga needed a parliamentary majority to govern, so Goga announced a new round of elections that were scheduled for 3 March 1938.

On 14 January Codreanu issued a circular ordering his legionaries to abstain from slander or negative comments about their electoral opponents and to "maintain an attitude of the greatest dignity."[5] At the same time, he arranged for legionaries to draw up blacklists of police officers and political opponents who tried to interfere with legionary propaganda. County chiefs were then supposed to inform these individuals that they would be "sanctioned according to the gravity of their actions once the Legion is victorious."[6] Fighting among legionaries, Cuzists, and the Siguranța—now under the control of Armand Călinescu—began even before the election campaign opened on 6 February. Within five days 2 legionaries had been killed, 52 injured, and 450 arrested.[7] With escalating violence, relations with Romania's allies at breaking point, and attempts at reconciliation among the major political parties meeting with repeated failure, King Carol II ended the parliamentary system on 10 February 1938.[8]

Royal Dictatorship

Carol abolished the constitution of 1923 and banned all political parties. He appointed the patriarch of the Romanian Orthodox Church, Miron Cristea (1868–1939), as his prime minister, with Armand Călinescu remaining as minister of the interior. Carol continued introducing new antisemitic legislation but reaffirmed his commitment to a pro-French orientation in foreign policy.[9] Carol's move signaled the end of the Legion as an effective social movement. His government was carrying out the antisemitic measures that ultranationalists

3. Jean Ancel, *The Economic Destruction of Romanian Jewry* (Jerusalem: International Institute for Holocaust Research Yad Vashem, 2007), 38–44.

4. Codreanu, *Circulări*, 221–224.

5. Ibid., 225–226.

6. AN—Iași, Fond Chestura de Poliție, dosar 7/1937, f. 454.

7. Codreanu, *Circulări*, 250–251.

8. Heinen, *Legiunea "Arhanghelul Mihail,"* 335–339; Shapiro, "Prelude to Dictatorship," 82–85.

9. Ancel, *Economic Destruction*, 48–68.

had demanded for decades, he had abolished Freemasonry at the beginning of 1937, and he had ostensibly ended "politicianism" by dissolving Parliament and prohibiting political parties. On 21 February 1938, Codreanu issued a circular disbanding the Legion on the grounds that it could no longer legally engage in politics and did not intend to stage a coup d'état: "We wait for our victory to come through the completion, in the nation's soul, of a process of human perfection," he said. "We will not use violent means because our historical mission and responsibility is too deeply rooted in the consciousness of today's youth to allow thoughtless actions that would transform Romania into a bloodied Spain."[10]

From this point onward, the everyday experience of fascism changed dramatically for legionaries at all levels of the movement. State functionaries and high school students now faced prison if they were found engaging in legionary activities.[11] The government insisted that Codreanu also close down legionary restaurants and businesses. He had trouble repaying his creditors on short notice, and some legionaries accused him of mismanaging the movement's funds.[12] Angry about these financial problems, Codreanu wrote an open letter to the king's counselor, Nicolae Iorga. He accused Iorga of betraying the ultranationalist movement that he had been instrumental in founding at the beginning of the century. Before World War I, Iorga had called on ethnic Romanians to establish their own businesses to undercut Jewish competition, but now his government banned legionary enterprises. "You are unfair!" Codreanu wrote. "You are, in spirit, dishonest!"[13] Iorga charged Codreanu with libel, and on 19 April a military tribunal sentenced Codreanu to six months in prison. Many of the Legion's leaders were arrested together with Codreanu, including 150 people in Bucharest alone.[14] In Constanța County the police raided 538 houses on the night of 16 April.[15] That month police began confiscating crosses (*troițe*) erected by legionaries and taking them to cemeteries, where they removed any legionary markings and began using them as gravestones.[16]

On 27 May, another military tribunal sentenced Codreanu to ten years in prison for treason and for inciting rebellion.[17] Most of the other legionaries arrested that spring were tried in July and remained in prison or under house

10. Codreanu, *Circulări*, 254–257.

11. AN—Iași, Fond Chestura de Poliție, dosar 118/1938, f. 2, 22.

12. Codreanu, *Circulări*, 260–263; ACNSAS, Fond Penal, dosar 011784, vol. 13, f. 329, vol. 19, f. 55.

13. The Romanian phrase is stronger than it sounds in English: "Ești un incorect! Ești un necinstit sufletește!" Codreanu, *Circulări*, 264–267.

14. Scurtu ed., *Ideologie*, vol. 5, 60–64.

15. Ibid., vol. 5, 96.

16. Ibid., vol. 5, 142–143.

17. Ibid., vol. 5, 112–123.

arrest for the rest of the year.[18] In December 1938 and January 1939, groups of legionaries who were still at large fled to Germany. Gathering in Berlin, they attempted to lead the movement in Romania, but personal rivalries made effective leadership difficult.[19] With all its senior leaders either behind bars or in exile, the Legion's hierarchy was in chaos, giving individuals more liberty to engage in desperate actions in the movement's name. No longer the organ of a confident social movement, the Legion began to resemble a clandestine terrorist organization. Those who took over as leaders did so as wanted men and women who could not come out of hiding for fear of arrest.

At the end of April 1938, legionaries formed an interim leadership team of five members, led by Ion Belgea (1909–1939) and including Radu Mironovici, Horia Sima (1907–1993), Ion Antoniu (?–1939), and Iordache Nicoară (?–1939). These men were arrested one by one, and by August 1938 Sima was the only one not in prison.[20] Sima had joined the Legion when he was a student in Bucharest in 1927, and he had proved to be a very effective organizer in Severin County during the mid-1930s.[21] He asked Codreanu's permission to officially take over as leader of the movement, but Codreanu ordered Vasile Cristescu to take formal command and for Sima to rely on Constantin Papanace for advice.[22] Even though many of the imprisoned leaders swore loyalty to Carol's regime, Sima managed to ignore their new oaths and bypass the old chain of command completely. From this point on, legionaries attempted to keep their hierarchy as anonymous as possible, such that each legionary would know only his or her immediate superior.[23]

Police reports show the authorities becoming increasingly paranoid over the summer. They speculated that legionaries had begun arming themselves, and they worried about prison revolts or peasant uprisings in support of Codreanu.[24] Legionaries continued doing muted propaganda, rebuilding their communications networks and raising money to help those in prison.[25] They also introduced secret codes. One police report claimed that legionaries in Iaşi began petitioning

---

18. Ilarion Ţiu, *Mişcarea legionară după Corneliu Codreanu*, vol. 1 (Bucharest: Editura Vremea, 2007), 51; ACNSAS, Fond Informativ, dosar 184933, vol. 3, f. 115, 117; dosar 184933, vol. 1, f. 46–48; dosar 210821, vol. 2, f. 234–240; Fond Penal, dosar 014005, vol. 3, f. 173–174. Cf. the numerous arrest warrants in AN—Iaşi, Fond Chestura de Poliţie, dosar 8/1938, f 140, 142, 150, 169, 358, 431; dosar 91/1938, f. 161, 217–219, 234, 237, 286, 456, 458.

19. Ţiu, *Mişcarea legionară*, vol. 1, 116–119, 132–136.

20. Ibid., 76.

21. Ibid., 70–71.

22. Ibid., 78.

23. AN—Iaşi, Fond Chestura de Poliţie, dosar 91/1938, f. 236.

24. Ibid., dosar 8/1938, f. 58, 62, 91; dosar 12/1938, f. 28; dosar 91/1938, f. 1.

25. Ibid., dosar 8/1938, f. 113, 127, 157, 274; dosar 12/1938, f. 10, 18, 25; dosar 91/1938, f. 153, 154, 179, 236, 302.

to have bus stops moved to locations near their houses or offices, making it easier to pass messages or packages on and off buses when they were stopped.[26] Officials even banned the Romanian premier of a Polish film that depicted the November Uprising (also known as the Cadet Revolution) of 1830, an armed rebellion that sparked the Polish-Russian War of 1830–1831. Censors feared that it might inspire legionaries to begin a civil war and demanded that all scenes involving rebellion—half the film—be cut.[27]

Publicly defending Codreanu while he was in prison was a punishable offence.[28] Legionaries began a wave of violent terrorist actions at the beginning of November.[29] That month, the first issue of *Curierul legionar* (The legionary courier, 1938) began by quoting the lyrics to Andrei Mureşanu's famous anthem, "Wake Up Romanian!": "Better to die gloriously in battle / Than to be slaves once again on this ancient soil."[30] Putting this dictum into practice, legionaries used dynamite and grenades to blow up synagogues and Jewish homes, factories, and theaters.[31] The violence culminated in the attempted assassination of the chancellor of the University of Cluj, Florian Ştefănescu-Goangă (1881–1958), on 28 November, by two young legionaries. They believed that Ştefănescu-Goangă had been behind the arrests of a number of students earlier that year. He was also the brother-in-law of Armand Călinescu, who had ordered Codreanu's arrest and subsequent trials.[32] King Carol II was visiting Berlin when Ştefănescu-Goangă was shot, and his audience with Adolf Hitler was constantly interrupted by phone calls from Romania informing him about the attempted assassination, making it look as though Carol did not have firm control of his own country.[33] Two days later, on 30 November, gendarmes drove Codreanu and thirteen other legionaries into a field on the outskirts of Bucharest where they strangled and then shot them.[34]

Legionary sources describe torture and beatings by the police during 1938 and 1939, overcrowded and unsanitary conditions in Romanian prisons, and

26. Ibid., dosar 8/1938, f. 366; dosar 2/1938, f. 28.

27. ANIC, Fond Ministerul Propagandei Naţionale—Direcţia Cinematografiei, dosar 20/1940, f. 1–2, 44.

28. Ţiu, *Mişcarea legionară*, vol. 1, 68, 96.

29. Scurtu ed., *Ideologie*, vol. 5, 183–187.

30. Ibid., vol. 5, 187.

31. Ţiu, *Mişcarea legionară*, vol. 1, 99–100, 103; ACNSAS, Fond Penal, dosar 014005, vol. 1, f. 17–19; Dana Beldiman, ed., *Dosar Horia Sima (1940–1946)* (Bucharest: Evenimentul Românesc, 2000), 66–67.

32. "D. Ştefănescu-Goangl şi arestarea preşedintelui [*sic*] Cercului studenţesc din Cluj," *Buna vestire*, 28 Jan 1938.

33. Andreas Hillgruber, *Hitler, Regele Carol şi Mareşalul Antonescu: Relaţiile germano-române (1938–1944)* (Bucharest: Humanitas, 2007), 63.

34. Scurtu ed., *Ideologie*, vol. 5, 196–199.

victims being buried or burned alive. According to a petition written by Ion Dumitrescu-Borşa in October 1938, "For some time now the police have begun using abhorrent torture. Scores of legionaries are beaten and thrown into prison every day. An entire system of torture inspired by the Cheka [Bolshevik Secret Police] is used. . . . Twisting the legs, striking and then stabbing the soles of the feet and under the fingernails with needles and splinters of wood, holding the head in a bucket of water until the person suffocates, and other horrors make up the ordeal. Many legionaries come out of the torture chamber completely destroyed; others deaf or maimed."[35] In February 1939, seven legionaries were interrogated then shot by police in Huedin, in Cluj County.[36] Dumitru Banea writes of a high school boy from Olt County named Gaman who was brutally beaten in the basement of a police station and then shot twelve times on the edge of town. He survived, and managed to crawl back into town before dying in hospital.[37] Nicoleta Nicolescu, who led the women's section of the Legion, was shot and then burned to death by police in Bucharest.[38] Another prominent legionary woman, Elena Bagdad, was tortured in prison and then shot. Her last words were "Long live the Legion and the Captain!"[39]

Horia Sima fled to Germany in winter 1938/1939, where he and other legionary exiles made plans and sent orders to legionaries inside Romania. He tried organizing a coup d'état during spring 1939, but this plan was quickly discovered by the police, leading to another wave of arrests.[40] Instead of staging a coup, the movement's leadership in Berlin decided to assassinate King Carol II; Armand Călinescu, who was now Romania's Prime Minister; or both.[41] A group of legionaries acting under Sima's orders shot Călinescu on 21 September then took control of the national radio station and announced the murder.[42] The government executed the assassins as well as scores of legionaries in prison and an extra two or three in every county.[43] The bulk of those who had led the Legion under Codreanu perished in this round of killings.

---

35. Ibid., vol. 5, 170.
36. Ibid., vol. 5, 225–228.
37. Banea, *Acuzat,* 113–115.
38. Dinescu, "Cetăţui sfărâmate," 13.
39. ANIC, Fond DGP, dosar 265/1940, f. 1–4.
40. Ţiu, *Mişcarea legionară*, vol. 1, 109–116.
41. Ibid., 137–144; Scurtu ed., *Ideologie*, vol. 5, 224, 229, 233, 234, 237–239, 272–276; Dumitru Groza, in *Ţara, Legiunea, Căpitanul*, ed. Conovici, Iliescu, and Silivestru, 204.
42. Scurtu ed., *Ideologie*, vol. 5, 270–272.
43. Ţiu, *Mişcarea legionară*, vol. 1, 145–146.

The National Legionary State

King Carol lost the support of Romania's political class after Romania was forced to cede Bessarabia and Northern Bucovina to Russia in June 1940. He then turned to prominent ultranationalists in order to form a new government, led by the industrialist Ion Gigurtu (1886–1959), that included three legionaries in ministerial posts—Horia Sima, Vasile Noveanu, and Augustin Bideanu. The legionaries resigned from the government after only a few days, claiming that they could not work with the king and disassociating themselves from his regime. Even during this brief period in power Sima and his colleagues used their new-found influence to get jobs for legionaries.[44] Gigurtu's government collapsed after the Second Vienna Award gave Northern Transylvania to Hungary on 30 August. General Ion Antonescu (1882–1946) assumed power five days later and the king abdicated on 6 September 1940.

After extensive negotiations between Antonescu and Sima, Romania was transformed into the National Legionary State. Senior government positions were filled by legionaries, including Sima as deputy prime minister, and five of his colleagues in other ministerial posts. Legionaries became prefects of Romania's fifty administrative districts.[45] Although the decision to create a legionary regime took place in the palace, teams of legionaries took power in regional cities by force. In Braşov a group of forty-five legionaries barricaded themselves in the police station and locked the police in their cells for three days.[46] In Constanţa County armed legionaries stationed themselves in important villages waiting for the signal to stage their coup.[47] Once the news became known legionaries and sympathizers crowded the streets cheering and singing legionary songs.[48]

The legionaries celebrated their victory by redecorating the streets and staging public spectacles. Father Ion Belenta, a parish priest in Poiana Mărului, a village near Sibiu, placed green wreaths on the walls of his church and proudly announced the Legion's victory from the altar.[49] General Antonescu called a day of prayer on 15 September, and at 11:45 a.m. loudspeakers mounted on the streets ordered everyone to kneel where they were and pray as church bells tolled all over Bucharest.[50] On 6 October, a month after the Legion had taken power,

44. AN—Iaşi, Fond Teatrul Naţional, dosar 10/1940, f. 124.

45. Dennis Deletant, *Hitler's Forgotten Ally: Ion Antonescu and His Regime, Romania 1940–44* (New York: Palgrave Macmillan, 2006), 57–60.

46. AN—Braşov, Fond Chestura de poliţie Braşov, Serviciul Administrativ, dosar 51/1940, f. 1.

47. Conovici, Iliescu, and Silivestru eds., *Ţara, Legiunea, Căpitanul*, 210–219.

48. Anania, *Memorii*, 22.

49. ACNSAS, Fond Informativ, dosar 157073, vol. 2, f. 88.

50. Aurică Simion, *Regimul politic din România în perioda septembrie 1940–ianuarie 1941* (Cluj-Napoca: Editura Dacia, 1976), 48.

legionaries staged a massive rally in the middle of the capital. Uniformed legionaries marched into the square in front of the royal palace, singing "Holy Legionary Youth" and cheering as bands played on the sidelines. Representatives from each section of the Legion presented themselves before Horia Sima and General Antonescu, singing songs specific to their units.[51]

Nichifor Crainic, now president of the Radio Broadcasting Station, wrote in his memoirs that as the new legionary minister of propaganda, Alexandru Constant, "immediately 'legionarized' the entire leadership of the Radio Broadcasting Station: the administrative council, the direction committee, [and] the director general. . . . He also introduced a so-called bodyguard, in place of the gendarmes, made up of snotty kids with revolvers who terrorized anyone who went there."[52] Radio programming now included hour-long lectures most evenings on themes such as "legionary spirit and doctrine," "legionary literature," and "Romanians in world history."[53] Unlike in Fascist Italy or Nazi Germany, where power caused fascists to embrace new aesthetics and ideologies, in Romania the National Legionary State reprinted legionary writings, poetry, and songs from the mid-1930s. Newspapers frequently carried mini-biographies of prominent legionaries who were now dead, arguing that their lives exemplified legionary virtues.[54] Publicists focused on themes of suffering and self-sacrifice, which they argued had paved the way for the Legion's victory in 1940.[55]

Within days of coming to power, legionaries began attacking Jews. Continuing the policies of the Goga-Cuza administration, the government boycotted Jewish businesses and expelled Jews from the civil service and certain other professions.[56] In Galați legionaries held sixty Jews hostage to ensure that others "kept the peace." Jean Ancel records that in Arad, forty Jews were "arrested, robbed, tortured, and jailed for several days" during the "week of romantic enthusiasm" that accompanied the beginning of the regime.[57] Jews were allowed to run their businesses only between certain hours each day. Those who broke the rules were arrested and charged.[58] Legionaries in Râmnicu Vâlcea rounded up all the Jews in the city, confiscated their property, and drove them out of town. In both Constanța and Brad gangs of legionaries forced Jewish shop owners to sell their

51. Tudor, *Un an lângă Căpitan*, 106–109.

52. Crainic, *Zile able*, 328.

53. ACNSAS, Fond Informativ, dosar 233726, vol. 1, f. 16.

54. For example, Petru Galiș, "Ilie Giulan," *Cuvântul* (22 Nov 1940).

55. Mircea Pop, "Din prigoană: Jilava 1938," *Bună vestire*, 4/2 (10 Sept 1940): 1; Grigore Manoilescu, "Lupta legionara," *Bună vestire*, 4/5 (13 Sept 1940): 1.

56. Matatias Carp, *Cartea neagră: Fapte și documente: Suferințele evreilor din România în timpul dictatueri fasciste, 1940–1944*, vol. 1 (Bucharest: Editura Diogene, 1996), 77–87.

57. Ancel, *Economic Destruction*, 72–73.

58. AN—Iași, Fond Chestura de poliție, dosar 36/1940, f. 6, 202, 254.

stores at gunpoint, at prices set by the legionaries.[59] Sometimes legionaries used Jewish collaborators to extort money from local Jews, and at others they extorted "protection money" from Jews in return for guarantees that no one would harm them.[60] Religious buildings were not exempt, and legionaries vandalized synagogues, breaking windows and destroying cult objects.[61]

A police circular from 7 October 1940 noted that legionaries had been searching homes and arresting suspects, demanding their files from local police stations, taking confiscated weapons from police stores, standing guard outside Jewish stores and inspecting the merchandise, and tracking down police officers who had persecuted legionaries in the past.[62] People with an antilegionary past were sometimes kidnapped and badly beaten.[63] Legionaries arrested people for fighting, begging, gambling, spitting, "looking suspect," using dishonest scales, engaging in price speculation, exhibiting drunken and disorderly behavior, or turning their backs on legionaries who shouted, "Long live the Legion!"[64] They searched homes of suspected Freemasons, destroying property and threatening their children with revolvers.[65] The regime established a formal legionary police force in October, but this was disbanded the following month following the disorderly conduct of the legionary police and their clashes with professional police.[66] Gendarmes complained that legionaries ignored and abused them, lamenting that "we no longer serve any purpose in the Legionary State."[67]

Despite the abuses being carried out in their names, legionaries proudly wore their uniforms and carried legionary identification cards to demonstrate their new status. The new director of the Central Theological Seminary in Bucharest began wearing a green cross with the legionary symbol in its center.[68] In an interview from 2001, Olimpiu Borzea recalled that his uniform gave him a new identity as a privileged member of the regime instead of his being just another anonymous individual: "Children turned their heads when they saw me on the streets, 'Look, a legionary! Look, a legionary!' I shivered from my head to my toes; something came over me and said: 'You are no longer yourself, from now on you

59. Ancel, *Economic Destruction*, 90.

60. ACNSAS, Fond Documentar, dosar 008912, vol. 23, f. 57–58; AN—Iaşi, Fond Chestura de poliţie, dosar 166/1941, f. 48.

61. Carp, *Cartea neagră*, vol. 1, 115.

62. AN—Iaşi, Fond Chestura de poliţie, dosar 8/1940, f. 49.

63. USHMM, Fond SRI Files, Reel #102, f. 549.

64. AN—Iaşi, Fond Chestura de poliţie, dosar 36/1940, f. 115, 160, 311, 427, 470 484–485, 487; dosar 109/1940, f. 86, 115, 134, 445, 461.

65. USHMM, Fond SRI Files, Reel #57, dosar 9039/31, f. 152–154.

66. ACNSAS, Fond Documentar, dosar 008912, vol. 23, f. 75, 134–137.

67. USHMM, Fond SRI Files, Reel #102, f. 493.

68. Anania, *Memorii*, 26.

do not belong to yourself, this shirt compels you!"[69] Some legionaries abused their uniforms, using them to eat and drink without paying and to destroy Jewish property.[70] Legionaries were rarely punished for such abuses, but people found committing offenses with forged legionary identification cards were arrested and tried.[71]

With the Legion in power, fascism now meant an opportunity for personal gain, and thousands of new members flooded into the movement. High school students became convinced that only legionaries would be admitted into universities the following year, and they joined Blood Brotherhoods in large numbers.[72] For their part, university students joined the Legion in order to get scholarships, and anyone with legionary connections who had been expelled before 1940 was automatically allowed to reenter university without penalty.[73] A similar pattern occurred in rural areas. Petre Simionescu, from Păroşi in Olt County, joined the Legion in the hope of attracting a team of legionary students to build his village a theater the following summer. In his testimony from 1948 he claimed that only villages with legionary connections received such assistance.[74]

The regime established a special charity known as Ajutorul legionar (Legionary Aid) modeled on the Nazi Winterhilfswerk (Winter Relief).[75] The charity provided food and shelter to needy families and was a reliable way of laundering stolen money and goods. In a letter to his superior from late 1941, Father Alex. C. Popescu of Caracal wrote that he raised 481,000 lei in donations for Ajutorul legionar. He put the money to use in several ways:

> [I] clothed 82 poor pupils and refugees, and provided clothes, shoes, food (beans, potatoes, sugar, meat, bread, etc) and firewood to 212 poor families. I subsidized the legionary canteen, where we fed poor and refugee children for free and office workers, teachers, lawyers and even soldiers below cost. Through Ajutorul legionar we gave medical assistance to the poor, including free medicine, paid school fees for poor children and helped the family of the legionary martyr Horia Orpovici.[76]

69. Olimpiu Borzea, in *Ţara, Legiunea, Căpitanul*, ed. Conovici, Iliescu, and Silivestru, 228.
70. AN—Iaşi, Fond Chestura de poliţie, dosar 8/1940, f. 87, 447.
71. AN—Braşov, Fond Chestura de poliţie, Serviciul Judiciar, dosar 9/1923, vol. 2, f. 53.
72. Anania, *Memorii*, 26.
73. ACNSAS, Fond Penal, dosar 014005, vol. 3, f. 100–101; AN—Iaşi, Fond Universitatea A.I. Cuza, Rectoratul, dosar 2072/1940–41, f. 1, 3–4.
74. ACNSAS, Fond Penal, dosar 014005, vol. 3, f. 123–125.
75. Veiga, *Istoria Gărzii de Fier*, 283.
76. ACNSAS, Fond Informativ, dosar 233726, vol. 1, f. 200–201.

In other places Ajutorul legionar collected Christmas presents for poor children or donated money to unemployed legionaries to fund their activism.[77] Popescu says that he collected donations for Ajutorul legionar from legionaries and sympathizers, and businesses sometimes gave goods or money directly to the organization.[78] Much of the charity's money was stolen from Jews. In Iaşi one security officer confiscated sixty-six pounds of meat from a restaurant and gave it to Ajutorul legionar, and legionaries took the Trianon cinema from its Jewish owners, using the proceeds to run thirteen soup kitchens feeding roughly twelve hundred people a day.[79] Legionaries did not always pass their thefts through the charity and sometimes just distributed stolen goods immediately. They invaded lumberyards and wheat and grain silos and gave away their contents for free. They also requisitioned buildings, cars, and furniture for legionary use.[80]

Legionaries often engaged in petty theft, but the most widespread thefts took place as part of the "Romanianization" campaign. This involved replacing Jewish workers with Romanians, who had to be trained by their Jewish counterparts.[81] In particular, Jews were no longer allowed to work as doctors, lawyers, of skilled tradesmen or to own cinemas.[82] Business owners frequently protested and tried to bypass this system, as many of the Romanians appointed to these posts refused to work and took their salaries without ever setting foot on the premises.[83] Other newly appointed legionaries interfered with the running of organizations even though they had no expertise in the area.[84] Through less official means, legionaries also drove nonlegionary professors from their university posts and appointed teachers who had long-standing legionary connections.[85] Once again, legionaries portrayed such abuses as charity. Gheorghe Ungureanu says that as commissar for Romanianization at the Norbert Juster factory in Bucharest, his first action was to visit the workers at home to ascertain their living conditions. Discovering their poverty, he forced the owner to supply them with firewood, foodstuffs, and

---

77. Ibid., dosar 209489, vol. 2, f. 2–6; ANIC, Fond Direcţia Generală a Poliţiei, dosar 244/1940, f. 80; USHMM, Fond SRI Files, Reel #102, f. 602.

78. ACNSAS, Fond Documentar, dosar 008912, vol. 23, f. 115.

79. AN—Iaşi, Fond Chestura de poliţie, dosar 109/1940, f. 461; dosar 166/1941, f. 71–74.

80. Ancel, *Economic Destruction*, 93–101.

81. "Românizarea muncii," *Cuvântul* (1 Nov 1940): 1; Dana Beldiman ed., *Statul Naţional Legionar: septembrie 1940–ianuarie 1941: Cadrul legislativ* (Bucharest: Institutul Naţional pentru Studiul Totalitarismului, 2005), 221–246.

82. Ancel, *Economic Destruction*, 77–79.

83. Ştefan Ionescu, "Implementing the Romanisation of Employment in 1941 Bucharest: Bureaucratic and Economic Sabotage of the 'Aryanisation' of the Romanian Economy," *Holocaust Studies*, 16/1–2 (2010): 39–64.

84. ANIC, Fond Ministerul Propagandei Naţionale, vol.3, dosar 20/1940, f. 87–88.

85. ACNSAS, Fond Informativ, dosar 185007, f. 7–9; dosar 15702, vol. 3, f. 7.

wine and set up a canteen at the workplace. He also established literacy programs and brought in a priest every Sunday to teach them religion.[86]

Legionary values quickly became law. After taking control of the National Theater, Radu Gyr told his employees to be "honest, patient, and modest in this time of victory, just as you were during the time of persecution. Be the first to work, to do your duties, and to sacrifice. Restrain your *personal interests* and seek, with faith and ardor, nothing but the realization of a new Destiny for Romanian Art."[87] Legionaries at theaters around the country persecuted Jewish actors or those with left-wing sympathies, sometimes dismissing or refusing to pay them.[88] Police officers were encouraged to attend church services and no longer had to respond to anything but the most urgent cases on Sundays and religious holidays.[89] On 28 September 1940, General Antonescu published a decree telling women that "the men who are building Romania will be warriors. Warriors in every moment. At home they must find goodwill, warmth, and order. You must make this happen. . . . Then shall we ask you to fulfill three great tasks: raising children, social welfare, and defending our borders."[90] The regime also cracked down on prostitution, using legionary informants to identify women, who were then arrested for soliciting. There were no penalties for the men involved in such transactions.[91]

Records of cabinet meetings show that General Antonescu soon became frustrated with the legionaries. On 21 September 1940, he warned Horia Sima that "legionaries are not allowed to demand audiences with the Ministers whenever they want, as happened at the beginning. That was a romantic period, which is understandable. . . . Now it is time for order and legality."[92] On 24 October, Antonescu complained that administrators appointed by the legionaries were consistently failing to carry out the most basic functions of their posts. Factories were nearing collapse and roads were blocked in the middle of Bucharest because the city council could not organize itself to clean up tiles that had fallen off roofs.[93] "You are achieving nothing but destroying your own regime!" he told them.[94]

86. Gheorghe Ungureanu, in *Țara, Legiunea, Căpitanul*, ed. Conovici, Iliescu, and Silivestru, 230–233.

87. AN—Iaşi, Fond Teatrul Național, dosar 10/1940, f. 163.

88. ACNSAS, Fond Informativ, dosar 209489, vol. 1, f. 94–99; dosar 184933, vol. 1, f. 1–3.

89. AN—Iaşi, Fond Chestura de poliție, dosar 8/1940, f. 60.

90. Apelul Conducătorul Statului Român, generalul Ion Antonescu, către femeia romãna, 28 Sept 1940; in *Statul Național Legionar*, ed. Beldiman, 259–260.

91. AN—Iaşi, Fond Chestura de poliție, dosar 36/1940, f. 12, 28, 76, 427, 484.

92. Marcel-Dumitru Ciucă, Aurelian Teodorescu and Bogdan Florin Popvici eds., *Stenogramele şedințelor Consiliului de Miniştri Guvernarea Ion Antonescu*, vol. 1 (Bucharest: Arhivele Naționale ale României, 1997), 72.

93. Ibid., 317–338.

94. Simion, *Regimul politic*, 203.

Social problems became even worse when an earthquake struck Bucharest on 10 November, demolishing buildings and killing at least seventy-five people.[95] Teams of legionaries and other volunteers worked together to rescue survivors and to rebuild, calling the earthquake a "trial from God."[96] Despite their efforts, the regime's disorganization made reconstruction difficult. The wartime disruption of international trade; territorial losses; refugees from Poland, Bessarabia, Northern Bukovina, and Northern Transylvania; and the disastrous Romanianization campaign meant that the country's economy was on the verge of collapse. On top of price fluctuations, the harvest of 1940 was 70 percent less than that of the year before.[97]

Some legionaries were also becoming hostile toward the regime. Codreanu's father, Ion Zelea Codreanu, despised Horia Sima, calling him "a Satan, in whom the soul of Stelescu lives."[98] On 13 November, he led a group of roughly twenty legionaries in a failed putsch by occupying the Green House, the Legion's headquarters in Bucharest.[99] There was even talk of assassinating Sima.[100] In an attempt to boost their popularity, Sima and Antonescu emphasized that they were continuing Codreanu's legacy.[101] Legionary newspapers investigated the treason charges on which Codreanu had been condemned in May 1938. They found legal irregularities and defended his innocence.[102] On 30 November the government exhumed Codreanu's body, together with those of other legionary martyrs, and reburied them at the Green House with state honors.[103] Funerals and commemorations for the dead became a regular feature of the regime, and police even arrested children for mocking the regularity and theatricality of such spectacles.[104]

The greatest scandal of the regime took place at Jilava prison, just as work was beginning to exhume Codreanu's body. On the night of 26 November, legionaries broke into the prison, where they murdered sixty-five political prisoners in their cells. Later that night, other groups of legionaries murdered Nicolae Iorga

95. "Pe urmele cutremurului din Capitală," *Buna vestire*, 4/51 (13 Nov 1940): 2.

96. "Păcatele noastre, Doamne!" *Buna vestire*, 4/52 (14 Nov 1940): 3.

97. Simion, *Regimul politic*, 110–112.

98. Nicholas M. Nagy-Talavera, *The Green Shirts and the Others: A History of Fascism in Hungary and Rumania* (Stanford, CA: Hoover Institution Press, 1970), 311.

99. Simion, *Regimul politic*, 210.

100. Nicu Cucoli, in *Țara, Legiunea, Căpitanul*, ed. Conovici, Iliescu, and Silivestru, 220.

101. "În spiritul lui Codreanu Generalul Antonescu constituie garanția cea mai sigură pentru renașterea poporului român," *Buna vestire*, 4/58 (21 Nov 1940): 6.

102. "Martorii Căpitanului împiedicați să se prezinte," *Buna vestire*, 4/49 (10 Nov 1940): 3.

103. "Au fost identificate rămășițele pământești ale Căpitanului, Nicadorilor, și Decemvirilor," *Buna vestire*, 4/65 (30 Nov 1940): 3.

104. AN—Iași, Fond Chestura de poliție, dosar 36/1940, f. 130.

and Virgil Madgearu in their homes.[105] Even loyal supporters of the regime were horrified and angry. Codreanu's funeral was the last time that Antonescu and Sima appeared together in public, and by December tensions between them had reached breaking point.

Rebellion

After five months of joint government, the legionaries turned against General Antonescu on 21 January 1941, in a rebellion that was put down after three days. Antonescu later argued that the rebellion had been well planned, with legionaries collecting arms for months before the revolt.[106] In fact, the rebellion caught most legionaries by surprise. Rumors spread throughout the movement, among them reports of a Soviet invasion and that a German officer had been murdered by British agents in Bucharest.[107] According to one legionary's account given several months later, prominent legionaries in Caracal awoke that morning to the news that a "revolution" had broken out in Bucharest. Assuming that the conflict was between communists and the current regime, they telephoned their colleagues in Craiova to find out what to do and were told to submit to the military.[108] Instead, they occupied the telegraph office but were forced to surrender when the military arrived.[109] That evening legionaries in Făgăraş were called to a meeting, where a local priest handed out guns and pamphlets. They occupied the telephone office and waited for someone to attack them.[110] Trucks carried peasants from villages around Sibiu into the city, where they received guns and were ordered to defend the government. None of the people interrogated by the police admitted to having understood what was happening.[111] Legionaries had good reason to plead ignorance, as they were facing treason charges for participating in the rebellion, but their testimonies consistently reflect a state of surprise, misunderstanding, and disorganization.

---

105. Stelian Neagoe ed., *Asasinatele de la Jilava . . . , Snagov şi Strejnicul, 26–27 noiembrie 1940* (Bucharest: Scripta, 1992).

106. Serafim Duicu ed., *Ion Antonescu şi "Garda de Fier": Pe marginea prăpastiei (21–23 ianuarie 1941)*, vol. 2 (Târgu-Mureş: Rom-Edition, 1991); USHMM, Fond SRI Files, Reel #52, dosar 9039/1, f. 1–340.

107. AN—Iaşi, Fond Chestura de poliţie, dosar 166/1941, f. 33–34.

108. ACNSAS, Fond Informativ, dosar 233726, vol. 1, f. 200–201.

109. USHMM, Fond SRI Files, Reel #58, dosar 9039/43, f. 7–8.

110. ACNSAS, Fond Pop Gavrila, MI.63517, Reel #690, f. 18–20; ACNSAS, Fond Pop Gavrila, MI.63517, Rola 690, f. 18–20; ACNSAS, Fond Informativ, dosar 163318, vol.3, f. 242.

111. ACNSAS, Fond Ţiţonea Mihai, MI.63515, Reel #690, f. 4–9. Cf. Simion, *Regimul politic*, 252, n. 26.

The nature of the rebellion differed from place to place. In Turda, Buhuşi, and Ploieşti, hundreds of legionaries marched down the streets singing legionary hymns before dispersing quietly.[112] Legionaries in the village of Ştefăneşti, in Botoşani County, heard about the rebellion on the radio but refused to believe that it was happening.[113] Two gangs of unarmed legionaries patrolled the main street of Vraţa in Craiova County, interrogating anyone who entered the village.[114] In Piatra Neamţ six hundred legionaries gathered to support Horia Sima, but the police intervened quickly and managed to prevent any violence. Later a small group of legionaries vandalized Jewish homes in the town.[115] Legionaries in Buzău met at the police station, only to be surrounded by soldiers and trapped inside.[116] In Târgu Frumos the mayor put groups of teenage legionaries on trains to Iaşi on 20 January. He immediately resigned when the situation deteriorated the following evening, but forty other legionaries armed themselves and tried to make it to Iaşi to take part in the fighting, only to be captured and disarmed en route.[117] More organized than in other provincial cities, legionaries in Braşov occupied the gendarmerie, the council chambers, municipal offices, the treasury, the post office and telephone exchange, the radio station, and gendarmerie posts in surrounding villages.[118] Elsewhere in the city, five armed legionaries hijacked a bus and held its passengers hostage for several hours.[119]

Even in Bucharest, where battle lines were more clearly drawn, legionaries joined the fighting spontaneously after seeing other legionaries in trouble and running to help them. Pamphlets circulated casting doubt on Antonescu's loyalty to Romania and calling for the dismissal of several of his ministers.[120] At least three thousand legionaries occupied the police headquarters, while others took control of the national radio station and protested on the streets.[121] Radu Gyr made speeches to a crowd of roughly one thousand legionaries from the balcony of the National Theater, calling on them to attack telephone and radio stations and leading them in song.[122] In many cases legionaries occupied their places of work. Legionary clerical staff at government offices barricaded themselves in

---

112. ACNSAS, Fond Informativ, dosar 163318, vol.3, f. 38–40; Fond Documentar, dosar 008912, vol. 23, f. 189–190; USHMM, Fond SRI Files, Reel #52, dosar 9039/1, f. 160.

113. Ion Constantinescu, in *Ţara, Legiunea, Căpitanul*, ed. Conovici, Iliescu, and Silivestru, 277–278.

114. ACNSAS, Fond Informativ, dosar 257541, vol. 1, f. 23–25.

115. ACNSAS, Fond Documentar, dosar 008912, vol. 23, f. 157–167.

116. Victor Moise, in *Ţara, Legiunea, Căpitanul*, ed. Conovici, Iliescu, and Silivestru, 275–277.

117. AN—Iaşi, Fond Chestura de poliţie, dosar 166/1941, f. 20–24, 29–30.

118. USHMM, Fond SRI Files, Reel #52, dosar 9039/1, f. 160–161.

119. AN—Braşov, Fond Chestura de Poliţie Braşov, Serv. Judiciar, dosar 9/1923, f. 10.

120. USHMM, Fond SRI Files, Reel #58, dosar 9039/43, f. 3.

121. Conovici, Iliescu, and Silivestru eds., *Ţara, Legiunea, Căpitanul*, 261–270; Simion, *Regimul politic*, 257.

122. ACNSAS, Fond Informativ, dosar 184933, vol. 1, f. 6–7.

their offices and forced nonlegionary employees to obey them at gunpoint.[123] Intense fighting took place at the factories of Nicolae Malaxa in Bucharest, where many legionaries worked. The rebels cut the telephone wires, stopped the trams running, and barricaded the streets around the factories. They threatened other employees with pistols and commandeered weapons, including a tank, from military storerooms.[124] Legionary newspapers reported that the rebellion was a Judeo-Masonic plot to destroy the Legion and claimed that peaceful protestors singing legionary songs were being fired on by the military.[125]

The army responded quickly and efficiently. On 20 January, Colonel N. Pătruţoiu gave orders for six regiments and one battalion to occupy Victory Square the following day.[126] Troops occupied the center of Bucharest as if it was enemy territory, shooting to kill and searching nearby buildings. Anyone who failed to keep 550 yards from the soldiers was to be shot.[127] Tanks fired into houses occupied by legionaries, and the rebels consistently had the worst of the pitched battles.[128] Soldiers strip-searched and sexually assaulted legionary women while looking for weapons.[129] Legionaries later claimed that secret police dressed as legionaries fired on the army, trying to spark a gun battle.[130]

The military convincingly defeated and arrested the rebels within three days but did little to halt the atrocities legionaries carried out against Jews during the rebellion. Legionaries began arresting Jews on 20 January, and the following afternoon gangs of legionaries invaded Bucharest's two largest Jewish neighborhoods. They loaded roughly two thousand Jews—including children and the elderly—onto trucks and transported them to prearranged sites, where they beat, raped, and tortured them.[131] Of the forty legionaries involved in torturing Jews at the police station on Matei Basarab Street, most were factory workers aged between fifteen and twenty-five years old.[132] The two hundred Jews held at the CML headquarters were forced to do gymnastics exercises in between beatings and those who asked for water were given a bowl filled with water and blood

123. ACNSAS, Fond Penal, dosar 014083, vol. 2, f. 197; Fond Informativ, dosar 15702, vol. 3, f. 7.

124. USHMM, Fond SRI Files, Reel #57, dosar 9039/22, f. 210–239; ACNSAS, Fond Informativ, dosar 160161, vol. 6, f. 196–209.

125. Crisu Axente, "Revoluţia legionară în plin marş," *Axa*, 10/64 (23 Jan 1941): 4.

126. Ordinul Comandamentului Militar al Capitalei, 20 Jan 1941, in Dan Vlad Radu, *Evenimentele din ianuarie 1941 în arhivele germane şi române* (Bucharest: Editura Majadahonda, 1998), 55–56.

127. Ordinul operativ al Secretariatului General al Ministerului Apărării Naţionale, 22 Jan 1941, in ibid., 59.

128. Constantin Malaxa, in *Ţara, Legiunea, Căpitanul*, ed. Conovici, Iliescu, and Silivestru, 265–266.

129. David Walker, *Death at My Heels* (London: Chapman and Hall, 1942), 156.

130. Titi Dobre, in *Ţara, Legiunea, Căpitanul*, ed. Conovici, Iliescu, and Silivestru, 260–261.

131. Ancel, *Economic Destruction*, 129–131.

132. Carp, *Cartea neagră*, vol. 1, 182.

from a rabbi's head wound.[133] After the rebellion friends and relatives found the bodies of eighty-four Jews in the forest near Jilava. The bodies were naked and mutilated, covered in cuts and burns and showing bullet holes. Each had had fingernails pulled out.[134] At Bucharest's largest synagogues survivors found little but broken glass and ashes.[135] A total of 1,274 buildings were attacked, among them 25 synagogues, 616 shops, and 547 homes. The authorities later found nearly two hundred trucks full of goods stolen from Bucharest's Jews.[136] Jews were not the only victims of the pogrom. Legionaries tortured and shot communist activists and there were reports of soldiers being burned alive.[137]

Living with General Antonescu

The movement's leaders decided to suspend all legionary activity after the rebellion, but the police still believed that isolated cells of legionaries were planning to assassinate Antonescu.[138] The general's repression of the Legion was harsh. Roughly four hundred legionaries fled to Germany, where they stayed in special quarters in Nazi concentration camps, most of them first in Rostock and then in Buchenwald. They worked in German armaments factories, but they also wrote treatises on legionary ideology, served as volunteer firefighters, and held weekly nest meetings and cultural celebrations.[139] Those who did not flee the country, including hundreds of high school students, were imprisoned. Prison exacerbated tensions between legionaries who had joined the movement in 1940 and those who had known Codreanu. Veteran legionaries held the newcomers in contempt and claimed that they quickly made compromises with the authorities to escape punishment.[140]

Legionaries who remained at liberty often tried to collaborate with the regime. Codreanu's father, for example, had long opposed Sima and praised Antonescu

---

133. Ibid., vol. 1, 185.

134. Filip Brunea-Fox, *Orașul măcelului* (Bucharest: Editura Hasefer, 1997), 40–41.

135. Ibid., 47–54.

136. Ancel, *Economic Destruction*, 132; Anca Ciuciu, "Images of Bucharest Pogrom," *Holocaust: Studii și cercetări* 2/1 (2010): 41.

137. Simion, *Regimul politic*, 252–254.

138. Tiberiu Tănase, *Fețele monedei: Mișcarea Legionară între 1941–1948* (Bucharest: Tritonic, 2010), 182.

139. Legionary accounts of life in Rostock and Buchenwald are available in Ciuntu, *Din Bucovina pe Oder*, 51–76; Nistor Chioreanu, *Legionarii români în Buchenwald* (Bucharest: Ramida, 1998); and Vasile Coman, *Amintiri*, vol. 4, in AN—Cluj, Fond Vasile Coman, dosar 4/1980.

140. Vasile Turtureanu, in Dragoș Ursu and Ioana Ursu eds., *Aiudule, Aiudule: Crâmpeie de memorie întemnițată* (Cluj-Napoca: Renașterea, 2011), 219.

for destroying the National Legionary State.[141] His supporters published a pamphlet admitting that the rebellion had been a mistake and swearing loyalty to Antonescu.[142] One enterprising legionary named Gheorghe Policala appointed himself head of the Legion in Sima's place. He had migrated from Greece in March 1940 and joined the Legion in November because he wanted a job. Policala wrote to Antonescu two weeks after the rebellion, offering to lead the Legion "in perfect conformity" with the general's opinions. Antonescu gave him permission, and Policala began issuing circulars insulting Sima. He was completely ignored by the rest of the Legion. Only his ex-wife took notice; she had him arrested for continued legionary activism later that year.[143] As ridiculous as the Policala fiasco was, the fact that a recent immigrant who had been a legionary for only three months would try to take control shows how confused and disorganized the movement was in the wake of the rebellion.

Despite their differences, both Antonescu and the legionaries were ultranationalists, antisemites, and pro-Nazi. Fascist newspapers and magazines such as *Porunca vremii* and *Sfarmă piatră* continued publication throughout Antonescu's time in office. Other periodicals that had expressed legionary sympathies continued unchanged. Some former legionaries received important functions within the new regime, one example being the historian Petre P. Panaitescu, whom Antonescu put in charge of proving to Hitler that Transylvania had historically been a Romanian region and should not be under Hungarian control.[144] Antonescu appointed Father Ion Dumitrescu-Borşa to a post in the Office of Romanianization and sent the sociologist Traian Herseni to Transnistria to organize education in the new province.[145]

Romania invaded Transnistria as part of Operation Barbarossa and occupied the territory from 19 August 1941 until 29 January 1944.[146] Antonescu moved the Jews and Roma of occupied Transnistria into ghettos and camps, where disease, starvation, and the brutality of their captors took a heavy toll. He also deported Jews from Bessarabia, Bukovina, and the Dorohoi region. Roughly 201,000 Jews died in Transnistria; this was 74 percent of the total

141. Eugen Weber, "Romania," in *The European Right: A Historical Profile*, ed. Hans Rogger and Eugen Weber (Berkeley: University of California Press, 1965), 567.

142. ACNSAS, Fond Penal, dosar 014408, vol. 2, f. 7–9.

143. Ibid., dosar 000324, vol. 12, f. 335–375, 397–402.

144. ACNSAS, Fond Informativ, dosar 234303, vol. 1, f. 57–60; P.P. Panaitescu, "Transilvania este a celor cari au muncit," *Transilvania noastra* (20 Feb 1944); "Panaitescu-Pacifistu!" *Semnalul* (15 Oct 1944).

145. ANIC, Fond MI-D, dosar 10/1936, f. 142; ACNSAS, Fond Informativ, dosar 163318, vol.1, f. 3.

146. Charles King, *Odessa: Genius and Death in a City of Dreams* (London: W. W. Norton, 2011), 201–228.

number of Jews who perished in the Holocaust in Romania, alongside approximately 11,000 Roma.[147] When typhoid fever broke out in Transnistria, killing tens of thousands of people, the former legionary eugenicist Iordache Făcăoaru was in the province carrying out "bioanthropometric measurements." Together with other Romanian doctors in the area, he did little or nothing to relieve the epidemic, which quickly reached genocidal proportions.[148] The Romanian Orthodox Church entered Transnistria alongside the soldiers, establishing almost three hundred new churches within a year.[149] Metropolitan Visarion Puiu (1879–1964), a former legionary, came out of retirement to organize the mission, as did other priests with legionary pasts.[150] In March 1943, Siguranța agents estimated that there were at least eight hundred legionaries working in the administration in Transnistria.[151]

Legionary prisoners at Aiud were given the opportunity to "rehabilitate" themselves by joining the army and fighting on the Eastern Front.[152] Many accepted, but others declared that they had nothing to atone for and dedicated themselves to religious exercises instead.[153] Later writers described these units composed of former legionaries as "suicide battalions" with very high casualty rates.[154] Given that these units were sent east just before the invasion of Odessa and at precisely the moment when the mass murder of Jews and Roma in Transnistria took place, it is even possible that former legionaries were among the perpetrators of the Holocaust. But too little is known about these units to speak with any certainty about their activities.

Legionaries were probably also involved in a major pogrom in Iași in June–July 1941. Soon after the war with the Soviet Union began, an estimated 1,500 Jews were massacred in the streets of Iași, and another 2,713 died on trains as they were deported from the city.[155] The area was under the control of German military commanders, although postwar testimonies suggest that the initial massa-

---

147. Raul Hilberg, *The Destruction of the European Jews*, vol. 2, 3rd ed. (New Haven: Yale University Press, 2003), 809, 847–848.

148. Maria Bucur, *Eugenics and Modernization in Interwar Romania* (Pittsburgh: University of Pittsburgh Press, 2002), 214–215.

149. Rodica Solovei, *Activitatea Guvernănmântului Transnistriei în domeniul social-economic și cultural (19 august 1941–29 ianurarie 1944)* (Iași: Casa Editorială Demiurg, 2004), 127–129.

150. ACNSAS, Fond Penal, dosar 000751, vol. 8, f. 290–303, 328–347; dosar 000324, vol. 7, f. 370.

151. Ibid., dosar 014083, vol. 2, f. 91.

152. Țiu, *Mișcarea legionară*, vol. 2, 65–68.

153. ACNSAS, Fond Informativ, dosar 184933, vol. 2, f. 166; Ioan Ianolide, *Întoarcerea la Hristos* (Bucharest: Christiana, 2006), 44–46.

154. A. G. Lepădatu, *Mișcarea legionară: Între mit și realitate* (Bucharest: Cartier, 2005), 305–307.

155. Deletant, *Hitler's Forgotten Ally*, 130.

cres were organized by Siguranţa agents and carried out by former legionaries.[156] Radu Ioanid also mentions legionaries leading pogroms in villages throughout Bessarabia later in July 1941.[157]

King Carol II's son, Michael I (1921–), staged a coup d'état against Antonescu on August 23, 1944. He quickly ordered a ceasefire and promised to support the Allies in their fight against Germany. Romania officially surrendered to the Soviet Union three weeks later, and legionaries fled the country together with the retreating German troops.[158] Others enrolled in the Romanian army still fighting to conquer Transylvania. They surrendered as soon as they came into contact with the German and Hungarian armies and traveled to Austria, where a sizeable community of legionary exiles had begun to form.[159] After King Michael I's coup, the Nazis moved those legionaries who had spent the war under their care at Buchenwald or Rostock to Vienna. Hitler planned to establish a puppet government in exile to challenge the legitimacy of Romania's new Soviet-backed regime.

After weeks of infighting between rival legionary factions, the Germans appointed Horia Sima president of the "government in Vienna."[160] With or without their consent, Sima forced several thousand men to join a National Army that included legionaries and other Romanians living in Germany. With minimal training and scarce resources, the National Army was deployed on the Eastern Front, where most of its soldiers were soon captured by Allied troops.[161] The Germans also parachuted legionaries into Romania to collect information and organize resistance forces. The missions were poorly planned and most parachutists were arrested soon after landing.[162] The "government in Vienna" quickly dissolved in the face of the Soviet advance, and its members fled to countries ruled by sympathetic regimes throughout the world.

---

156. Matatias Carp, *Holocaust in Romania: Facts and Documents on the Annihilation of Rumania's Jews—1940–44.* trans. Seán Murphy (Budapest: Primor, 1994), 136–147. The names of other legionaries involved in the Iaşi pogrom are given in Radu Ioanid, *The Holocaust in Romania: The Destruction of Jews and Gypsies under the Antonescu Regime, 1940–1944* (Chicago: Ivan R. Dee, 2000), 73, 89.

157. Ioanid, *Holocaust in Romania*, 94, 99.

158. AN—Cluj-Napoca, Fond Inspectoratul de poliţie Cluj, dosar 160/1945, f. 8.

159. Ilarion Ţiu, *Istoria mişcării legionare, 1944–1968* (Târgovişte: Cetatea de Scaun, 2012), 29.

160. Ţiu, *Istoria mişcării legionare,* 26–45; Tănase, 186–191; Ştefan Palaghiţă, *Istoria mişcării legionare scrisă de un legionar: Garda de Fier spre reînvierea României* (Bucharest: Roza Vânturilor, 1993), 241–278.

161. Ţiu, *Istoria mişcării legionare,* 48; Richard Landwehr, *Romanian Volunteers of the Waffen-SS, 1944–1945* (Brookings, OR: Siegrunen, 1991), 56–128; Aurel Sergiu Marinescu, *O contribuţie la istoria exilului românesc,* vol. 10 (Bucharest: Editura Vremea, 2011), 293–296.

162. Ţiu, *Istoria mişcării legionare,* 48–54; Tănase, *Feţele monedei,* 192–197.

Resistance

King Michael I's government did not last long. Even though in 1944 Partidul Comunist Român (the Romanian Communist Party, PCR) was tiny, disorganized, and its members mostly in prison, the communist Lucrețiu Pătrășcanu (1900–1954) represented Romania in peace negotiations with the Allies. Furthermore, the Soviet Union dominated the Allied Control Commission, which took control of Romania after 10 September 1944.[163] Under the terms of the armistice, members of dissolved organizations such as the Legion now faced between ten and twenty-five years in prison for continued activism. On the basis of existing criminal records and self-interested denunciations, the police arrested 972 legionaries between 10 October and 2 November 1944. The prison system was unable to process large numbers of political prisoners at such short notice, and legionaries were expected to pay for their food and clothing while in prison.[164] From the beginning of 1945 onward, the movement's leadership inside the country instructed legionaries to keep their heads down. Nests were reorganized so that members communicated with only their nest leaders and did not know who else was in the organization.[165]

Acquiescing to Soviet pressure, on 6 March 1945, King Michael I approved a coalition government led by the communist Petru Groza (1945–1952). With communists in control of key ministries, the government reorganized the civil service, replacing existing functionaries with communist sympathizers and purging "fascists" from public offices.[166] Nervous about their past affiliations with the Legion, large numbers of former legionaries began joining other political parties.[167] An investigation by the ministry of the interior in November 1945 found 15,538 former legionaries enrolled in those few political parties that were still legal, including 2,258 in PCR and 3,281 in Partidul Social Democrat (Social Democratic Party, PSD).[168] Tiberius Tănase argues that communists had begun infiltrating the Legion in September 1940 with the intention of destabilizing the National Legionary State. Police informers also suggested in mid-1941 that large numbers of workers who had joined the Legion in 1940 were now returning to PCR. Horia Sima then ordered legionaries to infiltrate PCR on 16 February 1945,

163. Dennis Deletant, *Romania under Communist Rule* (Iași: Center for Romanian Studies, 1999), 30–36.

164. Țiu, *Istoria mișcării legionare*, 57–63.

165. Ibid., 81; Sima Dimcică, in *Țara, Legiunea, Căpitanul*, ed. Conovici, Iliescu, and Silivestru, 367–369.

166. Deletant, *Romania under Communist Rule*, 42–45.

167. ACNSAS, Fond Documentar, dosar 008909, vol. 2, f. 171; Fond Informativ, dosar 210821, vol. 2, f. 234–240.

168. Țiu, *Istoria mișcării legionare*, 74.

so it is no surprise that the communists discovered large numbers of former legionaries in their ranks later that year.[169]

Nicolae Pătrașcu (1907–1966), who was a close friend of Horia Sima and had been active in the Legion since 1928, parachuted into Romania in March 1945 to reorganize the movement and to build ties with the other noncommunist parties.[170] In July he ordered those legionaries still loyal to Sima to return to their families and their jobs, ceasing any efforts at resistance. Several leading legionaries refused to follow Pătrașcu's advice, further entrenching divisions within the movement.[171] Pătrașcu also managed to negotiate a "neutrality pact" with the government in December. The government begrudgingly released some legionaries who had been in prison since the 1941 rebellion, and it issued ID cards to another 340 legionaries who wished to renounce their pasts.[172] Other former legionaries entered the Romanian Orthodox Church as priests, monks, or nuns, using monasteries as a place where they could develop a post facto legionary spirituality they claimed was based on Codreanu's teachings.[173]

When elections were held on 19 November 1946, under conditions that limited freedom of speech and facilitated electoral fraud, Groza's government won 84 percent of the votes. Nine hundred members of opposition parties were arrested without explanation in March and May 1947, and in October Iuliu Maniu and Ion Mihalache, the two most prominent opposition leaders, received life sentences on treason charges. Groza forced King Michael I to abdicate in December, and the People's Republic of Romania was founded on 30 December 1947.[174]

Despite Pătrașcu's neutrality pact, some legionaries did join the anticommunist resistance. Not all the resistance groups were willing to work with legionaries, and some rejected their overtures outright.[175] Legionaries turned to their former political opponents after discovering that other legionaries were uninterested in armed resistance.[176] At least 50 percent of those involved in resistance movements

169. Tănase, *Fețele monedei*, 208–219; Constantin Teja, in *Țara, Legiunea, Căpitanul*, ed. Conovici, Iliescu, and Silivestru, 359–360.

170. ACNSAS, Fond Penal, dosar 014408, vol. 2, f. 43–46; dosar 014005, vol. 1, f. 85–88.

171. ACNSAS, Fond Informativ, dosar 160161, vol. 2, f. 199–206; Gheorghe Jijie, *Vică Negulescu: Monografie* (Bacău: Vicovia, 2009), 104–170.

172. Țiu, *Istoria mișcării legionare*, 82–95.

173. George Enache, *Ortodoxie și putere politică în România contemporană* (Bucharest: Nemira, 2005), 299–400; ACNSAS, Fond Penal, dosar 000160, vol. 2, f. 33–38; vol. 3, f. 19–23, 186–222.

174. Deletant, *Romania under Communist Rule*, 48–51.

175. ACNSAS, Fond Informativ, dosar 160161, vol. 4, f. 24–25; vol. 5, f. 154–159.

176. Petre Baicu and Alexandru Salcă, *Rezistența în munți și în orașul Brașov, 1944–1948* (Brașov: Editura Transilvania Expres, 1997), 26, 56.

after 1945 had no political pasts, and the majority of those who did had been PNȚ members.[177] Moreover, many of the resistance movements were abortive. By the time a handful of legionaries joined resistance fighters from Bucovina in July 1945, the secret police were already following them and immediately crushed the whole movement.[178] In September 1947 one small group of legionaries joined with prominent Cuzists to establish a self-consciously ultranationalist resistance movement called Salvarea Neamului (the Salvation of the People). Members swore oaths on crucifixes and planned to commit terrorist activities that they thought might help stimulation an Anglo-American invasion. One of the earliest members was a Securitate informer. He helped persuade new members to join before betraying the entire organization to the authorities.[179] Others stockpiled weapons to use in a future anticommunist war.[180] Still others formed clandestine self-help organizations that delivered food and clothing to legionaries in prison or in hiding.[181]

One of the Legion's most prominent leaders inside the country, George Manu (1903–1961), formed contacts with British agents and wrote an extensive analysis of the Romanian situation, encouraging the agents to overthrow the regime.[182] Together with senior Liberals and Peasantists, Manu had been involved with Mişcarea de Rezistenţă Naţională (the National Resistance Movement, MNR) since April 1945. Not everyone in MNR was comfortable working with legionaries, and so when Pătraşcu put an end to legionary activism in December 1945 Manu gathered those legionaries who wanted to keep fighting into a new organization he called Chemarea Neamului (the Call of the Nation). Neither group managed to carry out significant attacks on the regime before their members were arrested or killed in 1948.[183] In Dobruja, where the forced collectivization of peasant holdings was particularly brutal, small groups of Aromanians who had been involved in the Legion since the early 1930s took to the forests, fearing repression from the authorities because of their legionary pasts.[184] They lived as outlaws (*haiduci*), defending themselves rather than

177. Ţiu, *Istoria mişcării legionare,* 149.

178. Ibid., 151–152.

179. ACNSAS, Fond Penal, dosar 000324, vols. 1–7, esp. vol. 7, f. 1–3, 31–33.

180. Conovici, Iliescu, and Silivestru eds., *Ţara, Legiunea, Căpitanul,* 360, 374, 380; Baicu and Salcă, *Rezistenţa în munţi,* 50–51.

181. ACNSAS, Fond Informativ, dosar 184933, vol. 1, f. 250; Fond Penal, dosar 014005, vol. 8, f. 323; Ţiu, *Istoria mişcării legionare,* 154–155.

182. Testis Dacicus (George Manu), *În spatele cortinei de fier: România sub ocupaţie rusească* (Bucharest: Kullusys, 2004); ACNSAS, Fond Informativ, dosar 160161, vol. 4, f. 31–52.

183. ACNSAS, Fond Informativ, dosar 160161, vol. 2, f. 10–28; vol. 4, f. 1–73; Gheorghe Jijie, *George Manu: Monografie* (Bacău: Editura Babel, 2010), 141–281.

184. Gail Kligman and Katherine Verdery, *Peasants under Siege: The Collectivization of Romanian Agriculture, 1949–1962* (Princeton: Princeton University Press, 2011), 143, 204.

attempting to overthrow the regime. Resistance cells in Dobruja survived until March 1950, when the Securitate successfully captured the last of the legionary outlaws.[185]

Several other resistance groups included young people who had joined the Blood Brotherhoods during the National Legionary State. Born in the mid-1920s or even later, they had not known Codreanu's Legion but had grown up hearing romanticized tales about legionaries and reading Codreanu's writings. They identified themselves as legionaries when they began forming resistance groups in the late 1940s, but in most cases they were arrested by the authorities after engaging in minor acts of sabotage.[186] This generation's most significant organization was led by Ion Gavrilă, who held out in the Făgăraş Mountains together with his high school classmates. All had been members of the same Blood Brotherhood and took to the mountains to escape arrest in 1948. They remained there, with the support of sympathetic peasants, until their arrests in 1956.[187]

The Securitate began a new wave of arrests on 14 May 1948. This time the regime arrested anyone with a legionary past, regardless of whether they were still engaged in subversive activities. Denunciations were often fabricated, and people turned in friends or acquaintances out of fear or for personal gain. A typical example is that of Alexandru Georgescu, who had joined the Legion in November 1940. Two friends visited him in 1949, and after several drinks they persuaded him to talk about how badly the Romanian army had fought during World War II. A few hours later they turned him into the police for treasonous utterances. Georgescu was freed after lengthy interrogations, but many others were not so lucky.[188] By January 1949 there were 4,782 legionaries in communist prisons, and 22 percent of the 17,728 political prisoners still in detention in 1959 were legionaries.[189] The state also used accusations of legionary activity to discredit and arrest priests who opposed the regime.[190] Although there was often little substance to such accusations, they did serve to associate the Legion more closely with the Orthodox Church and to identify the sufferings of priests with those of legionaries.

---

185. Ţiu, *Istoria mişcării legionare,* 152–155; Nicolae Ciolacu, *Haiducii Dobrogei* (Constanţa: Muntenia, 1998).

186. Marin Bărbulescu, *Centrul studenţesc legionar Timişoara* (Madrid: Editura Mişcării Legionare, 1988); Lăcrămioara Stoenescu, *De pe băncile şcolii în închisorile comuniste* (Bucharest: Curtea Veche, 2010).

187. Ţiu, *Istoria mişcării legionare,* 158–162; Ion Gavrilă Ogoranu, *Brazii se frâng, dar nu se îndoiesc,* vol. 1 (Baia Mare: Marist, 2009); Ioana-Raluca Voicu-Arnăuţoiu, *Luptătorii din munţi: Toma Arnăuţoiu, grupul de la Nucşoara* (Bucharest: Vremea, 2009).

188. ACNSAS, Fond Penal, dosar 014083, vol. 2, f. 248–266.

189. Ţiu, *Istoria mişcării legionare,* 176–177.

190. Cristian Vasile, *Biserica Ortodoxă Română în primul deceniu comunist* (Bucharest: Curtea Veche, 2005), 182; Adrian Nicolae Petcu, "Securitatea şi cultele în 1949," in *Partidul, Securitatea şi cultele 1945–1989,* ed. Adrian Nicolae Petcu (Bucharest: Nemira, 2005), 124–222.

Remembering a Religious Movement

Many of the students who had been Blood Brothers in 1940 understood the Legion primarily as a spiritual movement. During the National Legionary State the Brotherhoods had been extracurricular organizations, approved of by parents, teachers, and the state, in which outstanding students could excel and demonstrate their worthiness to enter leadership positions in the adult world. Blood Brothers reflected upon and were encouraged to try and emulate the sacrifices of earlier generations of legionaries.[191] The way that these students described the Legion in their later writings suggest that they knew little about what happened during the interwar period and believed the romanticized hagiographies of legionaries promoted by the National Legionary State. When they were arrested in the aftermath of the 1941 rebellion against Antonescu, roughly 250 Blood Brothers incarcerated at Aiud fell under the influence of Traian Trifan (1899–1990), a lawyer who had joined the Legion in 1933 and served as prefect of Braşov County under the legionary regime. Trifan emphasized prayer, introspection, and passive resistance as the most effective way of surviving prison.[192] Between 1948 and 1964, imprisoned legionaries and Orthodox priests inspired by Trifan's teachings began to engage in constant introspection, practiced the prayer of the heart, fasted, and sought to live the holiest lives possible.[193] Many had remarkable religious experiences behind bars, and their testimonies have inspired a large body of hagiographical writings since the end of communism.[194]

The majority of legionaries in communist prisons did not devote themselves to purely religious activities, however. Factions formed around which course of action was most appropriate under the circumstances, with people arguing for outright defiance, religious self-abnegation and prayer, or the renouncing of activism altogether.[195] Each faction had clearly recognized leaders who could rely on their followers to participate in hunger strikes or engage in other forms of passive resistance if necessary. Prisoners cared for and supported other members of their groups and those placed in supervisory roles in prison workshops actively discriminated against nonlegionaries on the grounds that only legionaries had the proper self-discipline and work ethic to function well in a team.[196] Prisoners

191. Ianolide, *Întoarcerea la Hristos*, 73.

192. Seiche, *Martiri şi mărturisitori.*

193. ACNSAS, Fond Informativ, dosar 233727, vol. 2, f. 1, 16; Moise, *Sfântul închisorilor*, 60, 76–77, 87–88; Ursu and Ursu eds., *Aiudule, Aiudule*, 57–59, 79–80, 112–115.

194. For example, Ianolide, *Întoarcerea la Hristos*; Moise, *Sfântul închisorilor*; Ursu and Ursu eds., *Aiudule, Aiudule*; Seiche, *Martiri şi mărturisitori*; and Stoenescu, *De pe băncile şcolii.*

195. ACNSAS, Fond Informativ, dosar 234687, vol. 1, f. 7–245.

196. ACNSAS, Fond Penal, dosar 000160, vol. 2, f. 35–36; vol. 9, f. 7–17.

taught each other foreign languages, history, philosophy, literature, mathematics, and theology.[197] Poets such as Nichifor Crainic and Radu Gyr wrote and distributed new poems, which prisoners memorized along with extensive Bible passages.[198] As with other aspects of everyday life in prison, these "schools" fostered a belief that legionaries were particularly self-disciplined, religious, and erudite, causing younger prisoners to look up to them as role models.[199]

Just before the state granted a general amnesty to political prisoners in 1964, inmates at Aiud were asked to compile a collective history of the Legion for the prison authorities as part of their "reeducation." Titled *About the Legionary Organization*, this two-volume work involved sixty-four collaborators, all members of Colectivul Cluburilor Cultural-Educativ (the Collective of Cultural and Educational Clubs). Hauntingly beautiful illustrations accompanied the text, which focused on scandals and libelous rumors surrounding Codreanu and other early leaders. The book claims that Codreanu's father was a murderer and an adulterer who beat his children and dwells at length on the foreign ancestry of Codreanu's mother. It details extramarital affairs between the families of leading antisemites of the 1920s and characterizes the early legionaries as thugs in the pay of the Germans. The book is clearly the work of demoralized men who were willing to write anything to secure their freedom. In addition to denigrating Codreanu's Legion, the authors described "reeducation" in detail, outlining methods of torture practiced in prisons at Suceava, Târgşor, Gherla, and Piteşti.[200] Many legionaries did not leave prison alive, and those who did were traumatized physically, mentally, and emotionally.

Unable to safely return to a communist Romania, after World War II legionaries in exile regrouped in France, Germany, and Italy and later in Spain and South America. Factional infighting continued to divide the movement in exile, and legionaries bickered with liberals, peasantists, and other exiles over who really represented Romania abroad.[201] Sima and his followers reinterpreted their movement's doctrine and history to appeal to a Western audience during the Cold War era. Denying the antisemitism and hooliganism of the interwar period, they reframed the Legion as a spiritual movement aimed at fighting communism.[202]

197. ACNSAS, Fond Informativ, dosar 160161, vol. 1, f. 1–4, 34–37.

198. Ibid., dosar 184933, vol. 1, f. 320–324.

199. Stoenescu, *De pe băncile şcolii*, 42–43, 113–114, 196.

200. ACNSAS, Fond Documentar, dosar 10160, vols. 1–2.

201. Faust Brădescu, *Opinii: Un deceniu de lupta in exil in slujba neamului si legiunii (1978–1988)* (Bucharest: Editura Majadahonda, 1997); Traian Popescu and Flor Strejnicu, *Din lupta exilului românesc din Spania împotriva comunismului* (Sibiu: Imago, 1994); Dinu Zamfirescu, *Mişcarea legionară în ţară şi în exil: Puncte de reper (1919–1980)* (Bucharest: Pro Historia, 2005).

202. Horia Sima, "Noi şi evreii," *România*, 1/5 (Sept 1949), reproduced in Pălăghiţa, *Istoria mişcării legionare*, 297–298; Horia Sima, *Antologie legionară*, 7 vols. (Miami Beach, FL: Colecţia Omul Nou, 1994).

According to Horia Sima, "After 1945 . . . the destiny of nationalism merges with that of democracy." Postwar nationalism thus "loses its aggressive characteristics and becomes a force of harmony between peoples."[203] Sima's attempts to court the United States paid dividends in 1949 when NATO began parachuting legionaries into Romania to fight communism. All thirteen parachutists were arrested and executed. The Central Intelligence Agency also provided resources to other resistance groups inside the country.[204]

When they preached "legionary values," post-1941 writers re-created the Legion as a Christian sect, projecting their religious teachings back into the 1930s.[205] They published collections containing the "testimonies" of former legionaries who portrayed the interwar movement in spiritual terms.[206] Once stories about suffering in communist prisons began to emerge from inside Romania, legionaries in exile circulated them as proof of the movement's spirituality.[207] With funds from all over the world, exiles in Spain erected a monument on the battlefield where Ion Moța and Vasile Marin had died, creating a pilgrimage site for former legionaries.[208]

Whereas legionary attempts to influence Radio Free Europe and major exile periodicals were largely ignored by other émigrés, former legionaries did have a significant impact on the Romanian Orthodox Church abroad. Under pressure from both the communist government and the Russian Orthodox Church, the Romanian patriarch, Nicodim Munteanu (1864–1948), could only watch as the regime slowly replaced his most loyal supporters and either attracted parish priests into pro-communist organizations or blackmailed them into becoming Securitate informers. After Nicodim died in February 1948, his successor inherited a church that was thoroughly under state control.[209] Romanians in Paris refused to subordinate themselves to a church under communist domination.

---

203. Horia Sima, "Menirea naționalismului," in Florin Dobrescu ed., *1950—Horia Sima leagă România de NATO: Documente* (Bucharest: Editura Sânziana, 2008), 27–28.

204. Țiu, *Istoria mișcării legionare,* 163–171; Traian Golea, *Procesul legionarilor parașutați în România* (Constanța: Ex Ponto, 2001).

205. Faust Brădescu, *Conducere și disciplină* (Rio de Janeiro: Colecția Dacia, 1966); Constantin Papanace, *Stilul legionar de luptă: Conecpția tactică a Căpitanului* (Bucharest: Editura Lucman, 2004).

206. Anonymous, *Corneliu Zelea Codreanu: Douazeci de ani dela moarte* (Madrid: Editura Carpații, 1958); Brădescu, *Mărturii despre Legiune*; Anonymous, *Mărturii despre Căpitan: Patruzeci de ani dela moarte (1938–1978)* (Madrid: Editura Dacia, 1978).

207. Ion Cirja, *Întoarcerea din infern: Amintirile unui deținut din închisorile României bolsevizate. Cruzimi, masacre și bestialități necunoscute* (Madrid: Editura Dacia, 1969); Nicolae Videnie, "Presa emigrației române—revista Bisericii Sfinții Arhangheli de la Paris," in *Partidul, Securitatea și cultele, 1945–1989*, ed. Adrian Nicolae Petcu (Bucharest: Nemira, 2005), 287.

208. See Anonymous, *Cultul dela Majadahonda și monumentul Moța-Marin* (Madrid: Biblioteca documentară "Generația Nouă," 1976).

209. Vasile, *Biserica Orthodoxă Română*; Olivier Gillet, *Religie și naționalism: Ideologia Bisericii Ortodoxe Române sub regimul communist* (Bucharest: Editura Compania, 2001).

After extensive negotiations they established an independent archdiocese in Paris headed by Metropolitan Visarion Puiu, who had been a strong supporter of the Legion for many years, and placed Father Vasile Boldeanu, a former legionary, in charge of the largest Romanian Orthodox congregation in Paris.[210] In the United States, the bishop of the Romanian Episcopate in America, Policarp Moruşca (1883–1958), retired suddenly in 1947 and the communist authorities refused to allow his successor to return to the United States to lead the already divided church. When the Romanian Patriarchate appointed a new bishop in 1950, church leaders from Detroit refused to accept the new "communist" bishop and instead appointed Valerian Trifa, another former legionary, effectively creating a schism within the church.[211] The schism was only resolved in 1966, when Bartolomeu Anania, who had been a Blood Brother under the National Legionary State and was arrested in 1958 because of his legionary past, visited the United States as an official of the state-controlled Church and appointed a new bishop acceptable to both parties.[212]

Although most of the mystics who gained celebrity for their endurance in prison were only children in 1941, their heroism has done a great deal to shape how contemporary Romanians remember the Legion of the Archangel Michael. Historical circumstances were such that legionaries formulated their memories of the movement for the first time while in prison and so the prison experiences influenced the nature of those memories to a significant extent. Exiles encouraged survivors to speak about their prison experiences in religious terms, further entrenching the idea that the Legion was a spiritual movement. This makes it difficult to speak of legionaries as villains in contemporary Romania, where many people, especially some Orthodox Christians and those on the extreme right, see legionaries as Orthodox saints.

---

210. Marinescu, *O contribuţie*, vol. 4, 125–150.

211. Ibid., vol. 4, 467–499; Valerian D. Trifa, *Marginal Notes on a Court Case* (Jackson, MI: Romanian-American Heritage Center, 1988), 7–16.

212. Anania, *Memorii*, 366–379.

Conclusion

It should be obvious by now how difficult it is to generalize about the experience of rank-and-file legionary activism between 1927 and 1938. In the words of Gilles Deleuze and Félix Guattari, when discussing the Legion, "A schizophrenic out for a walk is a better model than a neurotic lying on the analyst's couch."[1] The Legion brought together unique individuals just as a person with schizophrenia incorporates many voices and identities inside one body. Not a class-based movement, it appealed to peasants, factory workers, artisans, students, soldiers, intellectuals, and aristocrats. Despite their male chauvinism, legionaries attracted women as well as men. But the experiences of men, women, and children were not the same. Nation, race, rebirth, work, justice, purity, and discipline were all crucial elements of the legionary message, but their ideology was not "neurotic" in the way that Marxism is, in the sense that no one single idea drove Romanian fascism. "Out for a walk," legionaries used different strategies and rhetoric depending on the social and political conditions of the moment.

Examining everyday activism as I have done in this book emphasizes practical activity over abstract ideology. More effort went into printing and distributing legionary literature than into writing it, and building roads or fighting with gendarmes spoke more loudly about legionary values than the words of most propagandists. Rituals, singing, moments of silence, and oath taking took up more

1. Gilles Deleuze and Félix Guattari, *Anti-Oedipus: Capitalism and Schizophrenia*, trans. Robert Hurley, Mark Seem, and Helen R. Lane (London: Athlone Press, 1984), 2.

time in nest meetings than discussing ideology, and spectacles such as the funeral of Ion Moța and Vasile Marin showed clerical support for the Legion more effectively than any pronouncement of the Holy Synod could have. Legionaries forged fascist subjectivities as they engaged with potential supporters and clashed with police, communists, and Jews. Activism shaped individual life trajectories and identification with the movement gradually took priority over family, education, employment, and other considerations.

Opposing the State

Becoming a legionary aligned one against a variety of enemies. Assassinations, street battles, and religious ceremonies all provided opportunities for legionaries to portray themselves as more righteous and legitimate than the state authorities they were opposing. Violence was crucial both to the Legion's public image and to everyday experiences of fascism for rank-and-file activists. Joseph Goebbels's famous phrase "Blood cements us together" (*Blut kittet aneinander*) expresses a belief common to fascists throughout Europe that participation in group violence solidified bonds between activists.[2] In the words of Adrian Lyttelton, one of the foremost experts on the early years of Italian fascism, "The punitive expedition, even if it involved breaking someone's head, for the participants was often an outing with the lads, an excuse to make a lot of noise, eat and drink without paying, and have a good time generally."[3] Historians have noted a similar dynamic at work among members of the Nazi *Sturmtruppen*, the French Croix de Feu, the Spanish Falange, and the Croatian Ustaša.[4] While legionaries did engage in this type of violence, they rarely reflected on it as something that facilitated group bonding. Nor did they memorialize it as the Italian regime did during the 1930s.[5] When they spoke about violence, it was usually about Jewish and police violence.

Legionaries frequently portrayed themselves as victims of Jewish violence. A comparison between the legal records of Jewish violence and fascist accounts of those same incidents shows that fascists exaggerated the extent of Jewish violence

---

2. Joseph Goebbels, quoted in Reichardt, *Faschistische Kampfbünde*, 137.

3. Lyttelton, "Fascism and Violence in Post-war Italy," 269.

4. Bessel, *Political Violence*; Sheelagh M. Ellwood, "Not So Much a Programme More a Way of Life: Oral History and Spanish Fascism," *Oral History*, 16/ 2 (1988): 57–66; Kevin Passmore, "Boy Scouting for Grown-Ups? Paramilitarism in the *Croix de Feu* and the *Parti Social Francais*," *French Historical Studies*, 19/2 (1995): 527–557; Reichardt, *Faschistische Kampfbünde*; Rory Yeomans, *Visions of Annihilation: The Ustasha Regime and the Cultural Politics of Fascism, 1941–1945* (Pittsburgh: University of Pittsburgh Press, 2013), 126–176.

5. Roberta Suzzi Valli, "The Myth of *Squadrismo* in the Fascist Regime," *Journal of Contemporary History*, 35/2 (2000): 131–150.

and blamed Jews for starting conflicts that were often begun by the fascists themselves.[6] Antisemitic literature elsewhere in interwar Europe portrayed Jews as cunning, deceptive, greedy, and malicious but it was rare to find accusations that Jews were violent.[7] Romanian antisemites, on the other hand, portrayed Jews as perpetrators of violence against Christians and suggested that they posed a genuine threat to peace-loving citizens. Similarly, legionary newspapers and memoirs are full of accounts of police violence against legionaries. According to legionary writers, fascist violence was "necessary" to combat the problems posed by corruption and Jewish influence in public life.[8] Violence was important for legionaries because it established them as enemies of an illegitimate government.[9] Self-portrayals of legionaries as victims of violence fueled the idea that they were innocent and virtuous and willing to sacrifice themselves for their nation, in contrast to the greedy politicians.

Legionaries stood out for embracing religion just as they did for embracing violence. By controlling the police and the church, the state held a monopoly on both. Administrative reforms had gradually subordinated the Romanian Orthodox Church to the state from the late nineteenth century onward, a process culminating in the establishment of the Romanian Orthodox Patriarchate in 1925.[10] Ultranationalists complained about state involvement in church issues and suggested that they were more pious and holy than the state.[11] In 1925, ultranationalist mothers from villages near Focşani, with babes in arms, clashed with gendarmes who were trying to prevent A. C. Cuza and Codreanu from acting as godfathers at their children's baptisms.[12] In 1933, police fought with groups of students who wanted to erect a memorial cross commemorating the anonymous victims of World War I.[13] By forcing the authorities to censure their religious rituals, legionaries provoked symbolic conflicts in which the state appeared intolerant and anti-Christian.

---

6. For example, ANIC, Fond Ministerul de Interne—Diverse, dosar 3/1936, f. 217.

7. Brustein, *Roots of Hate*.

8. Radu Harald Dinu, "Die Legion 'Erzengel Michael'—Gewalt und Gemeinschaft im rumänischen Faschismus," *Jahrbücher für Geschichte und Kultur Südosteuropas*, 9–10 (2007–2008): 105–126.

9. Dinu, *Faschismus, Religion und Gewalt*, 130.

10. Lucian Leustean, "The Political Control of Orthodoxy in the Construction of the Romanian State, 1859–1918," *European History Quarterly*, 37/1 (2007): 61–80; Hans-Christian Maner, *Multikonfessionalität und neue Staatlichkeit: Orthodoxe, griechisch-katholische und römisch-katholische Kirche in Siebenbürgen und Altrumänien zwischen den Weltkriegen (1918–1940)* (Stuttgart: Franz Steiner Verlag, 2008), 68–79.

11. Arhimandrite Scriban, "O răspântie a mănăstirilor," *Calendarul*, 463 (4 Sept 1933): 3–4; Codreanu, *Insemnari*, 24; I. Diaconescu, "Ororile dela Biserica marcuţă," *Porunca vremii*, 5/531 (4 Oct 1936): 3.

12. "Cum se aplică starea de asediu la Focşani," *Adevărul*, 12785 (18 Aug 1925).

13. "Creştinismul în conflict cu francmasoneria," *Calendarul*, 280 (27 Jan 1933): 3.

Legionary propaganda that conflated the Romanian nation with the Romanian Orthodox Church involved much more than worshipping the nation-state as if it was a god. Legionaries saw the nation as a sacred community before God. They came to God corporately, as a group, and so the nation became a means to salvation. God demands purity, and if the authorities were not interested in purifying the nation then legionaries should do it for them. Moreover, the Christian community was much more democratic than the state, for whereas the nation-state lay in the hands of corrupt politicians, the Church belonged to God. Legionaries did not have to ask permission from the authorities to purify Romania, because they believed that God had already called them to do so as members of this sacred community. Regardless of how many rank-and-file legionaries could articulate this logic, what mattered was the sense of belonging and sacredness cultivated by legionary rituals. Commemorating the dead, celebrating national heroes, and carrying around soil from battlefields encouraged legionaries to believe that they, and not their elected officials, were truly in touch with, and responsible for, the Romanian nation.

The contest between legionaries and the state for leadership of the nation as a sacred community came to a head in the funeral of Ion Moţa and Vasile Marin in 1937. The government had not sent them to fight in Spain and it did not arrange their funeral. Yet legionaries treated them as national heroes, even as martyrs, and invited foreign dignitaries. The pageantry and oath taking associated with the funeral, and the presence of so many high-ranking clergy, suggested that the legionaries were the legitimate mediators between God and the nation. At least in terms of the funeral's theatrics, the legionaries had successfully replaced the state as the representatives of the Romanian people when it came before God. Moreover, the crowds, the collective prayers and songs, the uniforms, and the speeches encouraged legionaries to identify themselves with a bigger, national community rather than as individuals responsible only to themselves.

Fascist Subjectivities

When they joined the movement, legionaries subordinated themselves to its leadership and strove to remake themselves according to its image. They came to think of themselves not as individuals with their own needs and wants but as members of a nation, duty bound to serve it with all their strength. In 1933, as more and more fascist groups appeared all over Europe, Constantin Onu wrote in *Axa* that "the new systems, the epochal reforms which reorganized the lives of entire peoples exist thanks to a certain type of person . . . the new man [*omul nou*]. The Italian revolution succeeded through Mussolini; the German revolution through Hitler. Both had the unanimous and devoted support of the youth behind them; youth imbued with the novelty and virtue characteristic of those leaders and religions which illuminate its path." According to Onu, the new man was a leader like Codreanu, whose character could bring about revolutionary change. In Romania, he said, referring to Codreanu, "the new man is the one whose name Romanian youth speak with awe and in which they believe fanatically. Nameless multitudes come to him with a rare reverence and are inspired by his myth. He is, and apart from him there is no other."[14] The idea of the "new man" soon evolved to include all legionaries, not just Codreanu. Four years later, Ernest Bernea wrote that "the Legion is a revolutionary movement which goes to the heart of things and builds from solid foundations. It does not merely change forms or institutions; it remakes human nature itself according to its ideals."[15]

In a 1951 book the Orthodox priest and former legionary Father Ştefan Palaghiţă described joining the Legion as "conversion." It involved, he wrote, "a process in which a new life is grafted into the old one. . . . The convert moves vertically, from the sinful world toward God, and not horizontally, or in the ways of the world, as all political parties do."[16] Conversion for Palagiţă was a decisive, transformative change of self and requires a rupture with the past: "Conversion is not possible without a formal condemnation and a total repudiation of the old self."[17] Stories about this sort of conversion experience are rare. Of sixty-seven post–World War II memoirs that I consulted, only twenty-six included accounts of how the authors joined the Legion. Several of these mentioned becoming intellectually convinced of the legionary message after reading a book, hearing a propagandist speak, or discussing the issues with legionaries.[18] Others spoke about feeling unworthy to become legionaries and going through a time of self-examination that sometimes lasted several years before they finally joined.[19] Most common were accounts in which individuals joined because their friends or parents encouraged them to.[20] Nowhere did I find anything like the old-self/new-self metaphor that Palaghiţă used. This is a common trope in Western Christian conversion narratives but one that is rare in Eastern Orthodoxy.[21] Eastern

14. Constantin Onu, "Omul nou," *Axa*, 1/21 (29 Oct 1933).

15. Bernea, *Stil legionar*, 22.

16. Palaghiţă, *Istoria mişcarii legionare*, 83.

17. Ibid., 85.

18. Stănescu ed., *Corneliu Zelea Codreanu*, 11–16, 18–20, 49–50, 175–203; Ciuntu, *Din Bucovina pe Oder*; Corneliu Georgescu, *Pe drum cu Arhangheli: Însemnari din viaţa unui legionar*, vol. 1 (Bucharest: Editura Majadahonda, 1996).

19. Stănescu ed., *Corneliu Zelea Codreanu*, 208–214, 258–265.

20. Ibid., 36–48, 62–82, 89–116, 165–174; Păun, *Un soldat pe baricada*; Dinescu, "Cetăţui sfărâmate;" Horia Sima, "Cum am intrat în Legiune," in *Mărturii despre legiune*, 165–181.

21. On the former, see Heather Coleman, "Becoming a Russian Baptist: Conversion Narratives and Social Experience," *Russian Review*, 61/1 (2002): 94–112; and D. Bruce Hindmarsh, *The Evangelical Conversion Narrative: Spiritual Autobiography in Early Modern England* (Oxford: Oxford University Press, 2005).

Orthodox Christians prefer to frame their lives as a journey toward God through progressive refinement and purification from sin.[22] The fact that Palaghiță's work was written after the war and that this narrative frame is found only in postwar memoirs suggests that this particular way of thinking about conversion is a later interpolation by exiles seeking to reframe the Legion as a spiritual movement and was not characteristic of interwar legionary thinking.

So how did interwar legionaries conceive of conversion? A newspaper article from 1940 titled "A Slow Conversion" explained that the process of becoming a legionary involved a careful self-examination and then a conversion of the mind. Conversion, the article argued, was not a "breeze," but an "earthquake" in the soul.[23] Conversion of the mind becomes evident in a series of thirteen articles published in *Bună vestire* in December 1937. These articles were responses by colonels and generals, academics, public intellectuals, and political activists to the question "Why do I believe in the victory of the legionary movement?" Despite the title, only one article took on a confessional tone, and only three even used the first-person narrative voice beyond the initial sentence. The one confessional piece came from Mircea Eliade, a historian of comparative religion who wrote that he believed in a legionary victory "because I believe in the destiny of the Romanian people . . . because I believe in the victory of the Christian spirit . . . because I believe in love."[24] The others were all apologetics and took the opportunity to enumerate why the Legion was so great. Each broadly reflected the public persona of the writer. Colonel Cristodulo believed in legionaries because they had discipline and will.[25] Father Cristescu believed that the Legion was sent by God to save Romania from darkness.[26] Professor Rădulescu prefaced his thoughts by distinguishing between rationalist convictions and legionary convictions and then celebrated the latter because they were based on authentic instinctual belief.[27] Professor Bănică summarized his own recently published theory of ethical justice and then claimed that the legionaries put it into practice.[28]

What was happening here? Peter Stromberg's research suggests that rather than representing an event that happened in the past, conversion stories *are* the

---

22. John Chryssavgis, "The Spiritual Way," in *The Cambridge Companion to Orthodox Christian Theology*, eds. Mary B. Cunningham and Elizabeth Theokritoff (Cambridge, UK: Cambridge University Press, 2008), 150–163; and Paul Evdokimov, *Ages of the Spiritual Life* (Crestwood, NY: St. Vladimir's Seminary Press, 1997).

23. Ion Băleanu, "O convertire lentă," *Cuvântul* (30 Oct 1940).

24. Mircea Eliade, "De ce cred în biruința mișcării legionare?" *Bună vestire* (18 Dec 1937).

25. Em. Cristodulo, "De ce cred în biruința mișcării legionare?" *Bună vestire* (11 Dec 1937).

26. Grigore Cristescu, "De ce cred în biruința mișcării legionare?" *Bună vestire* (13 Dec 1937).

27. Dan Rădulescu, "De ce cred în biruința mișcării legionare?" *Bună vestire* (22 Dec 1937).

28. Vasile Bănică, "De ce cred în biruința mișcării legionare?" *Bună vestire* (17 Dec 1937).

change they wish to recount. "The conversion narrative itself is a central element of the conversion," Stromberg argues. "It is through language that the conversion occurred in the first place and also through language that the conversion is now re-lived as the convert tells his tale."[29] Stromberg's theory maintains that every conversion story is simultaneously an apologetic aimed at bringing both speaker and audience into the group through its ability to linguistically bridge the gap between everyday life and the supernatural reality upon which the religious community is posited.[30] In other words, the narrative takes a mystery and makes it socially explicable. This process is precisely what happens in each of these accounts. Like good evangelists, each writer uses an a priori virtue such as discipline, will, or incorruptibility and then logically derives the legionary victory from this starting point. Conversion narratives are basically attempts to explain to oneself and others why a person belongs to a particular religious community, and as proclamations of the legionary *kerygma*, these accounts do exactly that.

A similar process can be seen at work in a series of twenty-eight biographies published in *Cuvântul* in October and November 1940. The articles were written during the National Legionary State, but most of the legionaries mentioned had died during the persecutions of the late 1930s. Ostensibly these were eulogies, but their narrative structure has a lot in common with the 1937 articles from *Buna vestire*, particularly in terms of the primacy of the legionary message over presentations of individual selfhood. Even though they were supposed to be about the lives of the dead people, few of these articles included life histories, and only seven mentioned how the person joined the Legion. Individual personalities were muted, and each person seems to have embodied the virtues of the "new man" that legionaries were hoping to create. Twenty out of twenty-eight accounts, for example, described the departed as having had a noble and hardworking character. Eleven spoke about how strong, healthy, and handsome they were. Five mentioned an extraordinary capacity for suffering. Almost all mentioned dedication to the cause. Individuality emerges in these accounts primarily when the departed did not exhibit legionary virtues. Theodor Constantinescu, for example, was a great man *even though* he had a "slight build."[31] Ilie Giulan was a backbone of the legionary community in his village *even though* he was "not well read."[32] Like the columns on "why do I believe in the victory of the legionary

29. Peter Stromberg, *Language and Self-Transformation: A Study of the Christian Conversion Narrative* (Cambridge, UK: Cambridge University Press, 1993), 3.

30. Ibid., 17–18.

31. Anonymous, "Eri a fost condus la locul de veci camaradul Theodor Constantinescu," *Cuvântul* (15 Nov 1940).

32. Petru Galiş, "Ilie Giulan," *Cuvântul* (22 Nov 1940).

movement?" these hagiographies were less about creating an individual self than about expressing a corporate archetype. Community values were what counted, and a person's life history had value insofar as it expressed those values.[33]

In keeping with the lack of emphasis on individuality, there are also very few instances of before-and-after stories here. Time is remarkably vague in these hagiographies, as the actions of these heroes become subsumed into eternity. The biography of Father Ionescu, for example, describes him fighting in World War I and then teaching theology in Bucharest. All this was done in a legionary spirit despite the fact that he did not join the Legion until 1938. When he did join, the author tells us, Ionescu's soul "found an optimal climate for its realization."[34] Ilie Giulan came to legionary belief calmly and easily in his village, accepting it "as if it was Holy Communion."[35] Before he became a legionary, Petru Fleschin had felt so out of place in his environment that he declared when he took the legionary oath, "Comrades! If the Legion didn't exist I would have shot myself, or at the very least become a Communist."[36] The archetypal legionary was apparently born, not made.

These biographers thought that adopting a legionary identity should not involve taking on a new self, just new life. They describe vivification, not rebirth. In his memoir, Tudor Cicală mentions a time before he joined the Legion when he was working as a veterinarian. Codreanu visited him at work and explained that he should "organize the veterinary service with wisdom, developing a work plan based on the best systems from the countries in which [Cicală] had studied." "Suddenly," Cicală says, "I felt more sure of myself. I had a goal. I received his words as a mission."[37] Nowhere in this account was there any discussion of Cicală's changing who he was. Instead, Codreanu told him to intensify his commitment to the vocation that he already had—to vivify it, if you will. The same attitude is seen in Codreanu's own writings on the matter, which present fascism as a decision to fight for that in which one already believed.

Self-transformation, particularly the type of self-transformation that accompanies religious conversion, is traumatic not only for the individual but also for the community that he or she leaves behind.[38] Legionaries expressed their

---

33. Such a relational conception of personhood that conceives of the individual only as part of a group was being developed by Romanian theologians such as Dumitru Stăniloae at this time. See the extracts translated in *The Teachings of Modern Orthodox Christianity on Law, Politics, and Human Nature*, ed. John Witte Jr. and Frank S. Alexander (New York: Columbia University Press, 2007), 340–341.

34. Nic. Adameşteanu, "Părintele Duminică Ionescu," *Cuvântul* (20 Nov 1940).

35. Petru Galiş, "Ilie Giulan," *Cuvântul* (22 Nov 1940).

36. Ion Rodeanu, "Petru Fleschin," *Cuvântul* (24 Nov 1940).

37. Tudor Cicală, "Pe drumul tău, Căpitane!" in *Corneliu Zelea Codreanu*, ed. Stănescu, 49–50.

38. Gauri Viswanathan, *Outside the Fold: Conversion, Modernity, and Belief* (Princeton: Princeton University Press, 1998).

mission as being that of building the Romanian nation, not of tearing it apart. Of course, purification is necessarily painful, but they claimed to be creating a community that embodied the nation, not one that set itself apart from the nation. If they had said that radical, ontological change to one's selfhood were required for membership of the Legion, then it would have followed that simply being Romanian was inadequate. But for a nationalist, national identity is *completely* adequate. Legionary identity, then, was an intensification or vivification of national identity and not a transformation or conversion.

Legionaries emphasized the importance of intensifying preexisting beliefs in the courtroom too. On trial for treason in 1938, Nicolae Totu explained his trip to fight in the Spanish Civil War and the disturbances that he had been involved in in Iaşi as attempts to protect the king, and by extension the country, from the threat of communism. Totu further argued that he was motivated to action after having seen the poverty to which his natal village had been reduced as a result of "the Jews."[39] At no time did joining involve a suspension of one's faculties. As part of the same trial, Gheorghe Furdui wrote, "I participated with perfect lucidity in the legionary movement, conscious of my actions."[40] The Legion, according to Furdui, was about creating a new man, not about overthrowing a regime. Another of the defendants, Radu Budişteanu, agreed, emphasizing that joining the Legion was a continuation of his lifelong dedication to the Romanian people and was in no way an "annex."[41] Continuity between legionary and nonlegionary lives is a feature of most of these accounts and was a way for the accused to deny culpability for their actions. Father Georgescu admitted that, yes, he had conducted church services for legionaries, but he conducted church services for everyone. And the larger legionary services in which he had participated were also led by other priests and even hierarchs.[42] On trial for their lives, these men were certainly being disingenuous in the ways that they presented their pasts. But the recurrent themes of piety, rational decision, and continuity were typical of legionary lives recounted in a variety of contexts. Hagiographies, confessional or apologetic literature, and memoirs all emphasized that joining the Legion was a way for the legionaries to become more serious about an identity that they had been born into. Legionary writers would also have us believe that their "conversions" were not about them as individuals but were expressions of nationalism that any sensible Romanian would make.

39. Nicolae Totu, "Declaraţie," 13 June 1938, USHMM, Fond SRI Files, dosar 68.333, f. 372.

40. Gheorghe Furdui, "Declaraţie," 13 June 1938, USHMM, Fond SRI Files, dosar 68.333, f. 367–369.

41. Radu Budişteanu, "Declaraţie," 13 June 1938, USHMM, Fond SRI Files, dosar 68.333, f. 373–374.

42. Nicolae T. Georgescu-Edinti, "Declaraţie," June 13, 1938, USHMM, Fond SRI Files, dosar 68.333, f. 510–513.

What these joining narratives conceal is that developing a fascist subjectivity took time, as activists discovered politics as a domain newly available to ordinary citizens. They often read fascist newspapers or pamphlets before joining, and in many cases they already had a friend or relative in the movement who influenced their decision. Joining a nest introduced new recruits to other legionaries, and social occasions coupled with marches or propaganda campaigns cemented bonds of friendship and camaraderie that reinforced the ideals of loyalty and commitment that were emphasized in Codreanu's writings.

As Valentin Săndulescu has argued, far from being simply rhetoric for a gullible public, between 1933 and 1938 the idea of "new men" appeared at every level of the movement: from propaganda posters and Codreanu's writings to personal letters and orders from midlevel organizers to their subordinates.[43] Efforts to create "new men" structured legionary activities from work camps to nest meetings to funerals, but all these activities focused on the Legion itself—not on the Romanian nation, the "Jewish peril," or the grievances of peasants or workers. Joining the Legion meant opposing the status quo and obeying the movement while waiting for revolutionary change to happen. The Legion demanded a great deal of time from activists, it required learning new skills such as publishing or public speaking, it marked legionaries as members of an extremist organization, and it exposed them to the risks of imprisonment and physical violence. On the other hand, legionaries gained strong, supportive social networks; they had the opportunity to influence how other people thought and voted; they learned to be proud of their country, their work, and their image; and they could attack their enemies with the knowledge that other legionaries would support them when push came to shove.

43. Săndulescu, "Revolutionizing Romania," 2.

Bibliography

ARCHIVAL SOURCES

Lilly Library, Indiana University, Bloomington, Indiana, United States of America

Burton Yost Berry Collection

National Council for the Study of the Securitate Archives, Bucharest, Romania (ACNSAS)

Fond Documentar
Fond Informativ
Fond Penal

National Historical Archives of Romania, Bucharest, Romania (ANIC)

Fond Direcţia Generală a Poliţiei (DGP)
Fond Fundaţiile Culturale Regale Centrală
Fond Inspectoratul General de Jandarmerie
Fond Ministerul de Interne—Diverse (MI-D)
Fond Ministerul Propagandei Naţionale—Direcţia Cinematografiei
Fond Ministerul Propagandei Naţionale—Presa internă
Fond Teatrul National

Romanian National Archives in Braşov County, Braşov, Romania (AN—Braşov)

Fond Chestura de Poliţie—Serviciul Exterioare
Fond Inspectoratul Muncii
Fond Prefectura Braşov—Subinspectoratul Pregatirea Premilitară
Fond Prefectura Judeţului Braşov—Serviciul Administrativ

Romanian National Archives of the Municipality of Bucharest (AN—Bucharest)

Fond N. Malaxa
Fond Universitatea din Bucureşti, Rectorat

Romanian National Archives in Cluj County, Cluj-Napoca, Romania (AN—Cluj)

Fond Inspectoratul de Poliţie
Fond Personal Vasile Coman
Fond Universitatea Ferdinand I, Facultatea de Drept
Fond Universitatea Ferdinand I, Facultatea de Ştiinţa

Romanian National Archives in Iaşi County, Iaşi, Romania (AN—Iaşi)

Fond Chestura de Poliţie
Fond Inspectoratul de Poliţie

Fond Inspectoratul Regional de Poliţie
Fond Universitatea A. I. Cuza, Rectorat

United States Holocaust Memorial Museum Archives, Washington DC, United States of America (USHMM)

Fond Ministerul de Interne—Diverse (MI-D)
Fond Odessa Oblast Archives, Izmail Branch
Fond SRI Files

United States National Archives, College Park, MA, United States of America (USNA)

Records of the Department of State relating to Internal Affairs of Romania, 1910–1944.

PERIODICALS

13 Jilava (1940)
Acţiunea românească (1924)
Adevărul (1888–1913, 1924–1938)
Antisemitul (Bucharest) (1899–1901)
Antisemitul (Craiova) (1898–1901, 1904–1906)
Apărarea naţională (Iaşi) (1922–1938)
Arcaşul (1924)
Ardealul (1920–1943)
Aurora (1920–1937)
Axa (1932–1933, 1940–1941)
Biruinţa (1930–1933)
Braţul de fier (1935–1937)
Buna vestire (1937–1938, 1940–1941)
Calea nouă (1936–1937)
Calendarul (1932–1933)
Chemarea (1925–1929)
Conştiinţa (1919–1920)
Contimporanul (1922–1925)
Cruciada românismului (1935–1937)
Curentul (1928–1944)
Cuvântul (1924–1938, 1940–1941)
Cuvântul Argeşului (1935–1937)
Cuvântul studenţesc (1923–1940)
Dascălul (1909–1910)
Dimineaţa (1904–1938)
Ecoul Moldovei (1890–1918)
Facla (1910–1940)
Fascismul (1923)
Femeia satelor (1935)
Fraţia creştină (1923–1929)
Garda de Fier (Bessarabia) (1933)
Garda de Fer (Bucharest) (1930)
Garda de Fier (Oraştie) (1931)

Garda Jiului (1932–1933)
Garda Râmnicului (1932–1933)
Gândirea (1921–1944)
Glasul strămoşesc (1935–1941)
Iconar (1935–1938)
Ideea românească (1935–1936)
Înfraţirea românească (1925–1931)
Însemnări sociologice (1935–1941)
Lancea (1925–1926)
Libertatea (1902–1941)
Lumina satelor (1922–1952)
Lumina tineretului (1933–1938)
Luminătorul (1923–1944)
Luptă (1921–1937)
Muncitorul legionar (1936)
Naţionalistul (1922–1927)
Neamul românesc (1906–1940)
New York Times (1857–present)
Ogorul nostru (1923–1926)
Pământul strămoşesc (1927–1933, 1940–1941)
Păstorul creştin ortodox (1933–1943)
Păstorul ortodox (1904–1944)
Politică (1926–1928)
Porunca vremii (1932–1943)
Predania (1937)
Rânduiala (1935, 1937–1938)
România literara (1968–present)
Semnalul (1938–1940, 1944–1948)
Sfarmă piatră (1936–1941)
Sociologie româneasca (1936–1942)
Străjerul (1926–1928)
Studentul naţionalist (1935)
Svastica (1934)
Ţara noastră (1932–1938)
Telegraful român (1904–present)
Transilvania noastra (1944)
Unirea (Craiova) (1925–1927)
Unirea (Iaşi) (1912–1915, 1918–1920, 1924)
Universul (1884–1916, 1919–1953)
Vremea (1928–1938, 1940–1944)

PUBLISHED PRIMARY SOURCES

Anonymous. *Cântece legionare.* Bucarest: I. E. Torouţiu, 1940.
——. *Cultul dela Majadahonda şi monumentul Moţa-Marin.* Madrid: Biblioteca documentară "Generaţia Nouă," 1976.
Amzăr, Dumitru Cristian. *Naţionalismul tineretului.* Bucharest: Rânduiala, 1936.
——. *Rânduiala.* Bucharest: România Press, 2006.
Ancel, Jean ed. *Documents concerning the Fate of Romanian Jewry during the Holocaust.* New York: Beate Klarsfeld Foundation, 1986.

Arsene, Maria. *Iuda...* Bucharest: Atelierele "Adevărul," 1936.
Beldiman, Dana, ed. *Dosar Horia Sima (1940–1946)*. Bucharest: Evenimentul Românesc, 2000.
——. *Statul Național Legionar: Septembrie 1940–ianuarie 1941; Cadrul legislativ*. Bucharest: Institutul Național pentru Studiul Totalitarismului, 2005.
Bernea, Ernest. *Cartea Căpitanilor*. Bucharest: Serviciul Propagandei Scrise, 1940.
——. *Sociologie și etnografie româneasca: Ordinea spirituală*. Bucharest: Vremea, 2009.
——. *Stil legionar*. Bucharest: Serviciul Propagandei Legionare, 1940.
——. *Tineretul și politică*. Bucharest: Rânduiala, 1936.
Brădescu, Faust. *Conducere și disciplină*. Rio de Janeiro: Colecția Dacia, 1966.
——. *Opinii: Un deceniu de lupta in exil in slujba neamului si legiunii (1978–1988)*. Bucharest: Editura Majadahonda, 1997.
Brăileanu, Traian. *Politica*. Bucharest: Albatros, 2003.
Brunea-Fox, Filip. *Orașul măcelului*. Bucharest: Editura Hasefer, 1997.
Carp, Matatias ed. *Cartea neagră: Fapte și documente: Suferințele evreilor din România în timpul dictatueri fasciste, 1940–1944*, 3 vols. Bucharest: Socec, 1946–1948.
——, ed. *Holocaust in Romania: Facts and Documents on the Annihilation of Rumania's Jews—1940–44*. Translated by Seán Murphy. Budapest: Primor, 1994.
Chiricuța, Toma P. *Religia omului de știință (Răspuns dat liber-cugetătorilor)*. Bucharest: Tipografia Gutenberg, 1910.
Cioran, Emil. *Schimbarea la față a României*. Bucharest: Humanitas, 1990.
Ciucă, Marcel-Dumitru, Aurelian Teodorescu, and Bogdan Florin Popvici eds., *Stenogramele ședințelor Consiliului de Miniștri Guvernarea Ion Antonescu*, 12 vols. Bucharest: Arhivele Naționale ale României, 1997.
Codreanu, Corneliu Zelea. *Cărticica șefului de cuib*. Bucharest: Editura Bucovina, 1940.
——. *Circulări și manifeste (1927–1938)*. Bucharest: Blassco, 2010.
——. *Eiserne Garde*. Berlin: Brunnen, Willi Bischoff, 1939.
——. *Guardia di ferro*. Roma-Torino: SA Casa Editrice Nazionale, 1938.
——. *Însemnări*. MS, 1934.
——. *Pentru legionari*. Bucharest: Editura Mișcării Legionare, 1940
——. *Scrisori studențesti din închisoare*. Bucharest: Ramida, 1998.
Crainic, Nichifor. *Lupta pentru spiritul nou: Germania și Italia în scrisul meu dela 1932 încoace*. Bucharest: Editura Cugetarea, 1941.
——. *Nostalgia paradisului*. Iași: Editura Moldova, 1994.
Cristescu, Grigore. *Isus in viața modernă*. Sibiu: Tiparul Tipografiei Arhidiecezane, 1927.
——. *Jertfe, datorii și răspunderi de ieri, de azi și de mâine*. Sibiu: Tiparul Institutului de Arte Grafice "Dacia Traiana," 1929.
——. *Semănături de primavara: Gânduri inchinate tineretului*. Sibiu: Tip. "Dacia Traiana," 1927.
Cuza, Alexandru C. *Îndrumari de politică externă: Discursuri parlamentare rostite în anii 1920–1936*. Bucharest: Cugetarea—Georgescu Delafras, 1941.
——. *Naționalitatea în arta: Expunere a doctrinci naționaliste, principii, fante, concluzii*. Bucharest: "Minerva," 1915.
Dacicus, Testis (George Manu). *În spatele cortinei de fier: România sub ocupație rusească*. Bucharest: Kullusys, 2004.
Damé, Frédéric. *J. C. Bratiano: L'ère nouvelle—la dictature*. Bucharest: Bureaux de l'Indépendance Roumaine, 1886.
Diaconescu, Emil. *Agresiunea de la Cernăuți din ziuă de 7 octombrie 1926 împotriva profesorilor din Comisiunea No. 1 a examenului de bacalaureat*. Iași: Tipografia "Albina," 1926.

Dobrescu, Florin ed. *1950—Horia Sima leagă România de NATO: Documente*. Bucharest: Editura Sânziana, 2008.
Dobrogeanu-Gherea, Constantin. *Carp und die Judenfrage*. Vienna: Buchdruckerei "Industrie," 1900.
——. *Neoiobăgia: Studiu economico-sociologic al problemei noastre agrare*. Bucharest: Editura "Viaţa Românească," 1910.
Duicu, Serafim ed. *Ion Antonescu şi "Garda de Fier": Pe marginea prăpastie (21–23 ianuarie 1941)*. Târgu-Mureş: Rom-Edition, 1991.
Dumbrava, Dinu, *Fără ură! Pregătirea şi deslănţuirea evenimentelor din Focşani în zilele de 17 şi 18 martie 1925*. n.p.: n.p., n.d.
Georgescu, Corneliu. *Vremuri de restrişte*. Bucharest: Muntenia, 1940.
Georgescu, Ion V. *Actualitatea profeţilor*. Bucharest: Tiparul Academic, 1934.
——. *Demonologia Vechiului Testament: Satan in profeţia lui Zaharia*. Bucharest: Tipografia Cărţilor Bisericeşti, 1938.
Grosu, Gurie. *Denunţarea complotului apocaliptic*. Bucharest: Tipografia ABC, 1937.
Gusti, Dimitrie ed. *Enciclopedia României*, 4 vols. Bucharest: Asociaţiunea Ştiinţifică pentru Enciclopedia României, 1936–1940.
Herseni, Traian. *Mişcarea legionară şi muncitorimea*. Bucharest: Tipografia Legionar, 1937.
Ionescu, Nae. *Roza vânturilor*. Bucharest: Roza Vânturilor, 1990.
Ionică, Ion I. *Dealul Mohului: Cermonia agrară în cununii în ţară Oltului*. Bucharest: Minerva, 1996.
——. *Manifestările spirituale în cercetarea sociologică*. Bucharest: n.p., 1940.
Iorga, Nicolae. *Istoria evreilor în ţerile noastre*. Bucharest: Academia Romana, 1913.
Istrate, Gheorghe Gh. *Frăţia de cruce*. Bucharest: Fundaţiei Culturale "Buna Vestire," 2005.
L., E. *Cântecele lui Corneliu Zelea Codreanu*. Turnu-Severin: Editura Ziarului Ogorul Nostru, 1925.
Madgearu, Virgil N. *Agrarianism, capitalism, imperialism: Contribuţii la studiul evoluţiei sociale româneşti*. Cluj-Napoca: Dacia, 1999.
——. *Evoluţia economiei româneşti după războiul mondial*. Bucharest: Editura Ştiinţifică, 1995.
Maiorescu, Titu. *Istoria contemporană a României (1866–1900)*. Bucharest: Editura Universităţii Titu Maiorescu, 2002.
Manuila, Sabin. *Recensământul general al populaţiei României din decemvrie 1930*, 10 vols. Bucharest: Institutul Central de Statistică, 1938.
Marin, Vasile. *Crez de generaţie*. Bucharest: Tipografia "Bucovina" I. E. Torouţiu, 1937.
——. *Fascismul: Organizarea constituţională a statului corporativ Italian*. Bucharest: Serviciul şi Editura Colportajului Legionar, n.d.
Ministerul Industriei şi Comerţului. *Anuarul Statistic al României, 1937–1938*. Bucharest: Institutul Central de Statistică, 1939.
Moţa, Ion. *Corespondenţa cu Welt-Dienst (1934–1936)*. Munich: Colecţia Europa, 2000.
——. *Cranii de lemn*. 4th ed. Bucharest: Editura Mişcării Legionare, 1940.
——. *Prezent*. Bucharest: Tipografia "Bucovina" I.E. Toroutiu, 1937.
——. *Testamentul lui Ion I. Moţa*. Bucharest: Editua Sânziana, 2007.
Mugur, Gh. D. *Căminul cultural: Îndreptar pentru conducătorii culturii la sate*. Bucharest: Fundaţia Culturală "Principele Carol," 1922.
Nietzsche, Friedrich. *On the Genealogy of Morals*. Translated by Douglas Smith. Oxford: Oxford University Press, 1996.
Odell, Ralph M. *Cotton Goods in the Balkan States*. Washington, DC: Department of Commerce and Labor, 1912.

Papanace, Constantin. *Stilul legionar de luptă: Conecpţia tactică a Căpitanului*. Bucharest: Editura Lucman, 2004.

Paulescu, Nicolae. *Spitalul, Coranul, Talmudul, Cahalul, Francmasoneria*. Filipeştii de Târg, Prahova: Antet XX Press, 2001.

Polihroniade, Mihail. *Tabăra de muncă*. Bucharest: Tipografia Ziarului Universul, 1936.

Protopopescu, Ion D. *Pericolul Ovreesc*. Craiova: Editura Ramura, n.d.

Roşianu, Gheorghe. *Păţania lui Gheorghe Roşianu in Focşani*. Focşani: Atelierele Gh. A. Diaconescu, 1914.

Roventa, Haralambie, and Ion V. Georgescu. *Ioan Popescu-Malăeşti: Activitatea sa ca preot şi profesor*. Bucharest: n.p., 1939.

Savel, Mina. *Istoria Judaismului*. Iaşi: Tipografia M.P. Popovici, 1902.

Schifirneţ, Constantin ed. *Naţiune şi Creştinism*. Bucharest: Elion, 2004.

Scurtu, Ioan ed. *Ideologie şi formaţiuni de dreapta în România*, vols. 2–6. Bucharest: Institutul Naţional Pentru Studiul Totalitarismului, 2000–2007.

——. *Totalitarismul de dreapta în România: Origini, manifestări, evoluţie, 1919–1927*. Bucharest: Institutul Naţional pentru Studiul Totalitarismului, 1996.

Sebastian, Mihail. *De două mii de ani: Roman*. Bucharest: Editura Nationala-Ciornei, 1934.

Sima, Horia. *Antologie legionară*, 7 vols. Miama Beach, FL: Colecţia Omul Nou, 1994.

Stănescu, Dumitru. *Din trecutul nostru politic şi bisericesc*. Bucharest: Tipografia Curţii Regale F. Göbl Fii, 1921.

Stăniloae, Dumitru. *Viaţa şi activitatea patriarhului Dosoftei al Ierusalimului şi legaturile lui cu ţările româneşti*. Cernăuţi: Editura Autorului, 1929.

Şumuleanu, Corneliu. *Atetnatul jidănesc împotriva profesorului A. C. Cuza*. Bucharest: Tipografia "Cultura Poporului," 1925.

Sutton, Claud. "An Interpretation of 'Fascism.'" In *International Fascism: Theories, Causes, and the New Consensus*, edited by Roger Griffin, 257–258. London: Arnold, 1998.

Tua, Lorenzo Baracchi. *Garda de Fier*. Translated by Cesar Balaban. Bucharest: Editura Mişcării Legionare, 1940.

Ţurcan, Ion. *Ion I. Moţa şi Vasile Marin în lumina scrisului şi faptei lor*. Cernăuţi: Insemnări Sociologice, 1937.

Un bun român. *Chestiunea Ovreiască*. Bucharest: n.p., 1913.

Vulcănescu, Mircea. *"Tânară generaţie": Crize vechi în haine noi*. Bucharest: Compania, 2004.

Zeletin, Ştefan. *Burghezia română: Origina şi rolul ei istoric*. Bucharest: Cultură Naţională, 1925.

MEMOIRS, DIARIES, AND ORAL HISTORIES

Anania, Valeriu. *Memorii*. Bucharest: Polirom, 2008.

Anonymous. *Corneliu Zelea Codreanu: Douazeci de ani dela moarte*. Madrid: Editura Carpaţii, 1958.

——. *Mărturii despre Căpitan: Patruzeci de ani dela moarte (1938–1978)*. Madrid: Editura Dacia, 1978.

Baicu, Petre, and Alexandru Salcă. *Rezistenţa în munţi şi în oraşul Braşov, 1944–1948*. Braşov: Editura Transilvania Expres, 1997.

Banea, Dumitru. *Acuzat, martor, apărător in procesul vieţii mele*. Sibiu: Puncte Cardinale, 1995.

Bejan, Dimitrie. *Hotarul cu cetăţi*. Bucharest: Tehnica, 1995.

Brădescu, Faust, ed. *Mărturii despre legiune: Patruzeci de ani dela întemeierea mişcăriilegionare (1927–1967)*. Rio de Janeiro: Dacia, 1967.
Buzatu, Gheorghe, Corneliu Ciucanu, and Cristian Sandache. *Radiografia dreptei româneşti: 1927–1941*. Bucharest: FF Press, 1996.
Cantacuzino, Alexandru. *Opere complete*. Prahova: Antet XX, n.d.
Chioreanu, Nistor, ed. *Lacrima prigoanei: Din lupta legionarelor romånce*. Timişoara: Gorian, 1994.
——. *Legionarii români în Buchenwald*. Bucharest: Ramida, 1998.
Ciolacu, Nicolae. *Haiducii Dobrogei*. Constanţa: Muntenia, 1998.
Cirja, Ion. *Întoarcerea din infern: Amintirile unui deţinut din închisorile României bolsevizate. Cruzimi, masacre şi bestialităţi necunoscute*. Madrid: Editura Dacia, 1969.
Ciuntu, Chirilă. *Din Bucovina pe Oder (amintirile unui legionar)*. Constanţa: Metafora, 2004.
Conovici, Mariana, Silvia Iliescu, and Octavian Silvestru, eds. *Ţara, Legiunea, Căpitanul: Mişcarea Legionară în documente de istorie orală*. Bucharest: Humanitas, 2008.
Crainic, Nichifor. *Zile albe, zile negre: Memorii (I)*. Bucharest: Casa Editurială "Gândirea," 1991.
Cucu, Tudor V. *Totul pentru ţară, nimic pentru noi*. Braşov: Editura Transilvania Expres, 1999.
Dobre, Bănică. *Crucificaţii: Zile trăite pe frontul spaniol*. Bucharest: I. N. Copuzeanu, 1937.
Dumitrescu-Borşa, Ion. *Cea mai mare jertfă legionară*. Sibiu: Editura "Totul pentru Ţara," 1937.
Galaction, Gala. *Jurnal*, 5 vols. Bucharest: Minerva, 1980.
Georgescu, Corneliu. *Pe drum cu Arhangheli: Însemnari din viaţa unui legionar*. 2 vols. Bucharest: Editura Majadahonda, 1996.
Gheorghiu, Virgil. *Memorii: Martorul Orei 25*. Translated by Sanda Mihaescu-Carsteanu. Bucharest: Gramar, 1999.
Herovanu, Eugen. *Oraşul amintirilor*. Bucharest: Minerva, 1975.
Iancu, Nicu. *Sub steagul lui Codreanu: Momente din trecutul legionar*. Madrid: Dacia, 1973.
Ianolide, Ioan. *Întoarcerea la Hristos*. Bucharest: Christiana, 2006.
Iorga, Nicolae. *Memorii: Sinuciderea partidelor (1932–8)*, vol. 7. Bucharest: Tiparul Aşezământului Tipografic "Datina Românească," 1939.
Maria, Regina României. *Povestea vieţii mele*, vol. 2. Iaşi: Editura Moldova, 1991.
Marin, Ana Maria. *Poveste de dincolo*. Madrid: Editura Autorului, 1979.
Ogoranu, Ion Gavrilă. *Brazii se frâng, dar nu se îndoiesc*, 3 vols. Baia Mare: Marist, 2009.
Palaghiţă, Ştefan. *Istoria mişcării legionare scrisă de un legionar: Garda de Fier spre reînvierea României*. Bucharest: Roza Vânturilor, 1993.
Pană, Saşa. *Născut în '02: Memorii, file de jurnal, evocări*. Bucharest: Minerva, 1973.
Pandrea, Petre. *Garda de Fier: Jurnal de filosofie politică, memorii penitenciare*. Bucharest: Vremea, 2001.
Păun, Nicolae Nicu. *Un soldat pe baricadă idealului legionar: "Audiatur et altera pars."* Braşov: n.p., n.d.
Roth Jelescu, Ion. *Şi cerul plângea: Amintiri din prigoana cea mare*. Madrid: Dacia, 1974.
Sebastian, Mihail. *Cum am devenit hooligan*. Bucharest: Humanitas, 2006.
——. *Jurnal, 1935–1944*. Bucharest: Humanitas, 2005.
Sima, Horia. *Histoire du mouvement légionnaire*. Rio de Janeiro: Editôra Dacia, 1972.

Stănescu, Gabriel, ed. *Corneliu Zelea Codreanu şi epoca sa*. Norcross, GA: Criterion, 2001.

Stănicel, Stelian. *Lângă Căpitan*. Buenos Aires: Pământul Stramoşec, 1978.

Stoenescu, Lăcrămioara. *De pe băncile şcolii în închisorile comuniste*. Bucharest: Curtea Veche, 2010.

Sturdza, Mihail. *România şi sfârşitul europei: Amintiri din ţara pierdută*. Paris: Fronde, 1994.

Trifa, Valerian D. *Marginal Notes on a Court Case*. Jackson, MI: Romanian-American Heritage Center, 1988.

Tudor, Ilie. *Un an lângă Căpitan*. Bucharest: Sânziana, 2007.

Ursu, Dragoş, and Ioana Ursu, eds. *Aiudule, Aiudule: Crâmpeie de memorie întemniţată*. Cluj-Napoca: Renaşterea, 2011.

Walker, David. *Death at My Heels*. London: Chapman and Hall, 1942.

Index